THE CENTURY OF MODERN DESIGN

EXECUTIVE DIRECTOR
Suzanne Tise-Isoré

**EDITOR FOR THE LILIANE AND DAVID M. STEWART
PROGRAM FOR MODERN DESIGN**
Anne Hoy

EDITORIAL COORDINATION
Nathalie Chapuis

EDITORIAL ASSISTANT
Joy Sulitzer

**REGISTRAR AND COORDINATOR FOR THE LILIANE
AND DAVID M. STEWART PROGRAM FOR MODERN DESIGN**
Angéline Dazé

GRAPHIC DESIGN
Bernard Lagacé
assisted by Alain Bourdon

EDITORIAL ASSISTANT/PROOFREADER
Kate Clark

COPYEDITOR
Helen Woodhall

COLOR SEPARATION
IGS, France

Simultaneously published in French as *Un siècle de design*.

Flammarion SA
87 quai Panhard et Levassor
75647 Paris Cedex 13
France
www.editions.flammarion.com

Dépôt legal: 10/2010
10 11 12 3 2 1
ISBN: 9782080301611
Printed by CS Graphic, Singapore

Illustration following page: detail of the ceiling lamp *LED*
by Johanna Grawunder, c. 2005–06.

THE CENTURY OF MODERN DESIGN

Selections from the Liliane and David M. Stewart Collection

Edited with Introduction by David Hanks

Flammarion

The Liliane and David M. Stewart Program for Modern Design

Contents

The Liliane and David M. Stewart
Collection: Inspired Enterprise

Beginning in 2011, the Liliane and David M. Stewart Pavilion of the Montreal Museum of Fine Arts will be devoted entirely to the decorative arts and design, a collection unique in Canada and considered a model for North America and further afield. Moreover, the galleries will be open to everyone, free of charge. Given to the museum in 2000, the Liliane and David M. Stewart Collection is an inspired twenty-first-century enterprise. This publication is a tribute to the collectors.

Liliane and David M. Stewart have been great Canadian patrons dedicated to various causes since 1970, and Mrs. Stewart is rightly known as the "best friend of Montreal museums." In fact, her philanthropic work extends well beyond Canada's borders: the story told by the Stewart Collection of over five thousand works of decorative arts and twentieth-century design is truly without precedent on the American continent. From its inception, the collection was built with an eye to establishing an exemplary museum holding based on quality and excellence. The informed opinions of an expert advisory committee helped define the direction of the collection. In a novel approach, equal consideration was given to outstanding craftsmanship and industrial design. This acquisition program, a pioneer in its field, began with a focus on the American and Scandinavian schools and later extended to works from Italy, Japan, the Netherlands, Germany, France, and elsewhere.

The visionary venture took shape in 1979 with the establishment of the Montreal Museum of Decorative Arts. It occupied an historic monument, the restored stately mansion known as the "Château Dufresne," in which a selection of works was displayed. In 1997, due to lack of space, the museum moved its operations into a section of the new Jean-Noël Desmarais Pavilion of the Montreal Museum of Fine Arts, which three years later was given the collection. This gift—one of the most remarkable in the history of Canadian museums—was then reinstalled in the pavilion now named after Liliane and David M. Stewart.

The Stewart Collection represents another critical stage in the development of the Montreal Museum of Fine Arts' decorative arts department. In 1916, inspired by the model of the Victoria and Albert Museum in London, a "Museum Section" was created to bring together "all objects tending to the education of the designer and worker."[1] Previously restricted to the fine arts, the institution broadened its scope to become a truly encyclopedic museum. F. Cleveland Morgan, the tireless volunteer curator from 1916 to 1962, zealously strengthened the collection so that it offered a vast overview of artisanship from around the world, from ancient decorative arts to the crafts of Quebec. The generous gift of the Liliane and David M. Stewart Collection has brought the museum's collection to new heights.

The Montreal Museum of Fine Arts' Acquisition Committee for Decorative Arts, established in 2001, continues to acquire contemporary design, carrying on Liliane and David M. Stewart's original mission. With its new focus on twenty-first-century design, the museum collects works that reinterpret material and form through innovative technologies; for example in designs by Maarten Baas, Mathias Bengtsson, Patrick Jouin, Fabio Novembre, and Tokujin Yoshioka. New acquisitions reject any air of ostentatious luxury and look instead toward innovation, often with a certain taste for wit and humor. Mrs. Stewart recently shared her thoughts about collecting when she spoke enthusiastically about a new acquisition of which she is particularly proud: "the 'Louis Ghost' armchair by Philippe Starck [is] made from translucent polycarbonate and reinvents the Louis XVI medallion. I think the way the chair melds into the room, practically disappearing, is marvellous."[2] Highlighting this piece of furniture speaks to appreciation and promotion of good sophisticated design at a modest price. Mrs. Stewart's remarkable gift of the Eric Brill Collection of American industrial design, which includes once-ignored objects from offices and kitchens, is another example of her resolutely modern way of thinking. With the same daring, she mischievously remarked to me, following the exhibition of gold and silver contemporary jewelry from her unique collection of "wearable sculpture" at the grand State Hermitage Museum, Saint Petersburg, "All right then, next time we'll exhibit paper and plastic jewelry!"

Nathalie Bondil
Director and Chief Curator
The Montreal Museum of Fine Arts

Preface

Looking back at thirty years of collecting modern design is a source of great pleasure. Our collection has had three homes: first, the historic twin mansions known as the Château Dufresne in Montreal; next, Frank Gehry's extraordinarily exuberant galleries in the Montreal Museum of Fine Arts; and, finally, the Liliane and David M. Stewart Pavilion, at the same museum.

Not long after we saw the Château Dufresne some thirty years ago, my late husband and I agreed to undertake the renovation of the Dufresne brothers' home and return it to its original state. My husband's love of New World history and of his native Montreal impelled us to seek a use for the house we were restoring. It was natural that the historic house, with its large spaces and elaborate interiors, could become home to a decorative arts museum and a collection that we would assemble.

After considering other periods of the decorative arts, we decided to focus on mid-twentieth-century international design. This decision was based on the fact that collections of earlier periods were already well established and that available masterpieces were fewer, having been avidly sought by museums and private collectors, thus limiting the possibility of creating a new collection of distinction for Montreal. In 1980 we began in earnest to create the collection that we celebrate today.

Since my husband's death in 1984, I have continued to carry out these original goals so dear to his heart. The collection grew dramatically in its first decade, outgrowing the rooms of the Château Dufresne. In 1994, we leased unfinished space in the Jean-Noël Desmarais Pavilion of the Montreal Museum of Fine Arts and invited the acclaimed Canadian-born architect Frank Gehry to conceive a facility for us. The new galleries he designed for our collection opened in 1997. This was an exciting new venue, on Sherbrooke Street in the center of Montreal.

In 2000, a third significant step was taken: in order to assure the best use and preservation of the Stewart Collection for future generations, we decided to donate it to the Montreal Museum of Fine Arts, one of Canada's most eminent museums, and one with which we have always had a wonderful relationship. The Museum of Decorative Arts was merged with the Museum of Fine Arts, and the Stewart Collection was soon moved from the Gehry galleries to a new exhibition space in the museum christened the Liliane and David M. Stewart Pavilion. In the same year, we also created the Stewart Program for Modern Design, an initiative of the Macdonald Stewart Foundation, so that we could continue to enhance the collection through new acquisitions, and broaden its availability to the public through exhibitions and publications. I feel privileged on this occasion—the thirtieth anniversary of the Stewart Collection—to collaborate with Nathalie Bondil, Director of the Montreal Museum of Fine Arts, and her staff in the presentation of highlights from our collection in this celebratory publication.

I was delighted when our longtime friend and collaborator on previous publications, Suzanne Tise-Isoré, Editorial Director of the Styles and Design Collection at Flammarion in Paris, approached me to create a book that would mark the occasion of the thirtieth anniversary of our collecting. This volume is the latest project to fulfill our mission to share the Stewart Collection with the public.

Liliane M. Stewart
President
The Liliane and David M. Stewart Program
for Modern Design

The Creation of a Collection

1 Château Dufresne, Montreal Museum of Decorative Arts.

When in 1976 Liliane and David Macdonald Stewart decided to restore the Château Dufresne (fig. 1), they did not foresee that it would be their first step toward creating one of the most important design collections in North America. Mr. Stewart's interest in history and their shared desire to restore one of Montreal's historic houses, the original home of the Dufresne family, members of the French-Canadian bourgeoisie who developed the area, soon expanded. They acquired original furnishings from the Dufresne family in order to return the main rooms to their original grandeur, and then they determined to make the fullest and best use of the restored historic house by establishing a museum there, the Montreal Museum of Decorative Arts.[1]

The Stewarts developed the mission for the new museum guided by experts who recommended a focus on decorative arts from 1940 to 1960, a period from which it was still possible to create a significant collection with a limited budget. At the time, mid-century design attracted few museums or collectors, and there was little competition to acquire the works that the Stewarts sought. Rather than focus on Canadian design, already the mission of other institutions, they chose an international perspective. The principles and tastes that guided the development of the collection, from the outset and continuing without interruption for thirty years, were aesthetic excellence and inclusive range, without sociopolitical agendas or national bias. While its focus and funding concentrated on a narrow slice of design history, within those established boundaries the museum set out to be broad enough to incorporate the complete spectrum of media, in examples from one-of-a-kind and limited-edition works to industrial design, and to embrace examples of postmodern invention and irony along with models of Bauhaus modernism and later reductivist idioms.

When the Stewart Collection was initiated in 1980, there were few museums of decorative arts in North America, despite the long history of such museums in Europe. Creations of the nineteenth century, museums of decorative arts shared with museums of fine arts the mission of collecting broadly in many categories, from ancient to modern, and of seeking the choicest objects by recognized designers. Unapologetically elitist in their quest for time-honored examples of artistry, these institutions also sought to encourage contemporary designers by acquiring and displaying their work.

For example, at the turn into the twentieth century, the Musée des Arts Décoratifs in Paris acquired then-new works by René Lalique, Louis Comfort Tiffany, and Émile Gallé, both directly from the artists and from exhibitions it organized. For the period 1940–60 the Stewarts adopted the goal of seeking out acclaimed designers, but they also decided to remain open to works by lesser-known practitioners. And unlike their colleagues—in decorative arts museums in Europe and decorative arts collections within fine art museums—they did not seek to integrate their acquisitions with fine arts of the same period or to divide them into separate departments, devoted, for example to furnishings, textiles, graphics, or ceramics. Rather, all design media were displayed together, to allow visual comparisons or contrasts, and they were organized either chronologically or thematically.

While the fledgling Montreal Museum of Decorative Arts was developing its own path, a new museum model was rapidly evolving that threatened to make the older model of historic collections appear outdated. Design museums, as distinct from decorative arts museums, first appeared in the early 1980s, a time of economic expansion, and became immediately and internationally popular. Determined to educate consumer tastes by acquiring and exhibiting a broad range of contemporary design, and focused on mass-produced, industrial goods, they challenged traditional decorative arts museums for public attention. Most talked about was the Design Museum in London, established by Sir Terence Conran in 1982 in the basement of the Victoria and Albert Museum and by 1986 occupying an independent location in London's East End. Other design museums followed, in Chicago in 1988 and Toronto in 1994, and their proliferation in Europe and North America continues to the present day.

The Stewarts were aware of these developments and decided on a unique mission for the Montreal Museum of Decorative Arts. In the Château, modernized gallery spaces were on the lower floor level, and there, or in the more elaborate period rooms, the museum rotated installations of its holdings. There was also sufficient space for special exhibitions organized elsewhere, many brought from Europe both to enrich the cultural life of Montreal and, with equal ambition, to provide the Stewarts with opportunities to acquire new objects. Early on, the couple recognized the importance of relationships with designers, dealers, collectors, and other museums as sources of information, expertise, and new works for the collection.

The Stewarts made the first acquisition for the collection in 1980—a classic *LCW* chair designed by Charles and Ray Eames (p. 102–103). In subsequent years Mrs. Stewart acquired additional masterpieces, some of them quite rare or one-of-a-kind, such as the Carlo Mollino table (p. 163), as well as collections of objects assembled by others. In its early years, the collection was known as the Liliane Stewart Collection, but after Mr. Stewart's death in 1984, the name was changed to include both of their names to honor his memory. From the outset, Mrs. Stewart concentrated on collections: she saw that each opportunity to acquire a great object was limited to the moment and could easily be missed. The quality and scope of the Stewart Collection attest to the wisdom of that judgment.

During its first twenty years, the Stewart Collection's growth was linked closely to exhibitions organized and presented in the Château Dufresne, its first home. The purchase of a group of works might be the occasion for an exhibition, as was the acquisition in 1993 of ninety superb pieces of mid-century American jewelry, one of the most important gatherings of its type.[2] The resulting 1996 exhibition and book, *Messengers of Modernism: American Studio Jewelry 1940–1960,* led to a greater interest in jewelry within the collection and to the presentations of loan exhibitions such as *European Jewellery—A Matter of Materials* in 1998.

At the same time, special exhibitions organized by the Montreal Museum of Decorative Arts launched the search for new acquisitions for the collection. This method of collection-building was systematic but unusual in museum practice: most exhibitions display permanent collection works reframed by judicious loans. The Montreal Museum of Decorative Arts, however, began with an exhibition idea and then realized it primarily with new acquisitions. The resulting purchases and gifts enriched the particular exhibition as well as the permanent collection. The first instance of this approach was the major exhibition *Design 1935–1965: What Modern Was*, with an accompanying catalogue to which eighteen specialists contributed.[3] In the making between 1985, when research and planning began, and 1991, the survey sought to define modernism and its legacies, while celebrating the culmination of the Stewarts' first ten years of collecting. Scholarship for

2   3   4

What Modern Was made it clear that the starting date of the collection should be pushed back from 1940 to 1935, closer to the beginnings of prewar modern design, and that its terminus should be extended from 1960 to 1965 to reflect the dramatic cultural and aesthetic shifts at mid-decade. *What Modern Was* traveled to six North American institutions, and its catalogue became the bible for the field, establishing standards that other museums adopted. It went into a second printing a decade later and remains one of the museum's most important contributions to scholarship in the world of modern design.

The next synoptic exhibition of 1997, *Designed for Delight: Alternative Aspects of Twentieth-Century Decorative Arts*, was also organized over several years and explored new approaches to design. In this case Mrs. Stewart acquired works for the collection that drew on modernism's antitheses in exuberant, eccentric, individualistic conceptions. Whereas *What Modern Was* presented an in-depth study by a team of scholars, *Designed for Delight* relied primarily on the designers themselves to discuss the objects in the exhibition. Like *What Modern Was*, *Designed for Delight* traveled to institutions in North America, a total of five, and also to Italy. By 2000, even the publication of a book without an exhibition—*Designed for Living: Furniture and Lighting 1950–2000*—provided an opportunity for the museum to acquire objects to strengthen its decade-by-decade survey of design and the themes of the collection itself.

In giving a showcase to exhibitions organized by others, the museum also found auspicious collecting opportunities. In 1988, it presented the first display in North America of the furniture designs of Ron Arad,

organized by the New York gallery Art + Industrie; Mrs. Stewart purchased several major pieces from it. Such monographic displays also included *Eva Zeisel: Designer for Industry* in 1986; *Tea and Coffee Piazzas—The Alessi Collection* in 1987, and *Ettore Sottsass: Furniture for the Ritual of Life* in 1988. These exhibits of contemporary work provided opportunities to make purchases and they inspired artists, collectors, and manufacturers to donate works to the collection.

As early as 1985, Mrs. Stewart had seen that a larger, more cohesive museum facility was essential for the growing collection and active exhibition program, and she believed that a contemporary setting would enhance understanding of modern objects. Between 1980 and 1990, several detailed studies for the museum's future were undertaken. One of the studies confirmed that the museum should relocate to a more central area of Montreal if it wished to attract larger audiences. In 1990, Mrs. Stewart approached the Canadian-born architect Frank Gehry to create a new facility: this was his second commission in Canada. When subsequent economic conditions prevented the creation of a new museum building, she engaged Gehry to renovate part of the 1991 Jean-Noël Desmarais Pavilion of the Montreal Museum of Fine Arts. He designed new galleries, comprising ten thousand square feet, especially for the Stewart Collection (fig. 2), and conceived a sculptural sign (fig. 3) for the entrance to the galleries to give the decorative arts museum a clear identity.

This commission led Mrs. Stewart to acquire many of Gehry's unique prototypes for the furniture that Knoll introduced in 1991 (p. 372), in addition to examples of the chairs put into production. Again, an exhibition followed

2 Installation of *Designed for Delight: Alternative Aspects of Twentieth-Century Decorative Arts* at the Montreal Museum of Decorative Arts, in the galleries designed by Frank O. Gehry & Associates, 1997.
3 Frank O. Gehry and Associates, signage above the entrance to the Montreal Museum of Decorative Arts in the Cultural Corridor of the Montreal Museum of Fine Arts, 1996.
4 Installation of *Frank Gehry: New Bentwood Furniture Designs*, designed by Réjean Tétreault for the Montreal Museum of Decorative Arts, September 11 to November 15, 1992.
5 Installation of the Stewart Collection in the Liliane and David M. Stewart Pavilion, The Montreal Museum of Fine Arts, 2008.

with a catalogue: *Frank Gehry: New Bentwood Furniture Design* featured the museum's new acquisitions (fig. 4) and toured museums in North America in 1992 and 1993.

The presence of the Stewart Collection/Museum of Decorative Arts in its Gehry-designed galleries within the larger museum opened another chapter in the history of the collection, the beginning of a close, cooperative alliance between Mrs. Stewart and the Montreal Museum of Fine Arts. The year 2000 saw the next dramatic shift in the collection's history: Mrs. Stewart donated its more than five thousand objects to the Montreal Museum of Fine Arts, which, according to the MMFA's official history, "was one of the most valuable gifts ever received by a Canadian museum."[4] Mrs. Stewart wrote of the donation, "My decision to donate the collection and to establish a cooperative alliance with the fine arts museum reflects my conviction that entrusting these objects to a larger institution with ample support staff and gallery space will preserve it for future generations." The Museum of Fine Arts would also benefit from the addition of expert staff from the former Museum of Decorative Arts. Both

5

museum names were used in tandem until 2002, when it became clear that their juxtaposition was confusing to the public. The name Montreal Museum of Decorative Arts was dropped, and the Stewart Collection became the responsibility of an enlarged decorative arts department, housed and exhibited within the context of the traditional decorative arts collection of the Montreal Museum of Fine Arts. Also in 2001, the Stewart Collection moved from the space created for it by Frank Gehry into another wing of the Museum of Fine Arts, which had been built in 1976, adjacent to the original 1913 beaux-arts museum building. This third and permanent home, named the Liliane and David M. Stewart Pavilion, was inaugurated in 2001, and there the Stewart Collection, formed from 1980 through 2000, was united with the other decorative arts collections at the Museum of Fine Arts (fig. 5). Collecting has continued at an energetic pace with the relocation and change of ownership of the Stewart Collection. Mrs. Stewart is a board member of the Museum of Fine Arts, and she heads its Decorative Arts Committee, which is tasked with enhancing the museum's collection through an active acquisition program.

Since its inception in 1980, the collection has been shaped by the quick responsiveness of Mrs. Stewart and her advisors to design scholarship and to both leading and emerging designers. Focused initially on work of 1940–60, acquisitions reflected the primacy of design in Scandinavia, Italy, and the United States at that time and were first concentrated on those geographic areas. As the collection grew, it increasingly embraced contemporary works, moving beyond its original boundaries to choose the most inventive designs of the present and past, regardless of place. The prominence of Italian design in the 1980s and '90s coincided with an exceptionally active period of collecting for Mrs. Stewart. In particular, she added significant works of furniture, glass, and ceramics by the Italian architect Ettore Sottsass (sixty-four examples of his work are in the collection). After 1990, collecting expanded to include cutting-edge work from Japan, England, and The Netherlands, which had all become important centers of contemporary design.

Particular attachments to designers and their works are evident in the collection. The ceramic designer Eva Zeisel has been one of Mrs. Stewart's friends since 1981, when the Montreal Museum of Decorative Arts organized *Eva Zeisel: Designer for Industry*. The groundbreaking exhibition marked the rediscovery of this pioneer, now among the most famous of mid-century designers, and prompted the acquisition of an important group of Ms. Zeisel's ceramic designs for the collection. Diverse and extensive holdings by such pivotal figures as Gaetano Pesce and Jack Lenor Larsen are the result of similar relationships. In 1998 Mrs. Stewart invited Pesce to Montreal to design the installation of an exhibition of his work (fig. 6), and from it she made significant acquisitions.

Spontaneity and creativity played their part in building the Stewart Collection's special identity. This helped attract gifts and acquisition opportunities that more conservative institutions had refused. Such rare objects as a prefabricated bathroom patented by Buckminster Fuller in 1930 for his Dymaxion House was welcomed in the museum in 1996 when a New York collector offered it as a gift. The Dymaxion House was a prefabricated home, and only twelve examples of the copper-plated bathroom that Fuller designed for it were produced. In 1988, a collection of prototypes of coffeepots for Alessi, designed by internationally prominent architects (p. 290, 312–13), was offered for purchase, and the generosity of a single donor made it possible to acquire the entire collection. In 1991 a passionate New York collector gave more than one hundred design drawings by the American-Canadian abstract artist Rolph Scarlett; these studies ranged from refrigerators to cocktail shakers and added new depth to the collection's industrial design holdings. Here it can be noted that entire archives, such as the design drawings of Peter Todd Mitchell, were acquired as gifts for the Stewart Collection, as was the documentation gathered for publications such as *What Modern Was* and *American Streamlined Design*, including interviews and correspondence with designers, dealers, and collectors, as well as original catalogues. Such archives have made the collection a tool for researchers.

In 2000, at the same time the Montreal Museum of Decorative Arts merged with the Montreal Museum of Fine Arts, the Stewart Program for Modern Design was formed. This separate initiative, undertaken by the Macdonald Stewart Foundation, is dedicated to acquiring works for the Stewart Collection and to mounting and circulating design exhibitions based on the collection, when possible with publications. In 2004, the Stewart Program co-organized, with the Museum of Arts and Design in New York, the traveling exhibition *Jack Lenor*

6 Installation designed by Pesce of *The Presence of Objects: Gaetano Pesce*, The Montreal Museum of Fine Arts, September 29, 1998, to January 3, 1999.

Larsen: Creator and Collector, which drew upon the impressive holdings of the work of textile designer Jack Lenor Larsen in the collection.

From 2000 to the present, the Stewart Collection has grown by the addition of more than a thousand objects. Most acquisitions have gone to the Montreal Museum of Fine Arts, but other museums have also benefited from Mrs. Stewart's generosity. In 2002, she donated important examples of 1980s American design to the Denver Art Museum on the occasion of its organization of *US Design: 1975–2000*. In the 1990s gifts from the Stewart Program went to The Metropolitan Museum of Art and The Art Institute of Chicago, and, more recently, to the Wolfsonian-Florida International University in Miami. A recent gift to the Indianapolis Museum of Art was the catalyst for the development of its design collection.

Between 2001 and 2006, the American collector Eric Brill gave the Stewart Program his major collection of over nine hundred objects of American and Canadian industrial design. The size and importance of this acquisition was extraordinary. Selections from the Brill Collection became the subject of the exhibition *American Streamlined Design: The World of Tomorrow,* which was presented in six museums between 2005 and 2009. These and other acquisitions of the Stewart Program were offered to the Montreal Museum of Fine Arts and other institutions; the Brill Collection was accepted in its entirety by the Montreal Museum.

Meanwhile at the Montreal Museum of Fine Arts, the Stewart Collection has evolved within its larger context, integrated with the holdings of a major fine arts museum. Many pieces of Italian design from the Stewart Collection were featured in the exhibition *Il modo italiano: Italian Design and Avant-garde in the 20ᵗʰ Century,* organized in 2006 by the Montreal Museum of Fine Arts in partnership with the Royal Ontario Museum and Museo di Arte Moderna e Contemporanea di Trento e Rovereto.

The discrimination and determination behind the continuing acquisitions of both the Stewart Program and the Montreal Museum of Fine Arts, the imaginative use of the collection's diverse holdings, and a sequence of inventive and influential exhibitions and collaborations with other museums in the United States and Europe over the last thirty years constitute a history of which all those connected with the Stewart Collection can be proud.

An Introduction to Modernism, 1900–1929

1 Charles F. A. Voysey, Living Room Corner shown at the Arts and Crafts Exhibition, London, 1896.
2 Eugène Gaillard, Bedroom, Siegfried Bing's Art Nouveau Pavilion at the Universal Exposition of 1900, Paris, photograph from *Album de référence de l'Art Nouveau (Photo/Album Bing)*. Bibliothèque, Musée des Arts Décoratifs, Paris.

"What is modern design?" Edgar Kaufmann, Jr., asked in 1950. The influential director of The Museum of Modern Art's Department of Industrial Design proposed, as one of twelve qualities, that "modern design should be simple . . . and it should express the purpose of an object, never making it seem to be what it is not." This book, written some sixty years after Kaufmann's, answers his question more broadly. The full range of modern design reveals many contradictions: it has pattern and ornament, as well as bare surfaces and revealed structures; vivid color palettes, as well as strictly limited ones; historicizing references, as well as futuristic styling; distinct variations often associated with national or regional traditions, as well as global tendencies; and luxurious one-off or limited editions, as well as mass-produced designs priced for broad markets. The many "moderns" surveyed here include the streamlined modern of the 1930s and '40s, the biomorphism of mid-century, the Pop tendencies of the 1960s and '70s, and the Postmodernism and minimalism of the late twentieth century and today.

Reform movements in the late nineteenth and early twentieth centuries had in common a protest against the decline in the quality of design, which was associated with mechanized processes, especially those used in the nineteenth century to mimic historic styles. Many of these movements shared an admiration for designs of various earlier eras, in particular the medieval, but they shunned the historicism of the Victorian period's imitations of past styles. Reformists praised the period of the Middle Ages because the craftsman carried out a design from concept to production, there was a perceived unity of design expressing the spirit of the times, and there was little of the division of labor introduced by the Industrial Revolution. The reformists revived methods of individual craftsmanship, resulting in well-made, beautiful designs. Such designers often used historic models as vehicles for reform, primarily on aesthetic grounds but in some instances also to support ideas for social change.

In the first two decades of the twentieth century, the major tenets of modernism were established, rooted in the Arts and Crafts movement of the late nineteenth century. Established on principles that stressed simplicity, fitness to function, use of materials without disguise, and admiration for the craftsman's pride in his handiwork, the Arts and Crafts movement was inspired by the writings of Englishmen Thomas Carlyle and John Ruskin. William Morris, a leading figure in the English Arts and Crafts

3 René Lalique, Pendant, gold and enamel, c. 1898. Stewart Collection, The Montreal Museum of Fine Arts.

movement, put their ideals to work in 1862 by establishing an interior design firm, Morris, Faulkner & Co., aiming to revive an artisan guild system and to set high standards of craftsmanship as an antidote to the "soul-less" objects produced with new industrial processes. Morris lectured and wrote about these design principles, and put them into practice through his firm. He sought good design, affordable to all, and a restored pride in labor, but he decried machine production. Exhibitions such as those mounted by the English Arts and Crafts Exhibition Society also propagated the principles of the movement. Charles F. A. Voysey's Living Room Corner was shown at the 1896 Arts and Crafts exhibition in London (fig. 1). The rectilinear, unadorned forms and natural wood seen in his furniture designs looked surprisingly modern for the period. Unhappily for Morris's socialist cause, the return to handcrafted objects resulted in products that most buyers could not afford. Future reformists would have to come to terms with machine production, but in the 1890s designers focused on creating a new style.

(Design reform in the decorative arts in continental Europe at the turn of the century often appeared in organic flowing forms, quite distinct from the reductive, platonic style that later came to define "modernism.") In France, the new style of the *fin-de-siècle* was known as "Art Nouveau" after Siegfried Bing's chic shop in Paris, which opened in 1895. Art Nouveau was derived from diverse sources—including Rococo, Celtic Revival, and Japanism—and its champions rejected overt historicism. A bedroom designed by Eugène Gaillard for Bing's Art Nouveau Pavilion at the Paris Universal Exposition of 1900 illustrates this new style in its fluid lines and floral motifs (fig. 2). The celebrated jewelry designer René Lalique exhibited both at Art Nouveau Bing and at the Paris 1900 exposition. A gold-and-enamel pendant by Lalique illustrates the French Art Nouveau style with its abundant sensuous leaves wreathing a female head (fig. 3). The architect Hector Guimard and the furniture designer and glass artist Émile Gallé were also proponents of the voluptuous French version of Art Nouveau.

The style was international, though national names and expressions varied. In Germany it was known as "Jugendstil" from the magazine *Jugend* (Youth), founded in Munich in 1896; in Italy it was known as "Stile Liberty" after the English company Liberty, which sold fabrics and other objects in this style. Each country gave the style a national inflection.

In Austria, progressive designers joined painters to found the Vienna Secession in 1897, "seceding" from the traditional styles of the day in both decorative and fine arts. Leading designers and architects included Josef Hoffmann, Josef Maria Olbrich, and Kolomon Moser. The group shared a commitment to the Arts and Crafts movement and to the ideal of unifying architecture, interiors, and the decorative arts in an integral whole, much as Frank Lloyd Wright advocated with his Prairie School houses in the United States at the turn of the century. Although influenced by Art Nouveau, the Vienna Secessionist style was marked by flat, geometric motifs rather than by organic curves and vegetal metaphors. The Secessionist exhibition of 1900 presented works by the Scottish designer and architect Charles Rennie Mackintosh and the Englishman Charles Robert Ashbee, which influenced Viennese design with their strong, simple, upright forms (fig. 4). Secession products included metalwork, glass, ceramics, and other decorative arts. Such exhibitions, with their accompanying catalogues and press coverage, speeded the international spread of influential ideas. The porcelain dinnerware designed around 1901 by the Austrian Jutta Sika illustrates the bold, reduced forms with equally elemental, flat decoration associated with this reform movement (fig. 5).

In 1903 Hoffmann and Moser created the Wiener Werkstätte (Vienna Workshops), inspired by the English Arts and Crafts movement, in particular Morris's writings and Ashbee's Guild of Handicraft. The Wiener Werkstätte helped to popularize the Secession style in architecture and the decorative arts. An installation of the work of Hoffmann and Eduard Wimmer at the 1914 Deutscher Werkbund Exhibition, Cologne, shows a unified, harmonious design of carpets, walls, vitrines, and upholstery, with repeated flat patterns (fig. 6). Though these handcrafted products were expensive, like those of Morris's firm, they demonstrated the impact of an overall design conception and of a reticent planar aesthetic.

Founded in Munich in 1907, the Deutscher Werkbund (German Design Organization) was comparable to Arts and Crafts organizations in England and the United States, but it was explicitly dedicated to improving the quality of German industrial design. Leading the association of designers, artists, artisans, artists' associations, and manufacturers were Peter Behrens, Bruno Paul, and Richard Riemerschmid. The Werkbund sought to create low-cost yet beautiful products through industrial manufacture. Bruno Taut's Glass Pavilion at the 1914 Deutscher Werkbund Exhibition was exemplary in its geometric structure realized in mass-produced glass bricks held in a steel lattice (fig. 7). Interestingly, a glass vase by Josef Hoffmann of 1912 (fig. 8) has a similar division into geometric fields, but the flattened plant forms reflect the designer's crafts-based refinement.

The Werkbund published yearbooks from 1912 to 1920; the cover of the 1912 edition features the Werkbund's austere, geometricizing typography and design. After World War I, the Werkbund also published the periodical *Die Form* and continued to be influential in Germany through the 1920s. Its exhibition and book, *Die Form ohne Ornament* (*Form without Ornament*), which appeared in Stuttgart in 1924, included both craft and machine products and rejected historical ornament. Illustrated in this book were ceramics from the Bauhaus, the most influential of the organizations inspired by the Werkbund (fig. 9). The Deutscher Werkbund's designs for industrial production and exhibitions made an important contribution to modern design, although they were overshadowed by the fame of the Bauhaus. The same rationalist, or functionalist, principles were on display in the Weissenhofsiedlung exhibition in Stuttgart of 1927, where leading architects, including Marcel Breuer and Ludwig Mies van der Rohe, showed furnishings that fully utilized the machine.

The Bauhaus school was founded in Weimar in 1919 to unite the teaching of the fine and applied arts, with the goal of improving German manufacturing. Although the Bauhaus survived only until 1933, when it was closed by the Nazis, its philosophy and example shaped modern design and architecture for the rest of the twentieth century. Its founder and first director, the architect Walter Gropius, sought to teach all the arts under one roof and required all students to begin with a six-month foundation course focused on the exploration of materials and basic forms. Though it extended the ideals of the Arts and Crafts movement, such as unification of the arts, the Bauhaus unequivocally advocated the use of the machine. By 1925, when the school moved to Dessau and Gropius and his students designed its radically modern new building, the Bauhaus motto was "art and technology: a new unity."

In Dessau the 1925 dining room in the László Moholy-Nagy house (fig. 10) reflected the stripped, gleaming, industrial style of the new Bauhaus. The minimalist interior

4 The Eighth Secession Exhibition, interior by Charles Rennie Mackintosh, 1900.
5 Jutta Sika, dinnerware, designed c. 1901, glazed porcelain. Stewart Collection,
The Montreal Museum of Fine Arts.
6 Josef Hoffmann and Eduard Wimmer, Wiener Werkstätte room
at the Deutscher Werkbund exhibition, Cologne, 1914.
7 Bruno Taut, The Glass Pavilion, interior of the upper floor, Deutscher Werkbund Exhibition, Cologne, 1914.
8 Josef Hoffmann, vase, designed 1912, glass. The Montreal Museum of Fine Arts, gift of Roger Labbé.
9 Pottery and porcelain designed at the Bauhaus as illustrated in *Die Forme ohne Ornament*, 1924, 77.

4

5

6

7

8

9

included a color scheme and a geometric abstraction painted by Moholy-Nagy, a lighting fixture designed by Gropius and the Bauhaus metal workshop, and furniture designed by Marcel Breuer. Breuer headed the furniture workshops at the Bauhaus from 1925 to 1928, during which time he first began designing tubular steel furnishings, including the *B22* table manufactured by Thonet (fig. 11).[2] This example in the Stewart Collection was originally owned by Alfred H. Barr, Jr., the first Director of The Museum of Modern Art. Barr's Breuer furniture reflected his admiration for the Bauhaus and its functionalist principles when MoMA was founded in 1929, principles the museum would promulgate for the next half-century.

In contrast to the rationalist standpoint of the German design organizations, displays at the 1925 *Exposition Internationale des Arts Décoratifs et Industriels Modernes* in Paris largely advocated deluxe decor and ornamented objects. Much later the Paris show generated the term "Art Deco," but at the time the French design language was called "modernistic." This label was derogatory when used by functional rationalists for aspects of Art Deco, yet the style exerted international influence in the late 1920s. Derived from Synthetic Cubism and Futurism in painting, this was a popular language of flattened, mostly geometric forms, and bold outlines, often applied to traditional forms and executed in modern materials. A bravura example of Art Deco style is seen in Edgar Brandt's exuberant grillework for the central gate of the Porte d'Honneur at the exposition (fig. 12). Camille Fauré's *Sidney* vase (fig. 13) illustrates how the style celebrated at the 1925 show was used on decorative objects. Its geometric design of swirling, overlapping circles reflects the influence of the colorful abstract offshoot of Cubism known as Orphism.

Notwithstanding the triumph of deluxe decorative designs by expertly trained artisans at the Paris exposition, there were some advocates of industrial design present. A leading theorist of rational design in France was Le Corbusier, whose architecture and writings were already influential. His rational principles were realized at the exhibition in his Pavillon de l'Esprit Nouveau (fig. 14)—an example of his often-quoted line that the "house is a machine for living in."

The Russians were also represented at the exhibition, and theirs was the most radical design direction. Under the rubric of Constructivism, a movement in all

10 László Moholy-Nagy, Dining Room in the masters' duplex at the Bauhaus in Dessau, 1925, photograph by Lucia Moholy, BHA.
11 Marcel Breuer, *B22* side table, designed 1928, tubular steel, laminated plastic. The Montreal Museum of Fine Arts, gift of Victoria Barr from the Estate of Mr. and Mrs. Alfred H. Barr, Jr.
12 Edgar Brandt, Central Gate of the Porte d'Honneur of the *Exposition des Arts Décoratifs et Industriels Modernes*, 1925, Paris.
13 Camille Fauré, *Sidney* vase, designed c. 1925, enamels on copper. Stewart Collection, The Montreal Museum of Fine Arts.

14

15

16

the arts that thrived across the USSR and Eastern Europe from 1917 to the mid-1920s, Russian artists such as El Lissitzky, Aleksandr Rodchenko, and Vladimir Tatlin conceived visionary structures for the utopia promised by Communism. Tatlin's 1920 design for the *Monument to the Third International* was arguably the most memorable of these unbuilt public buildings (fig. 15). To house state communications bureaus, the giant spiraling tower of steel and glass had parts intended to rotate over the course of a week, a month, and a year, symbolizing the dynamism of the Russian Revolution.

Such idealism about the power of technology and design to improve public life gave immediacy to the ideas and practices of the reform movements in England, Scotland, and continental Europe of 1900–1930. They set the stage for the development of international modern design for the rest of the century and were directly developed during the 1930s. The Bauhaus had a lasting effect, while the French "modernistic" style was short-lived (though decorative countercurrents to functionalism would recur). A touchstone for modern style, certainly in the United States, was Ludwig Mies van der Rohe's design of the German National Pavilion for the 1929 International Exhibition in Barcelona (fig. 16). Its open plan, steel structure, and juxtaposed, unadorned planes of glass and marble were, and remain, the classic expression of what was dubbed the "International Style" in 1932.

The Bauhaus significantly influenced the structure and aesthetic ideals of The Museum of Modern Art, in New York. Through the museum's exhibitions and teachings, the Bauhaus had a tremendous impact on American design. Inspired by the organization of the school,[3] director Alfred Barr developed a multi-departmental museum that recognized equally a wide range of arts, including architecture, design, film, and photography, as well as painting, sculpture, and drawings and prints. For Barr, the Bauhaus had opened up a new world where "a community of artists" pursued arts, crafts, and industrial design and students worked in interrelation.[4] Enlarging the impact of MoMA's promulgation of Bauhaus ideals in the 1930s and thereafter was the emigration of leading European designers to the United States before and during World War II. In the 1930s the avant-garde design created largely in Europe found fertile ground in a number of key centers in the New World.

14 Le Corbusier, interior, Pavillon de l'Esprit Nouveau, *Exposition des Arts Décoratifs et Industriels Modernes,* 1925, Paris.
15 Vladimir Tatlin, *Monument to the Third International,* model in construction in Petrograd, 1920.
16 Ludwig Mies van der Rohe, German Pavilion in Barcelona, 1929.

1930
1939

Modes of Modernism

The economic and political turmoil of the bleak 1930s inevitably shaped design. In 1932, the depth of the Great Depression, one in four Americans was without a job, and 28 percent had no income at all.[1] In 1933, Hitler closed the Bauhaus, just months after his National Socialist party came to power in Germany, and the westward diaspora of modernist architects, designers, and artists began in force. In 1939–40, as the New York World's Fair was attracting thousands, most of the world was at war. The luxury trades survived in France, though for a diminished clientele, but middle-class consumers and technological innovators were arguably as formative on production as progressive designers in the 1930s.

"Hitler shook the tree, and America gathered the fruit," wrote one observer of the flight of Germany's progressive thinkers and creators, a shift of cultural capital that would help the United States dominate vanguard design and art practices after World War II. American academics welcomed the émigrés. Painter Josef Albers and his wife, textile designer Anni Albers, taught at Black Mountain College in North Carolina from 1933; designer-artist-theorist László Moholy-Nagy from 1937 and architect Ludwig Mies van der Rohe from 1938, both in Chicago; and designer Marcel Breuer and architect Walter Gropius at Harvard University from the same years. Their example and their fine-grained knowledge of the history, theory, and criticism of their fields would bring deeper professionalism to progressive design, art, and architecture among successive generations of students and liberal intelligentsia.

Even before the Bauhaus professors reached America, The Museum of Modern Art was championing the austere rational functionalism associated with these Germans, as well as certain Dutch and French architects and Russian Constructivists. When MoMA director Alfred H. Barr, Jr., architect Philip Johnson, and architectural historian Henry-Russell Hitchcock mounted the 1932 exhibition *Modern Architecture: International Exhibition*, they named the "International Style" and identified Gropius, Mies van der Rohe, Le Corbusier, J. J. P. Oud, and Frank Lloyd Wright among its avatars (fig. 1). The Europeans were drawing on Wright's Prairie Style homes of the 1900s and functional American structures, such as grain elevators, bridges, and factories, for their steel-framed, open-plan, and unadorned flat-roofed buildings. In *Vers une Architecture*, 1923, translated as *Towards a New Architecture* in 1927, Le Corbusier lauded the efficiency and formal clarity of anonymous U.S. construction (fig. 2), and Johnson echoed the widely read text in an essay introducing MoMA's *Machine Art* exhibition of 1934. "Pure engineering" offered models for design and building, he wrote: "The beauty of these designs consists of their simple geometric relations: the catenary curve and straight posts of the bridge, the interlocking cylinders of the silo, the spherical perfection of the ball bearing."[2]

MoMA showed ball bearings, a propeller, and laboratory glassware alongside equally no-nonsense housewares and appliances in *Machine Art* to confirm that mass production could generate standardized forms both functional and pleasing in their Platonic geometries: they were art by machine. Isolated and enshrined like abstract sculpture, the economical designs in shining metal and glass epitomized an aesthetic that had already captivated photographers and painters such as Paul Strand and Charles Sheeler in the 1920s.

While promoting modernist functionalism, MoMA spokesmen were equally clear about the kinds of new design they scorned. Objects with "neo-classical trappings and bizarre ornament," of "modernistic French"[3] or of "zigzag moderne style," were willful decorative distortions of true modern language. Classicizing and cubistic stylizations were trivia popularized at the 1925 *Exposition des Arts Décoratifs et Industriels Modernes* in Paris, and by the 1930s deluxe Art Deco designs were also condemned as out of touch with economic realities. By contrast, Bauhaus furniture in tubular steel by Breuer and all-metal lighting by forward-looking German, Dutch, and French designers had been industrially produced in the 1920s onward: these forthright examples were heralded as timeless, enduring types meeting practical, middle-class needs.

Yet a third version of current design offended MoMA critics. Streamlined forms failed to follow function; in fact, they defied it. The style, emergent around 1930, concealed working parts of products under windswept sheaths, adapting the aerodynamic cowlings of trains, planes, ships, and cars, intended to minimize wind or water resistance, to stationary objects (pp. 44, 60–61). The glamorous language was rooted in European precedents (e.g., Erich Mendelsohn's expressionist architectural drawings of the 1910s), but it was embraced as American by industrial designers and an avid public. Sweeping horizontal profiles accented by trios of "speed lines," teardrop shapes, and continuously curved surfaces replaced the jagged verticals and faceted planes of 1920s designs. The fluid forms of streamlining were efficiently molded from new plastics like Bakelite, and their sleek skins were easy to keep clean and gleaming. Identified with progress, goods from dinette sets and radios to electric fans, clocks, and cigarette lighters let consumers feel up-to-date for a modest price.

Designer Egmont Arens telegrammed President Franklin D. Roosevelt in 1934 offering to tour America speaking on "Streamlining for Recovery" with a van full of products illustrating the sales potential of streamlined packaging and design. The head of the first styling and design department in an American advertising agency, Arens asserted that "streamlining has captured American imagination to mean modern, efficient, well-organized, sweet, clean, and beautiful." Products updated with the style would attract customers to stores again, spur impulse spending, let manufacturers distinguish themselves from the competition, and improve brand loyalty, since such surface changes were seen as improvements. Postwar critics would decry "planned obsolescence" as wasteful, but Arens used his phrase positively: it would launch a needed capitalist renaissance.[4]

Sales figures proved Arens right. Just as General Motors had sparked car sales with annual style changes from 1927 on, so durable-goods manufacturers benefited from the mid-1930s by regularly altering the envelopes and materials of their household

1 View of exhibition, *Modern Architecture—International Exhibition,* The Museum of Modern Art, New York, 1932. At center: Model of Le Corbusier's Villa Savoye, Poissy-sur-Seine, France, 1930.
2 Pennsylvania elevator, James Stewart & Co., Baltimore, 1908, published in Le Corbusier, *Towards a New Architecture*, 1927.

3 Norman Bel Geddes, General
Motors Pavilion, New York World's
Fair, 1939.

machines. Most spectacular was Raymond Loewy's success in redesigning the Sears, Roebuck *Coldspot* refrigerator, not once but four times annually from 1935 on. Sales multiplied more than eighteen times in five years, from 15,000 to 275,000 units.[5] Loewy's fellow industrial designers, such as Henry Dreyfuss, Norman Bel Geddes, and Walter Dorwin Teague, were almost as celebrated for their streamlining of telephones and vacuum cleaners, stoves, and radios. Though the machinery inside might remain unchanged, the consumer liked the improved ease of use and maintenance, as well as the refreshed good looks that streamlined design provided.

The rise in such consumer purchases through the 1930s was aided by buying on time offers from retailers, low-cost government loans to homebuyers, and widespread electrification under the aegis of the New Deal. While dam-building projects to produce hydro-electric power provided jobs for middle America, the wiring of homes for refrigerators, washing machines, and the like improved the quality of domestic life across the country. These developments aided the adoption of streamlining for products large and small, and their creators contributed to making industrial design a full-fledged profession in America by the 1930s. Industrial design, according to a *Fortune* article of February 1934, was a way to lift the economy out of the Depression. In 1935 Peter Müller-Munk (p. 58) established the first academic degree-granting program in industrial design at the Carnegie Institute of Technology, Pittsburgh.

Between 1934 and 1939 modern design for popular consumption came to be identified with simplification and streamlining, if the Metropolitan Museum of Art's series of industrial design exhibitions, inaugurated in 1917, is any indication. The mandate for the 1934 display was "to show what might be achieved at low cost," and a participating designer remarked, "While we may still 'love the garish day' [referring to pre-Crash design], we welcome any opportunity to create a fine thing in a simple manner."[6] Of the 1938 survey a critic noted, "in only five years all the awkward points had been swept out . . . in favor of the circular smooth curves and contrasting textures which we have come to know as 'modern' or 'contemporary' design."[7]

In 1939 in New York, at the fair subtitled *The World of Tomorrow*, the industrial designer (not the architect) and streamlined design dominated. America's celebrity designers all had a hand in it: Arens, Loewy, Teague, Bel Geddes, Dreyfuss, Gilbert Rohde, and Russel Wright. (In 1931–41, Rohde's designs sold a quarter of a million chairs for manufacturer Herman Miller; in 1939–59 Americans bought more than eighty million pieces of Wright's *American Modern* dinnerware).[8] Streamlining was visible not only in the Fair's various buildings and the products on view, but also in the transportation systems used to move visitors around the park and especially at Bel Geddes's *Futurama* exhibit at the General Motors Pavilion, the most popular attraction. The giant structure itself, with its smooth, rounded forms and long, swooping entry ramp, evoked both Le Corbusier and submarines (fig. 3).

A comparison between the 1939 New York fair and the 1925 Paris Exposition illustrates the differences between the decades. Overall, Paris showcased individual, predominantly high-end designers who appealed to aristocratic connoisseurs and favored handcraftsmanship. New York featured American manufacturers, and streamlining symbolized their smooth corporate functioning for mass consumers. "The world of tomorrow" evidently belonged not to rosewood and silver but to plastics and aluminum, not to artists in their ateliers but to industrial designers in factories, not to a few knowledgeable art lovers but to a broad market of homemakers.[9]

That said, the fairs of the 1930s also demonstrated the hold of Neoclassicism on official public architecture worldwide. This was the style of the City of Paris pavilion at the 1937 *Exposition International des Arts et Techniques dans la Vie Moderne* in Paris (fig. 4), which again headlined René Lalique, Cartier, and Jean Puiforcat, the elitist stars of the 1925 Exposition (pp. 36–37). In New York in 1939, the Federal Building, situated at the end of the Constitutional Mall created for the fair, typified the retrospective style of U.S. government-funded construction, most visible in Washington, D.C., between the wars. Simplified and grandiose versions of Greco-Roman temples and arcades also rose to house government facilities and to frame public events in Mussolini's Italy and in Germany at the direction of Albert Speer, Hitler's architect. The modernized idiom of columned and pedimental façades, triumphal arches, and symmetrical plans appeared internationally, in democratic and totalitarian countries alike, while their symbolism—of antiquity, democracy, empire, or the Enlightenment—paradoxically reinforced the values of individual, opposed nations.

Symbolism was also crucial to the success of another idiom on view at the 1939 fair. Scandinavian design, and especially that pioneered by Finnish architect Alvar Aalto from the late 1920s, was identified with native craft traditions and the northern landscape of forests, lakes, and fjords. Aalto's Finnish Pavilion, with its rippling and canted interior walls of wood slats (fig. 5), triggered atavistic emotional responses from visitors, as his laminated wood furniture and freeform glassware did from their debuts in 1932 and 1937 respectively (pp. 68, 72). What won the popularity of such "organic" design was the human warmth of its curving forms, natural materials, and tactile appeal, in addition to its low cost. Aalto and other Scandinavians grasped the economic need for standardized production using the latest technology, but they gave these principles of the International Style a personal expression and acknowledged that designs should fill psychological as well as practical needs.

In 1934 the American cultural commentator Lewis Mumford wrote, "Until we have absorbed the lessons of . . . the mechanical realm, we cannot go further in our development toward the more richly organic, the more profoundly human."[10] An achievement of the 1930s was perceived mastery of the machine and recognition of its centrality to successful design production. In the 1940s organic design—uniting technical innovations in molded materials with a biomorphic form language—would dominate and enrich design in subsequent decades.

4 Jean-Claude Dondel, André Aubert, Jean-Paul-Émile Viard, and Marcel Dastugue, City of Paris Pavilion, *Exposition International des Arts et Techniques dans la Vie Moderne*, Paris, 1937.
5 Alvar Aalto, interior of Finnish Pavilion at the New York World's Fair, 1939.

Raoul DUFY

(1877–1953)

Tapestry
Hommage à Mozart
Designed 1934
Wool, silk, cotton
138.5 x 113 cm
Produced at Aubusson, France
The Montreal Museum of
Fine Arts, D87.189.1

One of the first Fauve artists, Dufy shared with this group "of wild beasts" an emphasis on warm color and lively brushwork. A great deal of his artistic output was in the decorative arts, including ceramic and textile designs. This tapestry and the creation of others by leading French artists was due to an atelier established in 1930 by Marie Cuttoli, wife of the French senator from Algeria. She was, wrote William Lieberman, "a gracious and spirited patron of the arts, she commissioned designs from masters of the modern movement: Braque, Derain, Dufy, Le Corbusier, Léger, Matisse. . . ."[11] Her efforts to revive the tapestry industry and win recognition for it as a contemporary art form led to an exhibition in 1936, for which she commissioned *Hommage à Mozart*. Almost all the artists included in this exhibition supplied paintings to be copied by the weavers. Dufy supplied a painting as well, and the house he depicted is Mozart's home in Salzberg.[12]

Clarice CLIFF

(1899–1972)

**Tea and coffee service
and soup tureen**
Coral Firs
Designed c. 1933
Glazed earthenware
Coffeepot: 17 x 22 x 8.5 cm
Produced by the Newport
Pottery, Newport,
Burslem, England
The Montreal Museum of
Fine Arts, D95.170.1–5a–b,
gift of Geoffrey N. Bradfield*

As the premier designer at the Newport Pottery, Clarice Cliff had her own studio. She was approaching the peak of her productivity in the early 1930s, and under her direction young artists hand-painted the ware she designed. One of her successful designs was this surprisingly modern service with its sharply truncated geometric forms and circular finials. She introduced the decoration in 1933, a bestselling landscape pattern inspired by the local Staffordshire hills, which are topped with ragged fir trees.[13] The rounded earthenware forms contain the stylized design, which laps over onto the lids, rendered in vivid colors associated with Fauvism, the French movement named in 1905.

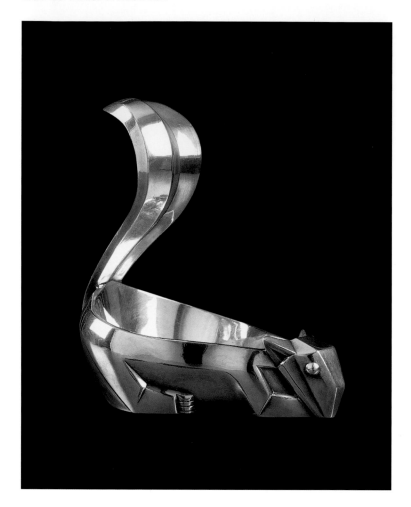

Antoinette Champetier DE RIBES

(1892–1972)

Nut dish
Écureuil (Squirrel)
Designed 1931
Silver-plated pewter alloy
19 x 18 x 11.2 cm
Produced by Orfèvrerie
Christofle, Paris, France
The Montreal Museum of
Fine Arts, D95.139.1

The sculptor Antoinette de Ribes, a pupil of Aristide Maillol, was known for her renderings of animals. Between 1929 and 1933 she designed several pieces for Christofle, the result of a commission from her cousin, André Bouilhet, who managed the company. This *drageoir* or sweetmeat dish was part of the Gallia Collection, begun by Christofle in 1930, referring to objects made in a new pewter alloy that was silver-plated.[14] De Ribes's designs, as in this example, exhibit a Cubist influence, seen in the flat angular shapes and simplified form of the squirrel. The sense of drama seen in Cubist sculpture is enhanced here by the light reflected from the faceted surfaces of silver.

Gilbert POILLERAT

(1902–1988)

Door grille
Designed c. 1939
Polished steel, gilded metal
175 x 70 x 2.3 cm
Probably produced by Baudet,
Donon et Roussel, Paris, France
The Montreal Museum of
Fine Arts, D93.273.1

Poillerat was an interior designer, painter, sculptor, and metalsmith. In 1921, he graduated from l'École Boulle, where he studied metalwork. From 1921 to 1927 he worked as a designer for the firm of Edgar Brandt, the acknowledged master of ironwork of the time. Poillerat introduced a sense of lightness and exuberant movement, distinctly different from the designs in iron in the Art Deco style for which Brandt was known and that had been so popular at the Paris Exposition of 1925.[15] Poillerat's work was light, spirited, and calligraphic, often made of steel rather than wrought iron. It recalled the Louis XV style of the Rococo era and showed that French design of the 1930s continued updating eighteenth-century styles, notwithstanding the leadership of Le Corbusier and the Bauhaus. This decorative door grille was exhibited at the 1939 *Salon des Artistes Décorateurs,*[16] a swansong for such goods before World War II.

Walter Dorwin TEAGUE

(1883–1960)

Camera and box

No. 1A Gift Kodak
Designed 1930
Camera: nickel-plated
and enameled brass,
steel, leatherette
9.6 x 21.2 x 4.4 cm
Box: cedar, nickel-plated
and enameled brass
11.2 x 22.5 x 6.3 cm
Produced by Eastman Kodak
Company, Rochester,
New York, U.S.A.
The Montreal Museum of
Fine Arts, D95.135.1

Like many of his colleagues in the emerging profession of industrial design, Teague began in advertising. Some of his early work was in typography and book design. In 1926, he went to Europe and studied the work of Le Corbusier, an experience that led to his abandoning the decorative "Teague borders" he used in his ads and turning to simplified designs associated with the Machine Age. One of his earliest clients was the Eastman Kodak Company, for which he designed a series of cameras, including the *Gift Kodak*, and four years later the very popular *Baby Brownie*. The geometric abstraction on this camera and its box, with a square overlapping a circle, derives from the flat, hard-edged shapes of Synthetic Cubism, as well as the precise, abstract beauty of modern machines. "A steadily quickening rhythm of life," Teague wrote, "—the automobile—the airplane—all tended to replace the irregular curve by the straight lines and parallels. . . . In the interests of economy, the machine was becoming more widely used and was largely limited to geometric lines."[17]

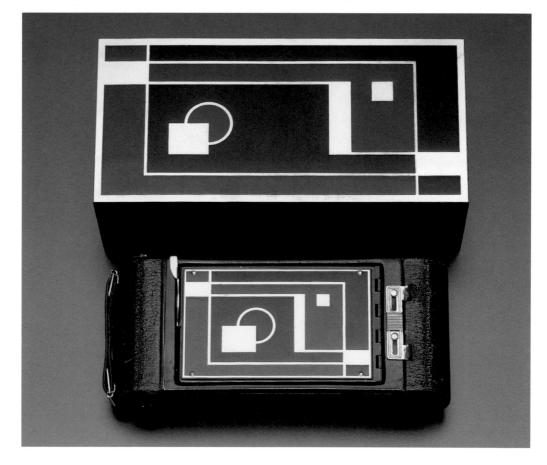

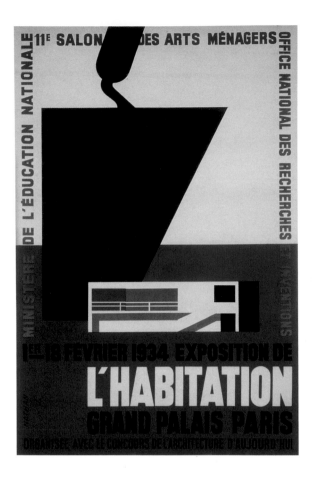

Jacques NATHAN-GARAMOND

(1910–2001)

Poster

11ᵉ Salon des arts ménagers (11ᵗʰ Domestic Arts Exhibition)
Designed c. 1934
Photolithograph
116.8 x 76.6 cm
Printed by Éditions de L'Architecture d'Aujourd'hui, Boulogne, France
The Montreal Museum of Fine Arts, D87.150.1

After studying architecture and training as a graphic artist in Paris, Jacques Nathan, as he was known, began his career working in interior design. He also created posters for product advertising and public service campaigns. His earliest experience in typography and layouts, from 1931 to 1933, was for the periodical *L'Architecture d'aujourd'hui*. This poster was commissioned for the 1934 *Exposition de l'habitation* for the eleventh *Salon des arts ménagers* (Domestic Arts Exhibition) at the Grand Palaisin Paris. Nathan placed a schematically rendered black trowel on the left and in front of it, in reduced scale, a "brick" representing a modern flat-roofed building in the style of Le Corbusier. With bold sans-serif typeface throughout, the poster reflects the geometric style of Bauhaus graphic design.

CARTIER

Necklace and bracelet

Designed c. 1935–40
Yellow gold, lapis
lazuli, diamonds
Necklace: 14.6 x 12.7 cm
Bracelet: 7.6 x 7 cm
Produced by Cartier,
New York, New York, U.S.A.
The Montreal Museum of
Fine Arts, D89.100.1–2

Founded in 1847 by the leading jewelry merchant Louis-François Cartier, the firm Cartier continues to be synonymous with the finest jewelry and *objets d'art* in the twenty-first century. During the 1930s, when this necklace and bracelet were made, most of the firm's creations continued the modern decorative style of the 1920s, which tended to be flat, but here the emphasis is on volume. The combination of semiprecious and precious stones—lapis lazuli and diamonds—extends Cartier's signature of the 1920s, yet here the circle shapes and clusters of spherical forms are associated with the Machine Age. In relation to the firm's earlier, polychromatic jewelry in the Egyptian and Art Deco styles, this set represents a new direction.

Jean PUIFORCAT

(1897–1945)

Tureen
Designed c. 1935
Silver, parcel gilt
25.4 x 27.6 x 27.6 cm
Produced by Puiforcat
Orfèvre, Paris, France
The Montreal Museum of
Fine Arts, D87.239.1

France's most important silversmith of the twentieth century, Puiforcat is associated with modernism and with the tradition of French luxury goods between the two world wars. Born into a silversmithing dynasty, he began as an apprentice in the family business at age seventeen. In 1929 he was a founding member of the Union des Artistes Modernes, an organization of architects and designers committed to modernism. By the time he designed this tureen, Puiforcat had grown to believe that "the circle, which explains the entire world, is the ideal figure, and the curve which approaches it is more noble than the straight line."[18] In this tureen, he enlivened his ideal form with bandings of gilt, creating a sense of speed and circular movement. Despite these aspects of modernism, Puiforcat has retained the traditional French sense of opulence in its massive form and heavy weight.

Karl TRABERT

(died 1968)

Desk lamp
Designed c. 1930
Plastic, aluminum, wood
41.6 x 32.2 x 32.2 cm
Produced by G. Schanzenbach &
Co., Frankfurt, Germany[19]
The Montreal Museum of
Fine Arts, D84.100.1

Although Karl Trabert was not a student of the Bauhaus, he clearly was influenced not only by Bauhaus principles[20] but also by specific Bauhaus solutions to lighting. In its emphasis on precise geometric forms, Trabert's table lamp resembles a William Wagenfeld design of 1924, executed in the Bauhaus's metal workshop. Likewise, Trabert's use of a cylindrical hinge at the base of the shaft recalls a design by noted Bauhaus designer Christian Dell, and the overall proportions and placement of the shaft and button switch at opposite sides of the base is reminiscent of a lamp by an anonymous Bauhaus student.[21] Trabert's lamp is documented in a catalogue of German goods published by Kunst-Dienst, Berlin, around 1935, which names him as the designer. Although Trabert's lamp has become an icon of German modernism, the career of this Frankfurt-based designer remains a mystery.

William LESCAZE

(1896–1969)

Armchair

Designed 1932
Chromium-plated tubular steel,
leather upholstery
82 x 57.5 x 59 cm
Produced by Garland Furniture
Manufacturing Company,
Chicago, Illinois, U.S.A.
The Indianapolis Museum of Art,
2008.218, gift of the Brooklyn
Museum to the Stewart
Program for Modern Design

This tubular steel armchair was one of a group of furnishings designed for the Charles Edwin Wilbour Memorial Library at the Brooklyn Museum, a commission of the Philadelphia firm Howe and Lescaze. Designed by the firm in 1933 and opened in 1934, the library served the Egyptian department. Square in plan, the room was divided by gray steel stacks forming alcoves around rectangular black-topped metal reading tables. These armchairs by Lescaze are identical to those he designed in 1932 for the safety deposit box floor of the Philadelphia Savings Fund Society, the famed International Style building by Howe and Lescaze. Here the material is bent into two rectangles, forming the arms, stiles, and legs of the chair as they support and echo its rectangular, upholstered seat and back. These cantilevered chairs were praised for their silvery gleam, which enlivened the library's somber setting.[22]

ABOVE, LEFT William Lescaze, Howe and Lescaze, Charles Edwin Wilbour Memorial Library, Brooklyn Museum, 1933–34.

Philip JOHNSON

(1906–2005)

Floor lamp
Steel, chromium-plated metal
175.9 x 33 x 33 cm
D88.144.1

Armchair
Chromium-plated tubular
steel, sailcloth
63.5 x 53.5 x 73.7 cm
D88.143.1

Designed 1932
Manufacturer unknown, U.S.A.
The Montreal Museum of Fine
Arts, gifts of Victoria Barr from
the Estate of Mr. and
Mrs. Alfred H. Barr, Jr.*

This armchair and floor lamp were part of the original furnishings of the Alfred H. Barr, Jr., apartment at 424 West 52nd Street in New York. Barr, as founding director of the Museum of Modern Art, had appointed Johnson head of the Department of Architecture and Design in 1932 and collaborated with him on the *International Style* exhibition held the same year. The armchair was inspired by Mies van der Rohe's 1927 *MR* chair of tubular steel with a woven cane seat. It reflects the interest of both Barr and Johnson in the architect's works. Like the *MR* design, Johnson's cantilevered chair is a continuous structure of tubular steel, characteristic of the machine aesthetic pursued by the Bauhaus and advanced by MoMA. The form of the lamp reflected similar lamp designs of the period, with its circular base and its round shade directing light upward to create dramatic luminosity in the room. Both the chair and the lamp reflect the International Style, as seen in the MoMA exhibit, in their display of unornamented industrial materials and simplified functional forms.

Max BILL

(1908–1994)

Poster

Der Schuh (The Shoe)
Designed 1936
Lithograph
127.3 x 90.5 cm
Printed by the
Kunstgewerbeschule
Zurich, Switzerland
The Montreal Museum of
Fine Arts, D87.172.1

Bill was one of the formulators of Switzerland's modern graphic design movement of the 1930s and beyond, combining Constructivist style with assertive typography. His approach to design reflected his training at the Bauhaus in Dessau from 1927 to 1929. This 1936 poster is from an influential series commissioned by the Zürich Kunstgewerbemuseum, and announces an exhibition on the history of footwear manufacture and fashion. The poster uses principles of layout and typography established by Herbert Bayer, as head of the typography department at the Bauhaus from 1925 to 1928. The lettering is laid out as a major compositional element in counterpoint with three blocks of primary colors and a graphic representing a foot in a shoe. Three different sizes of the same bold sans-serif type provide variety and distinguish the title, subtitle, and exhibition schedule. Bill's design of these elemental ingredients is both informative and dynamic, epitomizing the Bauhaus goal of no-nonsense communication.

Unknown German Designer

Coffee service
Designed c. 1930
Glazed terracotta
Coffee pot: 20 x 19.5 x 12 cm
Manufacturer unknown, Germany
The Indianapolis Museum of Art,
2008.230.1–4, gift of Dr. Michael
Sze to the Stewart Program
for Modern Design*

Although the designer has not been identified, the geometric forms of this service relate to products of the Bauhaus ceramic workshops. In 1919, the sculptor Gerhardt Marcks was appointed to head a ceramic workshop that the Bauhaus established in Dornburg, near Weimar, but when the school moved to Dessau in 1925, the shop was not reinstalled at the new location. Many of the Bauhaus potters and their students set up their own studios elsewhere, thus spreading the Bauhaus aesthetic. This service has certain characteristics of Bauhaus ceramics, such as unadorned geometric forms and a dense black glaze. On the other hand, the distinctive conical lid and exaggerated handles are perhaps more decorative than those of Bauhaus services.

Herbert MATTER

(1907–1984)

Poster

Winter Time Is Real Holiday Time:
Switzerland
Designed c. 1936
Rotogravure
102.2 x 65.2 cm
Produced by the Swiss National
Tourist Office, Switzerland
The Montreal Museum of
Fine Arts, D87.148.1

Educated in Geneva and Paris, Matter worked for both the graphic artist A. M. Cassandre and the famed architect Le Corbusier. As a photographer and graphic designer, Matter pioneered camerawork for advertising, particularly photomontage, which he used to focus his message in a simple, compelling form. From 1934 to 1936, he designed a series of travel posters for the Swiss National Tourist Office using photomontage and a minimum of typography. Each poster was printed in several editions, with a different language for each, to promote Swiss tourism. This poster is exemplary in its dynamic composition of type and photographs with a drastic contrast of scale. Matter juxtaposes the face of a skier and the diagonals of type with the red cross of Switzerland and tiny skiers on the mountainside background.

Clarence KARSTADT

(1902–1968)

Table radio
Silvertone Rocket
Designed c. 1938
Bakelite, plastic, fabric, rubber
16.5 x 30.7 x 16.5 cm
Produced by Chicago Molded
Product Corporation for Sears,
Roebuck, and Company,
Chicago, Illinois, U.S.A.
The Stewart Program for Modern
Design, B002, gift of Eric Brill*

This futuristically styled radio, named the *Silvertone Rocket* by Sears, Roebuck, resembles a streamlined train engine or a rocket. Karstadt, known for his patented household products for the mail-order retail company, designed the sheathing, streamlining it with horizontal, perforated banding that flanks the cylindrical form. The radio can be tuned by turning the rounded drum at the end, or the user can choose a favorite station from six push buttons on the top. Available in black, ivory, mottled walnut Bakelite, or in ivory Plaskon, it first appeared in the 1938 Sears catalogue, selling for $12.95, considerably less than the average cost for a radio five years earlier, $35.00.

Russel WRIGHT

(1904–1976)

Punch bowl with cups

Designed c. 1935
Aluminum, walnut
Bowl: 28.7 x 32.5 x 32.5 cm
Cups: 5.2 x 11.6 x 8.8 cm (each)
Ladle: 32 cm long
Produced by Wright Accessories/
Raymor, New York,
New York, U.S.A.
The Stewart Program for Modern
Design, L2010.4, promised
gift of Paul Leblanc

A leading champion of modernism from the 1930s through the 1950s, Wright designed a range of home furnishings for a casual American lifestyle. In addition to furniture and ceramics, he created simple tableware in aluminum that reflected a strict geometry of form. The spherical form of the punch bowl, echoed in its spherical walnut handles and twelve cups, embodies the gleaming minimalism of the Machine Age. Wright's interest in aluminum coincided with his aim to reach a broad range of consumers, especially in the Depression years. His designs in aluminum were not only inexpensive and lightweight, but also easy to maintain. His ware was produced by workers in his own workshop.[23]

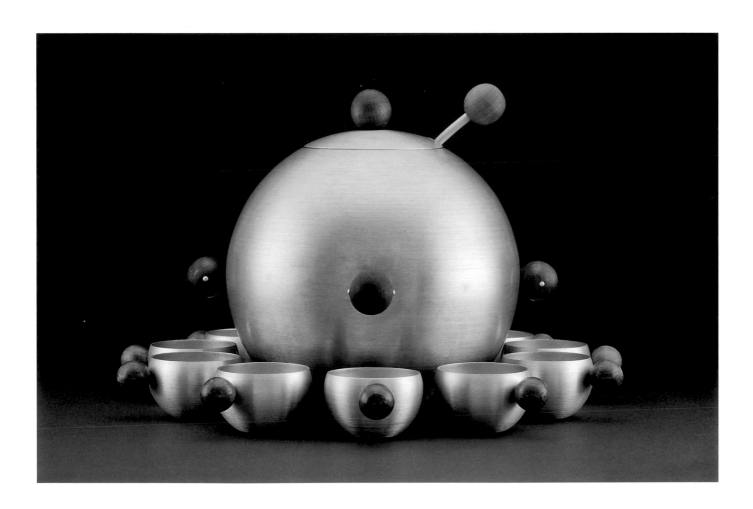

Peter SCHLUMBOHM

(1896–1962)

Garbage pail
Cinderella
Designed c. 1930–40
Aluminum, maple, cork
29 x 29 x 29 cm
Produced by Dr. Peter
Schlumbohm, New York,
New York, U.S.A.
The Stewart Program for Modern
Design, B025, gift of Eric Brill*

Schlumbohm, a chemist born and educated in Germany but working in New York, is best known for his *Chemex* coffeemaker, which is still in production. This design for a garbage pail follows the same principle: like the *Chemex*, the *Cinderella* pail has a paper liner insert that is removed for disposal. Intended for apartment living, the pail is the size of an ice bucket and looks stylish enough to be placed on a table in a bar or living room. Its dynamic streamlined form, in shiny aluminum, has space-age chic.

Hans CORAY

(1907–1991)

Armchair
Landi
Designed 1938
Aluminum, rubber
74.8 x 51.5 x 61.5 cm
Produced by Blattmann
Metallwarenfabrik AG,
Wädenswil, Switzerland
The Montreal Museum of Fine
Arts, D87.129.1, gift of Galerie
Metropol, New York

A self-taught artist and industrial designer, Coray made his first chair of metal wire in 1930. Nine years later he received the commission for this stacking chair from the *Schweizerische Landes Ausstellung* (Swiss National Exhibition) held in Zurich, from which its name, *Landi*, is derived. A major Swiss export, aluminum was selected to represent Swiss industry at the exhibition. Fifteen hundred examples of the *Landi* chair were produced for the exhibition grounds. Weighing just over three kilograms, the chair is strong and durable, and permits both indoor and outdoor use. The perforations are functional, allowing water or snow to drain, and also aesthetic, providing an appealing geometric pattern.

Marianne STRAUB

(1909–1994)

Textile
Howarth
Designed 1939
Cotton
126.4 x 101 cm
Produced by Helios Ltd., Bolton,
Lancashire, England
The Montreal Museum of Fine
Arts, D87.203.1, gift of Warner &
Sons Limited, London

Born in Switzerland, Straub studied weaving at the Kunstgewerbeschule, Zurich, and in 1932—33 continued her study of textiles at England's Bradford Technical College. From 1937 to 1949, she was the head designer for Helios in Lancashire and was responsible for woven and printed textiles. Wartime restrictions required the reduction of the number of colors for fabric to two or three, but Straub was inventive in her use of a variety of yarns, and she generated a nuanced palette of hues and textures, as seen here. Helios was one of the first English firms to retail a range of inexpensive avant-garde fabrics, including this 1939 curtain design.[24]

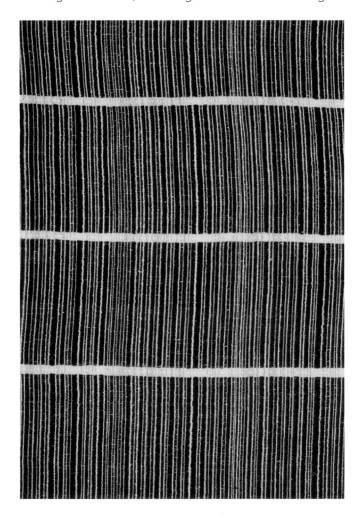

Donald DESKEY

(1894–1989)

Dining table
Designed in 1935 for the
Richard H. Mandel House
Bakelite, chromium-plated steel, glass
75.2 x 243 x 111.3 cm
Produced by Schmieg-Hungate
and Kotzian, New York,
New York, U.S.A.
The Stewart Program for Modern
Design, B920, gift of Eric Brill*

The Mandel home in Bedford Hills, New York, is a country house in the International Style. It was a collaborative design, with architecture by Edward Durell Stone, interiors and furnishings by Donald Deskey, and lighting by Kurt Versen. Deskey was then at the height of his career with his work on the interiors of Radio City Music Hall in Manhattan. Here he used new industrial materials, as seen in the white Bakelite top and the chromium-plated columnar legs of this table. Subtle indirect lighting comes through the frosted glass in the rectangular perforation at the center of the table, part of Versen's overall lighting concept.

ABOVE, LEFT Dining room, Mandel House, interior by Donald Deskey, 1935.

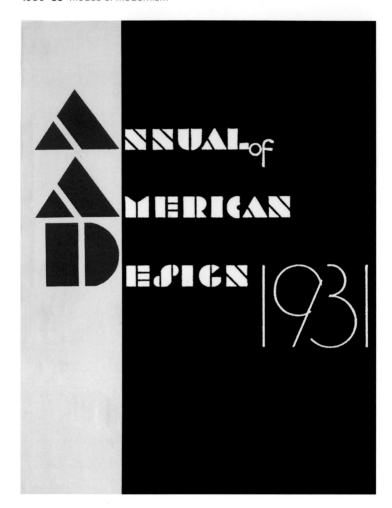

Robert L. LEONARD

(1879–1945)

Book
Annual of American Design 1931
Published 1930
Offset lithograph
31 x 23.2 cm
Published by Ives Washburn,
New York, New York, U.S.A.,
for AUDAC
The Stewart Program for Modern
Design, 2008.32,
gift of Dr. Michael Sze

Robert Leonard worked as an illustrator in Berlin before coming to the United States in 1923.[25] He became a member of the American Union of Decorative Artists and Craftsmen (AUDAC), founded in 1928, a professional organization of avant-garde architects and designers, and designed this catalogue to accompany its second exhibition. *Modern Industrial and Decorative Art,* held in 1931 at the Brooklyn Museum covered photography, advertising, and package design, as well as architecture and the decorative arts, and this catalogue includes essays by Frank Lloyd Wright, Kem Weber, Norman Bel Geddes, Edward Steichen, and other notable figures. The cover's stylized letters in two different typefaces—the white ones against a black ground contrasting with the red ones on a white ground—signaled the innovative work recorded inside.

John VASSOS

(1898–1985)

Book
*Ultimo: An Imaginative Narration
of Life Under the Earth*
Published 1930
Offset lithograph
26.3 x 19.5 cm (closed)
Published by E. P. Dutton, Inc.,
New York, New York, U.S.A.
The Stewart Program for
Modern Design, 2004.9.3

Ultimo was published as a limited edition with twenty-one illustrations designed by John Vassos to accompany text written by his wife, Ruth (1894–1965). The text, which resonates today, describes the devastation of an ice age caused by exploitation of our natural resources. In the Vassos illustration shown here, a huge streamlined ocean liner is blocked by masses of ice while dirigibles float helplessly above. For the cover Vassos provided a simple geometric design, setting the one-word main title and author's surname within a composition of vertical and horizontal lines. Vassos, a Greek-American painter and illustrator, was also an important product designer, active in the organization of the Industrial Designers Society of America.

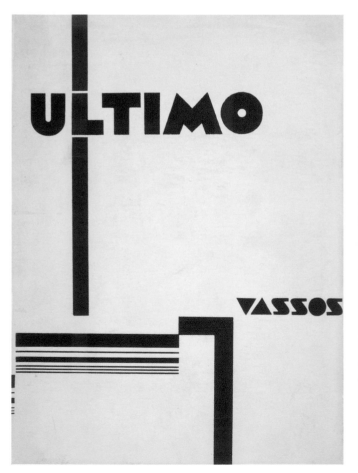

Harry BERTOIA

(1915–1978)

Drawing
Coffee Service
Executed c. 1937–43
Graphite, colored pencil, ink on
tracing paper mounted
on cardboard
33.5 x 88.7 cm
The Montreal Museum of
Fine Arts, D89.199.1

Known primarily for his later work as a sculptor, Bertoia was also an accomplished metalsmith. After graduating from the Cranbrook Academy of Art, Bloomfield Hills, Michigan, he taught in the school's metalshop from 1938 to 1943. This drawing for a pewter coffee service in the Stewart Collection reflects the work of Puiforcat in its combination of sphere and square. The inside of the coffeepot handle completes the perfect circle of its form. Bertoia used the overlapping of additional circles to estimate the size of the creamer's opening, creating a rhythmic dynamic. The drawing shows a service that combines functional modern characteristics with a streamlined aura.

Paolo VENINI

(1895–1959)

Three glasses
Esagonali (Hexagonal)
Designed 1933
Glass
15.7 x 7.1 x 7.1 cm
Produced by Vetri Soffiati
Muranesi Venini & C.,
Murano, Italy
The Montreal Museum of
Fine Arts, D84.185.2, gift of
Geoffrey N. Bradfield*

In 1932, Paolo Venini began to collaborate with leading Italian architects in the design of new glassware for his family's long-lived firm. Gio Ponti and Carlo Scarpa were among those he invited to participate, and in 1932 Scarpa became the firm's artistic director. Scarpa is sometimes credited with the design of the *Esagonali* glasses seen here, but they are more often attributed to Paolo Venini himself.[26] The delicate forms are typical of Venini glass-blowing, but their simple, modern design contrasts with the decorative wares of other glass produced by the Venini firm at the time. The design of the thin blown glass was technically challenging: the vessels taper gracefully from a circular coned base to a hexagonal lip, rimmed in red. For later achievements in modernizing Venini production, see p. 117.

René-André COULON

(1908–1997)

Radiator
Radiaver
Designed 1937
Glass, steel, nickel
50.7 x 42.5 x 13 cm
Produced by Saint-Gobain
Glass, Courbevoie, France
The Montreal Museum of
Fine Arts, D99.121.1

Coulon, known for his architecture and his designs in glass, collaborated with fellow architect Jacques Adnet in the design of the pavilion for the well-known glass manufacturer Saint-Gobain at the 1937 Paris International Exposition. With Adnet, he designed furniture combining glass and metal, which was first shown there. Coulon also collaborated with Robert Mallet Stevens to design the Pavillon de l'Hygiène at the same exposition. This electric radiator, illuminated by a light source in the base, is Coulon's most famous design. Made of *verre Securit* (safety glass), it exemplified a new concept in radiant heating, replacing the traditional use of metal with glass and providing both transparency and an impression of lightness. The unit thus harmonizes with the architectural style of the modernist interior.[27]

BELOW, LEFT Coulon and Adnet, Saint-Gobain Pavilion at the International Exposition of Arts and Technology, Paris, 1937.

Walter Dorwin TEAGUE
Edwin W. FUERST

(1883–1960) and **(1903–1988)**

Cordial glass and wineglass
Designed c. 1939
Glass
Cordial: 17.3 x 6.7 x 6.7 cm
Wineglass: 22.5 x 6.7 x 6.7 cm
Produced by Libbey Glass Company, a division of Owens-Illinois Glass Company, Toledo, Ohio, U.S.A.
The Montreal Museum of Fine Arts, D81.119.1–2

At the 1939 New York World's Fair, Teague and Fuerst collaborated to produce this elegant line of glassware for the United States Government's State Dining Room in the Federal Building. Teague also designed the building itself, and its Ionic columns, reflecting current international interest in classicism, inspired the stems of these glasses. Teague provided the design concept to Fuerst, head of the design department for the Owens-Illinois Glass Company, who was responsible for their execution. The glasses are etched with a stylized, spread-wing eagle surrounded by thirteen stars (for the thirteen original colonies). The pattern was sold by Libbey, without the crest, in its 1940 Modern American line and called *The Embassy*.[28]

Unknown Designer

Advertisement

Streamline Action with Texaco Fire-Chief
Published March 10, 1934,
in *The Saturday Evening Post*
34.7 x 26.7 cm
Photo offset on paper
The Stewart Program for
Modern Design, 2008.31

Speed enchanted the United States during the Depression. American unemployment in 1934, the year this advertisement was published, was at 26.7 percent, but the glamorous aerodynamic style in automobiles captured the American imagination. The metaphor of streamlining and its visual impact were used in marketing an array of products, from pencil sharpeners to gasoline, as seen in this advertisement. The strong diagonal format of the design and elongation of the streamlined automobile and lettering promote the sale of Texaco's product. "Speed lines," which often accompanied depictions of streamlined moving objects, are here added to "Texaco Fire-Chief," words bordered with longer repeated lines.

Kem WEBER

(1889–1963)

Armchair
Airline
Designed c. 1934–35
Birch, ash, wool upholstery
80.7 x 93.5 x 64.1 cm
Produced by Airline Chair
Company, Los Angeles,
California, U.S.A.
The Montreal Museum of
Fine Arts, D85.172.1, gift of
Geoffrey N. Bradfield*

Weber's declared aim—"to make a comfortable, hygienic and beautiful chair inexpensively"—is realized here. Designed to be mass produced of bent and laminated wood, the *Airline* chair is a knockdown design that was packed in a shallow square box for easy shipping and storage. Lightweight, portable, with a cantilevered seat that supports the sitter's body at ease, the chair in fact as well as in name shares with airplanes the principles of aerodynamics: low sweeping lines, no superfluous parts, a silhouette of unornamented minimalism. The design is based on an earlier prototype Weber had produced around 1930 for a "Bentlock easy chair," in which he experimented with a new way of joining the wood pieces.[29] Cantilevered chairs had been designed in tubular steel since the 1920s, and Weber here explores this modernist form in wood.

Peter MÜLLER-MUNK

(1904—1967)

Pitcher
Normandie
Designed 1935
Chromium-plated brass
30.4 x 24.4 x 7.7 cm
Produced by Revere Copper and
Brass Company, Rome,
New York, U.S.A.
The Stewart Program for
Modern Design, 2007.50.29,
gift of Roy Poretzky*

This industrially produced pitcher was inspired by the famous French ocean liner of the same name, whose maiden voyage took place the year the pitcher was introduced. As design historian Christopher Wilk points out: "Although the pitcher might have evoked the elliptical cylinders [smokestacks] that rose from the deck of the *SS Normandie,* it even more boldly embodied the smooth, windswept curves and, in plan, the teardrop shape of aerodynamic streamlining, a style that subjected all objects to the designer's imaginary wind tunnel."[30] Müller-Munk's inexpensive pitcher is one of the 1930s' most successful combinations of memorable design and mass-production processes.

Jean PUIFORCAT

(1897–1945)

Tea and coffee service
Designed c. 1933
Silver, gilt silver, cotton thread
Coffee pot: 14.3 x 19.9 x 8.3 cm
Produced by Puiforcat
Orfèvre, Paris, France
The Montreal Museum of Fine
Arts, D94.285.1–4, anonymous gift

Although streamlining was associated with work by American industrial designers in the 1930s, Puiforcat produced aerodynamic designs as early as the 1920s. Here he transforms traditional vessel forms into abstract volumes, and creates a sense of the sweep of streamlining in the downward sloping handles. This service is typical of his work during the early 1930s, when he began to give increasing emphasis to rounded shapes, especially distinguished by simplicity and unity of form and silhouette. The vessel lids have invisible hinges, a notable feature of his work, and bands of engraved horizontal lines, a device he employed frequently and that is repeated in the bands of black cord on the handles. The contrasting colors of silver, gold, and black are both decorative and opulent.

William B. PETZOLD

(1898–1983)

Duplicator

Duplicard
Designed c. 1940
Bakelite, rubber, painted wood,
flannel, steel
13 x 26.5 x 19.2 cm
Produced by Pac Manufacturing
Corporation, Terre Haute,
Indiana, U.S.A.
The Stewart Program for Modern
Design, B008, gift of Eric Brill*

In its bold teardrop form and curved top, this small machine recalls iconic images of American streamlining, such as Raymond Loewy's 1937 design for the Broadway Limited locomotive. Both use horizontal speed lines on an angled front to emphasize forward thrust. The name *Duplicard* in raised letters against a red ground is incorporated into a recess on the curved top. This streamlined sheath glamorizes an ordinary office machine that was used to address postcards. The user brushed ink on the flannel pad inside and turned the crank counterclockwise to print the address on an inserted card. Petzold patented numerous designs in Bakelite (the trade name for the first completely synthetic plastic). He also designed for General Electric in Pittsfield, Massachusetts, and Autopoint in Chicago.

BELOW Raymond Loewy, *Broadway Limited*, Pennsylvania Railroad, 1937.

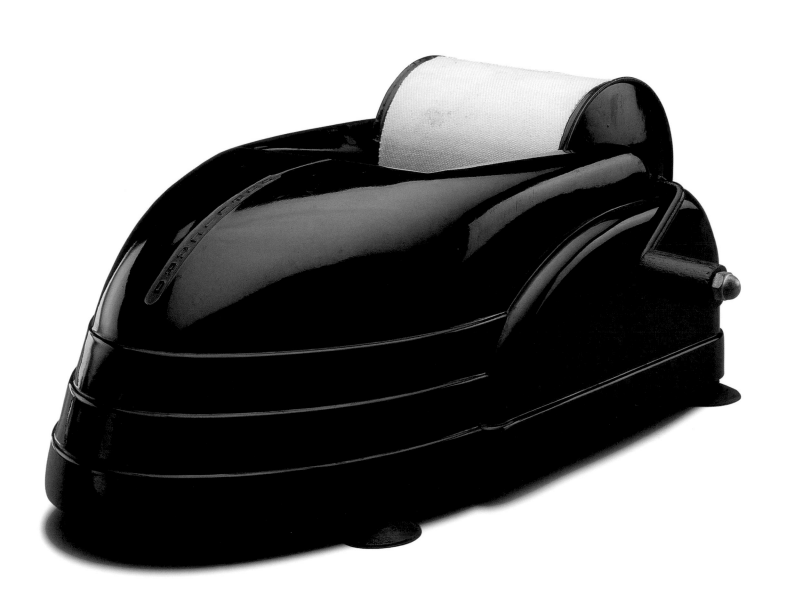

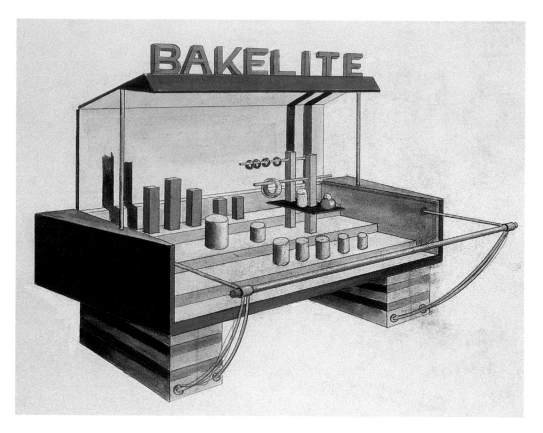

Rolph SCARLETT

(1889–1984)

Drawing

Bakelite Corporation Stand for the New York World's Fair
Executed c. 1939
Graphite, silver ink, and gouache on cardboard
39.4 x 50.9 cm
The Montreal Museum of Fine Arts, D91.395.282, gift of Mr. and Mrs. Samuel Esses*

Scarlett is best known as a painter whose Kandinsky-inspired work was among the early acquisitions of New York's Museum of Non-Objective Painting (now the Solomon R. Guggenheim Museum), but he began as a jewelry designer in his native Canada before moving to the United States in 1918. In addition to designing for industry, he was also a stage designer and created film sets in Hollywood. These experiences are reflected in this display for the Bakelite Corporation in the Industrial Science Building at the 1939 New York World's Fair. An illustration of that interior[31] demonstrates that many of Scarlett's designs were executed, but it is not known if this stand for Bakelite corresponds to one that was actually built. The versatile product is promoted in this streamlined booth, with its emphasis on horizontal banding and display of containers and jewelry in various colors and forms. Because Bakelite could be cast in rounded molds, it was widely used in streamlined products.

Louis V. ARONSON

(1869–1940)

Cigarette lighter
Touch Tip
Designed c. 1937
Enameled and brass-plated steel
8.5 x 11 x 5.7 cm
Produced by Art Metal Works,
Newark, New Jersey, U.S.A.
The Stewart Program for
Modern Design, 2004.14

Founder of the Art Metal Works, which later became the Ronson Company, Aronson took out many patents for cigarette lighters, including one for this example. He also took out a utility patent for the "Touch Tip," the innovative and popular mechanism for producing a flame. With its sleek curved form, conforming stepped base, and speed lines, this table lighter exemplifies American streamlined design at its best. The contrasting brass plating against the black ground added stylish refinement to the device in an era when smoking was considered glamorous and fashionable.

Frank Lloyd WRIGHT

(1867–1959)

Four Ottomans
Designed c. 1939
Cypress, mahogany,
vinyl upholstery
39.7 x 145.5 x 137.2 cm (each)
Produced by John T. Lyman,
Montclair, New Jersey, U.S.A.
The Montreal Museum of
Fine Arts, D81.149.1–4

America's most important twentieth-century architect, Frank Lloyd Wright developed a concept of an organic architecture to which he adhered throughout his career, requiring that all the furnishings of each of his houses express the spirit of the architectural whole. In the mid-1930s, after a half-century of prolific practice, Wright displayed a renewed creativity, evident in Auldbrass Plantation, Yemassee, South Carolina, commissioned by C. Leigh Stevens. Located in the heart of South Carolina's plantation district, Auldbrass was a working plantation. These modular grouped ottomans from the living room were part of Wright's specially designed furnishings and reflect the hexagonal open plan of the exterior and interior architecture. Their local materials (cypress) also reflect his concept of organic architecture. Wright's insistence on unity of design was also seen in European reform movements earlier in the century, and his example contributed to them.

LEFT Plan of Auldbrass Plantation, Yemassee, South Carolina, 1939. The Frank Lloyd Wright Foundation.

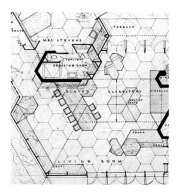

Marcel BREUER

(1902–1981)

Desk

Designed in 1938 for Rhoads Hall,
Bryn Mawr College, Philadelphia,
Pennsylvania, U.S.A.
74 x 127 x 63 cm
Pine, laminated plywood
Manufacturer unknown
The Stewart Program for
Modern Design, 2010.19.1,
promised gift of Paul Leblanc

After he emigrated from Germany, moving first to England and then to the United States, Breuer abandoned his favorite material—metal—and focused on creating wood furniture, which was more appealing to English and American domestic buyers, who associated the tubular steel furniture produced in Germany with commercial designs. This desk illustrates a continuation of his previous work with plywood, such as the *Isokon* lounge chair of 1935–36, seen in the bent, U-shaped desk support.[32] The desk is part of Breuer's first furniture commission in the United States, for Bryn Mawr College Rhoads Residence Hall. Intended for dormitory use, the Bryn Mawr furniture is straightforward and unaffected, reflecting minimalist principles.

Isamu NOGUCHI

(1904–1988)

**Shortwave
radio receiver**
Radio Nurse
Designed c. 1937
Bakelite
21 x 16.5 x 16.5 cm
Produced by Zenith Radio
Corporation, Chicago,
Illinois, U.S.A.
The Stewart Program for Modern
Design, B573, gift of Eric Brill*

The president of Zenith Radio Corporation commissioned the Japanese-American sculptor Isamu Noguchi to create this shortwave radio to allow families to monitor the elderly and infants away in other rooms of their homes. The device, which Zenith marketed successfully, reflects Noguchi's training in sculpture and the influence of Constantin Brancusi, for whom he worked in 1927 in Paris while on a Guggenheim travel fellowship. The design, resembling a head in a nurse's cap, suggests the affinity between streamlining and organic forms in the progressive art of the 1930s. The stylized teardrop-shaped head is crossed by the horizontal sound perforations resembling speed lines. The goal was "to create a device which will be simple, beautiful, and at the same time distinctively different from any inter-communicating set or radio now in use."[33]

Alvar AALTO

(1898–1976)

Armchair
Designed 1932
Birch-faced plywood,
laminated birch
66 x 61.5 x 78.2 cm
Produced by Artek,
Helsinki, Finland
The Montreal Museum of
Fine Arts, D85.113.1

One of the most significant architects of the twentieth century, Aalto also designed extraordinary examples of laminated wood furniture. This cantilevered armchair, known today as the *Springleaf,* is one of his more important designs. Like many of his Scandinavian contemporaries, Aalto focused on designs to be executed in wood, in this case the birch wood of his native Finland. The back and seat are made of a single thin piece of plywood, bent in sinuous curves and resting on horizontal supports. These are in turn held by flanking supports of laminated birch veneer, which form continuous arms, front stiles, and base. This treatment of wood was inspired by the bent tubular steel furniture of the Bauhaus, but the works were cheaper to produce and appeared warmer for the domestic interior.

Bruno MATHSSON

(1907–1988)

Chair
Working Chair
Designed c. 1933–36
Beech, jute
79.8 x 49.4 x 72.4 cm
Produced by Firma Karl
Mathsson, Värnamo, Sweden
The Montreal Museum of Fine
Arts, D88.145.1, gift of Victoria Barr
from the Estate of Mr. and
Mrs. Alfred H. Barr, Jr.*

Mathsson was apprenticed as a cabinetmaker in his family's workshop in Värnamo from 1923 to 1931. Between 1933 and 1936, he developed his first chairs with laminated bentwood frames and webbed seats, all of which his father's firm produced. Mathsson's chairs are contoured to follow the curves of the body and are comfortable without using conventional upholstery. The innovative design of the *Working Chair* was popular in both the United States and Europe and fostered a number of imitations. The chair was among the original furnishings in the New York apartment of Alfred Barr, Jr. (see p. 38), indicating his appreciation of the softer forms of Scandinavian wood furniture alongside Bauhaus geometry.

Russel WRIGHT

(1904–1976)

Dinnerware
American Modern
Designed c. 1937
Glazed earthenware
Pitcher: 27 x 20.6 x 20.6 cm
Produced by Steubenville Pottery
Company, Steubenville,
Ohio, U.S.A.
The Montreal Museum of Fine
Arts, D82.105.1, gift of David A.
Hanks; D873170.1–3, D88.180.1–10

Wright's most famous design was his colorful dinnerware, *American Modern*. In production for two decades, it has been claimed to be the best-selling dinnerware ever manufactured. Its softened forms reflect the rise of biomorphism in art and design in the late 1930s in Europe and the United States, although these fluid shapes with their sinuous curves and elongated shapes are predominantly symmetrical. Such shapes are also functional: the curving spouts allow easy pouring, and indentations on the salt and pepper shakers and serving bowls assure easier handling. The different colors were intended, giving buyers freedom to make their own combinations and acknowledging the more informal living by a servantless middle class recovering from the Depression. As scholar Martin Eidelberg has felicitously observed, *American Modern* "signaled the democratization of the American table."[34]

Carlo SCARPA

(1906–1978)

Vase
Tessuto (Textile)
Designed 1939
Glass
33.3 x 14 x 14 cm
Produced by Venini, Murano, Italy
The Montreal Museum of
Fine Arts, D88.109.1

Vase
Corroso (Corroded)
Designed c. 1936
Glass
16.5 x 16.5 x 15.5 cm
Produced by Venini, Murano, Italy
The Montreal Museum of
Fine Arts, D84.165.1,
gift of Susan A. Chalom*

One of Italy's most important mid-century architects, Scarpa graduated from the Accademia di Belle Arti in Venice in 1926. Early in his career he began to design glass for the Venini firm and served as its artistic director from 1932 to 1947. Intrigued with the virtuoso technical aspects of glassmaking, he created in 1939 a series he called *Tessuto*, represented by the vase on the left, because of its resemblance to a woven material. The technique uses flattened groups of glass canes that are drawn and rolled over a metal surface, fused, and then blown into shape. Adding to this complexity, half the vase is made from one set of colored canes, the other half from a contrasting set. The vase on the right is an irregular, organic form that uses the *corroso* surface, a 1930s version of acid-etching that Scarpa introduced to the firm.

Alvar AALTO

(1898–1976)

Vase
Aalto
Designed 1936
Glass
28.5 x 29.5 x 28.5 cm
Produced by Karhulan
Lasitehtaalla, Karhula, Finland,
and by Iittala Lasitehdas,
Iittala, Finland
The Montreal Museum of
Fine Arts, D87.149.1

Aalto's enormous contribution to modern design encompassed architecture, furniture, interiors, glass, and lighting. His glassware dates from 1932, when he and his wife, Aino, also an architect, participated in a Karhula-Iittala competition. While Aalto's first designs echo his hard-edged early architecture of the International Style, somewhat later in the 1930s he turned to a new vocabulary of organic undulant curves, which can be seen in his furniture, glass, and architecture. His new designs originated in his sensitivity to the contour lines of the hills and lakes of his native Finland, as well as in abstract Surrealism and the sculpture of Jean Arp and Alexander Calder. This Karhula vase was among a group, in various sizes and colors, that established the biomorphic style in design worldwide; it is still in production. Originally referred to as *Aalto* vases, these are generally known today as *Savoy* vases, a name introduced in the 1950s because some were ordered for the Savoy restaurant, designed by Aalto, in Helsinki.

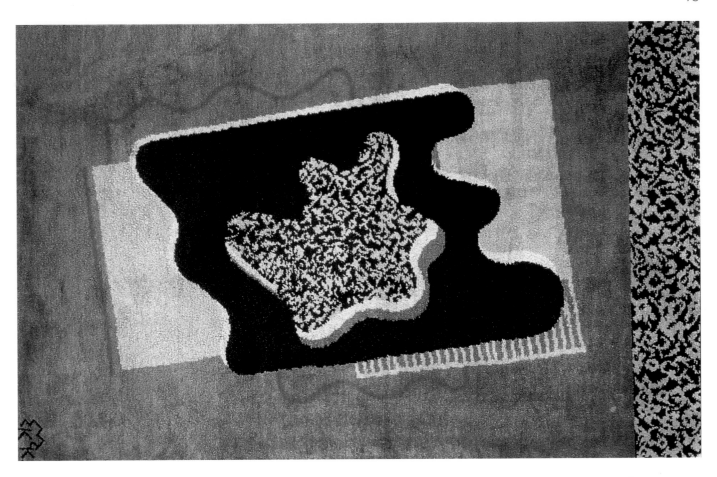

Edward McKnight KAUFFER

(1890–1954)

Rug
Designed c. 1935
Wool
229 x 151 cm
Produced by The Wilton
Royal Carpet Factory Ltd.,
Wilton, England
The Montreal Museum of Fine
Arts, D89.119.1, gift of Paul Leblanc

Although Kauffer is known primarily as a graphic designer of the interwar period with a reputation for Cubist-inspired posters and book illustrations, he began as a painter, studying at the School of the Art Institute of Chicago before moving to London in 1915. During the late 1920s and 1930s, he designed a series of avant-garde rugs, including this example, which demonstrates his shift to Surrealist biomorphic shapes. The apparent perforation in the center contributes to the movement and dynamic quality of this unique design. In 1940, Kauffer returned to the United States and continued his career as a graphic designer, contributing the catalogue cover for the *Organic Design* exhibition at The Museum of Modern Art in 1941.

1940
1949

Creativity in the War Years

The devastation of World War II made this a short decade for design. But the 1940s were surprisingly rich in design innovation, due in part to the technological advances required by the war. Necessity mothered the invention of nylon by DuPont in 1939, which replaced silk in parachutes, and fiberglass, or glass-filament-reinforced plastic, was created for radar domes on airplanes. Rationing of metal and timber led to the development of the nineteenth-century technologies of plywood lamination and bentwood. Plastics, protean composites, and synthetic materials known earlier were diversified with advances in polymer chemistry, producing polyethylene and latex foam, among other versatile substances. Perhaps most important, wartime government mandates among all combatant nations required designs of functionalism, simplicity, and economy. What a minority had espoused for design in the 1930s was now national policy.

When the world turned to peacetime production after 1945, the new materials and methods were redirected to furnishings and domestic goods and given new formal variety by ingenious emerging designers. In the United States, Bohn Aluminum and Brass was one of the companies that anticipated the coming need to retool for household uses, and it commissioned advertisements encouraging innovative applications for aluminum in the future (fig. 1). The aerodynamic uses illustrated for the lightweight material reveal the survival of streamlining into the 1940s.

During the war, as governments limited or shut down production for the domestic market, trade associations and museums gave designers a public platform with exhibitions and competitions and encouraged experiment by showing prototypes in advance of realization. Privations on the home front made "low cost" and "useful" the watchwords for desirable design. Before the United States entered the war, The Museum of Modern Art sponsored the competition *Organic Design in Home Furnishing* in 1940 (the catalogue appears on p. 83), and, two years after the Armistice, the *International Competition for Low-Cost Furniture* in the fall of 1947. MoMA had established its Department of Architecture in 1932, and industrial design was added to its purview the following year. From 1938 through the mid-1940s the museum earned a reputation for fostering the creation of progressive industrial design through its organization of the *Useful Design* exhibitions, including *Useful Objects in Wartime under $10,* in 1941–42.

For its *Organic Design* exhibition in 1940, its first major competition, the museum persuaded twelve major American department stores to sponsor the project and agree to put the winning designs into production. Eero Saarinen and Charles Eames collaborated on their entry and won in both of the categories they entered: seating and modular furniture. Their design for an armchair in molded plywood was a breakthrough in seating structure and use of materials, and it led to additional landmark seating designs by both architects (pp. 93, 94, 96–97).

In 1941, Eames and his spouse and fellow designer Ray Eames moved to Southern California where they conducted experiments in the bending of plywood in response to war demands, including scarcity of metal. That same year, they received a commission from the United States Navy to develop plywood stretchers and leg splints for injured war servicemen because the existing metal splints increased vibrations, making injuries worse. Building on their achievements in bending and molding plywood, they developed a plywood splint that conformed to the leg's shape (figs. 2 and 3)**.** Through this work, the Eameses developed a method of bending, gluing, and molding wood laminates in three dimensions that led to their later chair designs.

MoMA's *Low-Cost* competition, 1948, was inspired by the shortage of housing and inexpensive, good-quality furniture at the end of the war.[1] The Eames team was a co-winner of the second prize for seating, with their molded fiberglass chair (p. 94). Its technology had been generated during the war: to make it the Eameses commissioned Zenith Plastics Company to employ the same fiberglass technology used for domes on aircraft. The result was the first successful mass-produced molded plastic chair and a stunning transformation from wood to plastic of the shell aesthetic that Eames and Saarinen had developed earlier in the decade. Consumers for Eames and Saarinen chairs were waiting: according to an article in *Arts & Architecture* of June 1944, 4.7 million American families were planning to build homes as soon as materials became available again after the war.[2]

MoMA's pioneering exhibitions focused on furniture, but other types of design industries in America were healthy. The ceramist Eva Zeisel arrived in New York in 1938 and was recommended by MoMA to Castleton China as the designer of a dinner service. Conceived in 1942–43, though not produced until after the war, Zeisel's graceful, all-white *Museum* service was exhibited at the museum in 1946, which praised it as the first modern porcelain dinnerware created in the United States (p. 89).

In wartime Great Britain's government restrictions were the most severe among all the warring nations. Having declared war on Germany in September 1939, it began to ration industrial supplies and set quotas for the manufacturers of consumer products in 1940, including textiles and ceramics. The Utility Furniture Program, introduced in 1942, permitted the sale of new furniture only to newlyweds and those replacing homes destroyed by bombing. "Utility Furniture" was produced through 1951, under the supervision of the British Board of Trade and the chairmanship of the furniture designer Gordon Russell. A 1947–48 oak dining table from WM Birch's *Cotswold* line (fig. 4) exemplifies the sturdy sparseness of Utility's low-cost mass-produced designs, and their expression of Arts and Crafts principles of fitness to purpose and direct display of materials. One may speculate that such sobriety in national production—which continued long after the end of the war—made the "Youth Quake" of 1960s designs in Great Britain the more exuberant by contrast.

In the United Kingdom, where government initiatives were as seminal as private enterprise, if not more so, leadership in progressive design was taken by tax-funded bodies. In 1944, the Council of Industrial Design had been established by

1 Attributed to Arthur Radebaugh, advertisement for the Bohn Aluminum and Brass Corporation, c. 1942. Stewart Program for Modern Design.
2 Demonstration of Eames leg splint in use.
3 Charles and Ray Eames, traction leg splint designed for the United States Navy, c. 1941. Stewart Collection, The Montreal Museum of Fine Arts, gift of Judith Hollander.
4 Dining table, *Cotswold* range, stained oak, manufactured under the Utility Scheme, 1947–48, by WM Birch Ltd., High Wycombe, United Kingdom. Geffrye Museum, London.

the government to find means to improve design in British industry. In 1946, under its auspices, the exhibition *Britain Can Make It* was presented at the Victoria and Albert Museum, attracting nearly a half-million visitors. Its goal was to promote the best of British design in a range of consumer goods, and it was aimed primarily at export. Following in 1948 was *Design at Work*, which was also aimed at drumming up export trade. At the same time, organizers understood that progress could also be measured by the average British homeowner's improved standard of living. With such government support, postwar British textiles, ceramics, and glass achieved an unlikely but spunky originality.

After the war, France was unable to regain the artistic leadership it had enjoyed in the 1920s and 1930s, but it remained nonetheless a center for fashion and luxury goods. To counter its identification exclusively with deluxe objects, however, the Union des Artistes Modernes, led by René Herbst, initiated a series of exhibitions in 1949 called *Formes Utiles* (Useful Forms) in Paris. A room by Herbst for the first exhibition (fig. 5), for example, shows his molded plywood and metal chairs, simple and straightforward designs for an open-plan dining room and kitchen. Their resemblance to American innovations is unmistakable, and the metal-topped island opposite the sink would become a widespread convenience. The catalogue explained that the *Formes Utiles* series was meant to show that "there exist contemporary, everyday, affordable objects of quality, produced by both craftsmen and by industry, so designed that they can contribute to the harmony, health, and joy of life."[3] Adding to the well-being of the average consumer was the explicit goal of such design—in France and also internationally.

Italy, though defeated in the war, nevertheless experienced an energetic revival in design. Casting off the Neoclassical revivalism of Mussolini's Fascist regime, Italian designers produced innovative works in furniture, ceramics, glass, and enamel, which drew on their traditions of craftsmanship generated in small ateliers. Although Milan's series of Triennales had ended prematurely because of Italy's involvement in the war, this influential survey of current international design was resumed in 1947 and again became a barometer for important innovation worldwide. *Domus*, founded by architect Gio Ponti before the war and Italy's leading design periodical, published the competition entries. Achille Castiglioni, one of Italy's most creative postwar industrial designers, was on the organizing committee of the VIII Triennale of 1947, which was devoted to housing and reconstruction and included work by the Milanese architects Ettore Sottsass and Vico Magistretti. Swiss graphic designer Max Huber created the cover for the catalogue of the VIII Triennale: its de Stijl–derived graphics in primary colors dramatized "T8," a shorthand understandable in most languages. It could be read as announcing that the design on view was ready for international consumption.

Certainly such fairs helped the Scandinavian countries gain a leading position in international design following the war. Sweden had been neutral, Denmark and Norway were occupied by the Germans, and Finland had sided with Germany in the war. Despite the different experiences of each country, Scandinavia became known after the war for the quality of its design, which was exported internationally. Its beautifully crafted furniture, ceramics, and glass often explored traditional vernacular forms and natural materials, yet they were obviously modern in their simplicity, often ergonomic ease of use, and reasonable pricing. In aura, they contrasted with the more anonymous and mechanistic designs associated with the International Style of the 1930s.

5 René Herbst, dining room as shown at the *Formes Utiles* exhibition, Paris, 1949.

The International Style itself was modified during its migration beyond Europe. Admirers of progressive European artists pressured the U.S. government to give them refuge, and German émigrés helped to establish America as a center for the International Style and for Bauhaus teachings. Marcel Breuer first immigrated to England in 1935 and then to the United States in 1937, teaching at Harvard University from 1937 to 1946. His own house in New Canaan, Connecticut, designed in 1947 (fig. 6), was one of his best-known projects, and, in its incorporation of wood siding and local stone, was admired for these references to vernacular Yankee building within an obviously modern structure. Ludwig Mies van der Rohe moved to Chicago in 1938, where he worked until his death in 1969. His elegant, finely detailed Promontory Apartments at 5530 South Shore Drive, 1949, and later tall slablike buildings demonstrated that his modern design could appeal to an urbane American clientele. Lázsló Moholy-Nagy established the New Bauhaus in Chicago in 1937, which merged into the Illinois Institute of Technology in 1949. The curriculum, modeled on that of the German Bauhaus, required each student's aesthetic development in a wide range of arts. The chair by New Bauhaus students Harold Cohen and Davis Pratt (p. 135) illustrates the concepts taught at the transplanted school. Textiles by Angelo Testa (p. 99), who in 1945 was the first graduate of the Chicago institution, also illustrate the principles taught, including the creation of abstract printed patterns in affordable <machine-produced goods, principles that would influence American designers for decades.

European émigrés also shaped one of the most important design schools in the United States, still in operation today. The Cranbrook Academy of Art, in Bloomfield Hills, Michigan, outside of Detroit, was established in 1925 as a utopian, Arts and Crafts-inspired community. Directed from 1932 to 1946 by the Finnish architect Eliel Saarinen, Eero's father, the school offered specialization in weaving, ceramics, metalwork, and architecture, and later added graphic design and other disciplines. Like the Bauhaus, it taught both handicraft skills and design for industry, though it gave individual expression more freedom, in keeping with the Scandinavian values shared by Saarinen and the professors he attracted. Florence Knoll was a student in 1934; Charles Eames taught there in 1939—40; and subsequent teachers and graduates in the 1940s, such as Harry Bertoia, Jack Lenor Larsen, and David Rowland, went on to become major forces in American design (Larsen p. 141).

Interwar and wartime émigrés also helped promulgate vanguard art as a source of form languages for design. Piet Mondrian's arrival in New York in 1940 reinforced appreciation of de Stijl's flat geometries and their application to modular furnishings as well as textiles (p. 87, 88). The exodus of Surrealist artists from France was even more formative, as this movement in all the arts, named in 1924, espoused adaptable creative techniques and the idiom of biomorphism. Stylistically diverse Surrealists expressed themselves in liquid amoeboid forms, from the abstract sculptors and painters Jean Arp and Joan Miró to the flamboyant illusionist painter Salvador Dalí (p. 115), who arrived in America in 1940, followed in 1941 by André Masson and Max Ernst, who experimented with chance effects in their painting, and the Surrealists' leader André Breton in the same year. These artists claimed the authority of Freud and Jung for their exploration of dreams and "the collective unconscious" in pursuit of imagery and methods. Here was a rich source for design that was modern in its abstraction from nature but humanist in its allusions to changing organisms.

Biomorphism can be seen in most design media in the 1940s, especially in the United States and Scandinavia. Isamu Noguchi's furnishings (p. 105), Art Smith's jewelry (p. 104), and Henning Koppel's pitcher (p. 110) variously presented pierced and asymmetrical forms, voluptuous compound curves, and shapes suggesting bones or swelling branches. While some designs of the 1940s imitated nature, a time-honored source (note the flowers on p. 116), these works evoked natural processes and engaged the imagination with their multiple associations. The idiosyncratic and beautifully executed works resembled, and sometimes were, limited-edition art objects, giving consumers personal choices in an otherwise impoverished market for home products and fashion.

As the nations recovered from the war in the late 1940s and early 1950s, biomorphic design would continue to attract designers and the public, as would references to advanced art. Education, encouraged in America by the G.I. Bill for returning servicemen, played a role in broadening the definitions of the modern,[4] and design enjoyed growing respect for its aesthetic and economic impact. "Lines and forms have become communicative once more. They express the designer's moods and his sense of humor," said Eva Zeisel in 1946 in commenting on her *Museum* dinnerware. "Whether changes in production processes induced the designing of softer and more modeled shapes—I do not know. Nonobjective art, abstract sculpture particularly, which is now being taught in all art and design schools, may have been one of the influences."[5] The influence of these schools, in addition to the exhibitions and competitions organized by museums and trade associations, would continue to be felt in the 1950s.

6 Marcel Breuer's house, New Canaan, Connecticut, 1947.

Jean CARLU

(1900—1997)

Poster

Give 'em Both Barrels
Designed 1941
Offset lithograph
76.3 x 101.7 cm
Printed by the United States
Government Printing Office,
Washington, D.C., U.S.A.
The Montreal Museum of Fine
Arts, D84.187.1, gift of
Geoffrey N. Bradfield*

This poster was commissioned by the United States government to encourage Americans to produce supplies aiding the Allied war. Representing the factory worker's role to be nearly as important as the soldier's, the image is a visual pun on the slogan in which the riveter's cap and tool parallel the artillery man's helmet and machine gun. The poster's bold type is set in italic to simulate forward movement. The sobriety of color contributes forcibly to the earnestness of the sober bellicose message. Carlu, a Frenchman, was himself ineligible to fight in the war because of a physical disability, and he decided that he could best help the war effort by remaining in the United States designing posters like this one. Though trained as an architect, he became famous for his graphic art, which he pursued in both France and the United States.

Edward McKnight KAUFFER

(1890–1954)

Catalogue cover
Organic Design in Home Furnishings
Designed 1941
Offset lithograph
19 x 25.4 cm
Printed by William E. Rudge's Sons, Division of Harwyn Litho Inc., New York, New York, U.S.A.
The Montreal Museum of Fine Arts, D88.165.1, gift of Mrs. Stanley Hanks

This design was commissioned by The Museum of Modern Art for the cover of its catalogue for the exhibition *Organic Design in Home Furnishings* of 1941. Kauffer's bold graphic style, modernist image, and use of typography were in sync with the museum's aesthetic as advocated by its director, Alfred Barr, Jr., who admired Kauffer's work and had already exhibited some of his English poster designs. Kauffer resided in England from 1915 to 1940 and designed this cover shortly after he returned to the United States. The front cover is a stark contrast of white forms on black, with a red elliptical line adding a touch of color. The somber black ground is exchanged for vivid orange on the back cover. The use of a hand, the "ball and string" in silhouette, and the basic hues of black and red all reveal Kauffer's playful humanist aesthetic. The serif capitals for "organic" are associated with nineteenth-century American typography, while the sans-serif font was promoted by Bauhaus.

Eero SAARINEN
Charles EAMES

(1910–1961) and **(1907–1978)**

Modular furniture
four cabinets, two benches, and desk
Designed 1940–41
Mahogany-faced blockboard,
yellow poplar, cherry, elm
Cabinets: 55.8 x 45.8 x 45.4 cm (each)
Cabinet: 38.6 x 46 x 45.4 cm
Benches: 33.2 x 91.5 x 45.4 cm (each)
Desk: 76.8 x 125.1 x 53.4 cm
Produced by Red Lion Furniture
Company, Red Lion,
Pennsylvania, U.S.A.
The Montreal Museum of Fine Arts,
D83.111.1–6; D89.183.1–2

Although known primarily for their chairs, Saarinen and Eames won a prize for their modular series of wood storage units in the *Organic Design in Home Furnishings* competition organized by The Museum of Modern Art in 1940–41. The Saarinen-Eames entry was seven cabinets designed to be combined in a variety of arrangements on a group of four-legged benches. According to Christopher Wilk, "Standardized unit furniture offered the opportunity to produce economically a range of furniture from a small number of constructional elements that could cover a wide variety of needs as well as allow a relatively large number of unit combinations."[6] This modular furniture, which the exhibition organizers viewed as an American version of designs done by Marcel Breuer at the Bauhaus a decade before, would inspire modular furniture radically altered by the Eameses in 1946.

Eero SAARINEN

(1910–1961)

Armchair
Womb
Designed c. 1946
Steel; compound of fiberglass,
plastic, and wood particles;
cowhide
92.3 x 102.5 x 91 cm
Produced by Knoll Associates,
Inc., New York, New York, U.S.A.
The Montreal Museum of
Fine Arts, D83.109.1,
gift of Muriel Kallis Newman*

One of the most famous twentieth-century designs, this lounge chair, popularly known as the *Womb* chair, is produced by Knoll to the present day. It remains Saarinen's most successful synthesis of new materials, innovative structure, and arresting form. The design evolved from the award-winning entries by Saarinen and Charles Eames for the *Organic Design in Home Furnishings* competition at The Museum of Modern Art, 1940–41, their earliest experiments with a three-dimensionally molded shell mounted on a four-legged base. Their original designs were in plywood, but the arrival of plastics revolutionized their chairs—as well as the furniture industry. This seating is both immensely comfortable and satisfying to the eye. According to Saarinen, "People sit differently today than in the Victorian era. They want to sit much lower, relax their bodies more and rest their heads."[7] The Chicago art collector Muriel Newman bought this example when it was first introduced, and she selected the cowhide upholstery.

Ray EAMES
Charles EAMES

(1912–1988) and **(1907–1978)**

Storage unit

ESU
Designed c. 1949
Zinc-plated steel, birch-faced
plywood, plastic-coated plywood,
lacquered Masonite
148.9 x 119.4 x 42.5 cm
Produced by Herman Miller
Furniture Company,
Zeeland, Michigan, U.S.A.
The Montreal Museum of Fine
Arts, D83.144.1, gift of Mr. and Mrs.
Robert L. Tannenbaum,
by exchange*

Marketed by Herman Miller as "modestly priced" for both office and residential use, the *Eames Storage Unit (ESU)* series responded to the lack of space in postwar offices and homes in the United States. The units are lightweight, interchangeable boxes of steel and plywood held on a steel frame structure. Various arrangements are possible in assembling the unit sections, and the buyer could order the desired combination of open and closed shelving and drawers with facings in different colors and materials, or add units later to serve changing needs. Not just practical, the *ESU* lets the buyer personalize a beautiful, formal display of geometric design. The taut, linear composition of rectangles, some in primary colors, reflected avant-garde currents in abstract art of the 1930s and 1940s, such as de Stijl, and advanced architecture as well, for the series as a whole echoes the Santa Monica house the Eameses constructed for themselves after the war.

BELOW Variations of the Eames *ESU* storage unit, c. 1949, showing different combinations of unit types and heights.

Charles Edmund ROSSBACH

(1914–2002)

Textile
Designed and executed 1947
Cotton
223.7 x 93 cm
The Montreal Museum of
Fine Arts, D85.164.1,
gift of the designer

Rossbach created this fabric, inspired by the paintings of Piet Mondrian, while he was a student at the Cranbrook Academy of Art. The palette of its pattern of translucent rectangles and squares is limited to the primary colors, separated by opaque black lines, reminiscent of heavily leaded stained glass and de Stijl art works. Rossbach was bold in that he didn't weave or paint the design, but "resorted to a painstaking process in which he dyed sections of his warp threads while they were on the loom and inserted the weft at the same time."[8] This textile is characteristic of the continual experimentation throughout Rossbach's career.

Robert D. SAILORS

(1913–1995)

Textile
Designed 1944
Wool, cotton, linen, Lurex
139.7 x 76.2 cm
Produced by Contemporary
Textiles Weaving Company,
Bitely, Michigan, U.S.A.
The Montreal Museum of Fine Arts,
D89.136.1, gift of the designer

After graduating from the Cranbrook Academy in 1943, Robert Sailors taught in the school's Weaving Department under Marianne Strengell, a Bauhaus-trained émigré from whom he learned to experiment with man-made fibers of vivid colors and varied textures.[9] The introduction of industrial material in his woven work, such as Lurex, a metallic yarn used here, was a key to the success of his innovative designs. This example with its herringbone stripes and loose weave conformed to then-current avant-garde tastes in textile design and could be used for drapery or upholstery. This particular example was made from two pieces sewn together; it once covered a couch owned by the designer's parents.

Pierre JEANNERET

(1896–1967)

Lounge chair
Designed 1949
Birch, leather
76.9 x 58.9 x 78.2 cm
Produced by Knoll Associates,
New York, New York, U.S.A.
The Montreal Museum of Fine
Arts, D86.246.1a–c

Trained as an architect in his native Switzerland, Jeanneret moved to Paris in 1920, and from 1922 onward he worked as an architect in the office of his cousin Charles Edouard Jeanneret (Le Corbusier). The cousins collaborated with Charlotte Perriand on designs for several well-known examples of tubular steel furniture, but this wooden piece is credited to Pierre Jeanneret alone. It was listed in the 1950 Knoll catalogue as the *92* chair, shown in Florence Knoll's room installation in *An Exhibition for Modern Living* at the Detroit Institute of Arts,[10] but was later known as the *Scissors* chair, because the strongly canted legs splay from a large metal medallion at the juncture of the legs and the seat and back rail. A minimalist aesthetic is achieved here with simple upholstered pads for back and seat over a webbed wood frame.

BELOW Florence Knoll, combination living and dining room, *An Exhibition for Modern Living*, Detroit Institute of Arts, 1949, with Jeanneret chairs in the foreground.

Jupp ERNST

(1905—1987)

Poster
Neues Wohnen
Designed 1949
Offset lithograph
84 x 59 cm
Printed by Kölnische
Verlagsdruckerei,
Cologne, Germany
The Montreal Museum of
Fine Arts, D85.162.1

From 1929 to 1948 Jupp Ernst worked as a freelance graphic designer, and later as the director of the Werkkunstschule (Art and Crafts School) at Wuppertal, Germany. Ernst created this poster, *Neues Wohnen* (New Lifestyle), for a 1949 Cologne exhibition sponsored by the Deutscher Werkbund (here "dwb"). Suppressed by the Nazis, the Werkbund—or Design Organization—was revived in 1949 to meet postwar needs for home furnishings. The poster focuses on two modern chair designs. The armchair in the foreground, possibly by the Swedish furniture designer Axel Larsson, is shown against a divided yellow-and-white ground. The rear legs are aligned with the juncture of the two angled color planes, which creates a steep perspective and leads to the background of a modern terrace with a lounge chair. The use of lowercase sans-serif type combined with capital letters of the same size reflects the ongoing influence of Bauhaus principles, which was still strongly felt after the war. Cologne continues to host an important annual furniture fair today, much like the one promoted in this design.

Earl Silas TUPPER

(1907–1983)

Pitcher, bowl, covered bowls, creamer, iced-tea spoons
Tupperware
Designed c. 1946
Polyethylene
Pitcher: 24.5 x 18 x 13 cm
Produced by Tupper Corporation, Farnumsville, Massachusetts, U.S.A.
The Stewart Program for Modern Design, 2007.19, gift of Dr. Michael Sze

A self-taught Yankee inventor, Earl Tupper experimented in the early 1940s with polyethylene, a new synthetic plastic that was soft and flexible. In 1942 he founded the Tupper Corporation to manufacture a variety of food containers exploiting these properties. *House Beautiful* editor Elizabeth Gordon praised his airtight refrigerator bowls in an article, "Fine Art for 39¢": "Above all else, the bowls have a profile as good as a piece of sculpture."[11] Her opinion of Tupperware's aesthetic qualities was supported by The Museum of Modern Art, which acquired examples in 1956. Tupper's great commercial success came after 1951 when he began direct-marketing his pastel wares. Mobilizing housewives as representatives, he had them sell directly to their friends at Tupperware parties in their homes.

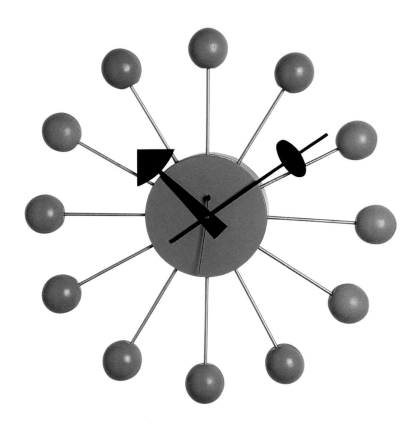

GEORGE NELSON Associates

(active 1947–1983)

Wall clock

Ball
Designed 1947
Painted birch, steel, brass
35.5 x 35.5 x 5.7 cm
Produced by Howard Miller Clock
Company, Zeeland,
Michigan, U.S.A.
The Montreal Museum of
Fine Arts, D86.150.1,
gift of Dr. Arthur Cooperberg

The whimsical *Ball* clock, designed by Irving Harper at Nelson Associates, was the best known of a series of wall clocks for the Howard Miller Clock Company. All of them can be related to American abstract sculpture of the period, especially the work of Alexander Calder. The *Ball* clock in particular refers to atomic structures with its small spheres surrounding the center as electrons orbit a nucleus. The Nelson clocks were considered radically modern in their day because they lacked a traditional numbered clock face. When Nelson's staff began developing them in 1947, his firm was only a year old. Trained as an architect at Yale University from 1928 to 1931, Nelson was also a designer, teacher, and writer. In 1946 he became the design director at Herman Miller Furniture Company, a position he held until his death in 1986.

Eva ZEISEL

(born 1906)

Coffee service
Museum
Designed c. 1942–43
Glazed porcelain
Coffeepot: 26.9 x 19.5 x 14.1 cm
Produced by Shenango Pottery,
New Castle, Pennsylvania,
for Castleton China, Inc.,
New York, New York, U.S.A.
The Montreal Museum of Fine
Arts, D83.113.1–2; D85.155.1–3;
D86.102.1–2, gift of Hans Zeisel*

This dinnerware service, the most elegant of Zeisel's ceramic designs, is the result of a collaboration of The Museum of Modern Art, the designer, and the manufacturer. MoMA wished to become closely associated with manufacturers to improve the quality of American design, and so it exchanged its imprimatur for the right to approve each piece of the *Museum* service. Modernism in American tableware was generally restricted to informal services such as Russel Wright's *American Modern* (p. 70). The *Museum* service proved that ceramic wares could be both modern and formal. Though this service alludes to various older styles, its harmony of curves and fluid lines reflects a contemporary sensibility.

Ruth Adler SCHNEE

(born 1923)

Textile

Bugs in a Booby Trap
Designed c. 1947
Printed cotton
160 x 125.6 cm
Produced by Ruth Adler,
Detroit, Michigan, U.S.A.
The Montreal Museum of
Fine Arts, D84.170.1,
gift of Geoffrey N. Bradfield*

During her youth in Dusseldorf, Schnee learned the basics of modern painting from Paul Klee, who was a good family friend and whose influence is seen in her postwar designs for textiles. As a teenager, she immigrated to the United States in 1939 and settled in Detroit. After graduating from the Cranbrook Academy in 1946, she designed this textile, which reflects her humorous style in its subject and title. Commenting on the print, she wrote: "For a few years after World War II, I was fascinated by rounded and pierced shapes. This was, no doubt, a reaction from the austere, square graphics which the Bauhaus produced. Undulating shapes and rounded holes played against each other in my dreams and then were put to paper and then to printing silk screens."[12]

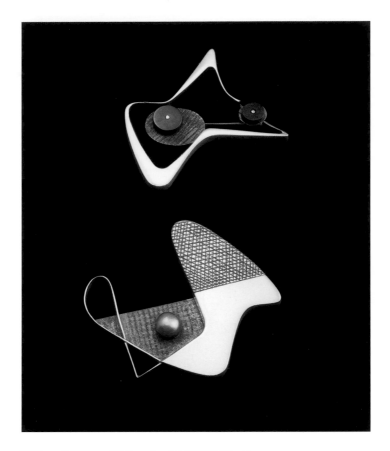

Margaret DE PATTA

(1903–1964)

Brooch
Designed c. 1946–50
Silver, malachite, jasper
7.7 x 7.7 cm
The Montreal Museum of
Fine Arts, D86.160.1

Brooch
Designed c. 1945
Silver, pearl
6.7 x 7.8 x 1 cm
The Montreal Museum of
Fine Arts, D94.230.1,
gift of Paul Leblanc

Originally a painter, De Patta became a seminal figure in American handcrafted "studio" jewelry. She studied at art schools in California and New York before establishing herself in San Francisco in 1929, and in 1935 she opened her own jewelry workshop. In 1940–41, she attended László Moholy-Nagy's Institute of Design in Chicago and began to evolve a distinctive visual vocabulary that included the geometric and biomorphic interplay seen in these brooches. Her stated aim was to take principles of modern design derived from abstract painting and sculpture and express them in jewelry.

Edgar BARTOLUCCI
John J. WALDHEIM

(born 1918) and **(1920—2002)**

Rocking lounge chair

Barwa
Designed 1947
Aluminum, canvas
112.2 x 56.4 x 140 cm
Produced by Ralph Elliot Co. for
Barwa Associates,
Chicago, Illinois, U.S.A.
The Montreal Museum of
Fine Arts, D82.112.1,
gift of Edgar Bartolucci

In 1944, Edgar Bartolucci and John Waldheim, two students at the Institute of Design in Chicago, started a design firm. This chair, titled with the first few letters of their last names, is their best-known work. Based on Le Corbusier's famous 1928 chaise longue, the design allows the user to achieve, with a slight shift of weight, several relaxed postures between sitting and reclining. At the time, reclining with the feet higher than the head was recommended as conducive to good health. Made of lightweight aluminum tubing with colorful canvas stretched over it, the lounging rocker was a comfortable, whimsical solution for seating that was extremely popular at mid-century. Various colors could be selected, and replacement canvas could be ordered for models frequently left outdoors. Although it was not intended as a toy, the *Barwa* has amused children, as well as adults, who delight in its many positions.[13]

Angelo TESTA

(1921–1984)

Textile

Little Man
Designed 1942
Printed linen
199 x 129 cm
Produced by Cohn-Hall-Marx Co.,
New York, New York, U.S.A.
The Stewart Program for
Modern Design, 2009.23,
gift of Dr. Michael Sze*

Textile

Textura Prima Solida
Designed c. 1945
Printed cotton
129 x 102.5 cm
Produced by Angelo Testa and
Company, Chicago, Illinois, U.S.A.
The Stewart Program for
Modern Design, 2009.13

Textile

Sportsmen's Blues
Designed 1942
Printed cotton
190 x 129.5 cm
Produced by Angelo Testa and
Company, Chicago, Illinois, U.S.A.
The Montreal Museum of
Fine Arts, D84.148.1,
gift of Geoffrey N. Bradfield

Testa began his education at the University of Chicago in 1939, but he soon transferred to the Institute of Design where he studied under László Moholy-Nagy and was one of the school's first graduates in 1945. Beginning in 1942, he focused on textiles, designing *Little Man* as a school assignment. When exhibited seven years later, it was admired for its "simplicity, boldness of form, and purity of color," which represented a break from the realistic patterns of traditional textiles.[14] In 1947 he established Angelo Testa and Company in Chicago, a firm that continued throughout his lifetime. He was one of the first Americans to specialize in abstract designs for textiles. His often linear and geometric patterns—printed on white or undyed fabric always made of such natural fibers as cotton or linen—were used for furnishings and draperies as well as clothing and carpets. Painting and sculpting throughout his life, he regarded his textile designs as works of art as well, describing them as "my first collection of abstract, non-objective designs to be mass-produced in the world."[15]

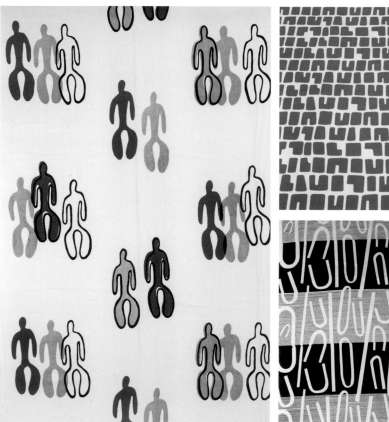

Ray **EAMES**
Charles **EAMES**

(1907–1978) and **(1912–1988)**

Armchair
LAR
Designed c. 1948
Fiberglass, zinc-plated
steel, rubber
64.1 x 63.4 x 62.1 cm
Produced by Herman Miller
Furniture Company,
Zeeland, Michigan, U.S.A.
The Montreal Museum of
Fine Arts, D81.111.1a—b

The thin sculptural shell of the *LAR* (for "low armchair") unites back, arms, and seat in a continuous shape and was based on Charles Eames and Eero Saarinen's plywood-shell furniture, which won first prize in The Museum of Modern Art's 1940—41 competition *Organic Design in Home Furnishings*. The designers' goal was to produce a chair that was comfortable and inexpensive: here the continuously curved shell replaced traditional upholstery and the use of molded plastic circumvented many of the problems inherent in working with plywood. The wire base structure replaced traditional vertical legs as a support for the shell. The *LAR* was one of the earliest mass-produced chairs in plastic and came in a variety of colors and forms, including a rocking-chair version.

Alexander CALDER

(1898–1976)

Textile
Model No. L-145, *Calder # 1*
Designed 1949
Printed rayon, fiberglass
84 x 126 cm
Produced by Laverne Originals,
New York, New York, U.S.A.
The Metropolitan Museum
of Art, 1984.565

Calder # 1 was part of the *Contempora* series of textiles and wallpapers issued by Laverne Originals. It features an abstract composition of stars, moons, and suns conceived in yellow, red, blue, and black on a white ground, reminiscent of Calder's mobiles. It reflects his interest in the solar system and delight in creating imaginary universes, which he began in the 1930s. He once said that "the underlying sense of form in my work has been the system of the universe."[16] In 1926, he went to Paris and began to make toy-like animals of wood and wire for his own amusement, influenced by Parisian artists, in particular Joan Miró, whom he met in 1928. The simplified forms and use of primary colors are seen in the work of these lifelong friends.

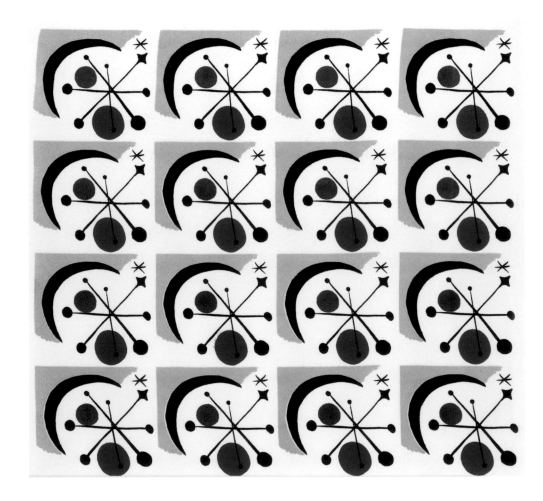

Ray EAMES
Charles EAMES

(1907–1978) and **(1912–1988)**

Screen
FSW
Designed c. 1946
Stained ash-faced plywood,
canvas
172.1 x 153.8 x 12.7 cm (extended)
Produced by Molded Plywood
Division, Evans Products
Company, Venice, California,
and by Herman Miller Furniture
Company, Zeeland,
Michigan, U.S.A.
The Montreal Museum of
Fine Arts, D81.134.1

Lounge Chair
LCW
Designed 1945–46
Stained laminated ash, stained
ash-faced plywood, rubber
67 x 55.8 x 55.5 cm
Produced by Molded Plywood
Division, Evans Products
Company, Venice, California,
and by Herman Miller Furniture
Company, Zeeland,
Michigan, U.S.A.
The Montreal Museum of
Fine Arts, D81.152.1,
gift of Ann Hatfield Rothschild*

Popularly known as the *Potato Chip* chair, this plywood seating created by the Eameses in the mid-1940s has become a modern icon, synthesizing technical and aesthetic achievements in a sculptural masterpiece of design. The *LCW* (for "lounge chair wood") was constructed from five separate plywood parts—seat, back, front and rear legs, and the "spine" connecting them all. The plywood is molded in three dimensions and offers comfort as well as visual appeal. It draws on the Eameses' wartime experience in California when they experimented with plywood on commission from the U.S. Navy for plywood splints and learned techniques of bending, gluing, and molding. The chair, produced in different finishes, was also available in a dining version, as well as another version with metal legs. Designed in the same year as the famous chair, the *FSW* (for "folding screen wood") was also made possible through the Eameses' experiments in the bending of plywood. This rippling organic form is remarkable for its method of construction of identical molded plywood sections joined together by long pieces of canvas sandwiched between the layers of wood. The screen can be folded into a compact form for shipping or storage. Made of ash or birch and stained in different colors, the design was available in heights of 86.5 and 173 cm.

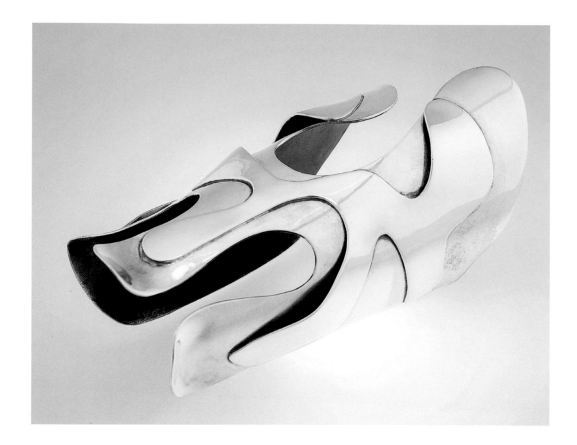

Art SMITH

(1917–1982)

Bracelet
Lava
Designed c. 1946
Silver
14.9 x 5.7 x 7.3 cm
The Montreal Museum
of Fine Arts, D87.213.1

In 1942, this African-American jeweler received a scholarship to Cooper Union, the respected art and design school in New York, where he studied architecture and pursued sculptural constructions on his own. In 1946, he opened his own shop in Little Italy, and two years later, to escape neighborhood racial prejudice, he moved to Greenwich Village, then a bohemian quarter that was home to many avant-garde artists. In this bracelet, two undulating, amoeba-like forms are layered to produce an outsized cuff. The dramatic work alluded to both the armor and the jewelry of African tribal culture and the sensuous biomorphic sculpture of European artists such as Jean Arp.

Isamu NOGUCHI

(1904–1988)

Chess table
Designed c. 1947
Plywood, aluminum, plastic
48.8 x 86 x 77.6 cm
Produced by the Herman Miller
Furniture Company,
Zeeland, Michigan, U.S.A.
The Montreal Museum of
Fine Arts, D85.132.1a–d,
gift of Jay Spectre, by exchange*

A leading American sculptor of the twentieth century, Noguchi was raised in both the United States and Japan. In 1927 he went to Paris and worked as an assistant to Constantin Brancusi, whose svelte abstracted sculpture was a strong influence. This biomorphic design is a piece of sculpture as well as a piece of furniture. It has an irregularly shaped, four-legged base, a thin plywood top into which red pegs and yellow dots of plastic have been set to denote the positions of a chessboard, and an undulating component supporting the top, with four containers that function as storage for the chessmen, accessed by swiveling the top. All the elements of the table are dynamic, powerfully conveying a sense of organic life. Though known as a sculptor, Noguchi designed furniture and lamps that helped define the engaging organic idiom of American Modernism at mid-century (pp. 138–39).

Eva ZEISEL

(born 1906)

Dinnerware

Town and Country
Designed c. 1945
Earthenware
Pitcher: 19 x 17 x 16 cm
Produced by Red Wing Pottery,
Red Wing, Minnesota, U.S.A.
The Stewart Program for Modern
Design, 2007.57.2/30/57, 2009.1,
2009.3.1–2, gift of Dr. Michael Sze

The biomorphic designs of the *Town and Country* line represent a radical departure for Zeisel as she moved away from the more geometric dinnerware she designed when she worked in Hungary, Germany, and the Soviet Union during the 1920s and '30s. *Town and Country* recalls Russel Wright's 1937 *American Modern* line (p. 70), which was also intended for America's more informal lifestyle and offered in colors that could be mixed and matched as desired. The asymmetrical, organic shapes of Zeisel's vessels suggest the influence of freeform sculpture by Arp. Some of the pieces even have human characteristics, such as the salt and pepper shakers, which can nestle together; Zeisel compared them to a mother and child.

Carol KRAMER
Sam KRAMER

(1918–1986) and **(1913–1964)**

Brooch
Dancers
Designed 1947
Silver, gold, peridots,
garnet, tourmaline
13.5 x 6.5 x 2.4 cm
The Montreal Museum of
Fine Arts, D93.319.1

One of the most significant American modernist jewelers of the postwar, Sam Kramer designed with the primal spirit of some Surrealist art, recalling expressive paintings by Miró. Like many of his works, *Dancers* is the result of a collaboration with his wife, Carol, also a jeweler, who executed this sizable brooch. Its sexually charged pair of pierced figures was built up from forged and assembled sheet silver. Kramer wrote: "Some people may say work like this is disquieting and has a quality deep-rooted and uncivilized. It is just another aspect of the new medium of jewelry that offers the artist one of the richest and most rewarding environments for his own kind of expression."[17]

Edvin ÖHRSTRÖM

(1906–1994)

Vase
Designed c. 1947
Glass
15.3 x 16.5 x 16.5 cm
Produced by AB Orrefors
Glasbruk, Orrefors, Sweden
The Montreal Museum of
Fine Arts, D87.111.1

Trained as a sculptor and a graphic designer, Öhrström created functional and decorative glass for the famed Swedish glass manufacturer Orrefors, where he worked from 1936 to 1957. The Matisse-like decoration on this vase is achieved through a technique known as *Ariel*, a process involving bubbles of air. A globe of molten glass is blown and cooled, and the design is then carved by means of sandblasting. The glass is reheated and a new layer of molten glass is added over it, here resulting in a modernist spherical form with the glass seeming to flow inward at the opening. The two layers fuse smoothly where there is no decoration, but where the design is carved away, pockets of trapped air form, creating a silvery pattern that hovers under the surface. This obviously difficult process is slow and labor-intensive.

Henning KOPPEL

(1918–1981)

Wine pitcher
Designed 1948
Silver
35.3 x 19.2 x 15.4 cm
Produced by Georg Jensen
Silversmithy,
Copenhagen, Denmark
The Montreal Museum of
Fine Arts, D86.244.1

After studying drawing and sculpture in Copenhagen, Koppel went to Paris in 1938 to study at the Académie Ranson. During the war he fled to Stockholm, where he worked for the sculptor Carl Milles from 1940 to 1945. Returning to Copenhagen in 1945, he joined the Georg Jensen silversmithy as a fully trained artist. This pitcher was one of the first in a series of jugs for Jensen. The curvaceous form represents a radical departure from Jensen's previous styles, which were straightforward, functional forms. The pitcher reflects Koppel's training as a sculptor, with a tense balance between the teardrop container section and the tall elliptical handle. It is both functional and aesthetically pleasing: Koppel generated it from a clay model to assure its interest from many angles.

Henning KOPPEL

(1918–1981)

Necklace
No. 89
Designed 1947
Silver
44.5 x 4.5 cm
Produced by Georg Jensen
Silversmithy,
Copenhagen, Denmark
The Montreal Museum of
Fine Arts, D88.121.1

Koppel was inspired by biomorphism, as seen in the irregular contours of the glass of Alvar Aalto (see p. 72). The silver links appear to grow organically from one another, like vertebrae, and create a continuous, animated whole. In the necklace, the piercing of the flying forms allows their linking.

Wilhelm KÅGE

(1889–1960)

Vase
Surrea
Designed 1940
Glazed stoneware
47.5 x 33 x 25.5 cm
Produced by AB Gustavsberg,
Gustavsberg, Sweden
The Montreal Museum of
Fine Arts, D93.274.1

A student of painting in Göteborg, Stockholm, and Copenhagen and of graphics in Munich, Kåge was the most influential of Swedish ceramic designers in the 1940s and the leading designer at Gustavsberg, where he had begun working in 1917. In 1940 he created the *Surrea* series of ceramics, which was inspired by Cubism and Surrealism. Greeting the introduction of the series to North America in 1953, a critic observed: "*Surrea*, Kåge's most recent chalky art ware, is an adventure in pure, glazeless ceramic sculpture. With the split personality of a Picasso half-face, a vase may be only half a vase, a branch blooming where its mirror image should be."[18] While the colorless, unglazed *Surrea* pieces were put into general production, and are back in production today, the Stewart Collection example is a rare type because it is painted. The lavender and brown glazing heightens the Cubist effects, emphasizing the main vessel's juxtaposition with a section of a pot and of a tall vase, both rounded on the far side.

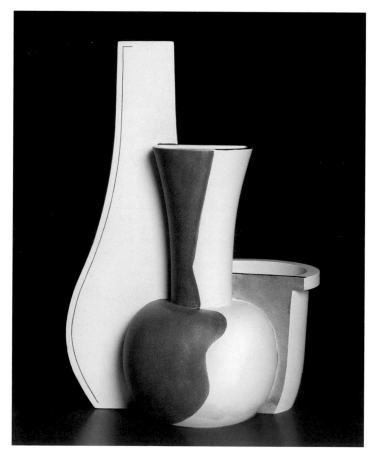

Fulvio BIANCONI

(1915–1996)

Candlestick
Designed c. 1948
Glass
28.8 x 14 x 10.5 cm
Produced by Venini S.p.A.,
Murano, Italy
The Montreal Museum of
Fine Arts, D94.308.1

Fulvio Bianconi is celebrated as one of the leading Italian glass designers of the postwar years. He began working for Venini in 1947 and remained with the firm until 1951. This candlestick depicts a man's coat (perhaps of the eighteenth or nineteenth century) on a coat rack, but it is far from inert: it is animated as if worn by an invisible person. In the same year he designed this candlestick, he also created a series of figurines in the humorous spirit of the *commedia dell'arte*. Although both Bianconi and Venini are known for their colorful palettes, this item is rendered in black and white, heightening its resemblance to a lively cartoon. In a 1986 article, art critic Marielle Ernould-Gandouet wrote, "Working at Venini, Fulvio Bianconi is able to express his sense of life in glass. . . . [He] animates the glass as easily as a humorist works with a pencil."[19]

Paul RAND

(1914–1996)

Poster

Subway Posters Score
Designed 1947
Offset lithograph
114.6 x 74.6 cm
Produced by the New York Subways
Advertising Company,
New York, New York, U.S.A.
The Montreal Museum of Fine Arts,
D87.152.1, gift of Mr. and
Mrs. Charles D. O'Kieffe, Jr.,
in memory of Mr. and Mrs. Charles
DeWitt O'Kieffe, by exchange*

In this poster for the New York Subways Advertising Company, Rand uses a simple stick figure with a target-like head and the forerunner of today's ubiquitous "smiley face." Reducing the human form to a humorous emblem, he indicates that the subway rider is a good target for advertising. Although his drawing is playful, Rand pursues modernist principles in his composition and geometric forms. Following Bauhaus precepts, the lines of lowercase typography are design elements set on contrasting diagonals. The large colorful balls, representing high-scoring hits near the center of the target, help balance the carefully arranged composition. Rand, who studied art in New York City at Pratt Institute, Parsons School of Design, and, later, the Art Students League, saw the close relationship between fine and commercial art, as witnessed by this Miró-like personage with its cheerful primary colors.

Salvador DALÍ

(1904–1989)

Brooch
The Persistence of Memory
Designed c. 1949–50
Gold, platinum, diamonds
6 x 6 x 1.9 cm
Produced by Alemany & Ertman,
Inc., New York, New York, U.S.A.
The Montreal Museum of
Fine Arts, D89.109.1

Like other examples of Dalí's jewelry, *The Persistence of Memory* brooch reflects an image from one of his paintings—the 1931 oil of the same title in The Museum of Modern Art. The motif of a limp watch hanging from a tree branch summons up a dreamlike world where time has been abolished. Dalí explained in 1959: "In American schools, my 'melted watch' is presented as a prophetic expression of the fluidity of time . . . the indivisibility of time and space."[20] Dalí's first jewelry designs, of 1948, were precious, one-of-a-kind items, but he later made some that were produced by Alemany & Ertman in a limited edition, like this one, with six or seven examples made of each model.

Paavo TYNELL

(1890–1973)

Chandelier
Designed 1948
Brass
106.8 x 83.8 x 83.8 cm
Produced by Taito Oy,
Helsinki, Finland
The Montreal Museum of
Fine Arts, D88.152.1a–y

A pioneer in Finnish lighting design, Tynell was trained as a metalsmith at the Central School of Industrial Design in Helsinki and taught there from 1917 to 1923. In 1918 he established his own firm, Taito Oy, where he produced a wide range of metal articles, and, beginning in the 1940s, lighting fixtures. This chandelier is primarily an aesthetic creation, as the functional element of the lamp is limited to the bowl of perforated sheet brass at the bottom of the shaft, which conceals the bulbs, and the light is reflected by the shining brass flower forms. Tynell sought to create a modern echo of an eighteenth-century chandelier. He designed several variations of the fixture in different sizes, and each was handmade by his metal artisans. Because of this expensive fabrication, production was limited.

Fulvio **BIANCONI**
Paolo **VENINI**

(1915–1996) and **(1895–1959)**

Vase

Fazzoletto (Handkerchief)
Designed 1949
Glass
26.4 x 21.1 x 19.1 cm
Produced by Venini S.p.A.,
Murano, Italy
Indianapolis Museum of Art,
2008.338, gift of Roy Poretzky
to the Stewart Program for
Modern Design*

The most celebrated design of the Venini firm was a series of *Fazzoletto* vases, the result of collaboration between Fulvio Bianconi, chief glass designer, and Paolo Venini. According to Venini's daughter, the glass historian Anna Venini Diaz de Santillana, "The design is prompted by Paolo Venini; thanks to Bianconi's gifts as an artist, the idea was developed with different techniques."[21] The vases were made with squares of free-blown glass allowed to fall into irregular, sculptural forms. The soft and pliable hot glass was held upside down on a rod until the glass hardened in curving peaks and folds. In this example, the opaque blown glass was cased in white and brown, producing a contrast that accents the form's amusing irregularities and its resemblance to a handkerchief in use (but inverted). The glassmaker's skillful manipulation is seen in the undulating rim, unique for each vase. Bianconi realized this idea in a range of sizes, colors, and decorations, and the series was put into production in 1949.

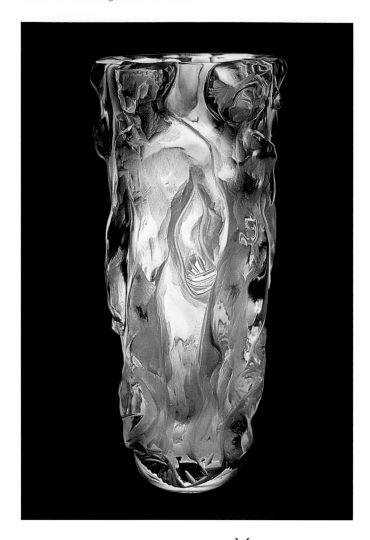

René ROUBICĚK

(born 1922)

Vase
Adam and Eve
Designed 1947
Glass
33 x 12.5 x 12.5 cm
The Montreal Museum of
Fine Arts, D83.121.1

Although working with a traditional vase form, Roubicěk achieves dramatic effects with his boldly curvilinear carving of the glass to create the intertwined figures of Adam and Eve here. From this high-relief sculptured vessel the Czech artist moved to executing monumental works in the 1950s, following the Communist takeover of his country. The vase was designed while Roubicěk, who had studied at the Academy of Applied Arts in Prague, was teaching at the specialized school of glassmaking in Kamenicky Senov (1945–52). As the chief designer of the Borske Sklo glassworks from 1952 to 1965, he was one of the most influential figures in the mid-century revival of Czech glass.[22]

Axel SALTO

(1889–1961)

Vase
Designed c. 1940
Enameled earthenware
32.7 x 22.8 x 22.8 cm
Produced by Royal Copenhagen
Porcelain Manufactory,
Copenhagen, Denmark
The Montreal Museum of
Fine Arts, 2001.17

Vase
Designed c. 1950
Enameled earthenware
20.8 x 26.4 x 26 cm
Produced by Royal Copenhagen
Porcelain Manufactory,
Copenhagen, Denmark
The Montreal Museum of
Fine Arts, 2001.16

Countering the functionalist aesthetics of his contemporaries, Salto was one of the first major ceramists to break away from the symmetry of wheel-thrown forms. Trained at the Copenhagen Academy of Art, he also was a painter and designer of textiles. He not only used an organic model, but also gave it a very expressive idiom, often on a large scale that prefigured the direction taken by "studio" ceramics (the work of individual ceramists in their own shops) in the later twentieth century under the American Peter Voulkos and others. Salto saw his works as reflections of three categories: budding, sprouting, and fluted, which refer to the forms of his pieces, with budding and sprouting shown here. He wrote: "The vase is like a living organism; the body buds, the buds develop, and a sprouting—even prickly—vessel results from the urgency of life within."[23]

Gunnel NYMAN

(1909–1948)

Vase
Designed 1947
Glass
17.5 x 10 x 10 cm
Produced by Nuutajärvi-Notsjö,
Nuutajärvi, Finland
The Montreal Museum of
Fine Arts, D85.115.1

"In certain ways, this vase summarizes Modernist glass in the years just after World War II," wrote Martin Eidelberg. "Its fluidity of form, its limpid mass, and its use of internal air bubbles were all distinctive features of the mid-1940s."[24] The drama of the design also derives from its unity, as the base seems to twist upward to merge with the vessel itself. Such forms are forecast in 1930s glass by Maurice Marinot and Steuben Nyman. She studied furniture design and interior decoration at the Central School of Industrial Design in Helsinki and graduated in 1932 and worked at three of the major Finnish glassworks: Riihimäki, Iittala, and Notsjö.

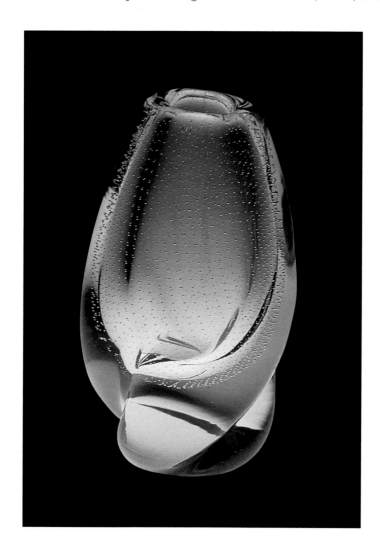

Tapio WIRKKALA

(1915–1985)

Vase
Kanttarelli
Designed 1947
Glass
22 x 16.6 x 17.5 cm
Produced by Iittala Lasitehdas,
Iittala, Finland
The Montreal Museum of
Fine Arts, D85.134.1

Vase
Varsanjalka
Designed c. 1950
Glass
38.1 x 11.7 x 10.8 cm
Produced by Iittala Lasitehdas,
Iittala, Finland
The Montreal Museum of
Fine Arts, D88.164.1

After studying industrial design from 1933 to 1936, Wirkkala began a career in advertising before turning to designing glass for Iittala, Finland's leading producer of glassware. He became his country's most important postwar designer, creating beautiful fluent forms in glass, wood, metal, and furniture. In the 1950s, he worked in a taut yet organic style, characterized by sculptural forms inspired by nature. The stunning *Kanttarelli* series for Iittala was inspired by the basic form of the chanterelle mushroom it was named for. Here swelling shapes are accented by the vertical lines of the machine-engraved decoration, as if the pierced and stringed sculptures of Barbara Hepworth had met Brancusi's *Bird in Space*. Wirkkala's work was recognized internationally at mid-century, notably at the Milan Triennales in 1951 and 1954.

Stig LINDBERG

(1916–1982)

Vases and bowl
Veckla
Designed c. 1949
Glazed porcelain
Vase 12 x 13.5 x 7 cm
Vase 35.5 x 17.4 x 8.3 cm
Bowl 4.8 x 14.5 x 9.5 cm
Produced by AB Gustavsberg,
Gustavsberg, Sweden
The Montreal Museum of
Fine Arts, D85.158.1,
D85.159.1, D86.144.1,
gift of Geoffrey N. Bradfield*

Veckla is Swedish for "folded," an apt name for Lindberg's eccentric line of porcelain for Gustavsberg. While traditional ceramic forms produced on a potter's wheel are primarily circular, Lindberg sought asymmetrical abstract forms, similar to sculpture, at mid-century. He achieved them by manipulating the cylindrical vessels, pinching and folding the clay while it was still pliant. Undulant forms were already part of the vocabulary developed in the 1930s by glass and ceramic artisans, but Lindberg's technique permitted the realization of such complex forms in inexpensive large-scale production.

Carl-Harry STÅLHANE

(1920–1990)

Vase
Designed c. 1948
Glazed stoneware
18 x 13.2 x 13.2 cm
Produced by AB Rörstrands
Porslinfabriker,
Lidköping, Sweden
The Montreal Museum of
Fine Arts, D86.139.1,
gift of Geoffrey N. Bradfield*

Vase
Designed c. 1947
Glazed stoneware
35 x 8.9 x 8.9 cm
Produced by AB Rörstrands
Porslinfabriker,
Lidköping, Sweden
The Montreal Museum of
Fine Arts, D86.140.1,
gift of Geoffrey N. Bradfield*

After studying under the Russian sculptor Ossip Zadkine at the Académie Colarossi in Paris, Stålhane joined the staff of the Rörstrands factory in Sweden in 1939, at age nineteen, and remained there until 1973. The simple forms and monochromatic glazes of Asian ceramics appealed to Scandinavian modernist designers like Stålhane in the 1940s and 1950s. This reductivist aesthetic is apparent in the two vases seen here, though their traditional forms are greatly modified in exaggerated silhouettes. Stålhane's globular sphere is astonishingly wide for its small foot, and its neck is thin in relation to its broad shoulders. The taller vase has extremely attenuated proportions and a small, mannered neck. This phase of what could be called linear lyricism, including the grouping of his work at the left was short-lived. By the 1960s, Stålhane had gone on to a more expressive mode in his ceramics, creating asymmetrical sculptural forms.

ABOVE, LEFT Carl-Harry Stålhane, vases, late 1940s, Rörstrands Porslinfabriker.

Carlo DE CARLI

(1910–1971)

Table
Designed 1945–50
Beech, glass
54.5 x 75.5 x 75.5 cm
Manufacturer unknown, Italy
The Montreal Museum of
Fine Arts, 2002.92.1–2

De Carli worked in the vanguard of modernist Italian design in the late 1930s with the architect-designers Gio Ponti and Giovanni Muzio and became a major mid-century designer with vigorous wooden furnishings like this. Like tentacles, twelve subtly carved arms support the round glass top of this table. The combination of the handmade organic forms of beech and the modernist, minimalist disc of glass recalls the better-known work of Carlo Molino and reveals the paradox and beauty of Italian postwar design. In these years, De Carli also pursued a career as an architect, organized exhibitions, and helped found the magazine *Il Mobile Italiano*, serving as its editor from 1958 to 1960. He was also a professor and the director of the Faculty of Architecture at the Politecnico di Milano.

Finn JUHL

(1912–1989)

Armchair
Chieftain
Designed 1949
Teak, leather
93 x 101.5 x 89 cm
Produced by Niels Vodder,
Allerød, Denmark
The Montreal Museum of
Fine Arts, D85.122.1

Juhl trained as an architect and became one of Denmark's most influential designers of furnishings. In 1937 he began what would become a long collaboration with the cabinetmaker Niels Vodder, producing a broad range of handcrafted furniture designs. The *Chieftain* chair is a functional sculpture in which the teak framework and black leather upholstery are carefully balanced. The curved armrests, oval seat, and shield-shaped back are three-dimensional upholstered shells that seem to float apart from the wood structure. The seat is supported on diagonal stretchers with chamfered edges, and the canted back panel is suspended from tapered stiles by bow-shaped, diagonally placed wooden elements.

ABOVE, LEFT Finn Juhl, *Chieftain* armchair with dining table and chairs shown in the 1949 Furniture Exhibition of the Cabinetmakers' Guild, Danish Museum of Decorative Art, Copenhaguen.

1950
1959

"Good Design"

By the early 1950s America's factories had completed their conversion from wartime to domestic production, and the country's standard of living was the envy of the world. Low-cost government-backed mortgages to first-time homebuyers fostered explosive building in suburbia. By the end of the decade the Jeep, that sturdy World War II vehicle, and Detroit's "insolent chariots" could speed across a growing highway system, which connected suburbs to cities and cities to one another across the country. Abroad, the United States aided postwar reconstruction with the Marshall Plan, sending more than $13 billion in aid to both Allied and Axis countries, including France, Italy, and West Germany. Though Winston Churchill had warned in 1948 that an Iron Curtain divided the West from the USSR, and nuclear arms buildups on both sides defined the Cold War, the world was spanned by jet travel for vacationers and businessmen. By 1949 a plane had circled the globe, refueling in midair. Design was enriched by the consequent interest in other nations and the purchasing power of peacetime. Though invention was not restricted to the former Allied nations, the consumer goods of America reflected its postwar economic supremacy.

Seizing the opportunity to shape consumer tastes, institutions defined "Good Design" through traveling exhibitions. *Gute Form* (Good Design), supervised by the German designer-architect-sculptor Max Bill for the Swiss Werkbund, was the first, in 1949. But arguably most influential was the series of competitive *Good Design* surveys of 1950–55 organized by The Museum of Modern Art in partnership with Chicago's Merchandise Mart, the country's leading wholesale furnishings center (fig. 1). Representing the museum's Department of Architecture and Design, Edgar Kaufmann, Jr., and his jurors chose objects that reflected his definition of Good Design: "a thorough merging of form and function revealing a practical, uncomplicated beauty."[1] The origins of their convictions were clear and derived from Bauhaus teachings. Using modern technology and materials, rejecting ornament, and, most of all, fitting the product to its purpose—these ways of making objects and architecture were at the heart of Good Design beliefs. They appealed to the American urge for self-improvement and, not incidentally, the desire to reform other people's lives. Advocates were confident that objects created on universal and rational principles would stir rational thinking and living in the men and women who used them.

The products of Good Design were intended to reach a broad market, so affordability was as important as style. This theme of the 1930s and '40s survived the conclusion of MoMA's *Good Design* exhibitions, partly owing to American periodicals, progressive manufacturers, and other museums. Notable champions of *Good Design* were the magazines *Everyday Art Quarterly* (later *Design Quarterly*), published by the Walker Art Center in Minneapolis, Minnesota; John Entenza's *California Arts & Architecture*; and the New York–based *Interiors*, edited by Olga Gueft, one of the most perceptive design critics of the day. The Walker Art Center had opened its Everyday Art Gallery of products for sale in 1946, and in 1951 and 1952 it presented *Useful Gifts* exhibitions. Their new products were selected for their "simplicity, intelligent use of materials, straightforward design, and pleasing appearance."[2]

Among manufacturers of furnishings, Knoll Associates and the Herman Miller Furniture Company distinguished themselves by marketing designs by the progressive Americans Charles and Ray Eames, George Nelson, Eero Saarinen, and Harry Bertoia (pp. 134, 137), and reissuing prewar furniture by Ludwig Mies van der Rohe and Marcel Breuer. Their lines, promoted by such interwar graphics pioneers as Herbert Matter (another émigré to America), ranged from moderately priced to expensive as consumers grew more prosperous over the decade.[3] Knoll and Herman Miller succeeded in making contemporary design de rigueur for offices and desirable in contemporary homes.

Since the 1940s Good Design had been promoted in Scandinavia with an organic form language that became popular worldwide in the 1950s. The rich craft traditions of these countries, their societies dominated by a comfortable middle class, proved adaptable to the modern beauty of understatement. Sweden and Denmark in particular produced household goods and furniture that looked and felt like crafts, though made by industrial methods. Practical and contemporary without appearing cold or mechanical, "Danish Modern" and "Swedish Grace" signified a humanized modernism far beyond national borders (pp. 147–48).

With notable unity, the governments and corporations of Scandinavia supported survey expositions of their products. *Scandinavian Design Cavalcades* circulated through the participating countries in the decade, and from 1954 to 1957 the more ambitious *Design in Scandinavia* traveled to twenty-two museums in the United States and Canada. By the 1950s Stockholm was a mecca for modern design. Sweden had been prominently represented at the first Triennale design exhibition in 1947; and at the 1954 Triennale, Finland won twenty-five prizes, a particular triumph for Tapio Wirkkala, who designed his country's installations and whose designs won three of the medals (fig. 2). At the 1954, 1957, and 1960 Triennales, Nordic designers won more prizes, firmly establishing themselves as leaders in Good Design.

Professional design organizations founded in Scandinavia during the late nineteenth-century Arts and Crafts movement were successfully revived in the 1950s. An especially significant postwar force was the Danish Society of Arts and Crafts and Industrial Design, which organized programs and exhibitions that promoted collaboration between industry and artists and published the periodical *Dansk Kunsthandwerk*. The Swedish design magazine *Form* is still issued.

While Italy also assumed leadership in the design world after the war, its defining note was not restrained Good Design but freewheeling invention, sometimes to the point of eccentricity. Italian designers were among the first to experiment with materials developed during the war: foam rubber, new wood laminates, and plastics. In these as well as traditional materials, Italians drew on their small-scale, artisanal heritage to create objects with organic shapes, sensual contours, racy curves, and sleekly elegant

1 Installation of Good Design exhibition, The Museum of Modern Art, New York, New York, 1952.
2 Tapio Wirkkala, design of Finland's exhibit at the tenth Triennale, 1954, with works by Timo Sarpaneva.

3 Jean Royère, *Hall d'un chalet à Megève*
(Room of a Cottage in Megève), 1953–56, graphite
pencil and gouache. Musée des arts décoratifs, Paris.
4 Oscar Niemeyer, Alvorada Palace, Brasília,
1956–58.

sculptural forms—in motor scooters, kitchen appliances, furniture, and more (pp. 161, 163). The question of whether the Italian rejection of the straight lines and sharp angles of functional modernism was a rebuke to the Germans and a nod to earlier Italian Futurist artists is an intriguing possibility.

Functionalism was not ignored, however, but given a wink of humor or sex appeal. At the 1951 Triennale, a celebration of Europe's economic recovery from the war, Italy featured new industrial products in an exhibition titled *The Form of the Useful*. The Castiglioni brothers displayed their lighting fixtures, and Olivetti introduced its latest portable typewriters, which won world recognition for their chic styling (pp. 156–57). In 1954 the Milan department store group La Rinascente teamed up with architect Gio Ponti to launch the Compasso d'Oro award for design excellence in Italian-made products, awards still given today. The Triennales themselves, especially those of 1954 and 1957, drew audiences from the international design world and were covered by print media around the globe.

Wartime shortages lingered in Britain, but government initiatives to revive industrial production were extensive. In 1949 the publication *Design* was inaugurated to become an influential tool of the government-funded Council of Industrial Design. The magazine was intended to illustrate the Council slogan, "Good Design and Good Business." In 1951 the agency undertook a trade fair, the well-received Festival of Britain; in 1956 it opened the Design Centre to display approved current products; and in 1957 it initiated the annual Good Design award for British manufacturers. To encourage interaction between artists and scientists—what C. P. Snow famously called "the Two Cultures"— the Council invited designers to use the patterns of natural crystals for both geometric and biomorphic embellishment (p. 162). Britain's textile industry responded with attractive prints and won kudos at the Festival.

Postwar France was faced with the same need as Britain to rebuild cities, factories, roads, and railways, but its response to Good Design was colored by its heritage of luxury trades. To support a French version of postwar modernism, it sponsored the Beauté de France label for well-designed products, and in 1956 it organized its own Triennale as a rival to Italy's. It is fair to say, however, that few of these well-intentioned efforts swayed a citizenry that viewed modern design with anxiety, suspecting it of threatening the good life. When Jean Royère, the best-known French designer at mid-century, adapted contemporary American design hallmarks to a ski chalet, the example was revealing (fig. 3). The language of biomorphism—of low-slung, foam-upholstered sofas and amoeboid coffee tables—was proving most acceptable in resorts and among the youthful.

In the Americas, by contrast, modern design was greeted effusively, especially in Brazil. The country, remote from World War II, had the money and the will to begin the monumental project of creating a new capital city, Brasília. Brazil's architects had admired the International Style since Le Corbusier's visits in 1929 and 1936; and they spearheaded support for Oscar Niemeyer's designs for the city, which used vast plazas and avenues to set off dramatic rectilinear and curvilinear buildings (fig. 4). The highly regarded Italian architects Pier Luigi Nervi and Gio Ponti embarked on major projects in Brazil that incorporated aspects of local modernism. Olivetti, among other Italian firms, also built factories there. São Paulo, inspired by the Venice Biennale, began a series of exhibitions surveying new art around the world; its first Bienal de Artes Plásticas in 1951 (p. 140) included design as well as fine art.

Germany and Japan faced the postwar period with more severe problems than the countries that defeated them. Major German cities were in ruins in 1945, and in 1950 the western part of Germany was still occupied by Allied troops. Yet it was beginning its "miracle" recovery. In 1950, the Hochshule für Gestaltung (Institute of Design) opened in Ulm, with a clear dedication to neo-functionalist ideals. Cofounded and led by the Bauhaus-trained Max Bill, the institution became one of postwar Europe's most respected design schools, attracting international students and faculty until its closing in 1968. There and in Zurich and Basel, the "International Typographic Style" was defined for the postwar generation, with the goal of easily understood trans-cultural communication. Bill's purist approach involved asymmetrical, grid-based compositions, sans-serif type, and graphically immediate photographs.[4] The product designs he advocated also aspired to universal validity. Electronic goods manufactured by Braun typified the clean lines, platonic geometries, and monochrome palette of the mechanistic aesthetic. Of compact elementary forms, the office furniture for Bofinger by Hans Gugelot was promoted as the first comprehensive modular furnishing system in laminates sold "flat-pack" or "knock-down," for the buyer to assemble (fig. 5). In Europe, where shipping was expensive and work and dwelling space was limited and sometimes temporary, such economy and flexible use were welcome. Everywhere, the easily understood functions of Ulm's reticent product designs and the legibility of its graphics assured the school's international influence.

Japan's recovery took place under American occupation, which ended in 1952. By that time Japan was again a major manufacturing country. Eager to be part of the international design community, Japanese designers adopted Western forms and concepts and took part in exhibitions in many countries. Isamu Kenmochi, one of the first Japanese designers to travel to the West after the war, wrote a report of his 1952 visit to the *Good Design* exhibition at MoMA for the *Kogei Nyusu (Industrial Art News)*. Taking Kaufmann's exhibition as a model, the Japanese Ministry of International Trade and Industry announced a Good Design Selection System in 1957. While before the war a label that declared "Made in Japan" had meant a cheap imitation, soon afterward that label identified well-designed and attractive products. Especially inventive in the field of electronics, Japanese firms such as Sony adopted the American transistor and by the end of the decade were preparing to dominate international markets with their miniaturized tape recorders, portable radios, and televisions.

By the late 1950s, Good Design still reigned supreme among most theorists and curators, but the abundant array of products and styles available in the marketplace gave consumers plenty of chances to ignore it. By 1960, new definitions and new designers would turn Good Design on its ear. In Italy, Ettore Sottsass applied the bright colors and flat stripes of abstract art to decorative objects and interior design with arresting results (p. 177). Was the effort worthwhile to seek universal forms and furnishing types? "This is a question," he said, that "supposes that somewhere, somehow, there is a place where GOOD DESIGN is deposited. The problem then is to come as close as possible to [it]. My idea instead is that the problem is . . . the need a society has for an image of itself."[5]

In 1960 British editor and critic Reyner Banham titled an article "A Throw-Away Esthetic," and therein defended the annual styling changes of American cars as more genuine expressions of culture than functionalist ideals. For him, popular and transient signs were the most valid aesthetic source in a consumer economy.[6] American Pop art—forecast in the 1956 London exhibition *This is Tomorrow* and named by the British critic Lawrence Alloway—would overtake Good Design as a touchstone in the 1960s. The appetite for a memorable "image" would sweep aside the beliefs in economy, simplicity, functionalism, and the moral imperative to right thinking and living that had been the dogma of the 1950s.

5 Hans Gugelot, *M 125* furnishing system, for Bofinger, Stuttgart, Germany, 1957.

GEORGE NELSON Associates

(active 1947–1983)

Sofa
Marshmallow
Designed 1954–55
Painted steel, latex foam,
vinyl upholstery
87 x 133 x 85.9 cm
Produced by Herman Miller
Furniture Co., Zeeland,
Michigan, U.S.A.
The Montreal Museum
of Fine Arts, D81.138.1,
gift of Mr. and
Mrs. George Nelson*

This prototype, executed in 1954–55, of the now iconic sofa was owned by George Nelson and given to the Montreal Museum of Decorative Arts along with other pieces from his country house. Anticipating Pop art in its humor and strong graphic sense, the sofa is composed of eighteen separate cushions (standard barstool seats), rather than one solid upholstered seat and back with springs, which would have been time-consuming and expensive to produce. The separate cushions are mounted individually on metal disks set on steel rods, which are painted white, and attached to a curved support. This prototype was quite different from the sofa that was put into production. The white tubular steel rods seen here were replaced by black crossbars, square in section, and the cushions are placed farther apart in the production models.
The cushions' resemblance to marshmallows later gave the name to a design that was initially described in the Herman Miller catalogue simply as "Model No. 5670."

Davis J. PRATT
Harold COHEN

(1917–1987) and **(born 1925)**

Chair
Designed 1951
Coated steel, nylon
73.5 x 50.9 x 77.1 cm
Produced by Designers in
Production, Chicago,
Illinois, U.S.A.
The Montreal Museum of
Fine Arts, 2001.88,
gift of Shan Sullivan

Both Pratt and Cohen studied at László Moholy-Nagy's School of Design in Chicago, a stronghold of Bauhaus design that was initially known as the New Bauhaus. In 1948, Pratt designed an inflatable chair that won an award in the *International Competition for Low-Cost Furniture* at the Museum of Modern Art. Pratt disliked the complex spring-and-pad upholstery process and attempted to create low-cost, portable furniture forms, seen in both the inflatable chair and this lounge chair. This design was based on Pratt's 1940 design for a "suspended chair" in plywood and steel tubing, which was the result of a course assignment at the School of Design "to change a flat sheet of material into a three dimensional structure."[7] In 1951, Pratt and Cohen's chair won an award in the MoMA *Good Design* exhibition. The same year, they founded Designers in Production to produce household furnishings, including this chair.

Dorothy LIEBES

(1899–1972)

Textile
Bon Bon
Designed c. 1950
Cotton and Lurex yarn
261.6 x 116.6 cm
Produced by Dorothy Liebes
Designs, San Francisco,
California, U.S.A.
The Montreal Museum of
Fine Arts, D88.129.1,
gift of Luc d'Iberville Moreau

Modern architects and designers sought the innovative woven fabrics of Dorothy Liebes for their sparse interiors. They were a welcome relief from the silk-screened printed patterns of commercially available lines. Although many Liebes textiles were monochromatic woven designs, the handwoven *Bon Bon* illustrates her color sense, combining pink and green with metallic Lurex yarn, an innovation in its day. Liebes introduced daring and unusual color combinations and yarn selections, which she or her assistants wove spontaneously in her studio. She described her clientele for handweaving as "a cross section of the top-flight decorators and architects in the country, and what they use for their clients is consistently the avant-garde of the textile world. They serve as a guinea pig for consumer acceptance."[8]

Eero SAARINEN

(1910–1961)

Armchair
Pedestal
Designed c. 1955
Plastic-coated aluminum,
fiberglass-reinforced polyester,
polyurethane foam, nylon
upholstery
80.8 x 67.5 x 60.2 cm
Produced by Knoll Associates,
Inc., New York, New York, U.S.A.
The Montreal Museum of
Fine Arts, D87.127.1a–b

The origins of this chair are in the molded shell designs that Saarinen and Charles Eames created in the 1940s, starting with their joint entry in the MoMA competition *Organic Design in Home Furnishings*. Both architects, then still at the Cranbrook Academy of Art, later developed multiple related designs independently. Saarinen's *Pedestal* chair is one of them: the shell seating, arms, and back have a single support, which replaces the normal four legs of a chair. This was a major innovation in seating design. Saarinen explained: "The undercarriage of chairs and tables in a typical interior make an ugly, confusing, unrestful world. I wanted to clear up the slum of legs." Although this appears to be molded as a single unit entirely of plastic, the chair combined plastic with metal. This elegant, flowerlike chair, which is also known as the *Tulip*, is a brilliantly integrated design in its structure of seat, stem, and base, an aesthetic triumph in the way that the individual parts flow seamlessly one into another.

Isamu NOGUCHI

(1904–1988)

Floor lamp and shade

Akari
Designed c. 1954
Mulberry-bark paper, bamboo,
cast iron, steel
191 x 57.7 x 57.7 cm
Produced by Ozeki & Co.,
Gifu, Japan
The Montreal Museum of
Fine Arts, D86.245.1a–b

The Japanese-American sculptor Isamu Noguchi turned to design to support himself in the 1940s and created a remarkable body of work in furniture, lighting, and stage design. Noguchi's interest in "light sculptures," like the lamp seen here, is derived from his 1951 trip to Japan. He was invited by the mayor of the city of Gifu to help revitalize the city's manufacture of traditional folded-paper lanterns. He designed the new lanterns to be collapsible for packing in flat boxes, and, instead of using candles, he wired them for electric light—in this case with a fluorescent bulb. "Akari," Noguchi's name for the lanterns, "in Japanese, means light as illumination just as our word light does. It also suggests lightness as opposed to weight."[9] Noguchi's lighting and furnishings helped to humanize modernism, especially in the United States.

BELOW Early promotional photograph of Noguchi's *Akari* lamps, 1950s.

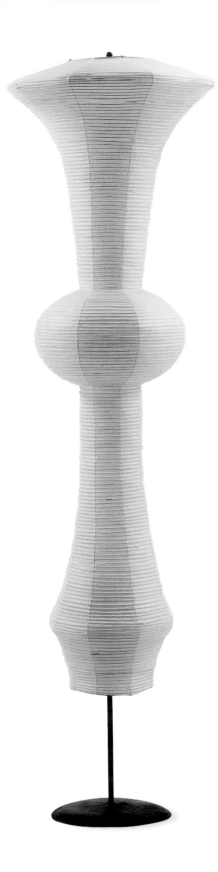

Antonio MALUF

(1926–2005)

Poster

1ª Bienal, São Paulo, Brasil, do Museu de arte moderna
Designed c. 1951
Offset lithograph
95.5 x 64.1 cm
The Montreal Museum of Fine Arts, D84.194.1, gift of Kathy Kurland

While much vanguard art in mid-century Europe and the United States was abstract expressionist, leading Latin-American painters extended the geometric abstraction they first explored in the 1920s and '30s. Maluf and other Brazilians were among them, and he explored the optical illusions seen in this poster in other media, notably paintings, some of mural scale, tiles, printed textiles, and book bindings. This poster derives from one of his *Art concret* paintings of the same year; it won the design contest sponsored for the first Bienal de São Paulo. The Bienal, inspired by the international Venice Biennale, became a showcase for contemporary Latin art by the late 1950s and continues in that role today.[10] The stylized typeface in red and gray anchors a perspective view of receding rectangles defined in yellow and black.

Jack Lenor LARSEN

(born 1927)

Textile
Remoulade
Designed 1954–55
Wool, cotton, rayon, linen,
Mylar, polyethylene, silk,
jute, metallic yarns
53.3 x 42.2 cm
Produced for Jack Lenor Larsen,
Inc., New York, New York, U.S.A.
The Montreal Museum of Fine
Arts, D88.154.1, gift of the designer

Trained on handlooms at Cranbrook Academy under Marianne Strengell, Larsen innovated by creating the look of handcraftsmanship with high-volume machine looms. This was his pioneering achievement in *Remoulade*. The pattern is elaborate in coloration and weave, incorporating approximately thirty natural and manmade yarns of different weights and combinations. He called it *Remoulade* after the French sauce of various spicy ingredients. The textile, designed shortly after Larsen established his own company in 1952, was produced in several color ways and was intended for upholstery. The designer said, "The fabric that came to be called *Remoulade* I first wove as a wall hanging by using up hundreds of leftover bobbins of all manner of yarns. . . . When I hung it in the foyer of our first showroom, our clients insisted we weave it for them, for upholstery!"[11]

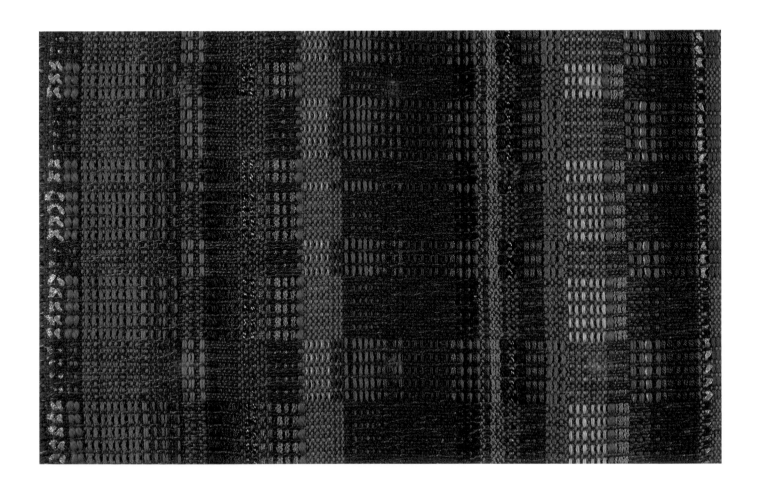

Eszter HARASZTY

(1923–1994)

Rendering

Knoll Paris Studio Living Room
Designed c. 1954
and executed c. 1955
Fabric and mixed media on paper
46.5 x 66.7 cm
The Montreal Museum of
Fine Arts, D88.178.1.25,
gift of the designer

Rendering

Knoll Paris Studio Plan
Designed c. 1954
and executed c. 1955
Fabric and mixed media on paper
46.5 x 66.7 cm
The Montreal Museum of
Fine Arts, D88.178.1.23,
gift of the **designer**

Rendering

Dallas Exhibition Perspective
Designed c. 1953
and executed c. 1955
Fabric and mixed media on paper
46.5 x 66.7 cm
The Montreal Museum of
Fine Arts, D88.178.1.10,
gift of the designer

Hungarian born, Haraszty immigrated to the United States in 1947 when the Communists took over her country. In 1949 she became the director of textiles at Knoll Associates. Her work was included in the *Good Design* exhibitions at MoMA. After she left Knoll in 1955, Haraszty repeated several renderings of interiors she had designed for Knoll using a collage of drawings and fragments of actual textiles. These renderings are part of a collection kept by Haraszty during her post-Knoll years, which she bound into a portfolio to serve as an example of her work for clients. They reflect Knoll's modern interiors at mid-century: the rooms are large, with open spaces divided into separate areas by the arrangement of the furniture and rugs in geometric sections, as seen in the studio plan. Haraszty was known for her bold color combinations, applied judiciously, which were startling at the time.[12]

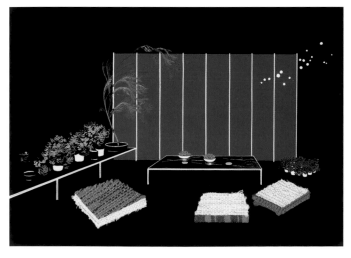

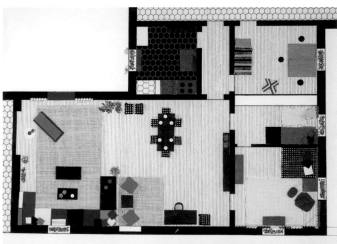

Louis Christiaan KALFF

(1897–1976)

Table lamp
Designed 1955
Brass, lacquered aluminum
42.5 x 32.5 x 32.5 cm
Produced by Philips, Eindhoven,
The Netherlands
The Montreal Museum of
Fine Arts, 2008.102,
gift of Roy Poretzky*

The geometric form of this Constructivist design is dominated by strong angles and circular elements. The lamp's light bulb extends through the perforation in the middle of the shade, becoming an integral part of the design and directing the light both upward and downward when illuminated. A similarly angled lamp was designed by Vico Magistretti in 1946.[13] Kalff began working for Philips in 1924, in the advertising department, and in 1929 he set up the company's light design studio. He later became the art director for the company, where he worked until he retired in 1960.

Hans WEGNER

(1914–2007)

Lounge chair
Flag Halyard
Designed 1950
Chromium-plated and painted
steel, halyard, wood, cotton
80.5 x 105 x 116.2 cm
Produced by Getama,
Gedsled, Denmark
The Montreal Museum of
Fine Arts, D97.173.1a–b

Wegner was one of the most famous and prolific of Danish designers at mid-century. Apprenticed at the age of fourteen to a cabinetmaker, he went on to earn a degree in architecture in 1938. He then worked as a furniture designer for the Danish architect Arne Jacobsen before setting up his own practice in 1943. Wegner's chair forms were usually modified from Chinese furniture and vernacular sources such as Shaker and Windsor chairs; these modern versions were made of beautiful wood with distinctive grains, often teak. *Flag Halyard* was an exception, as a strongly geometric design of steel and rope inspired by the 1928 chaise longue by Charlotte Perriand.

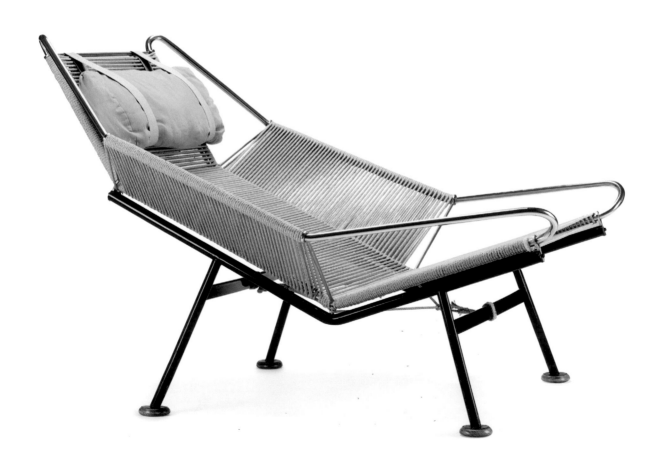

Timo SARPANEVA

(1926–2006)

Vase
Devil's Churn
Designed 1950–51
Glass
29 x 12 x 11 cm
Produced by Iittala Lasitehdas,
Iittala, Finland
The Montreal Museum of
Fine Arts, D86.159.1

Among the most renowned Finnish designers of the postwar period, Timo Sarpaneva worked in many media, including graphics and textiles. He is best known for his designs in glass, which he began in 1950 with an important line for Iittala, Finland's most famous glass manufacturer. The series known as *Devil's Churn* utilizes smooth, rounded, biomorphic forms with pierced sides. The name refers to a cavity in rock caused by erosion. For this series, the glass was pierced after its initial forming; its surface was then sandblasted and treated with acid, giving it a luminous appearance. The idea of cavities and piercings in rock forms is associated with the sculpture of British artist Henry Moore. In Sarpaneva's work, the results are sculptural masterpieces of design.

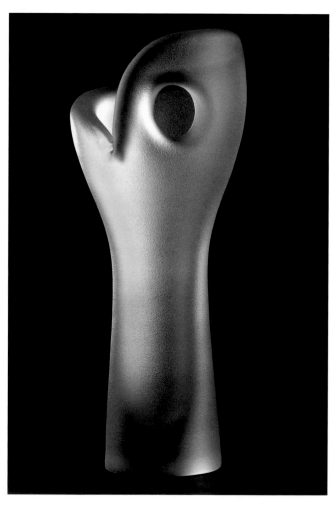

Arne JACOBSEN

(1902–1971)

Armchair
Egg
Designed 1957
Chromium-plated steel, fiberglass,
polyurethane foam, leather
106.2 x 87 x 78.7 cm
Produced by Fritz Hansens Eft.
A/S, Copenhagen
and Allerød, Denmark
The Montreal Museum of
Fine Arts, D87.131.1

Jacobsen designed this chair and a related model called *Swan* as part of his interior decoration for the lobby of the SAS Royal Hotel in Copenhagen. Derived from the traditional wingchair, the *Egg's* womblike form gives the same sense of protection as the eighteenth-century prototype. Also inspired by the pedestal furniture designs of Eero Saarinen, such as the so-called *Tulip* chair (p. 137), the *Egg* chair provided comfort and a sense of luxury. It is carefully crafted, and the original leather upholstery on this model, now worn with age, appears as a tight skin, emphasizing the sculptural quality of the design. The chair swivels and tilts on a steel base, which provides a contrast in material and form to the seat. The chair was offered for sale publicly, and became an internationally known modern design. Its production continues to the present day.

ABOVE, LEFT Arne Jacobsen, guest room at the SAS Royal Hotel and Air Terminal, Copenhagen, 1956–60, showing *Egg* chair.

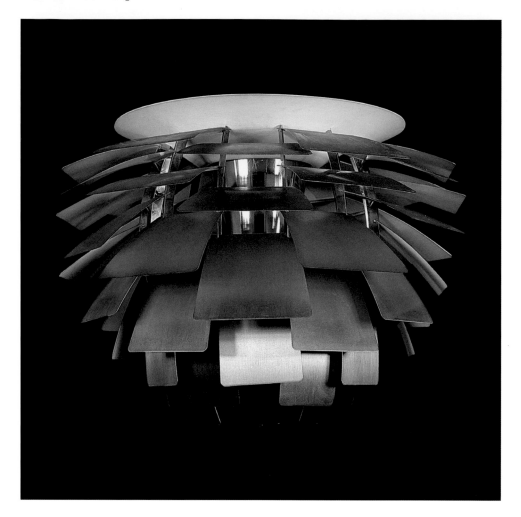

Poul HENNINGSEN

(1894–1967)

Hanging lamp
PH Artichoke
Designed 1958
Copper, enameled steel, metal
76 x 72 x 72 cm
Produced by Louis Poulsen & Co.
A/S, Copenhagen, Denmark
The Montreal Museum of
Fine Arts, 2001.20.1–3

A distinguished architect and critic, Henningsen is primarily known for his lamp designs for Louis Poulsen, and especially for the *Artichoke*. In 1924, he designed the first of his *PH* lamp series, based on his analysis of a shade's function. The *PH* shades were assembled from separate elements in such a way that they cover the bulb and direct the light down to avoid glare. The mid-century design differs from the 1924 debut model in its complexity and the addition of color. The overlapping parts projecting at different angles add to the dramatic aesthetic effect, with the copper "leaves" adding warmth to the model, as seen here.

Sven Gottfried MARKELIUS

(1889–1972)

Textile
Pythagoras
Designed 1952
Printed cotton
299.7 x 130.7 cm
Produced by Ljungbergs
Textiltryck, Floda, Sweden, for
Nordiska Kompaniet,
Stockholm, Sweden
The Montreal Museum of
Fine Arts, D85.160.1

Trained as an architect, Markelius designed many modern buildings, including the Swedish Pavilion for the 1939 New York World's Fair. The following year, he began to design fabrics, which he continued to do throughout his life. At the time he designed this, he had been the head of the Stockholm Planning Office for several years and had developed the city plan of Stockholm. His architectural training is reflected in *Pythagoras*, which is based on variations of a basic geometric form. Named for the Greek philosopher and mathematician who is famed for his theorem about triangles, the design uses the triangle in alternating bands within a bold yellow color scheme, one of three color ways. Originally designed as a stage curtain for the Folhets Hus (People's House) designed by Markelius in Linköping, *Pythagoras* later became commercially available from Nordiska Kompaniet.

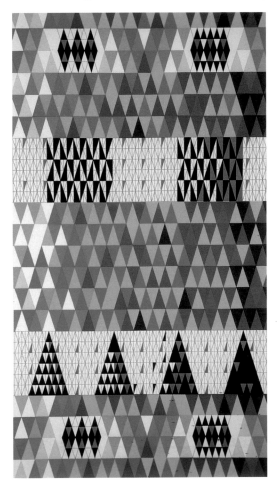

Peter MACCHIARINI

(1909–2001)

Necklace
Designed c. 1955; executed 1985
Silver, ebony, ivory
6.1 x 40 x 0.7 cm
The Montreal Museum of
Fine Arts, D94.250.1,
gift of Paul Leblanc

In the 1920s, Macchiarini trained as a sculptor while he and his parents lived in Italy. He joined the Works Progress Administration in San Francisco in 1935, and set up his first jewelry studio the following year and taught himself metalsmithing. A prolific and popular jewelry designer, he maintained the same studio and shop in San Francisco throughout his career. Its geometric patterning, structure, and order of parts are reminiscent of a piano keyboard. Contrasting paired ebony and ivory "keys" of gratuated size, separated by shaped pieces of silver, form the pendant, and the pattern is echoed in the smaller alternating black and white beaded collar.

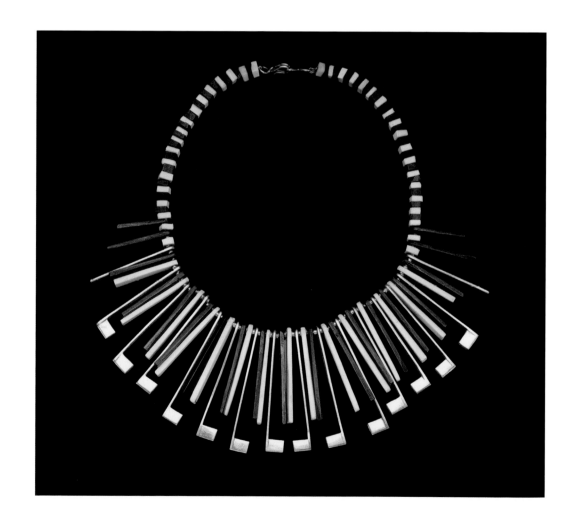

Stig LINDBERG

(1916–1982)

Vase
Designed c. 1951
Painted terracotta
40.4 x 34 x 34 cm
Produced by AB Gustavsberg,
Gustavsberg, Sweden
The Montreal Museum of
Fine Arts, D83.102.1

Exuberant, whimsical forms and decoration were an alternative to the spare minimalism so often associated with mid-century modern. Here Lindberg succeeded in combining humorous, colorful, pictorial ornament with a simple white form associated with Good Design. He depicted the round face of a woman, with her right hand at her ear, perhaps listening to the music of the flute player painted on the other side of the vessel. The use of such decorative elements aroused much protest from the advocates of purely functional modern design, but figurative folk art associations helped popularize "Swedish modern." Lindberg began working at Gustavsberg in 1937, where he designed lines for production as well as unique pieces, and succeeded Wilhelm Kåge as the company's art director in 1949. Lindberg achieved his renown for such works as this vase, executed c. 1951.

Piero FORNASETTI
Gio PONTI

(1913–1988) and **(1891–1979)**

Secretary
*Trumeau Architettura
(Trumeau Architecture)*
Designed 1950
Lithographs on Masonite,
painted wood, sheet metal,
glass, brass, felt
218 x 80 x 40.5 cm
Produced by Piero Fornasetti,
Milan, Italy, and by
Immaginazione s.r.l., Milan, Italy
The Montreal Museum of Fine
Arts, D97.172.1a–k, gift of Senator
Alan A. Macnaughton, Sr.

Fornasetti's background as a painter is seen in the decorative surface treatment of *Trumeau Architettura*, with the appearance of depth achieved through its blend of Renaissance trompe-l'oeil, seventeenth-century architectural drawings, and eighteenth-century stage scenery. The interior of the secretary reveals a depiction of the interior of a Renaissance palace with a deep perspective. In his designs for furnishings, Fornasetti was original and continued to use such decoration throughout his career. Perhaps he was ahead of his time, as interest in his work revived with the historicism associated with 1980s postmodernism. His collaborations with Ponti were some of his most successful creations. Ponti's straightforward case for this secretary reflects his work as an architect with roots in 1930s classicism.

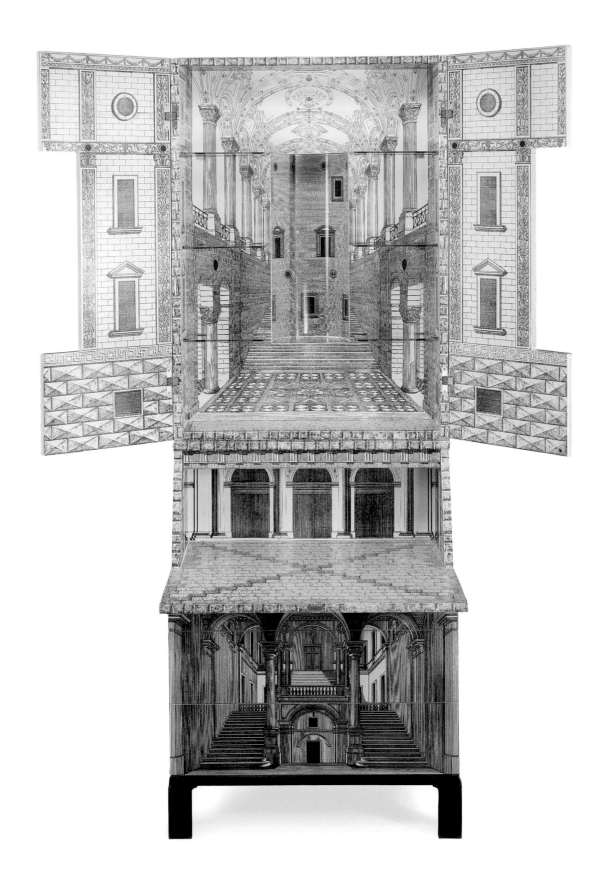

Gio PONTI

(1891–1979)

Side chair
Superleggera
Designed 1955
Ash, cellophane cane
85.3 x 40.4 x 44.9 cm
Produced by Figli di Amedeo
Cassina, Meda, Italy
The Montreal Museum of
Fine Arts, D83.115.1

Gio Ponti, as an architect, industrial designer, and founder-editor of the design magazine *Domus*, was an extremely influential spokesman for the modernist cause. His furniture designs often use traditional elements in a new way and tend to be light, with elegant, spare lines and tapering legs. *Superleggera* is an update of an earlier vernacular chair called *Chiavari*, named for the fishing village where this kind of light, wooden chair was made. This model was shown at the XI Triennale in 1957, and it won a Compasso d'Oro prize that same year.

Hans GUGELOT
Dieter RAMS

(1920–1965) and **(born 1932)**

Radio and record player
Phonosuper SK5
Designed 1956
Enameled metal,
plywood, Plexiglas
24 x 59 x 29.5 cm
Produced by Max Braun,
Frankfurt, Germany
The Montreal Museum of Fine
Arts, D86.196.1, gift of Barry
Friedman and Patricia Pastor*

Both Gugelot and Rams came from an architectural background and turned to industrial design. In 1954 Max Bill, a Swiss architect and graphic designer, invited Gugelot to teach at the Hochschule für Gestaltung at Ulm, where he later became the director of the product design department. Both Gugelot and Rams began to work for the Braun company in the mid-1950s. The two collaborated to design the *SK5*, which, with its transparent Plexiglas cover, became an icon of German functionalist design, following Bauhaus dictates. Each element has a clearly defined place in the abstract design. With refined composition and detailing and flawless white enamel, relieved only by the plywood sides, the *SK5* epitomized Braun's new modern aesthetic at mid-century. It further purified the Bauhaus aesthetic advocated at Ulm, which would dominate German consumer product design through the 1980s.

Marcello NIZZOLI

(1887–1969)

Portable typewriter
Lettera 22
Designed 1950
Enameled metal, chromium-
plated steel, plastic, rubber
11.5 x 30.1 x 31.4 cm
Produced by Ing. C. Olivetti & C.
SpA, Milan, Italy
The Montreal Museum of Fine
Arts, D86.198.1, gift of Barry
Friedman and Patricia Pastor*

Nizzoli was initially a painter before studying architecture at the Accademia di Belli Arte in Parma. He began working as a graphic designer for Olivetti in 1936 and was responsible for creating a forward-looking, integrated corporate image and for establishing the company's pioneering commitment to modern design. His sheathing for *Lettera 22* is rounded and sculptural, disguising the rigid machinery inside, designed by the engineer Giuseppe Beccio. Nizzoli's sensitivity to form is apparent in the fluid profile he gave to this housing and to the molded carriage handle, which opens at an acute angle for use and folds back to fit tightly for travel in a form-fitting case. The muted blue color is set off against the black keys and only one other accent: a bright red carriage return key.[14] The distinctive Olivetti style, seen in its business machines and advertising, resulted from the collaboration of architects, graphic artists, and industrial designers.

ABOVE, LEFT Studio Architetti B.B.P.R., Olivetti Corporation showroom, New York, c. 1954.

Achille CASTIGLIONI
Pier Giacomo CASTIGLIONI

(1918–2002) and **(1913–1968)**

Floor lamp
Luminator
Designed 1955
Steel
180.3 x 48.3 x 40.6 cm
Produced by Gilardi
e Barzaghi, Milan, Italy
The Montreal Museum
of Fine Arts, D85.171.1

This minimalist floor lamp reflects the interests of the Castiglioni brothers in combining the principles of structure, function, and modernist aesthetics in a single composition. Here they used a simple, vertical steel tube whose diameter perfectly accommodates the socket for the reflector bulb that fits into it, supported on a tripod made from slimmer steel tubes. Based on a 1933 lamp design of similar form by Pietro Chiesa, this elegant lamp was one of the first to project light directly onto the ceiling, from there to be diffused into the entire room. The idea, inspired by photographers' studio lighting equipment, became standard in progressive mid-century interiors. The designers were architects and together created a wide range of industrial design interiors from the 1930s onward.

Fulvio BIANCONI

(1915–1996)

Vase
Arlecchino (Harlequin)
Designed c. 1950
Glass
17.5 x 20.8 x 12.1 cm
Produced by Venini, Murano, Italy
The Montreal Museum of
Fine Arts, D86.162.1,
gift of Bombardier, Inc.

Made from pieces of glass cut into geometric sections and fused together in the glass blowing then pushed into an irregular form, Bianconi's *Pezzato* vases were exhibited at the Venice Biennale in 1950 to critical acclaim. This traditional technique of creating colorful patterns, derived from Roman glass-making, was introduced to the Venini workshop by the Italian architect Carlo Scarpa in the 1930s. Because of the bold hues in exuberant juxtapositions, this model was known as *Harlequin* in honor of the *commedia dell'arte* character's diamond patchwork costume.

Attributed to Anzolo FUGA

(1914–1998)

Vase
Designed c. 1955–56
Glass
50.6 x 24.5 x 14 cm
Produced by AVEM (Arte Vetraria
Muranese), Murano, Italy
The Montreal Museum of
Fine Arts, 2008.101,
gift of Roy Poretzky*

Born on Murano island, outside Venice, Fuga was apprenticed as a draftsman at the Cristalleria di Venezia e Murano (Glassworks of Venice and Murano) and from 1934 to 1938 attended the Instituto d'Arte di Venezia, where he specialized in book illustration. In 1943 he established a company with his brother Giuseppe, and in 1955 he began his collaboration with AVEM. A drawing helps to date this design and a group of similar vases made with vertical colored glass rods and an overlay of brightly colored spots.[15] This lively design on a relatively traditional vase form reflects the Murano industry's responsiveness to contemporary abstract painting and its efforts to modernize its output for an increasingly international and youthful clientele.

Marcello FANTONI

(born 1915)

Vase
Designed and executed 1956
Partially glazed earthenware
97 x 20 x 14 cm
The Montreal Museum
of Fine Arts, 2001.58

After graduating from the Instituto d'Arte at Porta Romana in 1934, Fantoni began working as a ceramist. In 1936, he established the Fantoni Ceramic Studio in Florence. With a staff of fifty workmen at mid-century, he created both unique pieces and limited productions "primarily as objects of art . . . by the artist craftsman who is frequently a sculptor as well as a ceramist."[16] This vase demonstrates Fantoni's use of pictorial motifs on large-scale sculptural vessels, typical of Italian contemporary painting, with its highly stylized elongated figures and plant forms set against an architectural ground. Its irregular form and coloration were expressive, influenced by the paintings and sculpture of Picasso from the 1930s and '40s. It demonstrates his training and skills as a sculptor and graphic artist.

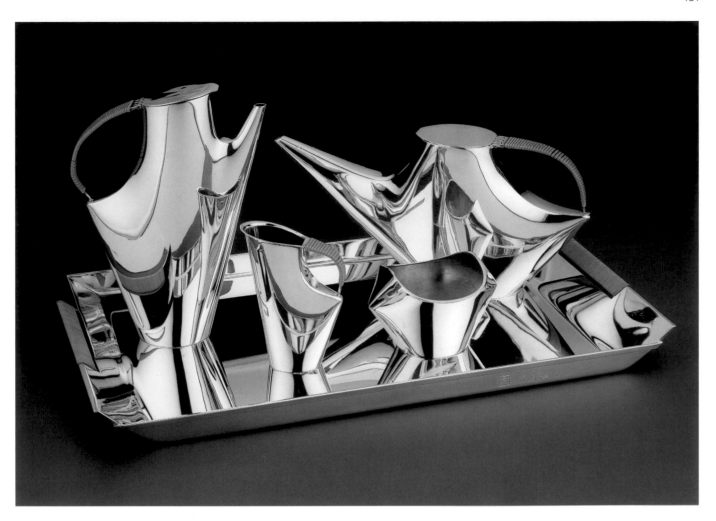

Lino SABATTINI

(born 1925)

Tea and coffee service

Como
Designed 1957
Silver-plated brass,
plastic cord, raffia
22.6 x 16.5 x 6.1 cm
Produced by L'Orfèvrerie
Christofle, Paris, France
The Montreal Museum of Fine
Arts, D86.164.1–4; D89.174.1,
gift of Sabattini Argenteria, S.p.A.

As a teenager, Sabattini first became interested in design through reading *Domus*, the architect Gio Ponti's influential magazine, founded in 1928. When he was thirty years old, he left his job selling brass objects and set up his own metal workshop in Milan. The *Como* tea and coffee service is a dramatic example of his distinctive style in silver and silverplate. Its thrusting asymmetrical forms recall the dynamism of futurist sculpture and forecast its revival among Italian designers of the 1980s. Ponti so admired this service that he published it in *Domus*. It was produced by Christofle, the Parisian firm, while Sabattini was the director of its design department.

Marianne STRAUB

(1909–1994)

Drapery textile
Surrey
Designed 1951
Wool, rayon, cotton
94 x 60 cm
Produced by Warner & Sons
Limited, London, England
The Montreal Museum of Fine
Arts, D87.204.1, gift of Warner &
Sons Limited

Swiss born, Straub began weaving as a child and later received training in Zurich before moving to England in 1932. One of the most memorable designs for the Festival of Britain trade fair, *Surrey* had its origins in an experimental project to unite advances in science and design. Straub represented the textile manufacturer Warner & Sons in the Festival "Pattern Group," whose mandate was to find innovative designs for the Festival exhibition, based on diagrams of crystal structures. In *Surrey*, Straub enlarged the naturally repeating biomorphic shapes she saw in the crystal structures of the mineral afwillite. The resulting textile, made with jacquard-woven twill in contrasting colors, served as curtaining in the Festival's Regatta Restaurant.

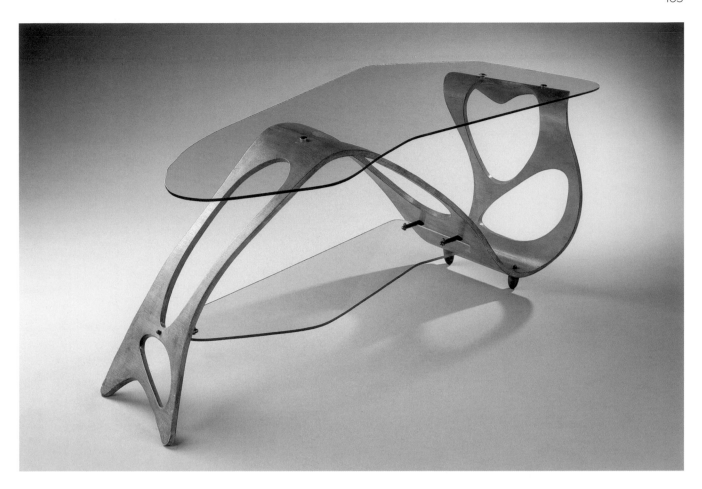

Carlo MOLLINO

(1905–1973)

Table
Arabesco (Arabesque)
Designed 1950
Maple-faced plywood,
glass, brass
50.2 x 122 x 49.5 cm
Produced by Apelli e Varesio,
Turin, Italy
The Montreal Museum of
Fine Arts, D88.128.1a–c

Trained as an architect, Mollino was one of the most important furniture designers of the 1930s through the 1950s, known for his dramatic biomorphic sculptural forms. This Italian designer called himself a "streamlined Surrealist," and his curved cutouts, flowing lines, and eccentric shapes remind one of earlier work by Joan Miró, Fernand Léger, Alexander Calder, and others. *Arabesco*, part of a large commission for the Lattes publishing offices in Turin, was one of his masterpieces. The one-piece bent plywood form followed the innovative designs of Mollino's contemporaries, such as Charles and Ray Eames, but it turns their practical designs into something humorous and faintly humanoid. The Lattes furniture was not manufactured, but made by artisans as unique objects.

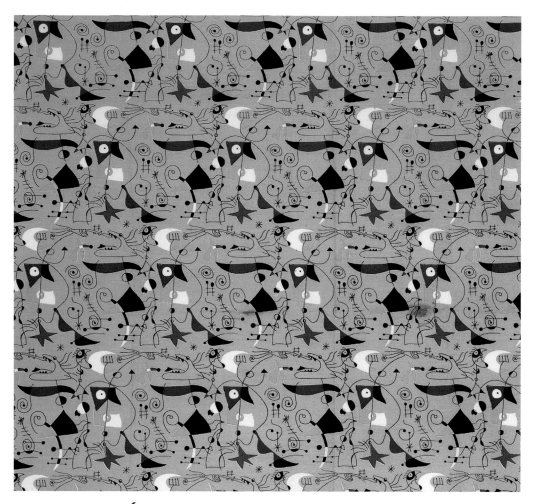

After Joan MIRÓ

(1893–1983)

Textile

Women and Birds
Designed c. 1955
Printed cotton
91.5 x 100.3 cm
Produced by Fuller Fabrics,
New York, New York, U.S.A.
The Montreal Museum of Fine
Arts, D92.102.1, anonymous gift

Joan Miró is identified with the abstract wing of the Surrealist movement and is considered one of the major artists of the twentieth century. Fuller Fabrics' adaptation of Miró's artwork evokes the painter's fantasy world, especially his *Constellations* series of 1940 with its schematic renderings of humorously ambiguous figures of women, birds, stars, and fish. This print was a commission to Miró, along with other celebrated artists of Paris, to lend their works for a textile line called the *Modern Master Print Series*. The adaptations of these works for repeat designs were made by draftsmen without the artists' direct assistance but were submitted to them for approval. In addition to textiles, Miró collaborated in the production of decorative arts in a variety of media, including ceramics, stage sets, and stained-glass windows.

Pablo PICASSO

(1881–1973)

Vase
Tripod
Designed 1951
Glazed earthenware
72.7 x 26.7 x 29.5 cm
Produced by Poterie Madoura,
Vallauris, France
The Montreal Museum of
Fine Arts, D96.109.1

Picasso, considered the greatest artist of the first half of, if not the entire, twentieth century, became involved in the decorative arts in the latter part of his career. Most significantly, he pursued ceramics, inspired by a 1946 visit to the Poterie Madoura. His ceramics were produced both in series, such as this vase, and as unique examples. They contain the same wit and spontaneity as his paintings and sculpture. The humorous quality of the sculptural work provides contrast to the cool demeanor and unornamented surfaces of Good Design in the same years. Picasso created this bulbous tripod vessel by assembling three small vase forms, connecting them at their openings to a larger, handled vase form. He then painted the assembly as a whole. After Picasso created a master ceramic for a series, each example was assembled and hand-painted by other artisans following the original.

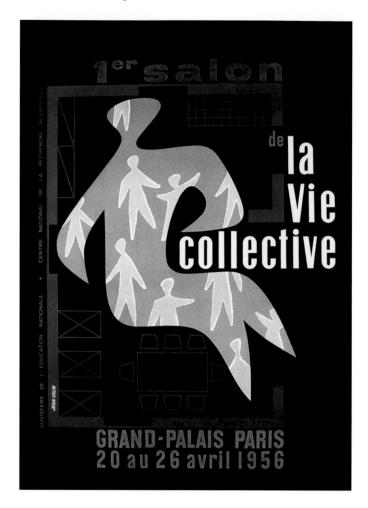

Jean COLIN

(1912–1982)

Poster

La Vie Collective (Community Life)
Designed 1956
Offset lithograph
164 x 123 cm
Produced by Bedos & Cie,
Paris, France
The Montreal Museum of Fine
Arts, D87.201.1, gift of Mr. and Mrs.
Charles D. O'Kieffe, Jr., in memory
of Mr. and Mrs. Charles DeWitt
O'Kieffe, by exchange*

Since the 1880s, posters have been a major aspect of the design arts in Europe, and Colin was among the outstanding graphic artists in France at the mid-twentieth century. He designed this poster for the first of a series of lifestyle exhibitions devoted to household furnishings held at the Grand Palais, Paris. His focus is on a curvilinear figure representing the consumer depicted in a seated position. Yellow gesturing figures may be visitors to the exhibition or simply part of the community referred to in the title. In blue against the black ground are plans of the installation of designs in the exhibition. The human figures are humorous and biomorphic; the plans are mathematical and rational.

Peter Todd MITCHELL

(1924–1988)

Drawing
Roman Monuments
Designed and executed 1950–54
Gouache on paper
71.7 x 63.8 cm
The Montreal Museum of Fine
Arts, D89.177.7,
gift of Priscilla Cunningham

Trained as a painter, Mitchell pursued an artistic career throughout his life, supporting himself by designing textiles and wallpaper for various firms. His designs were often decorative and whimsical rather than spare to adhere to the modernist aesthetic. In a 1946 article, Mitchell wrote that "to be a good fabric designer, you must be a serious artist too. . . . When I design a textile I use all the sense of color, form and composition that I use in a painting."[17] He often adapted architectural elements from his paintings into his design work, as seen in this design for wallpaper, which was inspired by several Roman monuments, such as Bernini's seventeenth-century elephant and obelisk. The drawing may have been made while Mitchell resided in Rome, between 1950 and 1954.

Raymond SAVIGNAC

(1907–2002)

Poster

Quinzaine de la Laine
Designed 1951
Offset lithograph
58.1 x 38.1 cm
Produced by Métivier, France
The Montreal Museum
of Fine Arts, D91.196.1,
gift of Miljenko and Lucia Horvat

Savignac is known for his posters, which often have a direct, humorous simplicity. In 1935, he began work as an assistant to A. M. Cassandre, the most famous graphic designer of the interwar period in France. Savignac often illustrated consumer products, as seen in this example celebrating a two-week promotional exhibition for wool. The designer cited film, especially American comedies, as his inspiration. Typical of his posters, this one centers on a single amusing figure. The lamb's wool is unraveling off its body into a skein of wool, captioned with a cunning rhyme—*quinzaine de la laine*, meaning "two weeks of wool"—and reminding us of the knitwear and other woolens to be seen during the fortnight.

Josef MÜLLER-BROCKMANN

(1914–1996)

Poster:

Proteggete i bambini!
(Protect the Children!)
Designed 1952–53
Offset halftone lithograph
127.9 x 90.2 cm
Produced by Lithographie &
Cartonnage, Zurich, Switzerland,
for Automobile Club Svizzero
The Montreal Museum
of Fine Arts, D85.167.1

Müller-Brockmann's use of photography to create visually powerful designs is well illustrated in *Proteggete i bambini!*, which was part of a series for the Automobile Club of Switzerland. He developed a grid principle for the placement of typography and illustrations to create order and thus more effectively communicate concepts, here a warning to drivers to be careful of children. The minimalist Helvetica typography is carefully placed to balance the design as a giant motorcycle wheel veers toward a little boy at a menacing angle. Müller-Brockmann studied architecture, design, and the history of art in Zurich at the Kunstgewerbeschule and at the University of Zurich. In 1936 he opened his own studio in Zurich, specializing in graphic design, exhibition, and stage design. During the 1950s, he was one of the leaders of the Swiss Typographic Movement, which "sought an absolute and universal form of graphic expression through objective and impersonal presentation."[18]

Vivianna Torun BÜLOW-HÜBE

(1927–2004)

Necklace
Designed and executed
c. 1954–58
Silver, rutilated quartz
23.2 x 11.6 x 15.2 cm
The Montreal Museum
of Fine Arts, D89.139.1

Torun Bülow-Hübe was born in Sweden and studied at the Konstfackskolan, in Stockholm. Her jewelry represents a radical departure from traditional jewelry forms of the prewar years. Made of hand-forged silver and semiprecious stones, her minimalist sculptural pieces are easy to wear as well as aesthetically pleasing. The gentle linear curves create a freeform, asymmetrical design that provides a comfortable fit for the wearer. The necklace reflects Bülow-Hübe's admiration for Romanian-born sculptor Constantin Brancusi, whom she visited in 1948 at his Montparnasse atelier. She wrote about his sculpture: "It changed my whole conception of being and I started making sculpture around the body of the woman, herself a living sculpture—to try to enhance her movements, light in her eyes—her laughter."[19]

Rudolph LUNGHARD

(1902–1983)

Mocha service

Oval
Designed c. 1950
Glazed porcelain
Mocha pot: 23 x 18.4 x 8.5 cm
Produced by Rosenthal
Porzellanfabrik,
Selb-Plössberg, Germany
The Montreal Museum of Fine
Arts, D93.218.1–4 and 10, gift of
Eric McLean, by exchange

Rosenthal, founded in 1879, is one of Germany's most famous porcelain manufacturers, known for its roster of distinguished designers. Following World War II, the firm developed a preference for elongated geometric forms, as seen in Lunghard's *Oval* series, which he designed soon after he started working for Rosenthal, among other German manufacturers. The oval shape is repeated rhythmically in the forms themselves, the handles, finials, and little painted decorations. The design's delicacy reflects the refined skills of the manufacturer, which was adopting modern styles for its relatively well-heeled customers. Lunghard's influence spread from designs such as this and from his teaching: from 1939 to 1967 he headed the Porzellanfachschule in Selb, Bavaria.

Sori YANAGI

(born 1915)

Stool
Butterfly
Designed 1954
Rosewood-faced plywood, brass
39.2 x 41.7 x 30.5 cm
Produced by Tendo Co., Ltd.,
Tendo, Japan
The Montreal Museum of Fine
Arts, D87.173.1, gift of Gallery 91

Yanagi's *Butterfly* stool is constructed of two identical plywood forms connected under the seat by a brass crossbar. The name is derived from the profile of the seat, suggesting a winged creature in flight. The outline of the stool is reminiscent of both Japanese calligraphy and the shape of a gateway to a Shinto shrine. While using traditional forms, here and in other designs, Yanagi employed modern manufacturing processes and factory-generated materials such as plywood. From 1936 to 1940, Yanagi studied architecture and painting at the Tokyo Academy of Fine Arts, and he initially worked as an architect. He left architecture in 1947 to study industrial design and opened his own design studio in Tokyo in 1952. His industrial designs cover a wide range of products, including appliances and ceramics, as well as furniture.[20]

Toshiko TAKAEZU

(born 1922)

Vase
Designed and executed 1953–54
Glazed stoneware
35 x 22.2 x 21.7 cm
The Montreal Museum
of Fine Arts, D87.101.1

Hawaiian born, Takaezu studied at Cranbrook Academy of Art, the seedbed for many leaders in American design and architecture at mid-century. Like her colleagues in the 1950s, she sought to escape the restraints imposed by traditional crafts making. Her first rebellion, she recalled, was turning a teapot she was making upside down and using the spout as a long neck for a vase. This initiated a series of vases with multiple spouts, such as the example seen here. Although this vase was still a thrown, spherical form, it was flattened and transformed with a paddle, and the spouts added to the asymmetry of the form. The use of the brushwork for the decoration reflected avant-garde art of the 1950s, such as Abstract Expressionism, although it also calls to mind the calligraphy on traditional Japanese ceramics.

Peter VOULKOS

(1924–2002)

Covered jar
Designed and executed 1956
Glazed stoneware
47.6 x 44.5 x 44.5 cm
The Montreal Museum
of Fine Arts, D88.201.1a–b

In the 1950s and 1960s, Voulkos revolutionized American studio pottery, transforming it into a dynamic art comparable to the best work of avant-garde sculptors and painters. While teaching at Black Mountain College, Voulkos met Robert Rauschenberg, and in New York he met Franz Kline, both artists whose Abstract Expressionist work influenced Voulkos's aesthetic. Not surprisingly, Voulkos focused on the experimental and the accidental in making his pottery. The scale of this jar was difficult to achieve and required heroic throwing. The painterly, expressive surface was created by hammering, which left a field of aggressive texture. Voulkos then added small sections of clay over the roughened surface to create a low relief. The two-handled lid and overall silhouette of the vessel recall Bronze Age Korean prototypes.

Stanislav LIBENSKÝ

(1921–2002)

Vase
Designed and executed 1954
Enameled glass
33 x 10 x 10 cm
The Montreal Museum
of Fine Arts, D83.118.1

Glassmaking in Czechoslovakia (now the Czech Republic and Slovakia, formerly the Autro-Hungarian Empire, Province of Bohemia) has had an honored tradition over several centuries. In this vase, Libenský combined irregular geometric shapes in multiple colors, creating a kaleidoscopic effect, reminiscent of Czechoslovakian Cubism from the 1910s and '20s. The simple, straight-sided form of the vase provides a contrasting background for the colorful abstract shapes and minimal figurative elements of what appears to be a Venetian scene with an Ionic capital and the prow of a gondola. Trained as a painter, Libenský was important in advocating the uses of glass for artistic rather than functional purposes during a period when his country was under Communist rule.

Ettore SOTTSASS

(1917–2007)

Vase
Designed 1959
Partially glazed earthenware
44.5 x 13.6 x 13.6 cm
D92.129.1, gift of Esperanza and
Mark Schwartz by exchange

Vase
Calice (Chalice)
Designed 1959
Glazed earthenware
46.8 x 17.8 x 17.8 cm
D87.240.1

Vase
Designed 1957
Partially glazed earthenware
32.7 x 10.4 x 10.4 cm
D87.159

Vase
Designed 1957
Partially glazed earthenware
13.4 x 16.8 x 16.8 cm
D87.160

Produced by Cav. G.
Bitossi & Figli, Montelupo, Italy
The Montreal Museum
of Fine Arts

Although best known for his furniture designs for the postmodern design group Memphis, named in 1981, Ettore Sottsass was equally creative in ceramics, graphics, industrial design, glass, and architecture. For much of the twentieth century, he was Italy's leading radical designer, constantly proposing new forms and images for objects of everyday life. As seen here, his ceramics reflect his work as an architect and resemble lathe-turned wooden objects. The bold color in jolly stripes on these vases might be traced to American chromatic abstraction, which Sottsass encountered when he worked in the George Nelson office in New York in 1956. The cheerful simplicity of these hard-edged cylinders, which make plain they were thrown on a wheel, forecasts the brash decorativeness of Pop art, emergent in the early 1960s.

Verner PANTON

(1926–1998)

Chair
Cone
Designed 1958
Stainless steel, polyurethane
foam, wool upholstery
80.7 x 57.2 x 60.4 cm
Produced by Plus-Linje, Denmark
The Montreal Museum
of Fine Arts, D88.187.1,
gift of Mrs. Lilian Korman

The *Cone* chair has no legs and appears precariously supported on a cross-shaped metal base: it looks as if it might topple over. In fact, beneath its padded upholstery is a frame of stainless steel wire. This ice cream cone–like chair is typical of Panton's proto-Pop designs of the 1950s. Vibrantly colored and fluid and futuristic in form, these designs brought startling invention and often humor to Scandinavian interiors at mid-century. Their surprise seems greater in view of Panton's relatively conventional schooling. He was trained first as an architectural engineer and then studied at the Royal Danish Academy of Fine Arts in Copenhagen from 1947 to 1951. From 1950 to 1952, he worked for Arne Jacobsen's architectural office. In 1955 he established his own architecture and design firm, which he moved to Switzerland in 1963. Recognized for his exploration of new technology and materials and for unconventional use of form and color, Panton became an international celebrity for his interiors, furniture, and lighting.

1960
1969

Contradictory Visions

If Mies van der Rohe's Modernist prescription "less is more" defined much of design in the 1950s, it was the retort of the architect-partners Robert Venturi and Denise Scott Brown that marked the 1960s: "less is a bore."[1] The appetite for more—for more variety in materials, methods, sources, shapes, colors, effects—looked to some like the fracturing of markets and taste, to others like an avalanche of fresh ideas. Form no longer followed function; form followed fun.

Italy dominated design in the 1960s. Building on its experiments in the 1950s, and emboldened by membership in the newly established European Common Market, Italy enjoyed a thriving economy and with it a flourishing design community. Its designers had begun working in the 1950s with national furniture and lighting manufacturers, such as Artemide and Kartell, to extend plastic's prewar association with futuristic technology and style. In the '60s synthetics were like teak in the '50s: a hallmark of desirable new design. Italian furnishings, engineered in novel ways and made of molded plastic, became international bestsellers. At the 1968 Milan Triennale, Italian dominance in plastic products was inescapable.

Plastic is derived from petroleum, so it was cheap to make when oil was cheap, as it was in the 1960s. But the molds needed to make plastic objects were expensive, so high-volume sales were essential to make manufacture in plastics profitable. The process for injection molding in Joe Colombo's 1961 polypropylene side chair illustrates the massive machinery required (fig. 1). While the designers of the 1950s had trusted that objects of "timeless and universal" character could help solve the problems of individuals and their societies, many artists and designers of the 1960s turned away from such design goals and ignored functionalist problem-solving. The built environment was now seen, especially in youth markets, as comparable to clothing fashions. Rapid style changes with broad-based appeal would pay for retooling and keep sales lively.

Designers took their cues from British and American artists who embraced banal mass-marketed products, such as Coca-Cola bottles and Campbell's soup cans, incorporating them and the ads created to sell them into their work. Andy Warhol, James Rosenquist, Roy Lichtenstein, and Claes Oldenburg, among other Pop artists, applied the language of advertising and packaging to painting, printmaking, and sculpture. Dominated by Abstract Expressionism in the 1950s, advanced contemporary artists now adopted mass advertising's instantly recognizable images, aggressive graphics, and blaring colors. When Robert Rauschenberg represented the United

States at the 1964 Venice Biennale and won the grand prize, international artists and designers noted this ratification of American invention and its artistic embrace of popular culture. Even the abstract artists emergent in the 1960s seemed to espouse Pop's immediacy. Color-field painters such as Frank Stella, Kenneth Noland, and Ellsworth Kelly devoted their mural-scale canvases to a few bold flat shapes in saturated hues. Designers of fashion, furniture, magazines, books, even architects and city planners absorbed these ideas.

Pop's comic transformations of scale and identity could be found in furnishings aimed at a youthful market. Lamps shaped like drug capsules and chairs resembling beach toys, beanbags, or rocks (pp. 193, 223) supplanted the sober objects of the 1950s. Rainbows of high-key colors replaced the restrained palette of the 1950s in graphic design, as seen in Massimo Vignelli's poster for Knoll (pp. 214–215), and industrial design, notably by Verner Panton (pp. 196, 218–19). The "go-go" stock market and the race to the moon were raising eyes and spirits, while providing buyers with disposable income and popular space-age imagery.

Additional stylistic inspirations were found by looking back. First in Europe and then in North America, designers rediscovered Art Nouveau, the international fin-de-siècle style of ornamental profusion. This phenomenon in all the arts, ostracized by strict modernist thinkers between the wars, was now rehabilitated in exhibitions like The Museum of Modern Art's *Art Nouveau*, 1960. Further, the museum identified works by Louis Comfort Tiffany and Hector Guimard as the first modern objects in its design collection.

In the San Francisco Bay Area, a home to the period's sex-drugs-and-rock-and-roll counterculture, Art Nouveau, along with Pop, became a source for psychedelic art and design. Posters for concerts and light shows rendered the serpentines and horror vacui of French and Austrian Art Nouveau in vibrating close-valued hues that imitated the optical distortions induced by hallucinogenic drug use. In New York, Peter Max's graphics and clothing printed with a benign amalgamation of flowers and feminine figures proved widely popular (p. 235). These explorations of a previously dismissed style were new and would foreshadow Postmodernism's cultural bricolage in the 1980s.

In the free-spirited environment of the 1960s, young artists relished the opportunity to explore their individuality in media set apart from mass production and industrial design. An explosion of new forms, described as "studio" ceramics, glass, or the like, represented defiance of 1950s' norms of function and social responsibility and showed the increasingly porous boundaries between media and between art and design. Were one-of-a-kind or limited-edition examples of studio glassblowing or weaving to be seen as artworks or usable objects or both? The studio movement was overlapping the sculpture world's "process art," in which Robert Morris, Richard Serra, Eva Hesse, and others were generating polymorphous works by exploiting the properties of unconventional materials—felt, rubber, molten metal, oozing synthetics.

From this matrix of exploration came fiber art, whose practitioners used the age-old crafts techniques of weaving and sewing pliable materials, but to create abstract works, often of large scale and primeval associations (fig. 2; pp. 226–27, 229). Here the expressionism in art of the 1950s joined hands with the nascent women's movement in art (though there were male fiber artists), and textile design was enlarged to encompass wall hangings and seating that owners could arrange as they saw fit. Exhibition labels sometimes read "dimensions variable": the exhibited works typified

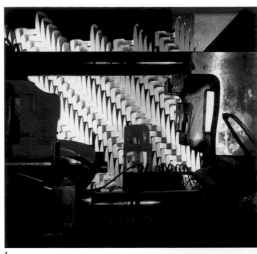

1 Injection molding in polypropylene of the *Universale* side chair, designed by Joe Colombo, 1965.
2 Magdelena Abakanowicz, *Abakan Round,* 1967, and *Yellow Abakan,* 1967–68.

the period's assault on previously rigid categories of artistic fabrication and aesthetic judgment.

Such rebellion against conformity marked the entire decade and the spectrum of expression from London and Paris fashions to American and Italian publications on design. Among "mod" youths were Edwardian dandies in ruffled shirts, disco girls in miniskirts and patterned pantyhose, minstrels in a motley of flea-market finds, and outer-space stewardesses in white vinyl by Courrèges. "Youthquake" apartments featured inflatable and disposable furniture with Marimekko-patterned pillows and silvery Mylar-covered walls, walls like those in Andy Warhol's Factory or the Italian Pavilion at the 1964 Triennale. This multiplicity of "signs"—all telegraphing the identities of their owners—was deconstructed in academe, and with early impact by Robert Venturi and Denise Scott Brown. In place of the mid-century aspirations to "universal" design, they illustrated vernacular solutions to local needs in *Complexity and Contradiction in Architecture,* 1966, and *Learning from Las Vegas,* 1972. In a culture of consumption, they praised the sales function of the duck-shaped road store for Long Island ducks and the billboards with messages readable at eighty miles per hour. The blessings that they and other thinkers gave to pluralism in design would bear fruit in the 1970s, while their parsing of architecture and design as culture-specific codes of communication would shape criticism for several decades.

Most quickly, Venturi and Scott Brown's architectural practice and theory generated Supergraphics, the painting of large-scale interiors indebted to the couple's designs with huge letters as both signage and decoration from 1962 on. The West Coast painter Barbara Stauffacher Solomon may be best known among those who altered perceptions of structure and space in new buildings by covering their walls, floors, and ceilings with sweeping planes of color and giant Helvetica letters.[2] In France from the mid-1960s, the *Art concret* painter Daniel Buren had applied his signature stripes to architectural features, making them freshly visible, but supergraphics artists were most praised in the United States for disguising or enlivening banal institutional architecture. This was a low-cost embellishment for malls and shops and a communications system for corporations and schools. Here graphic design gained environmental scale.

Amid such vibrant challenges to convention, big businesses worldwide continued to commission elegant steel-and-glass skyscrapers as their headquarters. The glass box also conveyed the postwar association between capitalism and sponsorship of masters of modern art when the New National Gallery opened in Berlin in 1968, Mies van der Rohe's last project. The state-supported museum was linked by critics to Karl Friedrich Schinkel's Altes Museum of 1825–28 in Berlin, a link that naturalized Miesian modernism as Neoclassicsm in industrial clothing. Inside International Style buildings in the 1960s, interiors continued to be furnished by Knoll International and Herman Miller of the United States and now by Vitra, the leading high-quality furniture maker in Germany. Italy's Olivetti dominated the European market for innovative office equipment.

Middle-class city housing remained a challenge, but the decade saw at least one stimulating solution to anonymous, crowded dwelling. Moshe Safdie's *Habitat 67* was an apartment complex designed for the 1967 Universal and International Exhibition in Montreal (Expo 67), which took as its theme "Man and His World." Safdie's modular system was a landmark experiment in construction as well as concept: he designed capsule-like, poured-concrete apartment units, mass-produced offsite, complete

3 Moshe Safdie, exterior view, *Habitat 67*, 1967, Expo 67, showing mass-produced apartment units being lowered into place by crane.

with built-in appliances and fiberglass bathroom and kitchen equipment. Each unit was hoisted into place by a crane (fig. 3), facing away from its neighbors to afford unobstructed views. Each unit—ranging in size from one to four bedrooms—had a private roof garden and separate entry.

There was fevered debate over the goals of city planning and design in general. In 1964, Archigram, a visionary group of young architects in Britain, designed what they called *Plug-in City* (fig. 4), relying on temporary add-on domestic and commercial services. Led by Peter Cook and Reyner Banham, they advocated design driven by systems of use rather than Modernist structure and style. Playful and experimental, Archigram's ideas were appropriated in 1966 by more radical groups in Florence, Archizoom and Superstudio (pp. 206, 209). With like-minded Italian collaboratives such as Gruppo 65 and UFO, they declared themselves "Anti-Design." They opposed Modernist style, which they saw as complicit with an authoritarian production system, and they adopted Pop art's populism, delighting in using any form or style that could irritate the devotees of Good Design and "good taste."

The radicalism of the young Italians was in part a response to the darkening political climate at the end of the 1960s. Across Europe and America there were angry marches against the U.S. war in Vietnam; the terrible year of 1968 marked the assassinations of Dr. Martin Luther King, Jr., and Senator Robert Kennedy in the United States, the Soviet Union's violent occupation of Czechoslovakia ending the brief "Prague Spring," and weeks of strikes throughout Paris as students and workers tried to overthrow Charles de Gaulle's government. These events dramatized fault lines that had already provoked many architects, designers, and city-planners to question their roles in shaping their societies.

In an echo of political events, in 1968 members of the Italian groups occupied the Milan Triennale building and delayed the opening of the exposition for more than a month, thus capturing world attention. The Triennale, they argued, purported to display design solutions that could be broadly applied, but in reality it promoted national rivalries with its national pavilions. Furthermore, Italian design, while internationally admired, often created only prototypes or limited-edition runs, which were by definition expensive and elitist, rather than products that could be mass-produced. The culprits were Italy's antiquated construction methods and labor relations. In sum, the young radicals asserted, the gulf between rich and poor in Italy was widened by the very designers and manufacturers who claimed to be trying to bridge it.[3]

Reaction to the occupation was dramatic, and in some quarters positive. The Japanese architect Arata Isozaki, who watched the events unfold, later wrote: "I consider the course of modern architecture pioneered by the avant-garde to have been changed definitely and qualitatively by the confrontation. . . . I later came to regard the year of the Triennale as a cultural watershed, comparable to 1527 when the Sack of Rome helped to stimulate Renaissance architecture."[4] The architect and designer Emilio Ambasz noted three profoundly different approaches to Italian design in his 1972 exhibition for MoMA, *Italy: The New Domestic Landscape*. "The first is conformist, the second is reformist, and the third is, rather, one of contestation, attempting both inquiry and action," he wrote. These contradictory but parallel approaches were true of design worldwide. In the first category, he noted efforts to "continue to refine already established forms and functions . . . exploring the aesthetic quality of single objects—a chair, a table, a bookcase—that answer the traditional needs of domestic life." Members of the second group, according to Ambasz, were convinced that design could not be changed without structural change in society, yet they were unwilling to undertake social changes themselves, instead "redesigning conventional objects with new, ironic, and sometimes self-deprecatory socio-cultural and aesthetic references."[5] In this group he included pieces by the Castiglioni brothers, Ettore Sottsass, and Gaetano Pesce. For the third group, which he saw as conceiving "environmental ensembles [that] permit different modes of social interaction . . . [and] allow the user to make his own statement about both privacy and communality,"[6] he cited works by Matta (p. 203) and Colombo. In this third group, whose goals dovetailed with those of Archigram, Ambasz clearly saw the most potential. Here design would serve both the individualism of the 1960s and its new social alignments by age and interest, and encourage active interrelations. Design was now defined as inseparable from social and political issues, whether one saw design as part of the problem or part of the solution.

4 Archigram, rendering, *Plug-in City*, 1964.

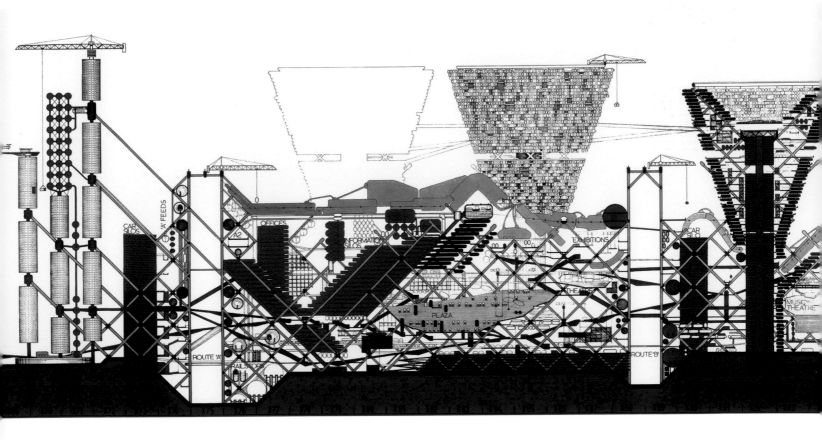

Pier Giacomo CASTIGLIONI
Achille CASTIGLIONI

(1913–1968) and **(1918–2002)**

Floor lamp
Arco
Designed 1962
Marble, stainless steel, aluminum
241.4 x 213.4 x 30.6 cm
Produced by Flos S.p.A.,
Nave, Italy
The Montreal Museum
of Fine Arts, D82.104.1a–c,
gift of Barbara Jakobson*

In this eight-foot-tall lamp the Castiglioni brothers created an elegant design, combining functionalism and high style. It has three simple elements: a rectangular base of marble, a swooping arc of stainless steel, and a hemispherical aluminum shade. The steel shaft can be adjusted in both its height and the extent of its arc to suit the space in which it is used. The oversize design solves the problem of providing overhead illumination where a ceiling fixture is inconvenient or undesirable, while allowing a flexible placement of furniture that other floor lamps would disrupt. The combination of marble, a traditional luxury material, with the modern materials of steel and aluminum suited both cautious and venturesome consumers: *Arco* popped up in a range of domestic and public spaces.

BELOW Publicity photograph showing *Arco* with the *Ball* chair (p. 198), the *Elda* chair (p. 204), a Vignelli sofa, and a Mascheroni coffee table.

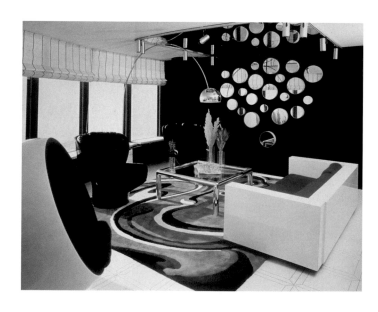

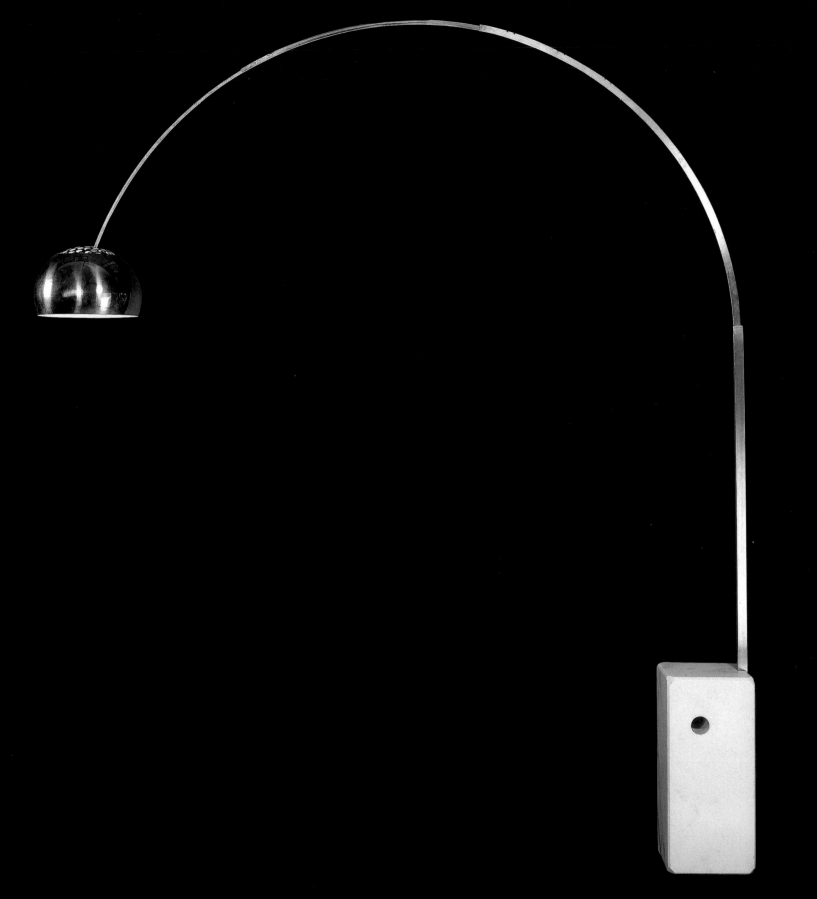

Hugh SPENCER
John MAGYAR

(1928–1982) and **(dates unknown)**

Hi-fi stereo cabinet
Project G
Designed 1963
Rosewood, leather, anodized and
brushed aluminum, plastic
72.5 x 214 x 48 cm
Produced by Clairtone Sound
Corporation, Toronto,
Ontario, Canada
The Montreal Museum of Fine
Arts, 2004.150.1–2, gift of Eric
Brill to the Stewart Program for
Modern Design*

Project G (for "globe") represented a radical departure from the traditional rectangular cabinets used to house stereo equipment. In this futuristic design, black spherical speakers flank an elongated rectangular container for the turntable and electronic equipment, and the total is supported on a four-pronged aluminum base. According to designer Karim Rashid, "*Project G* epitomized high design, pure form, the perfection of how sacred platonic geometry can bring our banal, everyday products to a higher spiritual art form."[7] Clairtone touted the *G*'s superior sound system in a 1964 press release: "By virtue of the freely rotating 'sound globes,' the instrument can be tuned to recreate any environment in which the music was originally recorded."[8] This stereo appeared in several contemporary films, and a later version of the system, the *G2,* was featured in the 1967 film *The Graduate*, an example of the clever promotion of products through popular cinema.

Studio Architetti B.B.P.R.

(founded 1932)

Desk and typewriter table extension

Arco
Designed 1960
Lacquered steel, laminated plywood, plastic
88.9 x 160.8 x 81.3 cm
(desk section only)
Produced by Olivetti, Milan, Italy
The Denver Art Museum, 2003.976, gift of Eric Brill to the Stewart Program for Modern Design*

The origins of Olivetti's innovative design for the office are in the German modular designs of the 1930s. Studio Architetti B.B.P.R. (an acronym of the initials of the designers' last names: Gianluigi Banfi, Lodovico Barbiano di Belgiojoso, Enrico Peressuttim, and Ernesto N. Rogers) designed a desk system with angled legs, interchangeable parts, and simple connections, which allowed users to choose and change configurations of desks and shelves. The *Arco* series reflected Olivetti's role as the leading manufacturer of avant-garde office furniture in its day—anticipating the advent of the open-plan office, such as Herman Miller's 1964 *Action Office*—and earned the Compasso d'Oro award in 1962.[9]

Maija ISOLA

(1927–2001)

Fabric
Lokki (Seagull)
Designed 1961
Printed cotton
158 x 132 cm
Produced by Marimekko Oy,
Helsinki, Finland
The Montreal Museum of
Fine Arts, 2004.151

Trained in painting in Helsinki, Isola is best known for her colorful cotton prints with giant flat motifs of the 1960s, which recall American Color-Field canvases. These designs were popular throughout the decade, becoming synonymous with the name of Marimekko, the Finnish company that produced them. Cartoon-simple patterns like this—dramatic waves in green, red, blue, and yellow—could be used for many purposes: drapery, upholstery, table linens, pillow coverings, or even for clothing. Lengths of fabric could also be stretched and framed as works of art. Though costly because of the high quality of the materials and production, the fabrics were readily available in the United States through the Design Research outlets, and the banner-like cottons added decorative zest to many interiors of the day.[10]

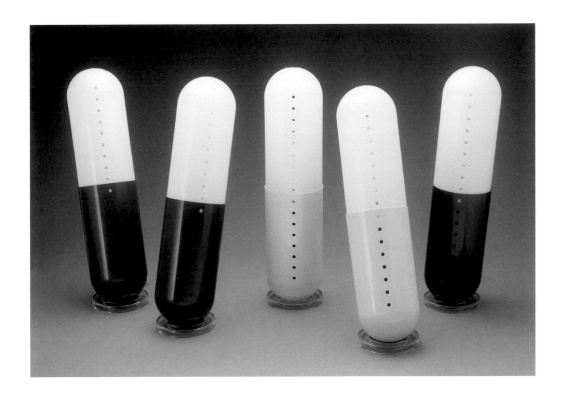

Cesare Maria CASATI
Emanuele PONZIO

(born 1936) and **(born 1923)**

Table lamps

Pillola
Designed 1968
ABS plastic, acrylic
55.1 x 13.3 x 13.3 cm
Produced by Ponteur,
Bergamo, Italy
The Montreal Museum of Fine
Arts, 2001.21.1–3, 2001.25.1–2

These brightly colored overscaled lamps create a bold Pop statement, typical of the Dada-like art and the "Anti-Design" of the 1960s. Allowing random arrangements, the capsule-like plastic lamps were created during the age of "The Pill" and "uppers" and "downers," reminding users of both contraceptives and recreational drugs. The lamp is composed of two vacuum-formed plastic sections, a translucent white upper section, and a boldly colored, weighted base resting on a clear acrylic ring. The design was included in the influential MoMA exhibition *Italy: The New Domestic Landscape* in 1972, grouped with two other enormous Pop objects, the *Joe* sofa (pp. 284–85) and a Pesce table lamp.[11]

Gaetano PESCE

(born 1939)

Armchair and ottoman

UP5 and *UP6, La Mamma*
Designed 1969
Polyurethane foam, viscose/
nylon/Lycra-blend fabric
Chair: 100 x 113.7 x 125.1 cm
Ottoman: 59.1 x 59.1 x 59.1 cm
Produced by B & B Italia,
Novedrate, Italy
The Montreal Museum of Fine
Arts, D84.179.1–2,
gift of B & B Italia

Pesce intended this anthropomorphic design to symbolize feminine fertility, but he said the addition of the "ball and chain" ottoman showed how "a woman is always confined, a prisoner of herself against her will."[12] Covered in stretch fabric, the polyurethane foam of the chair-ottoman duo is composed mainly of air, and so, after it was formed, all of the air could be removed by vacuum, allowing the upholstered furniture to be sealed into a flat, airtight package for easy, inexpensive shipping. Once the buyer opened the package and exposed the polyurethane to air, the chair and ottoman inflated instantly, and permanently, to their respective shapes—a process both brilliant in concept and immensely amusing to watch.

BELOW B & B Italia, 1969 publicity photographs showing phases of the inflation of the *UP5 La Mamma* chair.

Verner PANTON

(1926–1998)

Side chairs
Designed 1960–67
Luran-S thermoplastic
83.7 x 49.5 x 56.6 cm (each)
Produced by Vitra GmbH, Basel,
Switzerland, for Herman Miller
International, New York,
New York, U.S.A.
The Montreal Museum
of Fine Arts, D87.200.1,
gift of Luc d'Iberville-Moreau;
D92.209.1; D93.136.1

This icon of Pop design is one of Panton's most significant works. According to Christopher Wilk, "Throughout the twentieth century, designers dreamed of mass-producing a chair made from a single piece of material that would require no assembly of any kind. The notion of a chair stamped or cast into a single, finished unit was a potent one because of the possibility for large-scale, economical production."[13] Panton conceived this chair in 1960, but technical problems made its realization impossible until 1967. His final product, a stackable chair available in six bright colors, was not only strong, durable, and daring, but an aesthetic masterpiece in its dramatically cantilevered and curvilinear sculptural form.

Mario BELLINI

(born 1935)

Floor lamp
Chiara (Light)
Designed 1964
Stainless steel
144.8 x 73.2 x 52.7 cm
Produced by Flos
S.p.A., Nave, Italy
The Montreal Museum of
Fine Arts, D87.207.1

Bellini's dramatic lamp *Chiara* is constructed of a single thin and flexible sheet of steel, which is shipped flat and assembled by the consumer, saving costs. The rectangular section of the sheet is bent into a cylinder to make the tubular base, and the shade is formed from a flat pair of wings that are hooked together to create a broad hood. The light source is within the base, as evidenced by the glowing slits where the base meets the floor, and it reflects brightly off the interior of the stainless steel hood. *Chiara* is a floor lamp proportioned more like a table lamp, much wider for its height than most floor lamps, reflecting Pop art, and its large scale and unusual form command attention in any room.

Eero AARNIO

(born 1932)

Chair
Ball or *Globe*
Designed 1963–65
Fiberglass, aluminum,
polyurethane foam,
wool upholstery
119.5 x 103.5 x 85 cm
Produced by Asko Oy, Lahti,
Finland, and Adelta,
Dinslaken, Germany
The Montreal Museum of
Fine Arts, D87.245.1,
gift of Nannette and Eric Brill*

This large, womblike fiberglass semi-sphere rests on a swiveling aluminum pedestal. The interior is fully upholstered and provides a self-contained world that allows users to sit or curl up with the casual informality typical of the 1960s. Aarnio's geometric form reflects his quest for simplified design and structure. The *Ball* chair appealed to the fashion-conscious: the shell and fabric were both available in a variety of colors and reflected popular fascination with images of outer space. Some owners added optional audio equipment to the *Ball*, making it an acoustical environment for one.

Enzo MARI

(born 1932)

Vases

Pago-Pago
Designed 1968
ABS plastic
30.2 x 20 x 15.5 cm
Produced by Bruno Danese SNC,
Milan, Italy
The Montreal Museum of Fine
Arts, D87.216.1, gift of Geoffrey
N. Bradfield*; D88.125.1,
gift of Wistar Morris, by exchange

The manufacturer Bruno Danese commissioned these invertible vases to accommodate large and small flower arrangements. The lightweight plastic forms were manufactured easily and inexpensively in two-part molds. The designer wrote: "People already use craft objects of varying kinds as flower vases and prefer unique objects. I thought of the creation of a single object (and thus one set of tools), multipurpose so as to contain alternatively from one to many . . . flowers, multiform so that the form would be conceived in different ways according to the type of positioning."[14]

Ettore SOTTSASS

(1917–2007)

Cabinet
Designed 1964
Walnut, cherry veneer,
lacquered wood
251.5 x 152.5 x 61 cm
Produced by Renzo
Brugola, Milan, Italy
The Montreal Museum of Fine
Arts, D88.132.1, gift of Vivian and
David M. Campbell

This piece realizes a 1964 drawing by Sottsass of a whimsical cabinet that resembles a figure with large, round eyes and a rectangular set of antlers, or a chest-on-stand turned upside down. Sottsass designed several cabinets at this time that were produced by Poltronova, but this design was not made for another twenty-four years when he was celebrated as a Postmodernist. In the '60s, Sottsass was interested in abstract art and American Pop. He rejected the ideals represented by Good Design and sought designs to express the present. The Montreal Museum of Decorative Arts commissioned the production of this cabinet in 1988 for the exhibition *Design 1935– 1965: What Modern Was* to show Sottsass' prophetic design in three dimensions and to give background to its collection of 1980s Sottsass designs.

Grete JALK

(1920–2005)

Side chair
Designed 1963
Beech-faced plywood, steel
73.6 x 71.7 x 62.9 cm
Produced by Poul Jeppesen,
Stor Heddinge, Denmark
The Montreal Museum of
Fine Arts, D89.103.1

Although plastic was the favored material for progressive furniture in the 1960s, designers like Jalk continued to explore innovative solutions in bentwood, experiments that had been initiated by Charles and Ray Eames and by Alvar Aalto in the 1940s. The undulant surfaces of this chair, which call to mind origami or folded cloth, prove that new aesthetic results from bentwood were possible. Made from two pieces of plywood, each bent in one direction, the chair was easier to produce than chairs molded in three planes, such as the Eameses' plywood furniture (pp. 102–03). Jalk's chair is part of a laminated furniture series that she initiated in 1962.

Eero AARNIO

(born 1932)

Chairs
Pastille or *Gyro*
Designed 1968
Fiberglass-reinforced polyester
53.3 x 92.7 x 92.7 cm
Produced by Asko Oy,
Lahti, Finland
The Montreal Museum of Fine
Arts, D94.333.1–2, gift of Eleanore
and Charles Stendig in memory of
Eve Brustein and Rose Stendig*

Aarnio helped to establish Finland's international reputation in design in the 1960s with designs such as these chairs. Departing from traditional furniture forms with legs, backs, and joints, he created plastic sculptures that reflected the nonconformist spirit of the decade. His *Ball* chair of a few years earlier was simplified, but in the *Pastille* chairs he took reductivism a step further, eliminating the support structure and upholstery. The manufacturing process was simple, with each chair made of one material and molded in two parts. Like the *Ball,* these chairs reflect Pop art and were available in a variety of bright colors.

Roberto MATTA

(1911–2002)

**Modular
seating system**
Malitte
Designed 1966
Polyurethane foam,
stretch wool upholstery
160 x 160 x 63 cm (assembled)
Produced by Gavina, Foligno,
Italy; Knoll International,
New York, New York, U.S.A.
The Montreal Museum of
Fine Arts, D89.137.1a—e

The four lounge chairs and oval ottoman that compose *Malitte* were cut from a single slab of polyurethane foam. The availability of double-knit fabrics, like the stretch wool fitted over these forms, made designs such as this possible. When not in use, this lightweight seating system was intended to be stored or displayed as a work of art in the original square form from which it was cut. Matta was a student of architecture in his native Chile and worked in the Paris office of Le Corbusier in 1934—35. In 1937, he turned to painting and joined the Surrealists after meeting René Magritte, Pablo Picasso, and Joan Miró. *Malitte,* named after the designer's wife, was part of a series of sofas produced by Gavina. Some thought the company took a risk in using the designs of someone who was known only for his paintings, but the full spectrum of Matta's education and experience led to a new concept about what furniture could be.[15]

BELOW, LEFT *Malitte* seating system, separated.

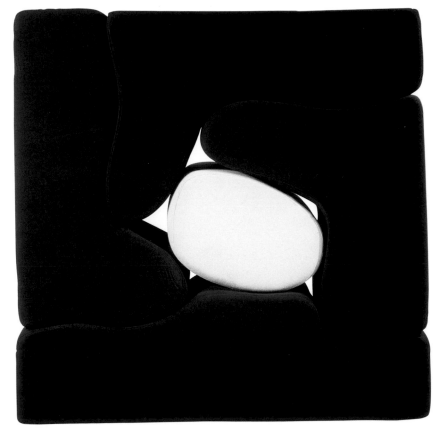

Cesare (Joe) COLOMBO

(1930–1971)

Armchair
Elda
Designed 1963
Fiberglass, polyurethane, leather
upholstery
92 x 92 x 92 cm
Produced by Comfort, Milan, Italy
The Montreal Museum of Fine
Arts, D90.147.1, gift of Paul Leblanc

One of the most original Italian designers of the 1960s, Colombo studied fine arts and architecture, and began his career as a painter in 1951. In 1962, he opened his own studio in Milan for interior and industrial design. The following year, he created *Elda* (named after his wife), the first large-scale armchair made of fiberglass. Two separate pieces form the front and rear structures, which are mounted together on a rotating base, and seven leather-covered cushions fit into the seat and backrest. Based on a traditional wingchair form, this chair has a cartoonish quality thanks to its exaggerated curves. Colombo's prolific, highly creative career was tragically cut short after only nine years by his death at the age of forty-one.

Livio CASTIGLIONI
Gianfranco FRATTINI

(1911–1979) and **(1926–2004)**

Lamp
Boalum
Designed 1969
PVC plastic, metal
187 x 6.7 x 6.7 cm
Produced by Artemide S.p.A.,
Pregnana Milanese, Italy
The Montreal Museum of
Fine Arts, D90.130.1, gift of Luc
d'Iberville-Moreau, by exchange

The *Boalum* lamp was designed for a hotel in Capri whose owner wanted to illuminate the pool area. "The idea came to us," wrote Gianfranco Frattini, "while we were observing the gardener, who was cleaning the lawn with a large vacuum cleaner fitted with a long flexible tube." Frattini and Castiglioni worked with Artemide's technical staff to create a lamp that could be draped, coiled, or twisted into a glowing arrangement placed virtually anywhere. "The result was therefore a two-meter-long module containing twenty bulbs, which was flexible and could be built up into a maximum of seven units; potentially, one could create a luminous snake fourteen meters long."[16]

ARCHIZOOM Associati

(active 1966–1974)

Sofa
Superonda
Designed 1967
Polyurethane foam, PVC plastic
89.5 x 237.5 x 36 cm
Produced by Poltronova,
Montale Pistoia, Italy
The Montreal Museum of Fine
Arts, D90.221.1a–b,
gift of Jay Spectre*

Superonda represents the playful, witty side of the "Anti-Design" movement in Italy in the late 1960s and shows the happy simplicity of the Supergraphics of that decade. Its undulating form of vinyl-covered polyurethane foam allows users to sit or recline in unconventional postures. Cut from one rectangular piece of foam, the two sections can be placed side by side, as shown here, or separately or even laid flat to form a bed. Because it did not require an interior structure, *Superonda* was relatively inexpensive to produce. Archizoom was founded in 1966 by rebellious architectural graduates of the University of Florence and took its name from the British design group called Archigram and from *Zoom*, the group's magazine. Rejecting the Bauhaus-based rationalism of the previous decades, such associations championed irrational and poetic design.

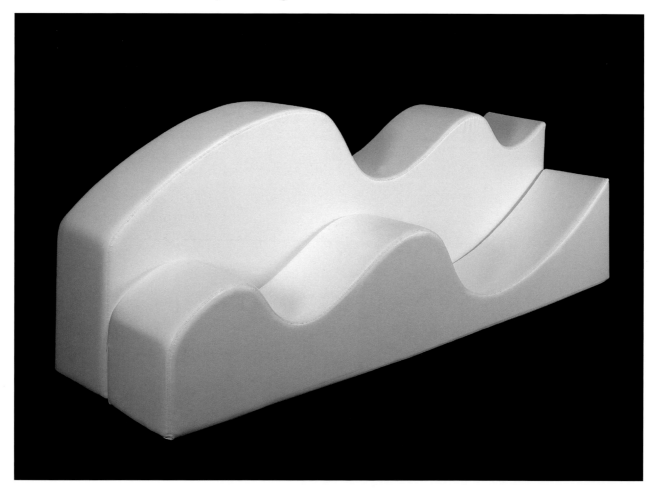

Cesare (Joe) COLOMBO
Gianni COLOMBO

(1930–1971) and **(1937–1993)**

Table lamp
Acrylica (Acrylic)
Designed 1962
Perspex acrylic, lacquered steel
23 x 23.7 x 24.7 cm
Produced by O-Luce, Milan, Italy
The Montreal Museum of
Fine Arts, D91.322.1,
gift of Guy Alexandre Miller

One of Joe Colombo's initial product designs, *Acrylica* was created in collaboration with his brother, Gianni, an artist who worked with light projections. The lamp won a gold medal at the Milan Triennale in 1964. A hidden fluorescent bulb in the lacquered steel base provides the light, which travels through the simple C-shaped curve of the clear acrylic and beams from the exposed end above, forecasting the look of light conducted through fiber-optic glass (a material that had not yet been invented). The sweeping curve of this lamp, which unites base, shaft, and light into a single form, reflects the Colombos' robust aesthetic.

Olivier MOURGUE

(born 1939)

Lounge chair
Bouloum
Designed 1968
Fiberglass, urethane foam, steel, nylon jersey
66.1 x 76.2 x 142.9 cm
Produced by Arconas Corporation, Mississauga, Ontario, Canada
The Montreal Museum of Fine Arts, D93.257.1, gift of William Prévost

For *Bouloum*, nylon jersey is stretched over a layer of polyurethane foam that, in turn, covers a fiberglass shell molded to resemble a reclining figure. This witty design is based on the silhouette of one of Mourgue's childhood friends who was nicknamed Bouloum. The elasticity of the jersey allows the curved forms to be upholstered inexpensively, and the bare fiberglass shells can be used outdoors, as they were at the French pavilion at the 1970 World's Fair in Osaka, Japan. These lightweight and stackable chairs were also used to great effect in the neutral domestic interiors that Mourgue designed.[17]

SUPERSTUDIO

(active 1966–1978)

Table lamp
Gherpe
Designed 1967
Perspex acrylic,
chromium-plated steel
20 x 42.9 x 20.3 cm (closed)
Produced by Poltronova,
Montale, Pistoia, Italy
The Montreal Museum of Fine
Arts, D94.139.1, gift of Eleanore
and Charles Stendig in memory of
Eve Brustein and Rose Stendig*

Founded in Florence in 1966 by a group of radical young architects, Superstudio was motivated by the political unrest of the period. For Superstudio and other such "Anti-Design" groups in Italy, the functional and practical were not enough: the design also had to convey a political message. Its young members sought to redefine consumer products as they considered Modernism out of touch with the new social realities. In *Gherpe,* six wide, concentric bands of acrylic provide a fan effect, forming an adjustable shade. The color of the plastic, its baseless form, and Pop style appealed more to young consumers than to the buyers of Good Design.

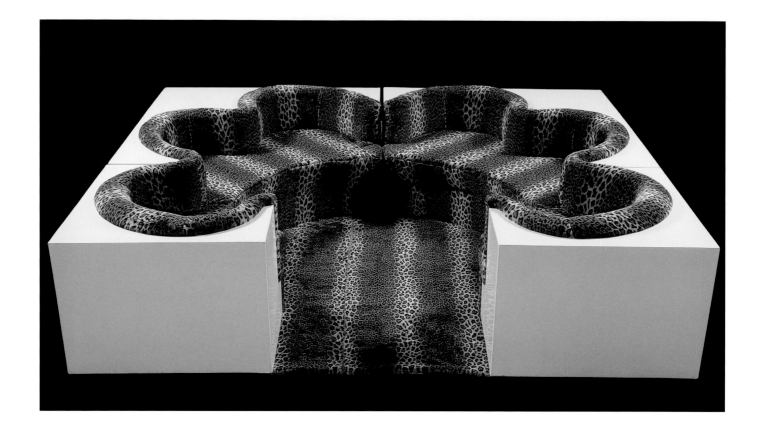

ARCHIZOOM Associati

(active 1966–1974)

Sectional seating unit
Safari
Designed 1967–68
Fiberglass, latex foam, cotton,
synthetic upholstery
64 x 261 x 216 cm
Produced by Poltronova, Montale,
Pistoia, Italy
The Montreal Museum of Fine
Arts, 2004.20.1–5

Founded in 1966 by Andrea Branzi with Paolo Deganello, Gilberto Corretti, and Massimo Morozzi, Archizoom challenged traditional views about architecture, design, and urban planning through their designs and theoretical writings. Their most publicized project was the urban plan *No-Stop City*.[18] Their furniture designs included the *Superonda* sectional couch (p. 206) and this seating, both dependent on imagery in contemporary painting and Supergraphics. *Safari* satirizes Good Design through its sense of kitsch, seen in the white fiberglass, the flower-shaped form, and the faux leopard-skin upholstery. The sectional seating is composed of four square fiberglass forms, each with scalloped seating areas: the total is a humorous version of the normally free-form "conversation pit" of the late 1950s.

Pierre PAULIN

(1927-2009)

Lounge chair
Tongue
Designed 1967
Steel, polyurethane, wool jersey
61.4 x 88.5 x 92.5 cm
Produced by Artifort, Maastricht,
The Netherlands
The Montreal Museum
of Fine Arts, 2007.254,
gift of Réjean Tétreault in memory
of Claude Beaulieu

Originally trained as a sculptor, Paulin brought his sense of organic form to this stackable lounge chair, which was available in a number of bright colors. A tubular-steel structure is covered with foam and upholstered in stretch wool jersey with a zipper. *Tongue* seats the individual in a relaxed position near the floor, and this typifies the informal style of the 1960s. Paulin recounted how the design overcame opposition to reach the marketplace: "Harry Wagemans, the head of Artifort, did not like the chair because it was too low and he couldn't get up from it easily, but he discovered that his son and his friends liked the chair and enjoyed it. Wagemans saw that the design was for the future, and so undertook production."[19]

Eleonore Peduzzi RIVA
Klaus VOGT Ueli BERGER
Hans ULRICH

(born 1939), (dates unknown), (1937–2008), and **(dates unknown)**

Modular seating

Nonstop
Designed 1968
Wood, metal, styrene and
urethane foam, Dacron,
leather upholstery
73.7 x 304.8 x 100.3 cm
Produced by de Sede,
Klingnau, Switzerland
The Montreal Museum of Fine
Arts, D94.156.1a–l, gift of Eleanore
and Charles Stendig in memory of
Eve Brustein and Rose Stendig*

Nonstop consists of multiple units that can be placed in various arrangements of different lengths. To create a sofa, these units can be hinged and zipped together, and leather strips between them cover any gaps. The owner can complete the ensemble at each end by adding segments with raised arms. On this and other designs for de Sede, the Italian designer Eleonore Peduzzi Riva was assisted by three Swiss designers. *Nonstop* anticipated other modular seating designs of curvilinear form, in particular Cini Boeri's *Serpentone* seating of 1970–71 for Arflex and Don Chadwick's units of 1974 for Herman Miller. *Nonstop* was retailed by Charles Stendig in the United States, who donated the seating to the Montreal Museum of Decorative Arts.

Angelo MANGIAROTTI

(born 1921)

Table lamp
Lesbo
Designed 1966–67
Glass, chromium-plated metal
36.2 x 48.9 x 48.9 cm
Produced by Artemide S.p.A.,
Pregnana Milanese, Italy
The Montreal Museum of Fine
Arts, D93.284.1,
gift of Loredana Occhiuto

Named after the Greek island of Lesbos, this table lamp, like Mangiarotti's closely related *Saffo* lamp, is made of hand-blown Murano glass. Its mushroom-like form rises from a metal base to a widely flared lip, emitting a soft, graduated light through the translucent shade. A modernist, Mangiarotti maintained a modified rational approach to his work, during the fermenting period of "Anti-Design" in Italy, seen here in the exaggerated organic allusion of the lamp. Born and trained in Milan, Mangiarotti moved to the United States in 1953 to teach at the Illinois Institute of Technology, at that time under the direction of Mies van der Rohe. Two years later he returned to Italy to open his own architectural firm, designing buildings in the international modern style.[20]

Massimo VIGNELLI

(born 1931)

Poster

Knoll International
Designed 1967
Offset lithograph
82 x 123 cm
Produced by Pirovano-Segrate,
Milan, Italy
The Montreal Museum
of Fine Arts, D88.169.1,
gift of Vignelli Associates

Massimo Vignelli, born and trained in Italy, moved to the United States in 1957 with his wife and design partner, Lella Vignelli. Some of Massimo's most important works were his graphic designs for Knoll, which the Vignelli firm began to serve in 1967. This poster, his first for Knoll, marked the beginning of a new graphic program for the company, a program that was, according to Vignelli, based on a "grid to assure basic uniformity in Knoll graphics through the world."[21] The Knoll logo, originally designed by Herbert Matter, was here redesigned in brilliant colors, each overlapping the next in the bold sans-serif letters of the firm's name. The bright colors and Supergraphic scale are reminiscent of Isola's textile for Marimekko (p. 192). Like a giant one-page catalogue, the back of the poster has line drawings of Knoll's furniture collection, inviting the recipient to hang the poster with either side on view.

Bertoia, Florence Knoll, Saarinen, Mies van der Rohe, Noguchi have designed for Knoll. Aulenti, Albinson, Catfiero, Christen, Colombo, Mangiarotti, Pearson, Pettit, Platner, Pollock, Schultz, and Stephens still do.

Knoll International, in 28 countries, has all these furniture and textile designs.

320 Park Avenue, New York

Knoll International

Kaj FRANCK

(1911–1989)

Plate
Rengaslautanen (Ring Plate)
Designed c. 1965
Glass
43.6 x 43.6 x 3.5 cm
Produced by Nuutajärvi-Notsjö,
Nuutajärvi, Finland
The Montreal Museum of
Fine Arts, D85.100.1

Franck excelled in designing tableware in both ceramic and glass. This plate, an assembled, laminated piece, is one of a group he called *Rengaslautanen*. It is reminiscent of modern paintings of the period, especially Kenneth Noland's concentric circles. The muted tones of this plate continue Franck's earlier, gentler palette, while other designs in this series "juxtapose intense reds and bright greens and blues, and thus approach more closely to the bold graphic system of the 1960s."[22] From 1945 to 1976, Franck worked for several factories, including Arabia, Nuutajärvi-Notsjö, and Oy Wärtsilä, with overlapping tenures and serving as an art or design director at each. He was the artistic director for Nuutajärvi-Notsjö from 1951 to 1976.[23]

Gaetano PESCE

(born 1939)

Textile panel
Motus (Movement)
Designed 1969
Printed cotton, nylon
413.4 x 132.8 cm
Produced by Expansion,
Bologna, Italy
The Montreal Museum of
Fine Arts, D.97.164.1

One of the most versatile and inventive designers of the last fifty years, Pesce studied architecture and industrial design in Venice from 1959 to 1965. He first began work as a designer in 1962 with overscale objects in the Pop design movement. *Motus,* a print of overlapping red and orange squares with rounded corners like Mickey Mouse heads, is influenced by Pop art in its scale and humorous allusion. According to Pesce, *Motus* was intended for upholstery and draperies. "It was conceived with three colors that could be superimposed in various ways to always create different patterns."[24] Additional color ways were yellow, blue, and red.

Verner PANTON

(1926–1998)

Chandelier
Spiral-Lampen SP2
Designed 1969
Plastic, nylon
170 x 45 x 45 cm
Produced by J. Lüber,
Basel, Switzerland
The Montreal Museum of
Fine Arts, 2001.19

Both futuristic and Pop in its fluid forms, intense hues, and synthetic materials, this chandelier is a dramatic example of the Danish designer's flamboyant style. The design suggests the fantastical total environments for which Panton was known, and examples were included in his installation *Phantasy-Landscape* in the 1970 Cologne furniture fair. The brightly colored plastic twists are grouped in double chandeliers and are based on *Fun*, a hanging lamp Panton designed in 1964, which was an assemblage of shell discs gathered into a globe-like form.[25]

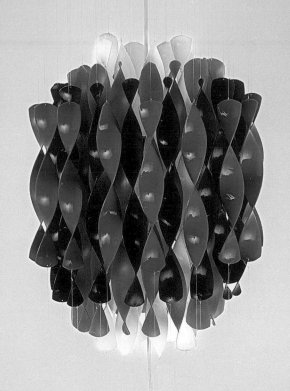
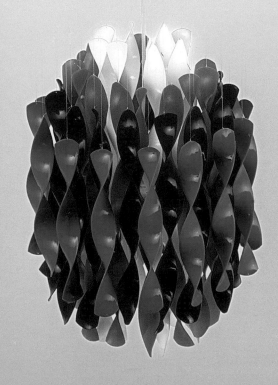

Bruno MARTINAZZI

(born 1923)

Bracelet
Goldfinger
Designed and executed 1969
Yellow gold, white gold
7.5 x 6.5 x 5.5 cm
The Montreal Museum of
Fine Arts, D93.203.1

Martinazzi is known for replicating human body parts in his jewelry. He described the hand as "creative, an instrument of knowledge and invention, meant to establish a relationship with others."[26] *Goldfinger*, a name perhaps inspired by the 1964 James Bond film, represents Martinazzi's transition in the early 1960s from jewelry focused on the entire human figure to specific body parts, including eyes, buttocks, and fingertips. For *Goldfinger* he cast the ends of a man's fingers and positioned them on a cuff so that they grasp the wrist of the wearer. The powerful image allows contradictory readings: of holding someone back, or the conveying of friendship.[27] Martinazzi began his career as a goldsmith's apprentice in 1951.

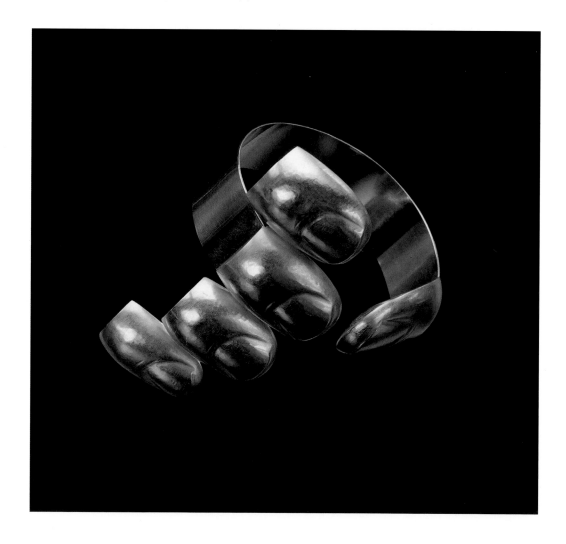

Robert EBENDORF

(born 1938)

Necklace
Eyeglasses
Designed and executed 1969
Metal chain, photographs,
seashell, copper eyeglass frame
6.5 x 10.7 x 1.5 cm
The Montreal Museum of Fine Arts,
D94.108.1, gift of Doug Green
and Marion Jambour*

"Growing up in the Midwest, Kansas, also in a family that had felt the hard times of the Depression," Ebendorf wrote, "there was a thinking: make do with what you have or make something of joy to play with."[28] He translated this experience into his art and created unique jewelry from assembled materials, making very personal objects such as this necklace. Here, he combines family photographs with a surrealizing photo of an apparently decapitated head set in found eyeglasses frames. As if inviting us to see fractured remains of the past, this necklace is mysterious yet communicative, the opposite of jewelry as ostentatious adornment.

Jonathan Donato Paolo Carla DE PAS D'URBINO LOMAZZI SCOLARI

(1932–1991), **(born 1935)**, **(born 1936)**, and **(born 1937)**

Armchair
Blow
Designed 1967
PVC plastic
76 x 83 x 98 cm
Produced by Zanotta S.p.A.,
Nova Milanese, Italy
The Montreal Museum of
Fine Arts, D99.134.1a–c

The initial collaboration by the firm of De Pas, D'Urbino, Lomazzi, and Scolari, *Blow* was one of the first inflatable chairs to be mass-produced. Without an internal support structure, it depends on the air filling the transparent plastic membrane for its shape. The advertising of the 1960s greatly influenced design of the day: this form was inspired by the Michelin tire company's *Bibendum* man, whose body is made of many tire-like rings. For outdoor or indoor use, *Blow* can be quickly deflated to be easily moved, shipped, and stored. Although it appealed to a younger generation, it proved to be uncomfortably hot during the summer, but it generated publicity for its novelty, becoming a design icon of the '60s.

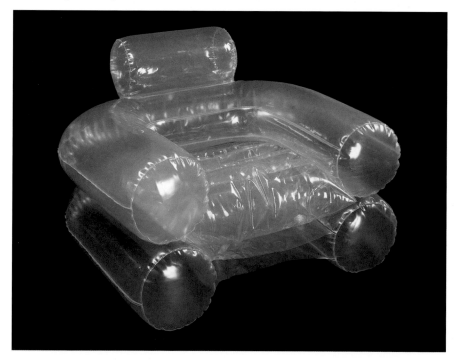

Piero GILARDI

(born 1942)

Seats

I Sassi (The Rocks)
Designed 1967
Painted polyurethane foam,
mica flakes
Largest: 45.7 x 67.3 x 59.7 cm
Produced by Gufram s.r.l.,
Balangero, Italy
The Montreal Museum of
Fine Arts, D94.154.1–3,
gift of Eleanore and Charles
Stendig in memory of Eve
Brustein and Rose Stendig*

Gilardi is best known for his art works of the 1960s, especially his "Tappeti-natura" ("nature carpets") in polyurethane foam, which were shown in art galleries internationally, and his few other designs became icons. *I Sassi* was included in MoMA's landmark 1972 show of Italian design, which described him as one of the designers who do not add anything or alter our environment but give their designs "the guises of nature."[29] Although the painted surfaces of the seating provide the visual illusion of hard, heavy stone, they are actually soft and light and give under the sitter's weight.[30] According to Gilardi, "My work is a kind of tactile art. I was trying to create a fantastic nature landscape for men living among all the modern city's concrete."[31]

Studio TETRARCH

(founded 1963)

Table

Tovaglia (Tablecloth)
Designed 1969
Fiberglass-reinforced polyester
38.4 x 111.1 x 111.1 cm
Produced by Alberto Bazzani,
Bovisio-Masciago, Italy
The Montreal Museum
of Fine Arts, D94.135.1,
gift of Eleanore and Charles
Stendig in memory of Eve
Brustein and Rose Stendig*

With this rock-solid form, the chief designer of Studio Tetrarch, Enrico De Munari, sent "a friendly admonition and a lighthearted reproach to our fellow designers. The *Tablecloth* table was created as a provocative answer to the incapacity prevalent among the majority of designers of that particular period to interpret correctly the use of a new material like plastic."[32] His surrealist surprise is the substitution of the firmer plastic material for a vinyl tablecloth, reminding us of the protean nature of synthetics, which designers embraced in the 1960s.

Marvin LIPOFSKY

(born 1938)

Vase
Designed and executed 1965
Glass
25.4 x 17.1 x 16.5 cm
The Montreal Museum of Fine
Arts, D93.303.1,
gift of Jean Boucher

Vase
Designed and executed 1967
Glass
18.4 x 25.4 x 12.7 cm
The Montreal Museum of Fine
Arts, D91.391.1, gift of Lilliana and
David Simpson

With a degree in industrial design, Lipofsky was initially more interested in sculpture until he enrolled in 1962 as one of the first students in Harvey Littleton's new glassblowing course at the University of Wisconsin, Madison. This class marked the beginning of the studio glass movement in the United States. In 1964 Lipofsky founded a glass program at the University of California, Berkeley. His experimentation in glass marks the transition in his work from traditional functional objects into abstract, sculptural objects. The seeming shapelessness of these forms from among his earliest works is actually part of a balanced artistic composition. "I always felt that glass was a sensual material," he said, "and I tried to use it in that way. I liked the excitement of 'doing it,' not so much conceptualizing things beforehand, but using the material at the instant of its forming, using it instantly and capturing it as floating in space."[33]

Sheila HICKS

(born 1934)

Banisteriopsis
Designed and executed 1965–66
Linen, wool
Variable dimensions
The Montreal Museum of
Fine Arts, D89.102.1–47

As a painting major at Yale University School
of The Fine Arts, Hicks received a B.F.A. in 1957 and
an M.F.A. in 1959. She studied under Josef Albers
and was influenced by his Constructivist theories
of color and composition. Her thesis, guided
by George Kubler, was on ancient Andean textiles.
After a Fulbright Grant in Chile, she set up studios
in Mexico and France. Hicks was a leader in
a radical movement in the textile arts in the 1960s,
expanding fiber into sculptural works. *Banisteriopsis*
(the title is based on an Amazonian hallucinogenic
plant that produces visions in bright colors)
is composed of forty-seven modules that can
be structured to create a changing work of art.
According to Hicks, her inspiration came
from viewing stacked leeks in an open-air
market in Paris.

Gunnar Aagaard ANDERSEN

(1919–1982)

Armchair
*Portrait of My Mother's
Chesterfield Chair*
Designed 1964–65
Polyurethane foam
69.8 x 100.5 x 100.5 cm
Produced by Dansk Polyether
Industri, Frederikssund, Denmark
The Montreal Museum of
Fine Arts, D87.182.1

To create this mudpie look-alike, Andersen made a highly toxic blend of urethane and water that expands when exposed to air and then solidifies. He built up the chair by spooning and spraying layers of the liquid plastic over the previous layers of solid foam. The result questions many of the basic assumptions of design, including definitions of beauty and structure, and it stands for free expression. Its title signals the 1960s defiance of an older generation, though Andersen was in his mid-forties when he designed the chair. He made few examples, and the foam has begun to decay in all of them—a fate that could not be anticipated with the new, then-untested material.

Magdalena ABAKANOWICZ

(born 1930)

Tapestry
Abakan Biz
Designed and executed 1965
Sisal
185.5 x 180.4 x 30.5 cm
The Montreal Museum of
Fine Arts, D88.258.1,
gift of Paul Leblanc

As aggressive and expressionist in weaving as Martin Lipofsky was in glass (p. 225), Abakanowicz invented a new artistic language for her medium of fiber, which transcended the use of sisal and other fibers in new ways as a vehicle for serious artistic expression. This work, although intended to hang on a wall like a traditional tapestry, is composed of a separately woven flap and tubular protrusions from the sisal surface. Abakanowicz wrote, "Ultimately it is the total obliteration of the utilitarian function of tapestry that fascinates me. My particular aim is to create possibilities for complete communion with an object whose structure is complex and soft. Through cracks and openings I try to get the viewer to penetrate into the deepest reaches of the composition."[34] Like Lee Bontecou, she challenges definitions of sculpture as hard, figurative, and male in references, and explores forms with female sexual allusions.

Milton GLASER

(born 1929)

Poster
The Sound Is WOR-FM 98.7
Designed 1966
Offset lithograph
75.7 x 90.8 cm
The Montreal Museum
of Fine Arts, D84.191.1

Reminiscent of the Beatles, the shaggy-haired rock band depicted in this poster recalls the famed group, then at the height of their popularity. In contrast to the vibrant illustration is the simple Helvetica type for the short text identifying the New York rock radio station WOR-FM. Capturing the beat of the music, the composition reflects a poster design by Roy Lichtenstein with a radiating sunburst ground. According to design historian Philip Meggs, Glaser's work helped express and define the 1960s. His images during this period incorporated flat shapes, formed by thin contour lines, echoing the simple iconography of comic books and the dynamic of Pop art.[35]

Gunnar CYRÉN

(born 1931)

Footed glasses
Pop
Designed 1965–66
Glass
16.2 x 10.2 x 10.2 cm
20.5 x 11.5 x 11.5 cm
Produced by AB Orrefors
Glasbruk, Orrefors, Sweden
The Montreal Museum of Fine
Arts, D84.156.1, gift of Susan A.
Chalom*; D95.203.1

Although initially trained as a silversmith, Cyrén received an appointment from Orrefors in 1959, which gave him an opportunity to learn skills in glassworking on-site. Cyrén introduced brightly colored opaque glass to Orrefors, including his *Pop* goblets seen here. Although the forms look traditional at first glance, their variations indicate a new design direction: the stems are short and thick to serve as a ground for the bands of bold colors, and the bowls have straight rather than flared sides. The glasses were made in a variety of sizes and shapes, traditionally associated with drinking glasses for wine and other spirits, and with varying widths for the banding. They did not come in matching sets for conventional use, but were sold as individual art objects for display.

Beth LEVINE

(1914–2006)

Shoes

Racing Car
Designed c. 1967
Vinyl, suede,
patent leather, leather
11.3 x 22.4 x 7 cm (each)
Produced by Herbert Levine,
New York, New York, U.S.A.
The Montreal Museum of
Fine Arts, D94.168.1, gift of the
designer; D93.260.1

Drawing on high art and popular culture, 1960s fashion provided the consumer with an accessible countercultural expression that was personal. These shoes, traditional in form, based on seventeenth-century men's buckled shoes, are enlivened by the dramatic graphic design of Pop motifs associated with racing cars, applied in red to the transparent vinyl. The flame shapes extending from the heels help form the *B* in Levine's first name. Levine recounted the background of her design: "*Harper's Bazaar* wanted to do something about cars. So we did the first car shoe. . . . Shoes can be very serious, or very funny. . . . I once said, 'These are shoes that you don't need, but you want.'"[36]

Paco RABANNE

(born 1934)

Textile

Chainmail
Designed c. 1967
Plastic
101.6 x 101.6 cm
Produced by Paco
Rabanne, Paris, France
The Montreal Museum of Fine
Arts, D91.441.1, gift of Louise
and George Beylerian*

Rabanne described the revolution in the arts in the 1960s, the abandonment of traditional materials, and how he became interested in plastic and aluminum, "which had never before been used in fashion design. I laid my needle and scissors aside and took up pliers and blowtorch."[37] Spanish by birth, Rabanne and his family moved to France when the Civil War began, and he later started his career in fashion by creating bold, plastic jewelry and buttons, which he sold to Givenchy, Dior, and Balenciaga. He started his own fashion house in 1966, using unconventional materials in dramatic designs such as *Chainmail,* more as bold Pop art than functional wear. The dazzling gleam of this linked design evokes the astonishing fashion of that decade. Rabanne's designs for films, especially his costume for Jane Fonda in the 1968 film *Barbarella,* added to his fame.

ABOVE, LEFT Paco Rabanne, *Paco Plastic*, dress made up of linked plastic squares, April 1967.

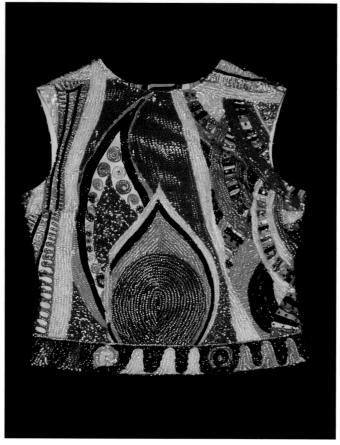

Emilio PUCCI

(1914–1992)

Bodice
Designed 1965
Silk, sequins, rhinestones
50.9 x 47 cm
Produced by Emilio Pucci,
Florence, Italy,
for Saks Fifth Avenue,
New York, New York, U.S.A.
The Montreal Museum
of Fine Arts, D91.381.1

"If I wanted to look and feel terrific, I always wore a Pucci," said Helen Gurley Brown, one of the fashion tastemakers of the 1960s. "They were sexy and in good taste at the same time."[38] Born into Florentine nobility, Pucci pursued several careers before turning to fashion in 1948. His colorful, abstract, stylized swirls reflected the exuberance of the 1960s, with economic prosperity and a young audience excited by the Beatles and Peter Max graphics. Such a garment could be worn with a contrasting simple satin skirt, as demonstrated by a Pucci model in 1962.[39] Sequins and rhinestones add a glittering glamour to the energetic patterns, which are very different on each panel.

Peter MAX

(born 1937)

Poster

Penney's Rainbow Lane
Designed 1967
Offset lithograph
91.3 x 61 cm
Produced by Peter Max
Enterprises, New York,
New York, U.S.A.
The Montreal Museum of Fine
Arts, D91.229.1, gift of Miljenko
and Lucia Horvat

Max began formal art studies at the Art Students League in New York in 1956, and in 1962 he established a small art studio. *Penney's Rainbow Lane* has some aspects of the psychedelic poster movement of the late 1960s, where "the art nouveau aspects of psychedelic art were combined with more accessible images and softer colors."[40] A rainbow dominates this Pop composition with multicolored centered typefaces and marbleized planets floating in the background. The title is derived from the Beatles' song "Penny Lane," released earlier the same year, and the poster appears to be selling Quant fashions, perhaps at a JC Penney store.

Pavel HLAVA

(1924–2003)

Vase
Designed and executed 1966
Glass
43.9 x 25.7 x 12.3 cm
The Montreal Museum of
Fine Arts, 2002.341

Pavel Hlava was among the first generation of new glass artists to emerge at mid-century in Czechoslovakia, and his work helped establish his country's primacy in avant-garde glass. This vase is an impressive early example of his art—large, colorful, and boldly worked. Although the flask form is conventional, its random spills of strongly colored glass reveal an Abstract Expressionist embrace of process and chance like a painting by Jackson Pollock. Traditional technical control was exchanged for expressive brio. The provenance of this piece is interesting: it remained with the artist until he gave it to the visiting American dealers and glass historians Ray and Lee Grover for their 1975 publication, one of the first studies of the then-new phenomenon of studio glass.[41]

Frances WHITNEY

(1912–2005)

Light fixture
Designed c. 1965
Glass, chromium-plated steel
25.5 x 88.9 x 88.9 cm
The Stewart Program for Modern
Design, 2009.10, gift of Anne and
Louis Rorimer in memory of their
mother, Katherine S. Rorimer

Trained in fashion, sculpture, and jewelry, Frances Whitney became known in the mid-1950s for her "millinery mobiles"—amusing sculptural hats influenced by the mobiles of her friend and mentor Alexander Calder.[42] Her work as an artist also included creating light sculpture from the 1960s through 2002. This light fixture, patented as an "Electroluminscent Lamp," is a flexible, removable, luminous tape sandwiched between glass leaves, to create a flowerlike form.[43] This fixture was not put into production but was a unique example commissioned for the New York apartment of Mr. and Mrs. James J. Rorimer. The fixture serves for radiant light and also as a light sculpture, evoking the neon art of the 1960s.

Alexander GIRARD

(1907–1993)

Textiles
Small Squares, Diamonds, and
Barber Pole
Designed 1964
Silkscreen-printed linen
and canvas
83.3 x 62.2 cm each
Produced by Herman Miller Inc.,
Zeeland, Michigan, U.S.A.
The Montreal Museum of Fine
Arts, D84.102.1, D84.110.1,
and D84.113.1, gift of
Herman Miller, Inc.

Girard was skilled in all aspects of interior, furniture, graphic, and industrial design, and his textiles are notable for their color and playful air. The three textiles here, intended for drapery or upholstery, reflect his sense of geometric design and harmonious colors in striking patterns. Girard once said of his theory for textile patterns, "In draped fabrics, since all pattern is distorted by the folds, I have tried [for] . . . strict avoidance of any representational forms."[44] In 1932, Girard opened an office in New York and in 1952 became the design director of Herman Miller's textile division. These three designs are among a collection of Girard textiles produced by Herman Miller in the 1950s and '60s.

Eddie SQUIRES

(1940–1995)

Textile
Archway
Designed 1968
Printed cotton
91.5 x 125.8 cm
Printed by Stead McAlpin & Co.,
Ltd., Carlisle, England, for Warner
& Sons Ltd., London, England
The Montreal Museum
of Fine Arts, D90.142.1,
gift of the designer

The radiating geometric forms printed on this textile are reminiscent of Art Deco patterns. According to Squires, this design was inspired by 1930s movie theaters and the artist Roy Lichtenstein.[45] The repeated starburst motifs suggest the elaborately decorated theaters of that period. Revived interest in Art Deco became more prominent in the 1960s, culminating in the landmark exhibition curated by English historian Bevis Hillier that gave Art Deco its name.[46] Squires joined Warner's design studio in 1963, and became its chief designer of printed textiles in 1971. By 1984 he was directing the firm, continuing Warner's tradition of superb craftsmanship and innovative designs.

Pierre CARDIN

(born 1922)

Textile
Environnement (Surroundings)
Designed c. 1969
Printed linen
370 x 137 cm
Produced for P. Kaufmann, Inc.,
New York, New York, U.S.A.
The Montreal Museum
of Fine Arts, 2005.126

After working for several Parisian fashion designers, Cardin established his own firm in 1950. From the 1960s on, he expanded his business to include furniture, textiles, and other goods, which were often hard-edged futuristic designs with geometric patterns and bright colors, influenced by abstract and Pop art.[47] The large geometric motif of this print reflects Cardin's fashion designs of the time, which ignored the female form and related to Supergraphics. Similar ideas can be found in the 1960s work of Archizoom, the Italian "Anti-Design" group,[48] and the reverberatory quality of the vertical color areas in this fabric shaded from dark blue to lavender to pink bears a relationship to Op art.

1970
1979

Pluralism and Responsibility

The 1970s opened with a memorable event, repeated annually ever since: on April 22, 1970, millions of concerned citizens in America gathered to celebrate "Earth Day" and to demand protection for Mother Nature. Industry, it was widely recognized, was poisoning its supposed beneficiaries, and fouled air and water and ever-growing dumps of obsolete products and dangerous wastes were no longer acceptable tradeoffs for abundant consumer choices and cheap energy. That same year the United States Environmental Protection Agency was created to regulate pollutants, and two years later a multinational conference in Stockholm developed programs to address environmental issues on an international scale. Across Europe and North America, new laws banned certain pesticides, required more stringent controls over auto fuel emissions, and taxed some consumer goods, like beverage bottles, to try to alter the individual's behavior toward throwaways and their damage. A few North American and European cities increased subsidies for rail and subway systems to lure commuters from their cars. By the mid-1970s, the annual celebration of Earth Day was gradually going global, and the Green Party, focused on ecological issues, was a significant voice in German politics.

Now taking center stage was the social concern nascent among some designers of the 1960s for mass production that inflicted little or no damage on the environment, and for the special needs of the disabled, the elderly, and citizens of Third World countries. Powerfully shaped by Victor Papenek's *Design for the Real World: Human Ecology and Social Change*, 1971, "Design for Need" was the theme of a 1976 conference in London, called by the International Council of Societies of Industrial Design (ICSID).

Plastics were a barometer of the consciousness-raising. In the 1960s synthetics were the affordable darling of designers who saw their potential for marrying high technology and style. But plastics are derived from coal, natural gas, and oil, and from 1973 forward their prices rocketed. In retribution for the support of Israel in the Arab-Israeli conflict, the Arab oil-producing nations embargoed oil to the United States, Western Europe, and Japan, and it quadrupled in cost between 1974 and 1979. Obviously, the supply of fossil fuels was finite, and it was substantially controlled by sometimes hostile powers. A line of plastic chairs no longer came cheap. Furthermore, plastics are virtually indestructible, adding to toxic waste heaps wherever they are discarded. Even before their damage to the environment was fully understood, some designers began to use plastics with greater deliberation, employing far less of them or molding them in objects with multiple uses and maximum efficiency.[1]

Joe Colombo's *Total Furnishing Unit*, for example, compresses a home's services and amenities into a sixteen-by-sixteen-foot plastic cube with all necessary appliances built in (fig. 1). On one side is a galley-style kitchen; on another is the living room—bedroom, with sleek trundle beds that roll under the storage and entertainment wall (note the TV) when not in use. Colombo wrote: "The space within this unit should be dynamic; that is, it should be in a constant state of transformation, so that a cubic space smaller than the conventional norm can nevertheless be exploited to the maximum."[2] His design was one of several commissioned by The Museum of Modern Art for its 1972 exhibition, *Italy: The New Domestic Landscape*. It united young Italian designers like Colombo, who saw design as immediate and practical problem-solving, with those who wanted to create social and environmental change through their involvement in social, political, and philosophical issues.

Representing the latter was the "Anti-Design" group formed in 1966 called Archizoom, whose 1970 exhibition, *No-Stop City*, had imagined communal living structures modeled on the factory and supermarket, organized as continuous open spaces (fig. 2). In these open, loft-like interiors, the people who lived there would have the freedom to place their stoves, beds, and motorbikes wherever they pleased, supplanting the fixed structures of kitchen, bedroom, and garage. The phrase "residential lots" described how interior space could be divided into rental units much like parking lots for cars.[3] "Anti-Designers" were more committed to opposing excessive consumption and planned obsolescence than to actually creating places and products, and so they were natural allies of ecologists and preservationists.

In the United States, architect Frank Gehry made seating from corrugated cardboard, a cheap packing material (p. 251). Although the environment was not Gehry's initial inspiration, James Hennessey and Victor Papanek recommended his reasonably priced works to do-it-yourself craftspeople in *Nomadic Furniture*, 1973, writing that they embodied "a concept of lamination from which you might develop your own design ideas."[4] Some companies were as practical as these critics: the German Blue Angel label was introduced in 1978 to designate products meeting specific environmental standards, and some firms in Great Britain, Canada, and Japan followed its example.

Passionate theories also flourished and a few visionary proposals for entire communities were realized. Some argued that unplanned suburban growth was an enemy of nature, and that only dense centers of population could protect the natural environment from being taken over; others insisted that the automobile was the true culprit and that only public transportation systems could prevent the pollution of the earth. Probably Paolo Soleri's design schemes attracted the most attention: the Italian-born architect applied his ideas about "arcology" (architecture and ecology) to the development of sixty acres near Phoenix, Arizona, which he called "Arcosanti" (fig. 3). His goal was to avoid suburban sprawl and the need for automobiles, and so he set aside most of the land for agriculture and recreation, condensing into a few multi-storied structures the places where people lived and worked. Solar power provided energy; greenhouses doubled as sources for food and heat. Arcosanti survived, and continues to be a destination for environmentalists.

Alerted to the natural world's need for protection, designers also recognized that the built environment was at risk. Important buildings, created by talented architects or heavy with history, were being demolished in cities across the globe. After the

1 Joe Colombo with collaborator Ignazia Favata, total furnishing unit commissioned for *Italy: The New Domestic Landscape*, 1972.
2 Paolo Soleri, *Arcosanti,* viewed from the South Mesa, Mayer, Arizona, 1970.
3 Archizoom Associati, *No-Stop City,* internal landscapes, 1970.

4 Carlo Scarpa, entrance to
Architectural Faculty Building,
Venice University, 1972.

Paris landmarks of Les Halles and the Gare Montparnasse were destroyed, and after nearly losing the Marché Saint Germain, the French government claimed protection for important monuments, offering financial and professional support for historic preservation. In New York City, the 1966 demolition of Pennsylvania Station galvanized citizens to protect other city landmarks. Similarly, the Japanese were mobilized by the destruction of Frank Lloyd Wright's Imperial Hotel in Tokyo in 1967. In Canada's Quebec province, a preservation group was organized in reaction to the 1973 razing of the Van Horne house in Montreal. Throughout the 1970s, privately funded organizations devoted to historic preservation grew more sizable, visible, vocal, and effective. At the end of the decade and through the 1980s, Postmodern designers would look to the past for inspiration and share some of the ideals of the preservation movement.

Efforts to design new buildings to harmonize with historic settings, and to adapt old buildings for contemporary needs, were further aspects of this new retrospection. The British architectural critic and historian Charles Jencks, who was the first to define Postmodernism in architecture, advocated reviving, rather than supplanting, past styles and urged preservationists to embrace many historic languages. He persuasively argued that preserving the architectural resources of the past was socially, ecologically, and aesthetically desirable: "[Postmodernists] claim positively that their buildings are rooted in place and history, unlike the abstract buildings of their immediate predecessors and competitors, and that they bring back the full repertoire of architectural expression: ornament, symbolism, humor, and urban context, to mention a few of their restorations."[5] Based in Venice, Carlo Scarpa was one of the most creative yet tactful of these preservationist designers. His additions to the entrance of the Architectural Faculty Building at Venice University are typical (fig. 4): they visibly coexist with the old building and establish a dialogue between carefully crafted traditional and new materials—dressed stone and poured concrete—and between the interlocking forms. Scarpa's many renovations of public interiors all demonstrate this respect for the past and continuity with it.

The foregoing images (figs. 1–4) could all be called designs with a conscience, but in the plethora of ideas and objects in the 1970s there was no dominant style. Furthermore, not every designer, or consumer, wanted significant change. Pop-flavored designs using plastics were still manufactured, especially between 1970 and 1973 (pp. 282, 290), before the effects of the oil embargo were felt in double-digit inflation and zero growth in the annual GNP. The casual, youth-oriented lifestyle of the 1960s continued, and was reflected in low-slung furniture for lounging (p. 275). Some notable designs were intended for the luxury market, employing costly materials or fabrication methods (p. 265), and designers such as Mario Bellini ignored trends they considered extremist and argued that the results of 1960s radicalism—in politics and design—were ambiguous at best.

Most important was the recognition that design could be its creator's compelling personal expression, and that designs themselves were meaningful cultural symbols. In Japan, where Western and especially Italian design were shaping aesthetics and means of production, the ICSID met in 1973 (designated "Design Year" in that country) and titled its conference theme "The Soul and Material Things." The message was that the participant design organizations "understood that the industrial society in which objects were measured in quantity and size was changing into a society that questions their communicative values."[6] In other words, personal and cultural expression mattered in design and should be appraised. Such Japanese designers as Shiro Kuramata created both traditional furniture types and expressive furnishings that challenged convention (pp. 260, 270–71). With similar simplification, the Italian Vico Magistretti designed the *Atollo* lamp (p. 259) from the Platonic shapes of cone, cylinder, and hemisphere, creating a poised sculptural juxtaposition. These designers were taking modernist abstraction to extremes, evoking the Spartan conceptions of earlier and contemporary Minimalist artists.

As Minimalists, the American Donald Judd and his colleague artists were touchstones, especially to Kuramata, who followed vanguard Western art and knew the furniture that Judd crafted in the idiom of his sculpture (fig. 5). Judd's elemental structures, initially carpentered and then industrially produced, were first exhibited in the early 1960s with similar geometric works by artists such as Robert Morris and Sol LeWitt; their constructions, often of repeated simple forms, were variously termed "primary structures" or "ABC art" for their refusal of illusion, symbolism, conventional scale, even pedestals. "The austerity of materials and simple, mass-manufactured forms of his 'specific objects' were necessary, according to Judd's thinking, to make viewers conscious of why and how one sees," observed a later critic.[7] "Judd insisted that the materials he used and their surfaces be read as 'themselves,' and not act as illusions of some material or somehow convey metaphoric meanings."[8] With these sculptors, generally sympathetic abstract painters like Yves Klein, Robert Ryman, and Agnes Martin helped compose Minimalism as an art movement. Their reductivist attention to perception—*how* we see materials and a gestalt of forms, rather than *what* they compose and stand for—led to a new literalism in advanced art and connected art and design. Judd's example in furniture-making also gave fresh encouragement to the tradition of artists designing useful items.

Related to Minimalist sculptors' frank displays of materials and industrial production methods were designs labeled "high-tech" in 1978 by *The New York Times* editors Joan Kron and Suzanne Slesin.[9] The persistent fascination with machines, which had been such a significant aspect of avant-garde thinking in the 1910s and '20s, here enjoyed a new burst of energy, and the phenomenon could be seen in designs from architecture to appliances. Among the most visible and influential of new high-tech buildings was the Centre Georges Pompidou in Paris, 1971–77, by Renzo Piano and Richard Rogers, a modern art museum that openly displayed its mechanical systems and services. Homes and offices began to bristle with metal and glass fixtures and furnishings that were aggressively industrial; such designers as Masayuki Kurokawa and Richard Sapper made desk lamps that were to be admired specifically for their efficiency. These high-tech designs bore no resemblance to streamlined prewar objects, nor the "black box" Braun company products by Dieter Rams that dominated postwar German manufacture. Gijs Bakker's *Paraplulamp* (pp. 278–79) marries a plain flood-lamp bulb to a shade derived from a photographer's reflector umbrella, and a zipper becomes a necklace by Frans van Nieuwenborg and Martijn Wegman (p. 281). The animating feature of such works is honesty, while aesthetic appeal is an unexpected bonus. The viewer recognizes the efficient adaptation of existing objects and admires the ideas.

Far from this abstemious tendency was the work of the Italian group Studio Alchimia, which helped pave the way for Postmodernism in Italy. Alchemy (*alchimia* in Italian) is the ancient effort to turn base metals into gold, a provocative name for young designers eager to turn common consumer objects into objects of delight and

5 Donald Judd, desk, 1977, in his studio in Marfa, Texas.

sometimes good-humored mockery. Founded in 1976 in Milan, the group exhibited works in 1979—under the tongue-in-cheek title *Bau.Haus*—in a hodgepodge of styles: polka-dotted bourgeois armchairs and Cubist sofas, for example. Alchimia's founders, Alessandro and Adriana Guerriero, chief theorist Alessandro Mendini, and members Andrea Branzi and Ettore Sottsass, went further than the designers of the 1960s who adopted Pop idioms: they linked high and mass culture and also revived, with great élan, discredited and ignored older styles. Most of these provocative designers would become design celebrities in the 1980s.

In sum, "Good Design" ceded to "Design for Need" in the 1970s, yet the giant baseball mitt *Joe* chair and the ergonomic *Balans* chair (pp. 284–85, 291) both went into production. Modernism was now comfortably into middle age, like The Museum of Modern Art celebrating its fiftieth anniversary in 1979. The forms that were fun in the 1960s continued, and in the 1980s would find new and more exuberant life.

5

Scott BURTON

(1939–1989)

Textile

Fabric for Window Curtains
Designed 1978
Printed cotton
277.2 x 107.7 cm
Produced by The Fabric
Workshop, Philadelphia,
Pennsylvania, U.S.A.
The Montreal Museum of
Fine Arts, D85.101.1

Burton emerged in the early 1970s with performance art, sometimes using furniture found in the street, and has made a mark with his public sculpture that functions as seating. This cotton print shares the aesthetics of art by minimalist colleagues such as Donald Judd, who also adapted his repetitive geometrics to furnishings from the '70s on. Somewhat romantically, Burton described his textile for The Fabric Workshop as evoking "the pattern of window mullions against the dark blue of the night's sky."[10] Interested in furniture and design from an early age, he studied literature at Columbia, graduating in 1962, and in the mid-1960s he worked as a freelance critic for *Art News*.

Frank O. GEHRY

(born 1929)

Armchair and ottoman
Experimental Edges: Little Beaver
Designed 1979
Corrugated cardboard
Armchair: 86.3 x 85.6 x 104.1 cm
Ottoman: 43.2 x 49.5 x 55.9 cm
Produced by New City Editions,
Venice, California, U.S.A., and by
Vitra GmbH, Basel, Switzerland
The Montreal Museum of Fine
Arts, D92.132.1–2

In the early years of his architectural career, Gehry designed two series of innovative furniture in cardboard—*Easy Edges*, introduced in 1972, and *Experimental Edges,* begun in 1979, of which this armchair and ottoman are a part. Whereas the first series was strongly linear, the second series, also echoing Gehry's evolving architectural aesthetic, was irregular, with varied thicknesses, and sturdy yet humorous. *Little Beaver* reflects his curiosity about the artistic potential of common industrial materials—and, with its shaggy edges, looks rather like it has been nibbled by a beaver. Its form is traditional, reminiscent of easy chairs of the 1930s, but the material and surface are obviously unconventional. According to Gehry, "I got interested in paper furniture when I was designing for department stores and had to invent display furniture that nobody really had to sit on, and then could be easily disposed of."[11] Although the *Experimental Edges* series was designed between 1979 and 1982, the furniture was not produced commercially until New City Editions was formed in 1986 for this purpose.[12]

Dale CHIHULY

(born 1941)

Goblet
Designed and executed 1971
Glass
29.2 x 15.2 x 10.1 cm
The Montreal Museum of Fine
Arts, D91.393.1, gift of Lilliana and
David Simpson

Chihuly graduated in 1967 with a degree in interior design from the University of Washington, his native state. He went on to receive a degree in sculpture from the University of Wisconsin-Madison, where he studied under the glassmaker Harvey Littleton. These diverse studies are reflected in his remarkable glassmaking career, as he moved from blowing individual pieces of functional sculpture, such as this eccentric goblet, to designing environmentally scaled works of glass, some as lighting, some for landscape installation, that he directed others to execute (owing in part to physical disabilities he suffered in the late 1970s). In the 1970s, the shapes Chihuly created were either quite restrained cylindrical forms or "completely crazy."[13] A rare example of his early work, this vessel can be used for drinking, but the comic sculpture—resembling a hybrid of plant and lobster on two cartoon legs—is hard to hold.

Flavio BARBINI

(born 1948)

Vase
Designed c. 1970
Glass
25.4 x 10.8 x 8.6 cm
Produced by Vetreria Alfredo
Barbini, Murano, Italy
The Montreal Museum of Fine
Arts, D84.160.1a–b,
gift of Susan Chalom*

Descended from the famous family of Murano glassmakers, Flavio is the son of Alfredo Barbini, who was also a distinguished glass designer. Flavio was trained in Venice at the Institute of Art and the Academy of Fine Arts. He has since worked at the Barbini glassworks as designer and art director. This sectional work is part of a series of geometric vases: "They are all geometric forms—superimposed, fixed, or mobile," Barbini wrote. "They have many positions; they are not static. This one is composed of two pieces, two pieces that lock together and share a single axis. The position of these two pieces in the rotation allows for different positions, constantly changing the look. It is like the tail of a peacock—it can be open or closed . . . like a zipper or a door or a hinge."[14] If one of the two pieces is flipped upside down, they can be fitted together to form a single rectangular sculpture, clear at the sides and opaque white down the center.

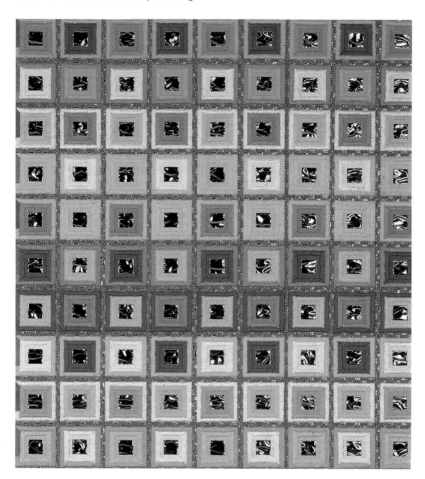

Jack Lenor LARSEN

(born 1927)

Textile

Magnum
Designed 1970
Mylar, cotton, vinyl,
nylon, polyester
136.5 x 140.7 cm
Produced by Jack Lenor Larsen,
Incorporated, New York,
New York, U.S.A.
The Montreal Museum of Fine
Arts, D86.110.1, gift of the designer

In many of his textiles, Larsen combines aspects of far-flung cultural traditions with new production technology. In *Magnum*, he created a vibrant pattern of colored yarns and mirror-bright Mylar, using the machine process to mimic handicraft work. According to Larsen, the fabric was "originally designed as a theater curtain for the Phoenix, Arizona, Opera House in colors reflecting Southwest Native American traditions, [and] the starting place was the mirrored cloths of India attached with stitches. . . . The square came from Hopi patterning." Though Larsen designed successful floral prints, he is best known for his weavings. "I feel geometric patterns are as old as time. . . . Their inherent sense of structure is the more welcome now when most spaces are without a sense of structure, and more adhesive than cohesive."[15] This design also suggests the 1960s in its use of Mylar and its apparent inspiration from the work of Victor Vasarely, seen, for example, in his 1963 collage in MoMA's influential Op art exhibition, *The Responsive Eye*.[16]

Paul RAND

(1914–1996)

Poster
Eye Bee M
Designed 1970
Offset lithograph
91.4 x 60.9 cm
Produced by Mossberg & Co.,
South Bend, Indiana,
for International Business
Machines Corporation (IBM),
New York, New York, U.S.A.
The Montreal Museum of Fine
Arts, D87.145.1, gift of the designer

Rand began his career in commercial art in the 1930s, and applied the aesthetic principles of the Bauhaus and avant-garde European art to American advertising and editorial design. He is best known for his outstanding work in corporate and product identification, notably for IBM—International Business Machines. In the 1970s, Rand updated the logo he had designed in the 1950s by introducing stripes, thus unifying the three letter forms.[17] Here he plays with the striped, slab-serif logo, demonstrating his use of visual puns to amuse viewers, in this case company employees: the poster was for an IBM in-house presentation of the Golden Circle award. Of the simple, humorous IBM poster, he wrote: "Of the twenty-six letters of the alphabet, the letters 'B' and 'I' [homonyms of 'bee' and 'eye' in English] are clearly the most graphic and the least subject to misinterpretation. The rebus is a mnemonic device, a kind of game designed to engage the reader and, incidentally, lots of fun."[18]

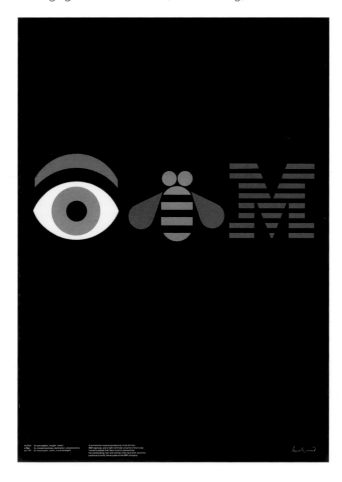

Gaetano PESCE

(born 1939)

Armchair and ottoman
Sit-Down
Designed 1975
Polyurethane foam, plywood,
Dacron upholstery
Armchair: 73 x 114 x 88 cm
Ottoman: 52 x 73 x 73 cm
Produced by Cassina S.p.A.,
Meda, Milano, Italy
The Montreal Museum of Fine
Arts, D89.187.1—2,
gift of Paul Pelletier

Sit-Down represents Pesce's rebellion against the uniform appearance of functional mass-produced objects, though he uses new materials and mass production to make this seating, of which no two examples are the same. The camouflage-like upholstery was lined with polyester, hung like sacks over the plywood frame of the chair, and filled with polyurethane foam. The foam expanded to fill the fabric and conformed to its limits and the frame, creating the permanent form. As described by the critic France Vanlaethem, "With this technique, each armchair comes out with a similar, but not identical, shape. The differences are accentuated by the mottled print of the fabric."[19] The armchair and ottoman are very comfortable, and reminiscent of both nineteenth-century overstuffed furniture and Claes Oldenburg's soft Pop sculpture, which Pesce admired.

Mario BELLINI

(born 1935)

Floor lamp, table lamp, and wall or ceiling lamp
Area 50
Designed 1974
Iron, Makrolon, fiberglass
Floor lamp: 160 x 44.5 x 44.5 cm
Table lamp: 50 x 44.5 x 44.5 cm
Wall/ceiling lamp:
20 x 44.5 x 44.5 cm
Produced by Artemide S.p.A.,
Pregnana Milanese, Italy
The Montreal Museum of Fine
Arts, D91.368.1a–d and D91.369.1,
gift of Artemide S.p.A.; D93.252.1,
gift of Bernard François Marcil

Bellini is interested in the built environment as a whole, but especially in industrial designs. Although best known as the chief consultant for Olivetti, he has also designed for other Italian companies, including Artemide. These minimalist lamps are both elegant and functional. Available in multiple heights for various installations, they can be used together to create a harmonious ensemble. The white shades, made of squares of fire-resistant synthetic material, resemble folded paper or falling handkerchiefs and have an ethereal, floating appearance. They represent a sculptural minimalism, appealing in their sensuousness, and are inspired by Japanese lighting in rice paper.

Andrea BRANZI

(born 1938)

Prototype tea and coffee set
Designed and executed 1974
Enameled acrylic, enameled wood
Teapot: 24.5 x 37.7 x 12.6 cm
The Montreal Museum of Fine Arts, D91.387.1–3, gift of the designer

Branzi's unorthodox, intellectual approach is reflected in the range of his designs, including this tea and coffee set, with its slanted forms and surprising shapes. He described this set: "This is the theoretical model of a group of objects that stand apart from visual rules, that is, they look asymmetrical."[20] Branzi is playing with the architect's drawing of buildings in two-point perspective. A founding member in 1966 of Archizoom, the Italian Anti-Design collaborative, he challenged conventional ideas about architecture, industrial design, and urban planning, in both his theoretical writings and his realized work.

Vico MAGISTRETTI

(1920–2006)

Table lamp
Atollo
Designed 1977
Lacquered aluminum
68 x 49.5 x 49.5 cm
Produced by O-Luce, Milan, Italy
The Montreal Museum of Fine
Arts, D99.157.1

Magistretti's skills as a draftsman—required of him during his architectural training—
are on view in this precise combination of cone, cylinder, and half sphere. That
they combine to form a functional table lamp seems almost superfluous, so perfect
are the proportions and the seeming suspension of the shade in air, though it is
supported by a thick hidden aluminum rod. It projects the light onto the conical
section of the base, allowing illumination to dramatize the composition further.
The lacquering of everything in beige accents the differences between the forms
and reflects a growing restraint in 1970s designs. The monochrome also assured
the lamp's adaptability to diverse interiors.

Shiro KURAMATA

(1934–1991)

Chests of drawers
Side 1 and *Side 2*
Designed 1970
Ebonized and lacquered ash,
brushed steel
Side 1: 170 x 44.7 x 60.5 cm
Side 2: 170 x 63 x 49.7 cm
Produced by Fujiko, Tokyo,
Japan, and by Cappellini
International Interiors, Arosio, Italy
The Montreal Museum of
Fine Arts, D91.414.1–2a–s

These curvilinear chests are a contemporary version of the high chest of drawers traditional in the Western world, often conceived in pairs. Tall and narrow, curving as if in movement or reflected in a funhouse mirror, the chests appear to fit together. Usually a ponderous form, these seem to float on their recessed, traditional castors, which allow them to be moved as needed. Kuramata was fascinated with such assemblies: with thirty-six drawers altogether, the pair offers ample space for precious objects and can serve as a space divider. The double curve distorts the conventional form more for play than function. With such a whimsical approach to design, Kuramata would readily join Ettore Sottsass's Memphis group in the 1980s.

Sergio ASTI

(born 1926)

Vase
Ruota (Wheel)
Designed 1972
Glazed earthenware
38.1 x 40.6 x 11.4 cm
Produced by Cedit, Lurago
d'Erba, Italy, for Knoll
International, New York,
New York, U.S.A.
The Montreal Museum of Fine
Arts, D92.134.1, anonymous gift

Asti studied art and architecture in Milan from 1947 to 1953, the year he opened his first studio. Like many Italian architects who lacked building commissions in the postwar period, Asti turned to designing interiors, furniture, and accessories. His surprising vase design with its wedge-shaped opening cut out of a wheel form is strongly graphic yet also functional. According to the designer, he sought "surprise, curiosity . . . the reference to other shapes, the sense of metaphor, the meaning of chakra in Hindu thought. . . . We share the belief that adding fantasy, ornament and emotional involvement (raga=strong emotion) to what we make (especially when they are objects close to us), beyond pure function, beyond a rational critical analysis (on the borders of a scientific approach proper to laboratories), carries a conspicuous weight, today as well as it did yesterday."[21]

Vico MAGISTRETTI

(1920–2006)

Armchair
Vicario (Vicar)
Designed 1970
Fiberglass-reinforced polyester
68.5 x 71.1 x 65 cm
Produced by Artemide S.p.A.,
Pregnana Milanese, Italy
The Montreal Museum of
Fine Arts, D91.379.1,
gift of Artemide Ltée

One of the leading Italian designers of the postwar period, Magistretti graduated from the Politecnico in Milan in 1945. Although he worked as an architect, he is best known for his furniture and lighting designs. He was not the first to create a single-molded plastic chair, but his *Vicario* is one of the most elegant and beautifully detailed. Fluid lines unite all parts of this design—the seat, back, arms, and legs—which form a single piece in the molding process and thus enhance cost-savings and efficiency in production. The grooving of the legs reduces the weight of the chair where previous designers achieved strength only through thickness.[22]

Cesare (Joe) COLOMBO

(1930–1971)

Bar stool
Birillo (Bowling Pin)
Designed 1970
Chromium-plated steel, fiberglass,
rubber, polyurethane foam,
vinyl upholstery
96.5 x 43.2 x 49.2 cm
Produced by Zanotta S.p.A.,
Nova Milanese, Italy
The Montreal Museum of
Fine Arts, D92.159.1,
gift of Muriel Kallis Newman*

Birillo's shapes have the cartoonish quality of Pop art, suggesting Colombo's background as an artist. The tiny disc for the back contrasts with the large squares of the seat, footrest, and base, creating a comic figure as well as an abstract sculpture. Not only witty, the stool is also functional, with a cross-shaped molding on the base concealing fully rotating wheels, which allow the chair to be easily moved. Once weighed down by a sitter, the rubber around the base grips the floor and the stool becomes stationary, a principal key to the success of the "kick stool" used in many kitchens. The seat also rotates on its columnar support with an automatic return. The vinyl upholstery and chromium-plated metal add attractive sheen. This example was used in the residence of famed Chicago art collector Muriel Newman, whose collection of abstract painting was complemented by contemporary design.[23]

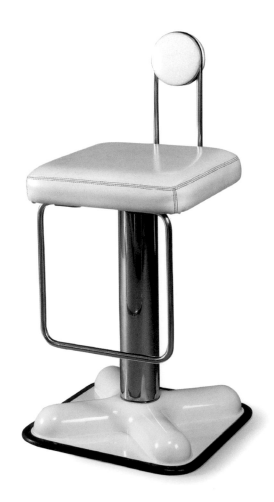

Lella VIGNELLI
Massimo VIGNELLI

(born 1934) and **(born 1931)**

Bar tools
Designed c. 1972
Silver
Stirrer: 24 x 1.5 cm
Produced by San Lorenzo,
Milan, Italy
Stewart Program for Modern
Design, L2010.12.1–4, promised
gift of Paul LeBlanc

The company that made these bar tools, San Lorenzo, was founded in 1970 and focused on producing high-quality sterling silver for architects, including Lella and Massimo Vignelli. In 1971, the year the couple established Vignelli Associates, Lella designed a carafe as part of a bar ensemble.[24] Strongly architectonic, the ensemble had contrasting textured and smooth surfaces. The following year, the Vignellis designed this set of four bar tools to accompany the ensemble. The smooth finish and elemental shaping was the same as that of the carafe's handle.[25] While some of the couple's designs for plastic dishware evoke Pop art in their bold simplification, these tools exploit the sheen, refinement, and flexibility of silver. Despite widely differing functions, the strainer, stirrer, tongs, and knife are all flat, rounded, and pierced forms—as graphic as the bold Helvetica typeface the Vignellis often used in their designs for signage.

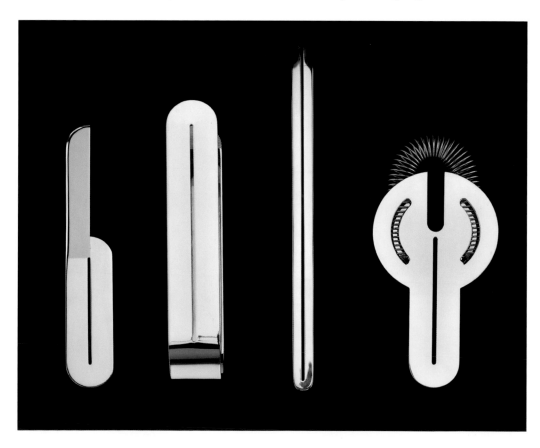

Mario BELLINI

(born 1935)

Chair
Cab
Designed 1976
Enameled steel, polyurethane
foam, leather
80 x 47 x 42 cm
Produced by Cassina S.p.A.,
Meda, Milano, Italy
The Montreal Museum of
Fine Arts, D93.254.1

As sleek as a diver's wetsuit, an innovative leather envelope is tightly fitted around the simple steel frame of this sturdy and comfortable chair. The leather upholstery of *Cab* is stitched and closed over each leg with a zipper, previously used only on slipcovers. Earlier tubular steel furniture revealed its structure on principle, emphasizing contrasting metal and upholstery, but here the leather conceals the chair's structure and softens its sharp lines and angles. *Cab* is short for *cabriolet*, an elegant one-horse carriage with a folding hood. Although a minimal design, *Cab* appeals to consumers with its luxurious material, obvious craftsmanship, and fine detail, displaying Italy's traditional skills in leatherworking.

ABOVE, LEFT Bellini, *Cab* chair, steel frame, and leather covering, 1976.

Cesare (Joe) COLOMBO

(1930–1971)

Caddy cart
Boby
Designed 1970
ABS plastic, steel
73.5 x 43.4 x 42.7 cm
Produced by Bieffeplast, Caselle
di Selvazzano, Italy
The Montreal Museum of Fine
Arts, D99.136.1a–d

Named after the dog star of a French series of children's books, this versatile cart will follow you anywhere like man's best friend on castors. Colombo's modular, multipurpose storage cabinet is designed to be assembled of different combinations of shelves and drawers stacked to several heights. Its modularity responded to postwar needs for versatile designs saving space and aiding efficient work. In this example, three tray-like drawers on one side swivel out, while the shelves below allow for open storage of large items. Visible on the other side are mid-sized shelves with higher rims—all contributing to the caddy's neatness and accessibility. Available in a variety of bright colors, this appealing design could be used in home or office, and its popularity is proven by its uninterrupted production to the present day.

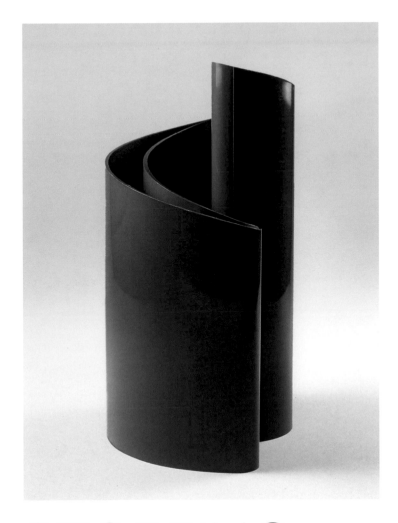

Giotto STOPPINO

(born 1926)

Vase
Deda
Designed 1971
ABS plastic
35.3 x 22.8 x 17.8 cm
Produced by Heller Designs, Italy
The Montreal Museum of
Fine Arts, D92.137.1,
gift of S. Bernard Paré

The architect and designer Stoppino created an arresting design for this vase with a streamlined silhouette and Pop colors. These hallmarks of his style attracted clients including the design firms Heller and Kartell. He said, "I have always been interested in developing the themes and investigating the specific characteristics of plastic materials and above all of injection-molded thermoplastics."[26] These plastics allowed an almost limitless range of cast forms and colors. The form of this vase for Heller—a tall, narrow vessel intended for long-stemmed flowers—is based on a spiral.

Tom PATTI

(born 1943)

Vase
Modulated Green with
Bronze and Burgundy Line
Designed and executed 1977
Glass
16.5 x 10 x 11.4 cm
The Montreal Museum of Fine
Arts, D91.392.1, gift of Lilliana
and David Simpson

Originally a painter, Patti studied at the Pratt Institute, exploring new ways to use common materials. Throughout the 1970s he experimented with the sculptural potential of glass while he pioneered techniques of fusing and laminating industrial glass. "It is integral," Patti said of his work, "to force the relationship of art and technology."[27] For example, he discovered that by blowing a bubble into a cube of plate glass squares, he could turn the cube into a sphere. He created variations on this basic technique by adding projecting elements. Here he transforms common green-tinged plate glass into a torso-like, one-of-a-kind vase. Although often architectonic, his works are surprisingly small in size, especially compared to the work of his contemporaries.[28]

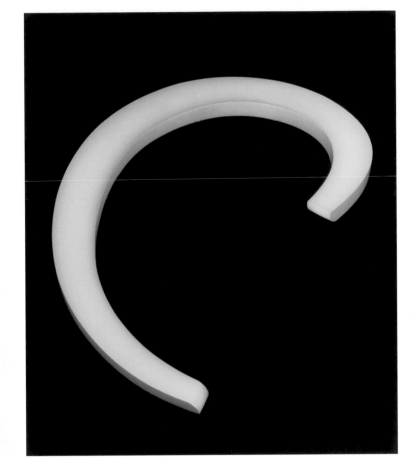

Susanna HERON

(born 1949)

Neckpiece
Neck-Curve
Designed and executed 1977
Painted acrylic
26.5 x 19 x 1.2 cm
The Montreal Museum of
Fine Arts, 2004.148

British-born, Heron studied at St. Martin's College of Art and Design in London from 1968 to 1971. She had begun making jewelry as a teenager, and in her senior year at St. Martin's she was already creating jewelry in silver and resin. In 1972 she had her first solo show in London.[29] Her use of color was unusual and can be attributed to the influence of her father, an abstract painter. She also attempted to explore the properties of materials and the effects of light, as seen here in her use of a translucent acrylic and paint. The tapering comma-like form is rectangular in section, and the opening is shaped for both easy wearing and aesthetic effect. This reductivism anticipated the art jewelry designs of the 1990s, but Heron had changed her focus to creating sculpture by 1983, giving up jewelry altogether.

ABOVE, LEFT *Susanna Heron wearing her acrylic neckpiece.*

Shiro KURAMATA

(1934–1991)

Chest of Drawers

Dinah
Designed 1970
Enameled steel, lacquered wood
175 x 60 x 50 cm
Produced by Cappellini
International Interiors, Arosio, Italy
The Montreal Museum of
Fine Arts, 2002.93.1–19

Kuramata saw the work of American minimalist artists Dan Flavin and Donald Judd in a 1967 exhibition in Tokyo, and he incorporated their reductive approach to sculpture into his design. His series of "Furniture with Drawers" multiplies its repetitive geometry and adds a refined linearity and sense of obsessiveness. He believed that "a chest of drawers is a kind of furniture that most strongly communicates with man, even psychologically . . . [with] a secrecy that is not found in a chair."[30] Kuramata's fascination with drawers and compartments is seen in his *Side 1* and *Side 2* designs (p. 252) as well as in the two views of the *Dinah* chest here. Resting on a flat black steel base, supported by rectilinear sides of the same material, *Dinah's* eighteen narrow drawers ascend like a miniature high-rise building.

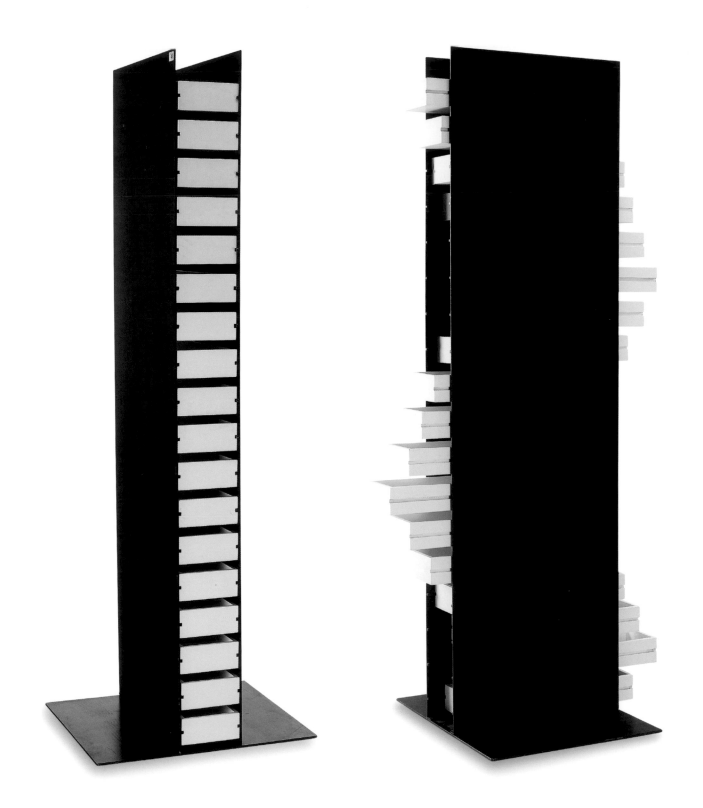

Alfredo BARBINI

(1912–2007)

Vase
Designed 1970
Glass
26.9 x 17.3 x 5.8 cm
Produced by Vetreria Alfredo
Barbini, Murano, Italy
The Montreal Museum of
Fine Arts, D84.159.1,
gift of Susan A. Chalom*

Descended from a family of Murano glassmakers, Alfredo Barbini studied at the art academy in Murano and in 1950 founded his own factory where he produced his own designs and those of others. This vase reflects his adoption of a modern sculptural idiom, paralleling the artistry of his son Flavio, who also designed for the Barbini glassworks. The slab form of this vessel is composed of three stacked concentric rectangles of ice-blue glass, each with an air bubble trapped at its center. On the side of this transparent solid form is a darker vertical, a tapering hollow spine that serves as the functional opening of the vase. Barbini's most adventurous glass between 1945 and 1970 is characterized by bold sculptural forms, with a minimum of functionalism.[31] Distinct from the decorative glass popularly associated with Murano, Barbini's minimal forms anticipated glass design of the following decades.

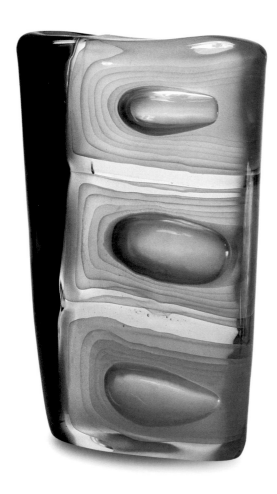

Astrid SAMPE

(born 1942)

Textile
Computer Column
Designed c. 1975
Printed cotton
223.7 x 130.8 cm
Produced by Lars Ljunaberg
Prints AB, Floda, Sweden
The Montreal Museum of Fine
Arts, D86.181.1, gift of the designer

Though the Op art aesthetics of this textile were not cutting-edge in 1975, its production was. In collaboration with Sten Kallin, an IBM programmer in Sweden, Sampe used the computer as a design tool to generate the print's closely grouped lines, symmetry, and repetition. In fact, with the IBM Plotter 1627 and Kallin's help, she was able to produce a textile collection for Lars Ljunaberg. In the same period, Sampe had aided the development of Swedish textile design by experimenting with an innovative photo print process in which photographic images were directly transferred from photographic film to the surface of a flat woven fabric. Throughout her life Sampe was known for her textile designs in abstract patterns, particularly those intended for architectural settings.[32]

Mario BELLINI

(born 1935)

Calculator
Divisumma 18
Designed 1972
ABS plastic, synthetic rubber
4.5 x 30.5 x 11.5 cm
Produced by Olivetti, Milan, Italy
The Montreal Museum of
Fine Arts, D87.185.1,
gift of Geoffrey N. Bradfield*

Bellini began to work for Olivetti as its chief industrial design consultant in 1963, following in the footsteps of Marcello Nizzoli and Ettore Sottsass. In business offices worldwide, the decade marked a turning point between reliance on mechanical devices, like adding machines, and microelectronic technology, such as this battery-powered calculator. According to MoMA curator Paola Antonelli, "Bellini was able to link the necessities of the developing electronics industry to contemporary visual culture by emphasizing tactile qualities."[33] Here Bellini molds a simple design in plastics to replace the heavier metal casing of older office machines and draws a skin of rubber taut over the keys, unifying and concealing the mechanical parts under a smooth and friendly surface.

Ana Maria NIEMEYER
Oscar NIEMEYER

(born c. 1942) and **(born 1907)**

Lounge chair and ottoman

Designed 1972
Stainless steel, aluminum,
polyurethane foam, wool
Chair: 67 x 77.5 x 104.1 cm
Ottoman: 27.9 x 76.8 x 76.8 cm
Produced by Mobilier
International, Paris, France
The Montreal Museum of
Fine Arts, D97.105.1–2

Although the architect Oscar Niemeyer is best known for designing Brasília, the capital city of Brazil, which he began to shape in the late 1950s, he also designed buildings in Europe and the United Nations in New York in 1947, using a modernist approach influenced by Le Corbusier. For many buildings he designed furniture, sometimes in collaboration with his daughter Ana Maria, as seen in this example. In 1966 Niemeyer moved to Paris and began to design furniture for Mobilier International. In this luxurious lounge chair, a single wide band of stainless steel connects the tufted cushion sections and provides resilience. The chair is very low to the ground and reflects the informal style of living that first became popular in the 1960s. The contrasts of form within this elemental seating reflect those in Niemeyer's architecture—the play of concave and convex, solid and void.

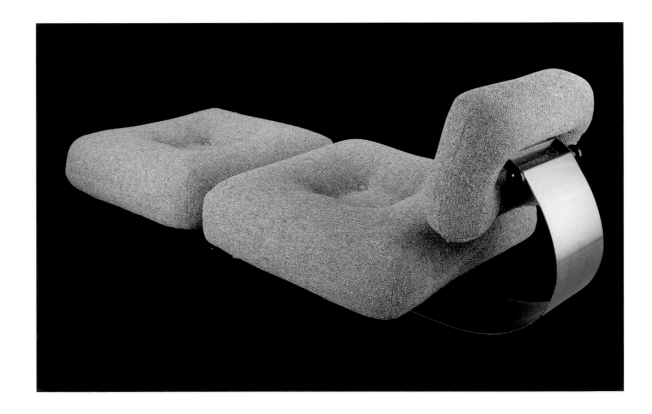

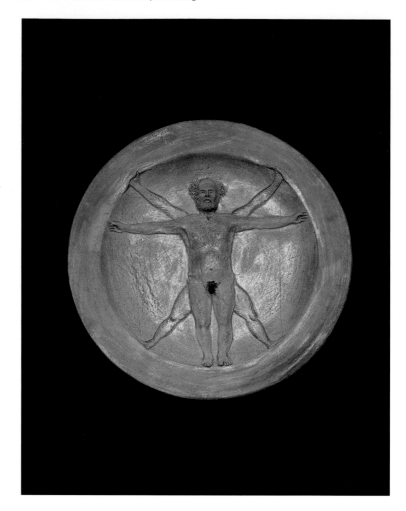

Robert ARNESON

(1930–1992)

Charger
Describing the Diameter
Designed and executed 1977
Glazed earthenware
3.8 x 47.6 x 47.6 cm
The Montreal Museum of
Fine Arts, D93.306.1,
gift of Jean Boucher

In the 1950s, California developed into a center for nontraditional ceramics, beginning with Peter Voulkos and followed in the '60s and '70s with Robert Arneson's satirical figurative work. In this charger, Arneson replaces Leonardo da Vinci's ideal male figure—his *Vitruvian Man* study drawing of c. 1485—with a depiction of himself, satirizing the idea that man is the measure of all things and the most perfect in creation.[34] Arneson himself said, "The things that I'm really interested in as an artist are the things you can't do—and that's really to mix humor and fine art. I'm not being silly about it, I'm serious about the combination. Humor is generally considered low art, but I think humor is very serious—it points out the fallacies of our existence."[35]

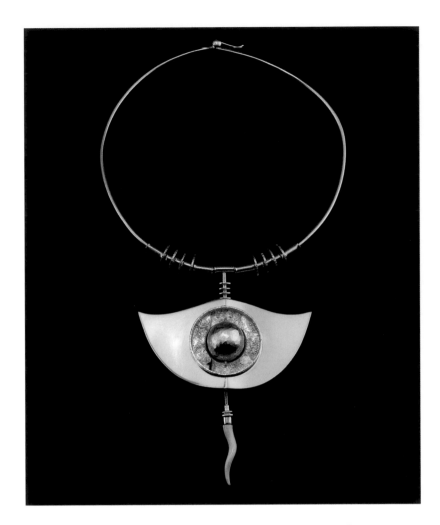

Olaf SKOOGFORS

(1930–1975)

Pendant
Designed and executed 1973
Silver, ivory
10 x 5.6 cm
The Montreal Museum of
Fine Arts, D90.224.1,
gift of Edna Sloan Beron

Skoogfors came to Philadelphia from Sweden as a small child. He studied silversmithing and jewelry making under Hans Christensen, and in 1957 he established his own studio in Philadelphia. This pendant necklace is complex in association, but it is basic in composition, made of two geometric shapes. From the circular neckpiece hangs an eye-like pendant with a forged and cast ball within a circular recess, with a talismanic ivory drop dangling at the bottom. It reflects Skoogfors's ongoing fascination with images from the first moon landing in 1969. Some of his pieces are constructivist, but he worked in a variety of styles that reflected his interest in African jewelry and traditions of primitive cultures.[36]

Gijs BAKKER

(born 1942)

Table lamp

Paraplulamp (Umbrella Lamp)
Designed 1973
Chromium-plated steel, nylon
72.4 x 22.9 x 22.9 cm
Produced by Artimeta, Heerlen,
The Netherlands
The Montreal Museum of Fine
Arts, D93.207.1, gift of Helen
Williams Drutt English in honor
of the Emmy Van Leersum
retrospective

In addition to his formal art training at the Rietveld Academy in Amsterdam, Bakker explored new concepts and techniques in jewelry. He became known primarily as a pioneer designer in jewelry, but also designed furniture and objects, such as this lamp in the form of an umbrella (*paraplu* in Dutch). The shade opens on the same principle, above an exposed floodlamp. Photographers use such shades as reflectors to reduce shadows and create ambient lighting in the studio. Bakker incorporated photographs in a series of jewelry creations, often with the same wit and irony as seen in this design. "For me the concept always is the most important," he wrote, "but then the problems start, how to solve all the details."[37] In this case, he supported the umbrella shade on five verticals rather than one so that the bulb could hang on a ring connecting them.

STUDIO 65

(founded 1965)

Chair
Attica
Designed 1972
Polyurethane,
polyurethane foam, cotton
64.4 x 70.8 x 70.8 cm
Produced by Gufram s.r.l.,
Balangero, Italy
The Montreal Museum of Fine
Arts, D94.144.1a–d, gift of Eleanore
and Charles Stendig in memory of
Eve Brustein and Rose Stendig*

Studio 65, founded by five architecture and art students in Turin in 1965, was an "Anti-Design" collaborative like Superstudio and Archizoom. Resembling a segment of an Ionic column, *Attica* is named after the mainland of Greece where the classical order originated. This chair's allusion to monuments of antique architecture is ironic: the angled slice allows for seating, but also suggests this is a broken column. Poking fun at a pompous Italian heritage, such fanciful and satiric designs characterized many of the radical creations of the 1970s and anticipated postmodernism in art in the following decade.

Frans VAN NIEUWENBORG
Martijn WEGMAN

(born 1941) and **(born 1955)**

Necklace
Zipper
Designed and executed 1973
Aluminum zipper, rubber
34.5 x 0.4 cm
The Montreal Museum of
Fine Arts, D96.127.1,
gift of Dr. René Crépeau

In 1973, the year they designed this necklace, Van Nieuwenborg and Wegman opened an industrial design studio in Leiden, The Netherlands, to collaborate on limited-edition jewelry as well as industrial objects. They often based the forms on prefabricated materials, such as metal tubing, strips of stainless steel, or, as in this instance, a zipper.[38] By simply removing the pull tab of a heavy-duty zipper and attaching its two ends, they created an oval neckpiece with an adjustable-size opening and a long pendant, following the outline of a zipper, but unattached to fabric. The results are amusing and surprisingly elegant, recognizing the technical and aesthetic marvel of the common zipper. The partnership continued until 1990, and today the firm is maintained by Van Nieuwenborg alone and focuses on lighting designs.

Gruppo STRUM

(active 1966–1975)

Seating
Pratone (The Big Meadow)
Designed 1971
Painted polyurethane foam
95 x 140 x 140 cm
Produced by Gufram s.r.l.,
Balangero, Italy
The Montreal Museum
of Fine Arts, 2006.54

Founded in Turin in 1963 by a group of architects—Giorgio Ceretti, Pietro Derossi, Riccardo Rosso—all graduates of the Turin Politecnico, Gruppo Strum was active in Italy's Radical Design movement of the late 1960s. Its name is an abbreviation of the Italian *strumentale,* meaning functional. Made of polyurethane foam, *Pratone* looks solid but it is soft and gives under a sitter's weight. Examples of *Pratone* can be grouped—with the wavy edges of the bases fitted together—to simulate giant turf, or used singly to accommodate one or more individuals. This seating reflects Gruppo Strum's experimental approach and their dissatisfaction with the dominance of industry. The concept of grass on such a scale is surreal and indicates the influence of Pop art. The appearance of *Pratone,* according to architect and curator Emilio Ambasz, "contradicts the behavior one would expect from the form . . . no longer does 'form follow function' but, on the contrary, it aggressively conceals it."[39]

Marzio CECCHI

(1940–1990)

Table lamp
Fagotto (Bundle)
Designed 1972
Cotton, polyester resin, iron
25.4 x 39.3 x 37.9 cm
Produced by Studio Most,
Florence, Italy
The Montreal Museum of Fine
Arts, D94.332.1a–b, gift of
Eleanore and Charles Stendig in
memory of Eve Brustein
and Rose Stendig*

Critic Cesare Birignani said, "Although the functional aspect of objects is always present, what undoubtedly prevails is the ironic spark, the intellectual provocation. . . . And maybe it is because of that very reason that, more than a quarter of a century later, we look at these objects with amazement and (why not) amusement: for luck, fantasy, and irony will never go out of style."[40] Cecchi's early work reflected the International Style, but in the 1960s she first began to employ a more personal idiom with fanciful metamorphoses, as seen in this table lamp, which resembles a bundle tied in cloth, like a hobo's pack. This surreal gesture, recalling both Christo's wrapped monuments and Arte Povera's use of debased materials, was perfect for the reformists of "Anti-Design." A lamp displaying its parts with cold functionalism could not have said so much about the social concerns of young Italian designers.

Jonathan
Donato
Paolo

DE PAS
D'URBINO
LOMAZZI

(1932–1991), **(born 1935)**, and **(born 1936)**

Sofa
Joe
Designed 1970
Polyurethane foam, leather
upholstery
94 x 191 x 120 cm
Produced by Poltronova S.p.A.,
Pistoia, Italy
The Montreal Museum of Fine
Arts, D95.163.1, gift of Eleanore
and Charles Stendig in memory of
Eve Brustein and Rose Stendig*

Like other progressive Italian designers, De Pas and his colleagues were intrigued by American popular culture and the work of contemporary American artists. Named in honor of the famed homerun hitter Joe DiMaggio, this Pop chair was inspired by Claes Oldenburg's soft sculptures, which were first created in 1962 and introduced to Europe at the Venice Biennale in 1964. The humor of transforming a baseball glove into a gigantic seat appealed to hip consumers in Europe and North America.[41] Donato D'Urbino said of the *Joe* sofa, "The baseball glove has more ironic content than any real reference to any 'icon of American life.'"

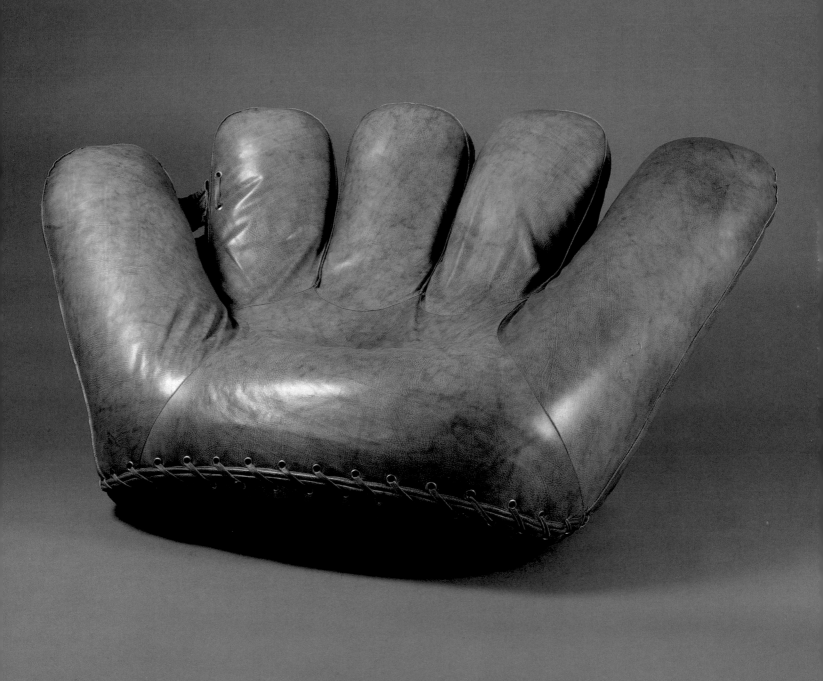

Helena HERNMARCK

(born 1941)

Tapestry

Crystal Glasses
Designed and executed in 1970
Wool, plastic, polyester, cotton
112.5 x 156 cm
The Montreal Museum of
Fine Arts, D98.147.1

Educated at the University College of Art, Craft and Design in Stockholm, Hernmarck moved to Canada in 1964, living there for seven years. *Crystal Glasses* was designed and woven in the artist's Montreal studio. This is one of six tapestries made for the restaurant of the Sheraton Hotel, Stockholm. According to the artist, three of the designs were translucent and two-sided to be used as room dividers, and three were wool and used as wall hangings. Although Hernmarck bases her compositions on photographs cut out of magazines[42]—and was the first to create woven works of art using photographs—the images in her works include surprising effects in perspective and color and no longer appear realistic after she transfers them to the tapestry medium. Plastic is integrated into the wood elements for sturdiness and it also produces a translucent two-sided effect.

BELOW Reverse side of *Crystal Glasses* tapestry.

Stephen FRYKHOLM

(born 1942)

Poster

Fruit Salad
Designed 1977
Silkscreen
103 x 63.5 cm
Produced by Continental
Identification Products, Sparta,
Michigan, for Herman Miller, Inc.,
Zeeland, Michigan, U.S.A.
The Montreal Museum
of Fine Arts, D87.202.1,
gift of Herman Miller, Inc.

Not long after the furnishings manufacturer Herman Miller was founded in 1936, the company's president, D. J. De Pree, and his wife, Nellie, began giving an annual picnic for all employees with home-cooked food in their backyard or a local park. As the company grew, so did picnic logistics, which included the creation of annual posters to commemorate the summer occasion.[43] Frykholm, the company's head of graphic design, had the assignment from 1970 to 1989, and featured a summer theme in each poster. With amusing flattened shapes in bold colors, this design depicts a vertical slice of a scalloped, scooped-out shell of a watermelon piled with fruit salad. As with Knoll and IBM, the creation of a graphic identity for Herman Miller was important, and Frykholm's work in the '70s continued the tradition established by George Nelson, who was the company's consultant design director.

Franciszek STAROWIEYSKI

(born 1930)

Cinema poster
*Dyskretny urok burzuazji
(The Discreet Charm of the
Bourgeoisie)*
Designed 1975
Photo offset
81.1 x 56.9 cm
The Montreal Museum
of Fine Arts, D91.115.1, gift of
Milikenko and Lucia Horvat

In the 1960s and '70s Polish posters moved toward the metaphysical and surreal, perhaps as a somber reaction to the constraints of Communist rule. One of the most renowned designers to express this in a new idiom was Starowieyski, who had studied painting in Cracow and Warsaw in the 1950s.[44] His film posters convey his sometimes shocking surrealistic visions, his use of the grotesque and macabre, and his interest in anatomy. All of these are reflected in this surreal poster of a lady with a bird's head in a red evening gown, designed for the film *The Discreet Charm of the Bourgeoisie*, written and directed by the famous Spanish filmmaker Luis Buñuel, who was at the heart of the Surrealist movement. The story focuses on a group of upper-middle-class people and the bizarre interruptions that prevent them from having a dinner together, intermixed with equally bizarre dream sequences.

Guido DROCCO
Franco MELLO

(born 1942) and **(born 1945)**

Coat rack
Cactus
Designed 1972
Painted polyurethane foam, steel
168.4 x 71.8 x 63.2 cm
Produced by Gufram s.r.l.,
Balangero, Italy
The Montreal Museum
of Fine Arts, D91.371.1,
anonymous gift

Although this hat stand is nominally functional, it is also a sculpture, relying on the ironies of Pop art as used by members of the Italian Radical Design movement. According to Drocco, "the attitude towards design during this period was closely linked to the Italian cultural experience of 1968, which was contesting rule-based attitudes."[45] *Cactus* evokes the open desert of the American Southwest and kitschy symbols of Mexico, so it is ironic to use this sculpture in an urban home or office. A steel frame supports the polyurethane, permitting it to serve as a coat rack, but polyurethane tends to fade in color and disintegrate over time, as has occurred in this example. A further irony is that the design was intended to be outmoded by fashion changes, but no one considered whether the material would speed obsolescence.

Peter OPSVIK

(born 1939)

Chair
Balans Variable
Designed 1979
Beech, wool upholstery
48 x 51 x 72.5 cm
Produced by Varier Furniture AS,
Ålesund, Norway
The Stewart Program for
Modern Design, 2009.23,
gift of Dr. Michael Sze

This simple, functional seating is aesthetically pleasing, using a minimum of materials. *Balans* provides comfort and relieves back strain by shifting the weight and pressure from the spine to the knees, allowing sitting in a kneeling position. It also emphasizes rocking which improves blood circulation. While studying in Germany, Opsvik became interested in ergonomics. He was one of a number of Scandinavian designers concerned about the social and ethical responsibilities of design. In the U.S. patent,[46] Hans Christian Mengshoel is listed along with Opsvik as the inventor of the "Seating Device," but the design itself was Opsvik's.

Gianfranco FINI

(born 1936)

Lamp
Quanta
Designed c. 1970
Methacrylate, steel
92.7 x 92.7 x 21 cm
Produced by New Lamp,
Rome, Italy
The Montreal Museum of
Fine Arts, 2004.93

Fini began as a painter who exhibited in Paris in the 1950s. In 1976, he opened a studio in Rome where he worked as an architect, interior designer, and designer of objects, as well as continuing as an artist who made functional sculpture. Although he referred to *Quanta* (the plural of "quantum") as a lamp, it is not especially useful as a light source. It is really a light sculpture, incorporating rods of frosted methacrylate, a transparent plastic, which gently transmits the illumination from a concealed light source.[47] Fini's work is reminiscent of Op art of the 1960s, seen in the work of Bridget Riley, and also of the minimal neon grids in reliefs and installations by the American light artists Dan Flavin and Larry Bell.

1980

1989

Postmodernism and Other Currents

Much of the 1980s looked like a new Gilded Age: an effervescent stock market, unapologetically conspicuous consumption, and a slogan from the 1987 film *Wall Street* that summed it up: "Greed is good." The creation of a cornucopia of eye-catching vanguard designs for the new moguls seemed almost inevitable. Manhattan's investment bankers and their counterparts in Margaret Thatcher's deregulated United Kingdom were only the most visible—and most envied—customers for the new luxuries; having the money to buy costly, exotic, and freshly minted objects was a badge of success nearly everywhere.

Though oil shortage made 1979–80 a year of global recession, 1989 saw the fall of the Berlin Wall—the symbolic triumph of capitalism over Communism—and Russia embraced materialism as the new religion. In the West, some designers enjoyed art-star celebrity; more artists and architects were designing products, while couturiers licensed their names for perfumes, purses, and the like with the result that middle-market buyers could afford status symbols.

Many groups were loosely gathered under the label "Postmodernism," which stood for the rejection of Modernism in architecture, design, and fine arts. Postmodernists shook off responsibilities to ideals of functionalism and social utility and rejected the idea of vanguard expression as unitary and future-oriented. No style was privileged; all were available for the artist-as-magpie or art director. The resulting eclecticism drew on the plural movements and multicultural currents of the 1970s, and also on Pop art's happy embrace of the motifs and techniques of Madison Avenue and Hollywood. At the same time, all of art history was fair game for appropriation. The new role models were not engineers, technicians, or utopian city planners, but social critics, anthropologists, psychologists, and some artists, as well as fashion consultants, socialites, and media observers. Design became a popular commodity and a subject for widespread and ardent debate.

The books by American architects Robert Venturi and Denise Scott Brown were cited earlier as prescient arguments for design as a popular sign language. The British architect and theorist Charles Jencks, writing in the mid-1970s and in *What is Post-Modernism?*, 1986, did most to make "Postmodernism" a familiar term and to give its variety of directions a history. In midtown Manhattan, the Seagram Building, 1954–58, and the AT&T (now Sony) Building, 1978–82, embodied the paradigm shift. Their office functions were identical, but now Philip Johnson, once the avatar of the International Style, and his partner John Burgee clad the skyscraper slab not in plate glass and steel but marble, with a broken pediment termination and a triumphal arch entrance. A poster by Michael Vanderbyl dramatized the contrast of aesthetics: a multicolored Postmodern high-rise sticks out its entry canopy tongue at a plain Bauhaus box (fig. 1).

The poster recalled architectural designs by Michael Graves, perhaps the most publicized of a new and elegant generation of New York architects, including Richard Meier, Charles Moore, Peter Eisenman, and Robert A. M. Stern. Fluent in practice and argument about Modernist and older design traditions, they were variously termed Late Modernists or Mannerists, after the sixteenth-century group that inverted Renaissance principles or gave them eccentric inflections. Of the group, Graves proved especially adept at alluding to past masters in beautifully finished designs, from showroom interiors to luxury goods (p. 308) and mass-market products. His whistling teakettle with a bird attached to its spout raised eyebrows among purist designers but pleased the crowd.

More thought-provoking were Venturi and Scott Brown's historically inspired chairs for Knoll International. The company was hedging its longtime bet on the International Style, and its new owners commissioned the Venturi firm to design its Manhattan showroom, while it continued to reproduce Modernist classics by Mies van der Rohe, Marcel Breuer, Eero Saarinen, and Harry Bertoia. A Knoll publicity shot shows Venturi among the new chairs (fig. 2), which quote Neo-Gothic, Regency, Art Deco, and eight other styles, as if mocking the Modernist pursuit of a single, perfect solution to seating. The seat-cushioned designs were all relatively comfortable, but they also flattered those who recognized the aesthetic allusions. Venturi said that his concept was to "adapt a series of historical styles involving wit, variety, and industrial process, and consisting of a flat profile in a decorative shape in a frontal dimension. Like a building with a 'false' façade, you see the 'real' structure from the side and you attribute a symbolic rather than an authentic quality to the ornamental surface in front."[1] On the West Coast, Frank Gehry attacked Modernism on both structural and surface levels. In the 1980s his home looked like a work in progress, and it was, with angular forms in undisguised industrial materials like chain-link fencing and plywood.

In Milan, the Italian group Memphis was the first to produce Postmodern furnishings. Formed in late 1980 by veteran designer Ettore Sottsass, it flourished by using all Italy's postwar design strengths: creative atelier-manufacturer relations, interest in aesthetic movements from around the world, and a tradition of craftsmanship and experimentation. Though Memphis drew members from the radical design movements of the 1970s such as Studio Alchimia, their oppositional attitudes were now expressed aesthetically. In 1981, Andrea Branzi described the group's aims in the design magazine *Modo*: to abandon "the myth of the 'unity' of a project," to see "a new linguistic 'expressive quality,'" to identify "decoration and color as signs of freedom and nobility," and to concentrate "on an affective relation between man and his things."[2] Sottsass articulated the difference between Memphis and Bauhaus values: "Memphis, which allows the surface to send more sensorial information and tries to separate the object from its schematic idea of functionalism, is an ironic approach to the modern notion of philosophical pureness. In other words, a table may need four legs to function, but no one can tell me that the four legs have to look the same."[3]

Steadfastly opposing the International Style's reductivism, Memphis advocated eclecticism with its very name, taken from Bob Dylan's song "Stuck Inside of Mobile with the Memphis Blues Again." For the Memphis spokesperson, this conjured up

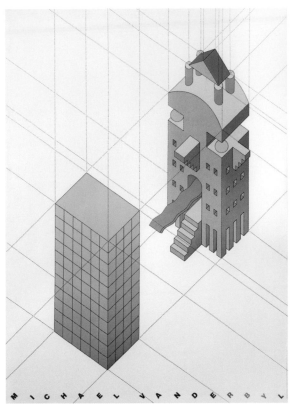

1 Michael Vanderbyl, postmodern architecture poster, 1984.
2 Knoll International publicity image showing Robert Venturi and his chair line, 1984.

"Blues, Tennessee, rock n' roll, American suburbs, and then Egypt, the Pharaohs' capital, the holy city of the god Ptah."[4] Memphis welcomed many levels of culture and history; it was international. Besides the Italians Sottsass, Branzi, Michele De Lucchi, and Alessandro Mendini, it included two Americans, Michael Graves and Peter Shire; the Japanese Shiro Kuramata, Arata Isozaki, and Masanori Umeda; Xavier Mariscal of Spain; Hans Hollein of Austria and the Austrian-born Italian émigré Matteo Thun; and Nathalie du Pasquier of France.

At the 1981 Salone del Mobile, the annual international furniture fair in Milan, Memphis presented its first exhibition with fifty-two works of furniture, lighting, and ceramics. On opening night alone, the display attracted 2,500 viewers. Quirky, animated surface decoration and intensely bright colors made startling juxtapositions with plastic laminates and luxurious materials. The cover for the 1986 *Memphis: Milano* catalogue shows the intentional "semantic confusion" of the mixture of vibrant patterns, demonstrating the group's conviction that no single standard could identify vital design (fig. 3). Memphis marketed its lines worldwide and commercial success quickly brought the company from limited editions to mass production. Although Sottsass began to exhibit apart from the group by 1985 and the collaborative effort dissolved by the end of the decade, Memphis continues to exist.

3

4

3 *Memphis Milano* catalogue cover, 1986.
4 Riccardo Dalisi, exhibition of Alessi prototypes for the *Tea and Coffee Piazza* series, 1988.

The Italian lighting and furnishings manufacturer Artemide had backed Memphis financially. Earlier, in 1979, the Italian firm Alessi commissioned silver tea and coffee services from eleven internationally known architects, including Graves, Venturi, Hollein, Mendini, Aldo Rossi, and Charles Jencks (p. 320). The *Tea and Coffee Piazza* series was presented in Milan during the Congresso Internazionale di Design in October 1983, and, in November of the same year in New York, they were displayed with cases designed by the Italian sculptor Riccardo Dalisi (fig. 4), whose whimsical coffeepots were also part of the Alessi collection. Two years later, the American firm

Swid Powell made its debut with tableware designed by Graves, Gwathmey Siegel, and other architects. The companies won cachet through associations with progressive builders, and the builders spread their design philosophy to audiences far larger than those who knew their buildings. Most twentieth-century Italian designers were trained as architects; from the 1980s onward architects in other countries became known through their product designs.

France's prosperity in the 1980s was most visible in Paris, where President François Mitterand initiated mammoth building projects at the Grand Louvre and the Bibliothèque Nationale de France complex. In opposition, the Parc de la Villette designed by Bernard Tschumi in 1984 reflected a deconstructivist philosophy, countering both Modernism and the historicizing side of Postmodernism. The French government spent generously to sustain international appreciation of French culture and to encourage its designers, who enjoyed the longtime association of French design with the luxury trades. Designers also filtered Postmodernism through the artistic traditions of Surrealism and Primitivism. At the market's highest end were exquisitely finished works by Sylvain Dubuisson (p. 344), while Philippe Starck captured global media attention with his svelte, disquieting designs. His hotel and restaurant interiors attracted glitterati in New York (fig. 5), Miami, Tokyo, and Paris, while his clever, stylish housewares were sold at a wide range of prices. More shocking to design professionals and the public was the Neo-primitivist movement, exemplified by the designs of Elisabeth Garouste and Mattia Bonetti, whose 1981 exhibition, *The New Barbarians*, evoked the French colonial past while incorporating found ingredients, such as tree branches, into chairs.

The exchanges between Japan and Italy that had begun at mid-century, and between Japan and other countries, bore significant fruit in the 1980s. Sottsass visited Japan, where Memphis designs were widely sold, and he appeared on Japanese television. Memphis produced Isozaki's and Kuramata's designs in Italy. Toshiyuki Kita opened an office in Milan, where Cassina manufactured his *Wink* armchair (p. 308).

In the 1980s Japanese couturiers won international success, and they commissioned Japanese designers to create interiors for their stores around the world: Shiro Kuramata, for example, designed eight for Issey Miyake. The Miyake showroom in Kobe, 1986, typifies Kuramata's polished use of industrial materials, such as steel mesh, corrugated aluminum, and Plexiglas, to create effects of transparency and dematerialization. This cool, minimalist style would characterize much design of the following decade. The reputations of Japanese designers spread through internationally circulated exhibitions and books such as *Japan Style* in 1980 and *Tokyo: Form and Spirit* in 1986, and their reductivist beauty was lauded in opposition to Italian Postmodernism. At the same time, certain progressive Japanese designers embraced Postmodernism's stylistic allusiveness, some emphasizing its roots in popular culture, others deconstructing Modernist language.

Among Japanese electronic companies winning world dominance, Nintendo and Sega led the craze for video games; Sharp and Canon competed with IBM to produce and market the microchip-powered office equipment of choice; and Sony with its *Walkman* portable cassette player, available in dozens of colors, and its compact disc player, introduced in 1985, provided music for a generation on the move. Like Japanese consumers, youths in the Western world viewed such lifestyle luxuries as necessities, and Japanese companies anticipated their changing tastes, using design (increasingly assisted by computer technology) as a marketing tool more swiftly and astutely than companies elsewhere.

Computer technology, pioneered by Japan and the United States, entered businesses and homes worldwide. Increasingly, the computer became a tool for architects and designers, replacing the time-consuming drawing and mockup process of the past. IBM launched its personal computer in 1981; in 1984 Apple introduced its friendlier version, the Macintosh, with a click-and-drag mouse and a screen with a menu of icons, humanized by design and quickly adopted by professionals in the design field. On the West Coast, April Greiman (p. 332), Rudy Vanderlans, and Zuzana Licko were pioneers in exploring the creative potential of the new software in generating new, seamlessly layered images and fonts. By the early '90s most graphic designers were computer-literate, and desktop publishing was commonplace.

While technology launched the Information Revolution, its flaws in relation to nature became obvious by the mid-1980s. Ecological problems that had emerged in the 1970s worsened in the face of previously unimaginable environmental tragedies: the deaths of three thousand people from a toxic gas leak at the Union Carbide chemical plant in Bhopal, India, in 1984; radiation leaks at Chernobyl in the Soviet Ukraine in 1986; the release of thousands of tons of toxic chemicals into the Rhine River near Basel, also in 1986; and the tanker Exxon Valdez's spill of crude oil in Alaska in 1989. These and longer-term alarms, like global warming and a damaged ozone layer, focused new attention on what was now called Green Design. The Design Centre in London hosted the exhibition *The Green Designer* in 1986, and *The Green Consumer Guide* was published in 1988, both focusing on "energy-conscious design" in buildings and products. In Denmark, the Irma chain of supermarkets banned the use of PVC in packaging, forcing suppliers to use other packaging materials. These were early signs of conservationist currents that became a tsunami by the turn of the century.[5]

Before the 1980s ended, a reaction to the extravagances of Postmodernism set in. The Memphis style had lent itself to cheap imitations with decorative features easily mimicked by lesser designers, filling stores around the world with clichéd reproductions. Spain, England, and Japan were identified as new contenders for Italy's status as the international leader of design. In the 1987 stock market crash, prices plunged nearly twice as far as they had in 1929, signaling that greed was not so good after all, and fear took its place. Though the market regained its pre-crash level within two years, there was a new sobriety in the air, for designers and for everyone else.

5 Philippe Starck, cocktail lounge, Royalton Hotel, New York, 1988.

Alessandro MENDINI

(born 1931)

Cabinet
Calamobio
Designed 1985
Inlaid and stained koto, maple,
tulipwood
83.5 x 131.8 x 43.2 cm
Produced by Zabro, a division of
Zanotta, Nova Milanese, Italy, for
Nuova Alchimia, Milan, Italy
The Montreal Museum of Fine
Arts, D91.107.1

This Milanese architect, designer, artist, and theorist was a major figure in the Italian radical design movement, and an influential contributor to important design magazines such as *Casabella* and *Domus*. Mendini worked with Studio Alchimia from its founding in 1976. His focus on the decorative rather than the functional is seen in this cabinet, which is conceived in terms of geometric surface patterns. Mendini explained: "As in other investigations into vibrations, colors, and geometry undertaken in other objects, here, too, the basic idea is to render the volume of the furniture evanescent and indefinite. The hint of an atmosphere overlays and replaces the form, giving the work an immaterial appearance."[6]

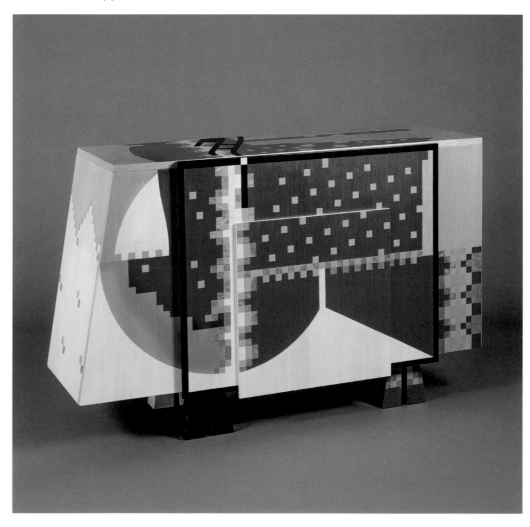

Gaetano PESCE

(born 1939)

Sofa

*Tramonto a New York
(Sunset in New York)*
Designed 1980
Polyurethane foam,
Dacron, plywood
116.9 x 231.7 x 90.9 cm
Produced by Cassina S.p.A.,
Milan, Italy
The Montreal Museum of
Fine Arts, D91.415.1a–j

Pesce's designs are characteristically bold and eye-catching, as in this cartoon-like sofa. It is made of foam cushions covered in gray fabric with a pattern of rectangles imitating Manhattan's skyscraper grid of windows and armrests of different heights mimicking the skyline. A semicircular red cushion at the back represents the setting sun. To Pesce, Manhattan's day as a cultural capital was over. "When I came to New York for the first time, I found it full of energy," he wrote. "But on a subsequent visit, I felt that vitality was less strong. I thought the lack of it was a sign of the city's decadence. Certainly New York was the capital of the twentieth century, but . . . which city will be the capital of the twenty-first?"[7]

Ramón Puig CUYÁS

(born 1953)

Brooch
The Choral Mermaid
Designed and executed 1989
Partially enameled silver,
ColorCore
15 x 7 x 1 cm
The Montreal Museum
of Fine Arts, D90.116.1

Cuyás studied at the Massana School in Barcelona between 1969 and 1974 and has been teaching jewelry design there since 1977. In this brooch, he combines traditional silver with brightly hued plastic, creating a stylized figure of a mermaid. "There is a truly ironic game between the supposedly poetic title and the material actually used, ColorCore, an absolutely synthetic, practical, and functional material," Cuyás stated. "Nothing has awakened my fantasy with such power as the half-fish, half-woman figure—the Siren. I have always been fascinated by the image of Ulysses tied to the mast of his ship by force, enduring the irresistible song of the Sirens' voices."[8] ColorCore was a Formica Corporation surfacing material intended for large-scale use in kitchen countertops and the like, but jewelry and accessories designers soon saw the potential of its colors, which are uniform throughout the malleable material.

Nathalie DU PASQUIER

(born 1957)

Textile
Cerchio
Designed 1982
Printed cotton
406.4 x 150.5 cm
Printed by Rainbow B & B, Milan,
Italy, for Memphis, Milan, Italy
The Montreal Museum
of Fine Arts, D86.165.1,
gift of Geoffrey N. Bradfield*

Without formal education in art or design, du Pasquier learned by collaborating with other designers. In 1979, she moved to Milan to work with the British designer George James Sowden, and both contributed to the first Memphis exhibition in 1981. Her textiles were startling at the time in juxtaposing strong, vibrant, and sometimes discordant colors in angular patterns. The pattern of *Cerchio*[9] is geometric, with a grid of decorated rings joined by black bars against a mottled ground. The Memphis scholar Barbara Radice described the designer's eclecticism: "It absorbs everything like a sponge, and nothing in particular. In the end it's the collage that counts. Her hard, aggressive, acid patterns, her harsh, sharp, flat colors, her broad, black angular marks make no compromise. They are impervious to logic . . . they embrace Africa, Cubism, Futurism, and Art Deco."[10]

BELOW LEFT Nathalie du Pasquier and George J. Sowden, *Royal* sofa, Memphis, 1983. HPL Print laminate and *Cerchio* cotton print.

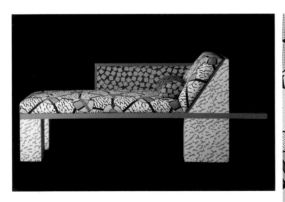

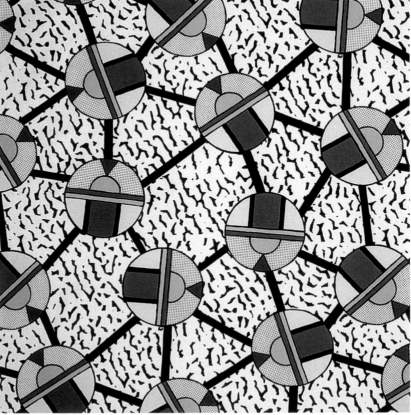

Ralph BACERRA

(1938–2008)

Charger
Designed and executed 1986
Glazed and lustered earthenware
8.9 x 56.5 x 56.5 cm
The Montreal Museum
of Fine Arts, D93.202.1

After graduating with a fine arts degree from Chouinard Art Institute in Los Angeles in 1961, Bacerra returned to teach there in 1963, the same year he opened his pottery studio. Experimenting with various innovative techniques, he created complex decorated polychromatic surfaces through a difficult process involving multiple firings. "By using simple geometric shapes," Bacerra wrote about this charger, "I transform a two-dimensional plane into a three-dimensional surface. I let the basic circle, square, and triangle evolve into shapes and forms to disorient the viewer. Pattern and color enhance the new orientation. My interest in Asian ceramics, Chinese cloisonné, and Persian painted miniatures has enhanced my way of dealing with clay surfaces."[11]

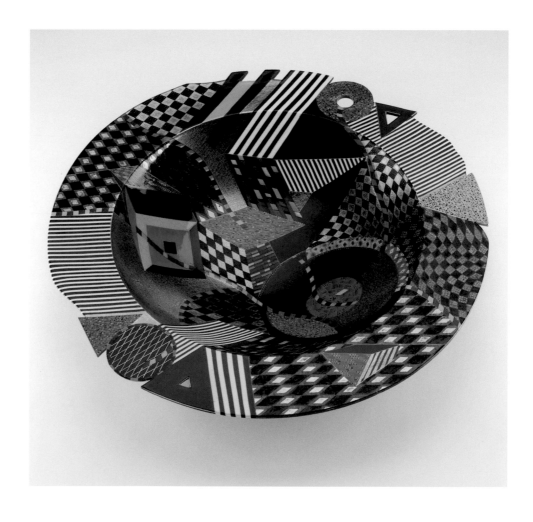

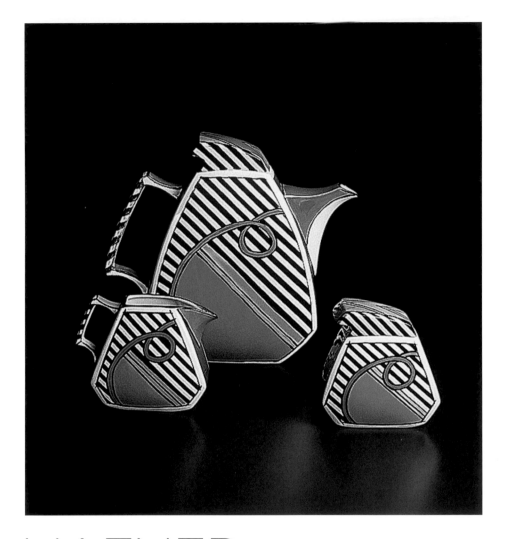

Dorothy HAFNER

(born 1952)

Coffee service

*Fred Flintstone, Flash Gordon,
and Marie Antoinette* (form); *Blue
Loop with Headdress* (decoration)
Designed 1984
Glazed porcelain
Coffeepot: 26.9 x 30.2 x 10.1 cm
Produced by Dorothy Hafner,
New York, New York, U.S.A.
The Montreal Museum
of Fine Arts, D94.305.1–3

Trained as a painter and sculptor, Hafner began working in ceramics in 1973. She is known for her brightly colored, patterned dinnerware, such as this coffee service, which she conceived as a graphic design. In Hafner's words: "There are combinations of decoration that seem modern, regimented. But things like checkerboards, which we think are really modern, go back to medieval heraldry and beyond. And we associate racing stripes with highway barricades, but they're primitive in art, on baskets and gourds. So each is both modern and primitive. It was interesting to contrast them so that the beauty and dynamic of each was enhanced."[12] Her title for the form of this service refers to its blend of low and high art, typical of much Postmodern design.

Toshiyuki KITA

(born 1942)

Armchair
Wink
Designed 1980
Steel, polyurethane foam,
Dacron, ABS plastic, cotton
upholstery and slipcover
100 x 83.4 x 200 cm (extended)
Produced by Cassina S.p.A.,
Meda Milano, Italy
The Montreal Museum of
Fine Arts, D90.105.1

In 1964 Kita graduated with a degree in industrial design from the University of Osaka, and in 1969 began working as an independent designer for clients in Japan and Italy. Since 1979, he has kept offices in both countries, finding Italian manufacturers enthusiastic to produce his designs. *Wink* is ingenious in its mechanical innovations: the chair can be adjusted by the round black knobs on the sides; the two-part headrest or "ears" can also be moved for comfort, hence the name *Wink*; and the front can be unfolded to make a chaise longue. With its bright Pop colors and humorous silhouette, the chair appears to be an entirely new invention, but the form derives from the traditional wing chair, which was also designed for comfort. In addition, the slipcovered upholstery allows the owner to change colors easily, while the ears, separately covered, can wear different hues and patterns, again part of the fun of owning *Wink*.

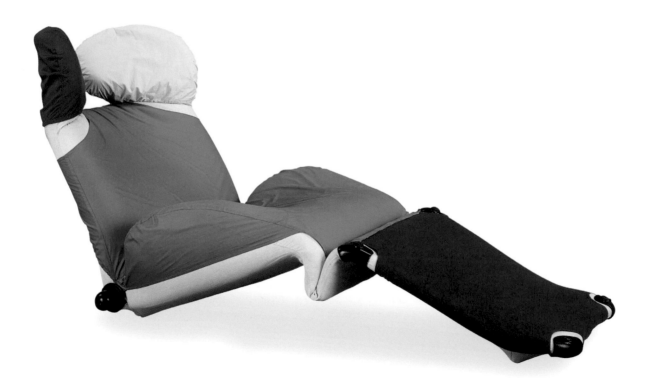

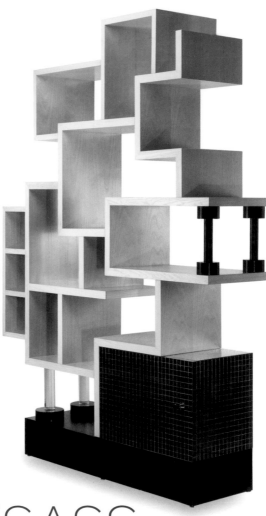

Ettore SOTTSASS

(1917–2007)

Cabinet
Lemon Sherbet
Designed 1987
Ash, mirror, Plexiglas, Formica
226 x 162 x 40 cm
Produced by Renzo Brugola,
Milan, Italy
The Montreal Museum of
Fine Arts, D88.135.1

This was the most spectacular of the works commissioned for *Furniture for the Ritual of Life*, an exhibition devoted to Sottsass' furniture organized by the Blum-Helman Gallery, New York. Owing to their size, all the designs were intended to be produced as one-of-a-kind examples or in limited editions and for high-ceilinged lofts rather than apartments. But *Lemon Sherbet* dominated the gallery space by its sheer scale, color, and dramatic asymmetrical play of solid and void. The small squares of mirror set into the cabinet surfaces were meant, Sottsass said, to evoke 1950s bars and restaurants, and add a touch of kitsch.[13] Recalling a de Stijl construction, the open cabinet shelving is cantilevered in an irregular rhythm and adds to the exuberance of this irrational design. Such popular and museum-art allusions were among Sottsass' contributions to Memphis design, while the bright colors and energetic shapes of the *Ritual of Life* collection recall his furniture for Memphis at its debut in 1981.

Catherine-Marie-Agnès Fal (Niki)
DE SAINT-PHALLE

(1930–2002)

Armchair
Clarice
Designed 1981–82
Painted polyester
120 x 112.5 x 88.9 cm
Produced by Plastiques d'art
R. Haligon, Périgny, France
The Montreal Museum
Fine Arts, D91.420.2, gift of
Esperanza and Mark Schwartz

Table
Designed 1980
Painted polyester
40 x 30 x 30 cm
The Montreal Museum of
Fine Arts, D89.202.2, gift of
Esperanza and Mark Schwartz

This French-born artist moved to the United States as a young child in 1933 and began to paint in 1951 while living in Cambridge, Massachusetts. In the 1960s she began sculpting her famous *Nanas* series, goofy female figures made of polyester on a wire framework, reflecting the ongoing influence of Pop art, which was conducive to the merging of sculpture and furniture. In describing *Clarice*, the artist wrote: "I have always enjoyed juxtapositions which create a visually ambiguous situation or psychological provocation. Chairs are simply expected to be nondescript in look and form. By fashioning them as human figures, the chairs . . . become 'unexpected guests,' assuming a presence of their own. They confuse the seat with the sitter, merging the identities of the two."[14]

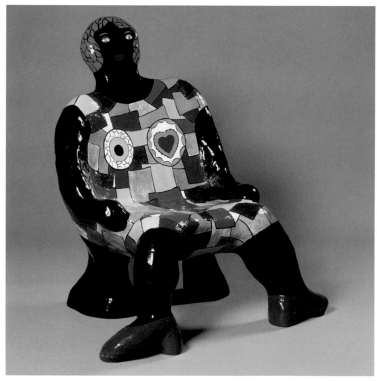

THE KNIFE/SHIP II BY CLAES OLDENBURG AND COOSJE VAN BRUGGEN IS A GIFT FROM GFT USA CORP., A COMPANY OF GRUPPO GFT.

Michael BIERUT

(born 1957)

Poster

Knife/Ship II: The Museum of Contemporary Art, Los Angeles, 1988
Designed 1988
Offset halftone lithograph
63.5 x 81.3 cm
Produced for the Museum of Contemporary Art, Los Angeles, California
The Montreal Museum of Fine Arts, D88.176.1, gift of Vignelli Associates

The original *Knife/Ship* was a large-scale sculpture designed by Pop artist Claes Oldenburg and his partner Coosje van Bruggen in collaboration with the architect Frank Gehry. The enormous Swiss pocketknife, its handle transformed into a gondola, was conceived as part of a performance on land and water in Venice entitled *Il Corso del Coltello* (The Course of the Knife). *Knife/Ship* combined the mass-produced tourist souvenir with the boat emblematic of Venice, but both functions were denied when *Knife/Ship II* was installed in the sculpture garden at California Plaza, Los Angeles, as part of an exhibition organized by the city's Museum of Contemporary Art. MOCA commissioned this poster from Bierut to celebrate the installation.[15] Before becoming a partner in Pentagram's New York office in 1990, Beirut worked for ten years at Vignelli Associates, an office that championed the International Typographic Style. The poster dramatizes the contrast between the sculpture and the plaza architecture, with discreet type in white across the top and dropped out of black across the bottom. It has the clarity of Vignelli's crisp style, but it is distinctive in its witty contrast between line and airbrushed color.

Leopold FOULEM

(born 1945)

Teapot

Teapot with Banana Spout
Designed and executed 1986
Ceramic, found objects
18 x 30 x 18 cm
The Montreal Museum of Fine
Arts, D98.173.1, gift of Dawn
Bennett and Marty Davidson*

A native of New Brunswick, Canada, Foulem has been influential in the international ceramic field, not only in Montreal where he lives, teaches, and writes, but also as a leader of a movement exploring themes of gay sexuality and identity in ceramic design. In this teapot, his replacement of the spout with a plastic banana is unmistakably sexual. Also transgressive is his use of a found lid and a curled wood branch as a handle—booty from his customary forays to the markets for parts. Here he unites three disparate objects with his combined saucer and body, clay he fired with an aesthetically appealing copper luster. A final irreverence is that the sculptural design follows the form of a traditional teapot, but it cannot pour, perhaps referring to taboos about homosexuality in the AIDS-panicked 1980s. In his reworking of a conventional "minor art" type to make a personal, sculptural statement, Foulem's work can be seen as part of the blurring of media boundaries that began in the 1960s and part of the contemporary expressionism in ceramics.[16]

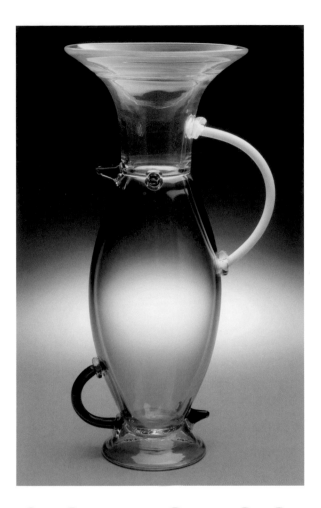

Ettore SOTTSASS

(1917–2007)

Vase
Altair
Designed 1982
Blown glass
45 x 22.5 x 19.4 cm
Produced by Toso Vetri d'Arte,
Murano, Italy, for Memphis
The Montreal Museum of
Fine Arts, 2007.251

This vase was part of the first collection presented by Memphis, the loosely organized but highly creative and influential group of designers and architects formed in 1981 by Ettore Sottsass. According to his wife, Barbara Radice, Memphis abandoned the search for social utopias of the 1960s and '70s and created "an open and flexible design culture that is aware of history, conscious of consumption as a search for social identity, and of the object as a sign through which a message is conveyed."[17] Sottsass had begun designing glass objects in the early 1970s and thus knew the work of the famous Venetian glass workshops. As with his furniture and ceramics, his designs in glass were complex and emphasized unexpected combinations of form and color, as seen here. *Altair* is based on an ancient vase type, with an extra loop handle and decorative prunts, or cones of glass, applied at the base and neck.

Dan FRIEDMAN

(1945–1995)

Poster
Gallimaufry
Designed 1989
Photo lithograph
99 x 68.5 cm
The Montreal Museum of
Fine Arts, D89.132.1,
gift of the designer

Trained at the Ulm Institute of Design in 1967–68, Friedman was among the Americans who created a new typography in the 1980s by mixing typefaces and pictorial elements in defiance of Modernist rules. Inspired by a wide range of sources, Friedman called his design philosophy "radical modernism," that is, "a reaffirmation of the idealistic roots of our modernity, adjusted to include more of our diverse culture, history, research, and fantasy."[18] This poster for Gallimaufry, a New York shop that sold housewares by modern designers, includes the boutique's logo at the bottom and the definition of its name across the top: "1. a medley 2. a delightful collection of unrelated objects." The illusionistic clouds recalling Magritte's surreal paintings, the stool drawn in two-point perspective, and its curious appendages, like work by his friend Alessandro Mendini, suggest Friedman's own design gallimaufry.

Shigeru UCHIDA

(born 1943)

Table clocks
Dear Vera 1 and *2*
Designed 1989
Aluminum, plastic, metal
1. (right) 13.3 x 4.7 x 2.9 cm
2. (left) 13.3 x 4.5 x 4.5 cm
Produced for Alessi, Milan, Italy
The Montreal Museum of
Fine Arts, D93.105.1a–c and
D93.105.2a–c, gifts of Gallery 91

Although these two desktop clocks are small, they appear monumental thanks to their architectonic proportions and elongated supports. The *Dear Vera* clocks are smaller versions of Uchida's tall clock *Dear Morris* (a tribute to William Morris), a design of the same year. In general, Uchida enjoys playing with similarities and oppositions, as seen here in the two nearly identical rectilinear forms, which differ in their perforated supports. This visual tour de force calls to mind both modern and Postmodern attitudes toward functionalism as well as traditional and contemporary Japanese forms. The clocks were conceived for Il Palazzo Hotel in Fukuoka, Japan, designed by Uchida and Aldo Rossi in 1987, and they were named after Rossi's daughter.[19]

Robert VENTURI

(born 1925)

Side Chairs
Queen Anne and *Art Deco*
Designed 1978–84
Plywood, printed plastic
laminate, rubber
Queen Anne: 98 x 67.6 x 61.7 cm
Art Deco: 80.5 x 56.7 x 58 cm
Produced by Knoll International,
New York, New York, U.S.A.
The Montreal Museum of
Fine Arts, D99.156.1 and D85.117.1,
gifts of Knoll International

Venturi and Scott Brown are one of the most influential architectural teams of the twentieth century, through both their theoretical writings and their buildings, which helped to change the direction of modern architecture. The husband and wife pursued Postmodern ideas in both forms before the term came into widespread use. The line of furniture for Knoll, designed by Venturi alone,[20] included nine different but comparable chairs based on historic models ranging from Chippendale and Sheraton to Gothic Revival and Art Deco. In profile, the thin members are similar, while "the fronts are signs reminiscent of Western false-front stores,"[21] the designers wrote. The radiating decoration of the *Art Deco* chair and the flowers punctuated with pairs of parallel lines in the *Grandmother* pattern on the *Queen Anne* chair challenged strict functional modernism, which forbade applied ornament and extraneous color.

Robert VENTURI

(born 1925)

Candlesticks
Designed 1985–86
Silver-plated metal
22.9 x 10.2 x 10.2 cm
Produced by Cleto Munari,
Vicenza, Italy, for Swid Powell,
New York, U.S.A.
Denver Art Museum, 2001.313

These designs are based on early eighteenth-century English baluster-form candlesticks, which Venturi rendered as flat, two-dimensional silhouettes. The silhouettes were cut out of two sheets of silver-plated metal and joined at right angles to echo the Georgian prototype. Venturi had originally presented this design concept to Alessi in 1980,[22] and the segmented form of the candlesticks closely follows a similarly segmented table he created for Knoll, prior to this commission from Swid Powell. The reduction of the sculptural, lathe-turned form to a cut-out accords with Venturi's notion of design (and architecture) as primarily a system of signs.

Michael GRAVES

(born 1934)

Ice bucket
Designed 1988
Silver, resin
20 x 22 x 36 cm
Produced by Cleto Munari,
Vicenza, Italy
Denver Art Museum, 2001.580

The historicism in Graves's work is emblematic of an aspect of Postmodernism. Although he is best known for his inexpensive designs for Target in the 1990s, he also created objects in deluxe materials, such as sterling silver, as seen in this octagonal ice bucket, produced by Cleto Munari expressly for the Denver Art Museum. This example is a duplicate of a prototype owned by Munari.[23] It was inspired by French silver of the 1920s, and resembles covered sugar bowls in silver coffee services designed by Jean Puiforcat.[24] The only embellishments of this simple form are the stepped molding around the base, the octagonal finial of black resin, and the reeded handles of the same material.

Michael GRAVES

(born 1934)

Tea service
The Big Dripper
Designed 1987
Teapot: 22.5 x 26.5 x 17cm
Enameled and gilt porcelain
Produced for Swid Powell,
New York, New York, U.S.A.
The Stewart Program for
Modern Design, 2009.9

In the late 1970s, Graves moved from a formal late modernism to become one of the leading figures of the Postmodern movement. His new buildings were based on historic and cultural references to the past; his colorful and extravagant decorative designs included work for Memphis in 1981. He was one of the architects invited to design tableware for Swid Powell, a company founded by Nan Swid and Addie Powell in 1982 to produce innovative products by internationally known architects. This commission was instrumental in what would become prolific output in furniture, textiles, glassware, and ceramics. The humorously titled *Big Dripper* combines stylistic influences from the past, including Wiener Werkstätte and Bauhaus designs, as seen in its spherical forms and horizontal wavy-line and dot decoration. Graves has simplified both the form and decoration so that the design is distinctly his own and of the 1980s. Although the spheres appear to be separate from their bases, each is a continuous porcelain form. The color of the base, he noted "represents the heat and color of coffee, and the blue signifies water. This is a direct association to some extent, but with an abstract touch."[25]

Charles JENCKS
Kazumasa YAMASHITA
Paolo PORTOGHESI

(born 1939), **(born 1931)**, and **(born 1937)**

Charles Jencks
Coffeepot (1)
Designed 1982
Brass
21.5 x 9 x 8.3 cm
Produced by Alessi, Milan, Italy
The Montreal Museum of Fine
Arts, D88.209.1a–b, gift of Vivian
and David Campbell

Kazumasa Yamashita
Coffeepot (2)
Designed 1982
Brass
24.1 x 23.2 x 7.6 cm
Produced by Alessi, Milan, Italy
The Montreal Museum of Fine
Arts, D88.212.1, gift of Vivian
and David Campbell

Paolo Portoghesi
Coffeepot (3)
Designed 1982
Partially enameled brass, ebony
15.9 x 17.9 x 8.3 cm
Produced by Alessi, Milan, Italy
The Montreal Museum of Fine
Arts, D88.213.1a–b, gift of Vivian
and David Campbell

In 1979 Alberto Alessi commissioned eleven internationally renowned architects to design services for the *Tea and Coffee Piazza* series, which he produced in 1983 using handcraft techniques.[26] Each coffeepot was designed to be part of a complete service. The four here represent a selection from a large collection of prototype coffeepots acquired by the Montreal Museum of Decorative Arts. Jencks conceived of the coffeepot as a swelling Ionic column; Portoghesi was inspired by Viennese turn-of-the-century design; and Yamashita created a form with sinuous double spouts and handles by bending brass tubing. The series represents the involvement of Postmodern architects in designing objects, an area traditionally left to the industrial designer. The project is regarded as seminal work of Postmodernism, and it also, according to Alberto Alessi, gave the Alessi firm "a definitive international presence, both in the view of the media and of the most influential outlets in the world."[27]

BELOW Charles Jencks, coffee service for Alessi, 1982.

1

2

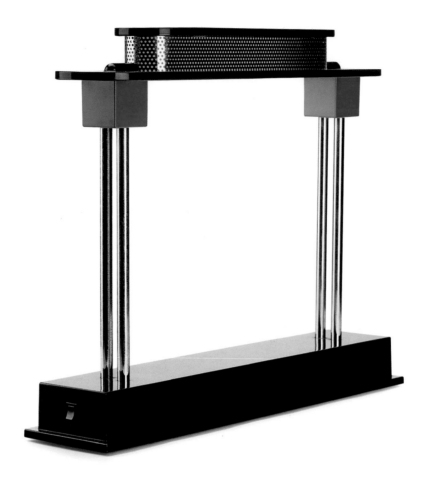

Ettore SOTTSASS

(1917–2007)

Table lamp
Pausania
Designed 1982
Plexiglas, chromium-plated steel,
aluminum, glass, rubber
39.5 x 48 x 11 cm
Produced by Artemide,
Pregnana Milanese, Italy
The Stewart Program for
Modern Design, 2007.50.10,
gift of Roy Poretzky*

Sottsass designed this lamp for Artemide as a simpler, less expensive alternative to the exuberant lamps he conceived for Memphis, a group he founded the previous year with financial backing from Artemide's founder, Ernesto Gismondi. Sottsass' lamps for Memphis were more complex, multicolored, and had funkier forms, especially *Ashoka*.[28] Based on a traditional lamp form seen in bank lobbies earlier in the century, *Pausania* was mass-produced and enjoys sales to the present, which attests to its popular appeal. Its stepped base supports two columns that rise to block-shaped capitals and a stepped oval "roof" containing two neon tubes, all architectonic features characteristic of Sottsass' objects.

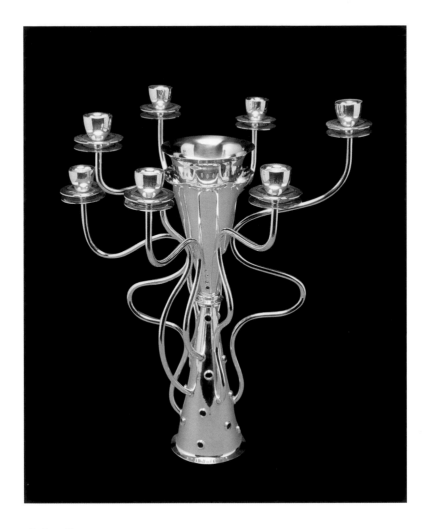

Bořek ŠÍPEK

(born 1949)

Candelabra
Simon
Designed 1988
Silver-plated stainless steel
45.8 x 35 x 38.5 cm
Produced by Driade,
Fossadello di Caorso, Italy
The Montreal Museum of
Fine Arts, D93.219.1a–b,
anonymous gift

Šípek's neo-Baroque composition is an updated epergne, a combination of a vase and a candelabra. Its undulating branches and double bobeches add drama to this vigorous, fanciful, and opulent work. *Simon* can contain flowers in its removable cone-shaped vase. This vase is mirrored in the reverse cone shape of the base, punctured with holes, some of which accommodate the calligraphic branches. A prominent Czech architect and designer, Šípek admired the vitality and invention of the Baroque style, which "always allows you to think up something new, almost endlessly. Baroque has far more principles than solutions. . . . I am impressed even by the lifestyle of the Baroque, the liberations from the Church and freedom."[29]

Julia MANHEIM

(born 1949)

Vase

Scarlet and Grey Vase with Collar
Designed and executed 1984
Painted and crayoned newspaper
68.5 x 21 x 51 cm
The Montreal Museum of Fine
Arts, 2003.282

A British-born jewelry designer, Julia Manheim lives and works in London. Although she initially made experimental jewelry, she has focused on sculpture and installation art since 1984 and often transforms discarded material, an ongoing theme in her work. The newspaper composing this vase has been hardened through the application of acrylic paint and wax crayon, leaving few traces of the newspaper visible. From its diamond-shaped base the vessel rises to a semicircular top, with one side pulled down to resemble a flower opening. The vase was part of a series that Manheim made for *Paper Containers*, her 1984 solo exhibition at Gallery Ra in Amsterdam.[30]

Issey MIYAKE

(born 1938)

Jacket
Designed 1988
Mulberry paper
73 x 148.6 cm
Produced by Issey Miyake
Permanente, Tokyo, Japan
The Montreal Museum of
Fine Arts, D94.207.1,
gift of Yvonne Brunhammer

After graduating from Tama Art University, Tokyo, in 1964, with a degree in graphic design, Miyake worked in Paris and, in 1969, New York. When he returned to Tokyo in 1970, he opened the Miyake Design Studio. Like his contemporary Japanese textile designers, such as Reiko Sudo (p. 427), he is known for his innovations in the manipulation of fabrics, and his experiments with new techniques. For example, pleating of fabrics for clothes allowed easy care and preserved the wearer's flexibility of movement. His *Pleats Please* project of 1988 was the same year as his exhibition *Issey Miyake: A-ŪN* at the Museum of Decorative Arts, Paris. On this occasion he gave this short jacket of crinkly Japanese paper to Yvonne Brunhammer, then director of the museum. "We have clothes made of iron, paper, cane, bamboo, stones," Miyake wrote. "There are any number of possibilities once you let your imagination roam."[31]

Gerd ROTHMAN

(born 1941)

Neckpiece

*Schmuck einer Tänzerin
(Jewelry of a Dancer)*
Designed and executed 1986
Silver
4.7 x 64.3 x 0.4 cm
The Montreal Museum of
Fine Arts, D93.220.1

Educated in metalworking in his native Germany, Rothman opened his own jewelry workshop in 1965. In the late 1970s, after exploring acrylics, he began to employ precious metals almost exclusively, casting body parts and turning them into jewelry. For the series he later called *Body Prints*, he cast each part in gold from plaster-of-Paris molds.[32] In this necklace, each disk is made from the mold taken of the nipple of a friend who was a dancer. Rothman then arranged the ten disks into a circular necklace reminiscent of jewelry from antiquity. Rothman observed: "At first one sees the discs with an emphasis on the central point—attractive as jewelry, not exceptional or classical. On second glance, one discovers the origin of this delicate modeling."[33]

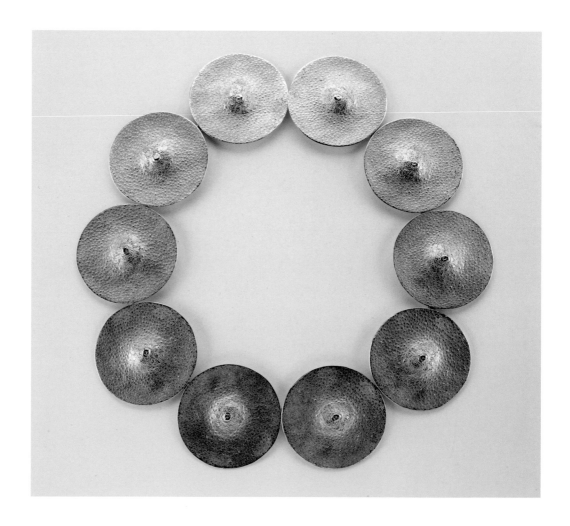

Lella VIGNELLI Massimo VIGNELLI
David LAW

(born 1934), **(born 1931)**, and **(born 1937)**

Stacking chair
Handkerchief
Designed 1982–87
Fiberglass-reinforced
polyester, steel
73.7 x 56.2 x 46.4 cm
Produced by The Knoll Group,
New York, New York, U.S.A.
The Stewart Program for
Modern Design, 2009.4.1–2

Known for its graphics, packaging designs, and interiors, all of a decidedly Minimalist bent, the firm Vignelli Associates also designed furniture, including this stacking chair for Knoll, which the Vignellis noted was many years in development. They added that the final design was heavier than desired.[34] Its represents the opposite of the ornamental overkill of the Postmodernist 1980s, a modernist stance maintained by the Vignellis to the present day. The *Handkerchief* chair was available in several bright colors, in armchair and side-chair versions. The back and seat are molded of one piece of polyester, with curves like those of a handkerchief, supported by a black steel skeleton. These chairs were among the seating ordered for office use at the Montreal Museum of Decorative Arts when it was located in the Château Dufresne.

Tom DIXON

(born 1959)

Chair
Fat
Designed 1988
Steel, rush
81.9 x 71.8 x 83.8 cm
Produced by Space,
London, England
The Montreal Museum of
Fine Arts, D93.250.1

Dixon dropped out of art school in 1986, and, while repairing his motorcycle, discovered welding techniques. This chance experience helped him become a furniture designer. He welded his first furniture designs and sold them in limited editions in his shop, Space. This chair is a welded steel-rod structure with a woven rush covering, and was a prototype for his first mass-produced collection. He wrote: "I started working in a period in which people were using predominantly angular forms and applied finishes. Finding these unsatisfactory, I started my search into more natural and softer materials which could be used in a decorative way without having to add decoration as an end in itself. . . . [They] evolve in an organic way and my main concerns have to do with elegance of lines and the nature of materials."[35] Dixon's designs in rush are reminiscent of furniture forms of the 1950s, transformed by the exaggeration of lines into new designs.

Thom MAYNE

(born 1944)

Side Chair
Nee
Designed 1988
Metal
61 x 61 x 76 cm
Produced by Farrage &
Company, Culver City,
California, U.S.A.
Denver Art Museum, 2001.408

Thom Mayne, the founder of the architectural group Morphosis, created
this chair as part of his design for the Los Angeles showroom of fashion designer
and retailer Leon Max.[36] Made of cast, welded, and perforated sheet metal, *Nee*
has the taut skeleton of Mayne's deconstructivist architecture, with each joint
defined. Deconstructivism in American architecture of the time opposed both
Modernism and Postmodernism, shunning rationalist forms as well as historical
references. The industrial, technical look of the *Nee* chair became part of design
in the 1980s, while its air of science-fiction menace, with its crest rail tapering
to dagger-like ends, characterized many of Mayne's designs then.

April GREIMAN

(born 1948)

Poster

*Design Quarterly 133:
Does it Make Sense?*
Published 1987
Offset lithograph
192 x 65 cm
Denver Art Museum, 2001.595,
gift of R. Craig Miller to the Liliane
and David M. Stewart Collection

While some graphic designers denounced the new digital technology, in 1986 Greiman was early in embracing it and exploring the layering and overlapping of computer-screen information. Commissioned by *Design Quarterly*, published by the Walker Art Center, to design an issue, she created *Does it Make Sense?* as a single-sheet magazine entirely on a Macintosh computer. This huge, double-sided print is her digital collage of found video images focusing on communication systems from cave paintings to sign language. To create it, wrote design historian Philip B. Meggs, she "integrated words and pictures as part of a single computer file. The juxtapositions and combination gained new symbolic meaning and graphic dynamism. Uniting the whole was her life-size, bit-mapped self-portrait."[37]

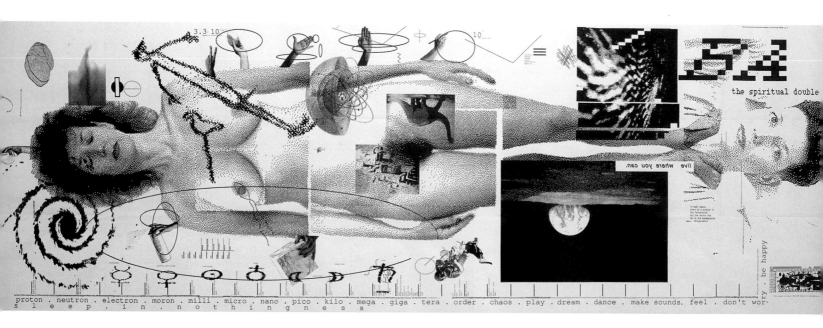

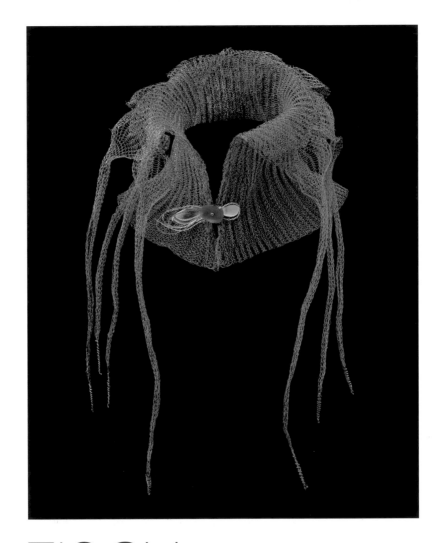

Arline M. FISCH

(born 1931)

Collar

Collar MKC43
Designed and executed 1985
Copper, silver, carnelian
50 x 31 x 24.5 cm
The Montreal Museum of
Fine Arts, D95.180.1a–b

Trained in fine arts at Skidmore College and the University of Illinois, Fisch turned to jewelry after graduation and began experimenting with different materials and techniques. She learned how to use knitting, weaving, and braiding of various metallic threads to create adornments for the body, first by hand and then by weaving on a loom. "Teaching on a Fulbright grant at the Academy of Applied Art in Vienna in 1982, Fisch was able to develop [her 'garment jewelry'] concepts with machine-knitting, allowing larger expanses of metal 'fabric' to be made more quickly into ornament for the body."[38] This collar is related to a general interest among certain artists in the 1980s who sought to break down barriers between crafts and fine arts.

Stephen PEART

(born 1958)

Wetsuit
Animal
Designed 1988
Neoprene rubber, nylon jersey
152 x 56 cm (widest diameter)
Produced by O'Neill, California,
California for Vent Design,
Campbell, California, U.S.A.
The Montreal Museum of Fine
Arts, D92.121.1, gift of Vent Design

Peart's wet suit is an aesthetically pleasing design whose function is to retain a diver's body heat in cold water while allowing full body movement. The solution to providing both flexibility and thermal insulation lies in the incorporation of thin hollow channels in the rubber. Their spacing, diameter, and overlapping position give the suit a futuristic appearance, as well as thermal insulation. The Neoprene material is a stretchable synthetic fabric, allowing a close fit, which is crucial to the effectiveness of the suit. Although the suit was technologically advanced, it had to be hand cut with scissors. According to design curator Paola Antonelli, "the suit's design owes its success to the studies of the kinetics of the human body and the advanced technological development of synthetic-rubber injection and molding processes."[39]

Gaetano PESCE

(born 1939)

Side chair
Greene Street
Designed 1984
Fiberglass-reinforced
polyester, stainless steel
94.3 x 54.3 x 57.6 cm
Produced by Vitra GmbH,
Weil am Rhein, Germany
The Montreal Museum of
Fine Arts, D90.112.1

Pesce's inventive use of new materials, expressive forms, and challenges to expectations about furnishings are key components of all his designs. The wacky *Greene Street* chair, named after his studio's location in New York's Soho district, appears to have landed from outer space. According to Pesce, "I tried to represent the instability of our times with the *Greene Street* chair, which gives when you sit on it. . . . It is not as rigid as a traditional chair that gives you a feeling of security—you sit on it, you stay on it. The *Greene Street* chair is a more flexible structure. It has eight very thin legs that allow a kind of movement."[40]

Ron ARAD

(born 1951)

Armchair
Big Easy Volume II
Designed 1989
Mild steel
101.9 x 136 x 97.8 cm
Produced by One-Off Ltd.,
London, England
The Montreal Museum of
Fine Arts, D90.200.1,
gift of Paul Leblanc

Born in Israel and trained as an architect, Arad has long been fascinated with the philosophical and sculptural aspects of furniture design. In 1973 he moved to London and started his studio and workshop, One Off, in 1981. His one-of-a-kind designs challenged the basic modernist premise that design should be functional and mass-produced. Although the form of this chair derives from the traditional, comfortable, overstuffed armchair, Arad has transformed it into a hollow form in cold, hard sheet metal with crudely forged seams. This armchair does not provide much comfort, but as a work of sculpture it has a metaphorical meaning: according to the designer, its silhouette was inspired by the three-part shape of the Hebrew letter Shin (ש).[41] Arad also used the Hebrew alphabet for the shape of eight other chairs he designed between 1986 and 1992.

Adelle LUTZ

(born 1948)

Jacket and pants
Ivy Suit
Designed and executed 1986
Wool blend, polyester,
cotton, acrylic paint
Jacket: 77.5 x 44.5 cm
Pants: 109.5 x 38 cm
The Montreal Museum of
Fine Arts, D95.186.1–2,
gift of David Byrne*

For this clothing, the actress, model, and costume designer Adelle Lutz created a surreal fantasy, transforming a suit into a tree, with the pants as the trunk and the jacket as leaves. The suit is worn here by David Byrne captured in an image by the American portrait photographer Annie Leibovitz. The suit was designed for Lutz's *Urban Camouflage* series, which was "part of a fashion show for the film *True Stories*," according to the designer. The film was co-authored and directed by David Byrne (who also acted in it). Best known as the lead singer of the popular band the Talking Heads, Byrne was Lutz's husband from 1987 to 2004. "These outfits allow one to blend into one's own town rather than stand out. Middle-class folks disappearing into their suburban environment. Secondly, it was important that the outfits be fantastic yet truly wearable; they could be improbable but not preposterous."[42]

Mario CANANZI
Roberto SEMPRINI

(born 1958) and **(born 1959)**

Sofa
Tatlin
Designed 1989
Lacquered wood, chromium-plated tubular steel, polyurethane foam, cotton velvet upholstery
Produced by Edra S.p.A., Pisa, Italy
The Montreal Museum of Fine Arts, D93.258.1, gift of Maurice Forget

This seating is based on the Russian architect Vladimir Tatlin's most famous design, his 1920 *Monument to the Third International*. Although the spiral form is Tatlin's tribute to revolutionary Communism, the architects Cananzi and Semprini satirize this ideology by turning a conception for a giant steel and glass tower into a red velvet upholstered pouf or tête-a-tête, staples of bourgeois Victorian interiors. The designers assume a Postmodern stance by mocking the visionary Constructivist building, transforming a symbol for revolution into a useful, marketable object. *Tatlin* also reflects Semprini's fascination with forms evocative of speed: he became a member of the Bolidist group—dedicated to this form language—after he and Cananzi established their architectural practice in Milan.

Massimo IOSA GHINI

(born 1959)

Pitcher
Simulata (Simulated)
Designed 1989
Silver-plated alpaca
25.1 x 24.8 x 7.5 cm
Produced by Design Gallery
Milano, Milan, Italy
Indianapolis Museum of Art,
2008.332, gift of Dr. Michael
Sze to The Stewart Program for
Modern Design*

Iosa Ghini began his architectural studies in Florence and graduated from the Polytechnic Institute in Milan. In 1982 he was one of the founding members of the Bolidist group of architects and designers (from *bolide*, or fast-moving object), and in 1986, Sottsass invited him to join Memphis. From boyhood, Iosa Ghini had made skillful cartoons, especially outer-space fantasies, and he created cartoon-like drawings for his futuristic architectural projects, and for furniture and objects, such as this pitcher. *Simulata*, which is part of a collection commissioned by Design Gallery Milano in 1989, has an undulant silhouette like a reflection in a funhouse mirror. Its swooping curves also suggest the designer's appreciation for streamlined works of the 1930s. The malleability of the metal alloy alpaca also appealed to Iosa Ghini. "Expressions of extreme virtuosity," he said, the collection was intended to show "you can give every kind of shape to material."[43]

BELOW, LEFT Massimo Iosa Ghini, architectural drawing, *Fluid City*, quadriptych 4, 1986.

Matteo THUN

(born 1952)

Vase
Volga
Designed 1982
Glazed porcelain
55.6 x 24.7 x 17.9 cm
Produced by Porcellane d'Arte
San Marco, Nove, Italy,
for Memphis,
Pregnana Milanese, Italy
Indianapolis Museum of Art,
2008.235, gift of Dr. Michael
Sze to The Stewart Program for
Modern Design*

Thun studied architecture in Florence, before moving to Milan in 1978 to work for Ettore Sottsass. When the veteran designer launched the collaborative Memphis in 1981, Thun was among the young designers represented in its first collection. In 1984 Thun established his own studio. *Volga* is one of a provocative series of ceramics, which, like other radical designs by Memphis, challenged conventional ideas about functionalism. On a bulbous base, the canted, torpedo-shaped body with applied zigzag ridges evokes a cactus and a fish: the total is a humorous phallic sculpture more than a functional vase. Nonetheless, a flower can be inserted into the conical mouth of the vessel. Thun recalled designing the vase "while I was drunk and discussing [things] with Sottsass in early '81."[44]

Philippe STARCK

(born 1949)

Two kettles

Hot Bertaa
Designed 1987
Aluminum, polyamide
25 x 31 x 15 cm each
Produced by Alessi, Milan, Italy
Indianapolis Museum of Art,
2008.330–331,
gift of Dr. Michael Sze to
The Stewart Program for
Modern Design*

France's most famous contemporary designer, Philippe Starck studied interior architecture at the École Camundo in Paris and in 1968 founded his first firm there. Since 1972, he has worked independently as a designer of products and interiors. His career advanced with the publicity he received from a prestigious commission to design the private Elysée Palace apartments of French President François Mitterrand, and he became internationally famous with his designs for boutique hotels for Ian Schrager in the 1990s. Starck's tea kettle for Alessi is a streamlined, sculptural design that he described as "aerodynamic and useless."[45] Alberto Alessi wrote, "The kettle has the obliquely styled shape of a Howitzer, as if it was pierced by a conical tube, by an arrow, functioning at the one end as a handle into which the water is poured and at the other as a spout for the water to pour out. It has the appearance of a religious object, and the original idea was to have a Latin inscription embossed in ancient lettering."[46] Beauty, not functional efficiency, is key to Starck's product designs—and in fact to many Postmodern objects of desire.

Sylvain DUBUISSON

(born 1946)

Desk
Designed 1989
Parchment- and leather-
covered wood
72.5 x 150.5 x 82.5 cm
Produced by Édition
Fourniture, France
The Montreal Museum of
Fine Arts, 2009.02.12

Dubuisson graduated from the École Supérieure d'Architecture de Saint-Luc, in Tourai, Belgium, in 1975. In addition to his role as an architect, he has designed furniture and glass. This desk is a dramatic piece of sculpture, conceived in curves and counter-curves and requiring skilled artisans to make. The tapering form is covered in parchment with a leather inset. The use of these sumptuous materials recalls the luxurious furniture of Art Deco designers such as Jacques-Emile Ruhlmann. It also calls to mind biomorphic sculpture at mid-century. In its suave elegance, it shuns the decorative extravagance of the 1980s and forecasts the minimalism of the 1990s. A shallow storage space is hidden beneath the desk pad for holding papers and small items.[47] The Stewart Collection example was fabricated in 2002, duplicating the 1989 model, of which only a few examples were made.

Masayuki KUROKAWA

(born 1937)

Table lamp
Lavinia
Designed 1988
Enameled aluminum
47 x 50.8 x 59 cm
Produced by Artemide, S.p.A.,
Pregnana Milanese, Italy
The Montreal Museum of
Fine Arts, D94.167.1

A Tokyo-based architect and industrial designer, Kurokawa designed for Italian manufacturers, like many of his Japanese colleagues in the 1980s, and this helped him win international recognition. His artistic sensibility is seen in this dynamic design, which transforms a functional table lamp into a piece of sculpture. *Lavinia* looks futuristic in its forward thrust and large, overscaled aluminum shade. The shade, which can be tilted to direct the light, seems to float over the conical base, and it protects against glare as it supplies subtle lighting. The white eggshell finish and the balance of the two forms appear miraculous. In opposition to the excessive decoration of the 1980s, Kurakawa's designs represent the quiet minimalism often associated with traditional Japan.

Mario BOTTA

(born 1943)

Floor lamp
Shogun Terra
Designed 1985
Painted aluminum, steel, cast iron
217 x 32 x 31.5 cm
Produce by Artemide S.p.A.,
Pregnana Milanese, Italy
The Montreal Museum of
Fine Arts, D91.378.1,
gift of Artemide S.p.A.

Armchair
Seconda
Designed 1982
Epoxy-painted tubular steel,
perforated sheet steel,
polyurethane foam,
rubber upholstery
73 x 52 x 59.5 cm
Produced by Alias, Milan, Italy, for
International Contract Furnishings,
New York, New York, U.S.A.
The Montreal Museum of
Fine Arts, D85.120.1,
gift of Luc d'Iberville-Moreau

This Swiss-born architect studied architecture in Milan and Venice, and worked in the office of Le Corbusier, the master of modernist architecture. In 1970 Botta opened his own practice in Lugano, Switzerland, and became known for his late Modernist designs in the 1980s. This chair and lamp share crisp lines and geometric forms: *Seconda* is conceived within a cube, with a cylindrical back rest composed of a pair of foam cushions that rotate. *Shogun Terra* is a tall cylindrical form with a perforated tilting shade and horizontal black stripes. While the lamp incorporates ornament in these stripes, they are contained within the structure and help to articulate it. These designs demonstrate the survival of the International Style and, in fact, its refinement in opposition to the decoration of Postmodernism.

Carlo FORCOLINI

(born 1947)

Coffee table with lamp
Apocalypse Now
Designed 1984
118 x 120 x 120 cm
Cor-Ten steel, galvanized steel,
chrome, rubber
Produced for Alias, Milan, Italy
The Montreal Museum of
Fine Arts, 2004.30.1—2, gift
of Eric Brill to The Stewart
Program for Modern Design*

This table is named for the 1979 film about the Vietnam War by Francis Ford Coppola and recalls the military helicopters of that film. According to Forcolini, the specially treated Cor-Ten steel in this table "rusts only on the surface, so that whoever uses the table leaves marks on it. I think we have a twentieth-century distortion in the way we always think of object as being new. In fact things change as we use them."[48] Trained as a painter and sculptor, Forcolini initially worked in kinetic art from 1970 to 1974, and his training is reflected in the conceptual nature of his deconstructivist furniture designs. In 1979 he was one of the founders of the Italian company Alias, which is known for experimenting with materials. Unlike that of Memphis, furniture by Alias was characterized by minimalism.

Shigeru UCHIDA

(born 1943)

Floor lamp
Tenderly
Designed 1985
Steel with baked Melamine finish, aluminum
136.8 x 49.5 x 42 cm
Produced by Chairs, Tokyo, Japan
The Montreal Museum of Fine Arts, D92.192.1, gift of Toshiko Mori

Uchida studied design in Tokyo in 1966, and in 1970 established his own studio. In 1981, he was one of the founding members of the interior design firm Studio 80, and in that capacity designed this floor lamp, modeled on a professional photographer's light stand with a telescoping rod and lamp supported by a tripod. The halogen bulb in its pyramidal shade points directly upward to a perforated metal grid, which both reflects the light and allows it to pass through. The name *Tenderly* comes from the Elvis Presley song "Softly and Tenderly," reflecting the designer's interest in American popular music of the mid-twentieth century. He based his initial sketch for this tilting screen, he explained, on "the image of Japanese men holding up their sun visors to see who is good looking."[49] Uchida's work, like that of Kuramata, anticipated the new minimalism of the 1990s.

1990

1999

A New Minimalism

Optimism surged following the fall of the Berlin Wall in 1989 and the subsequent dissolution of the Soviet Union. But the end to the great postwar conflict between Communism and capitalism unleashed multiple older hatreds and ideologies. Genocide based on ethnic and tribal differences swept the former Yugoslavia, Rwanda, and Somalia, while religious fundamentalism took deeper hold in the Middle East. Participants in what financial pundits called the Predators' Ball of the 1980s were humbled by a recession in 1990–91, and Japan entered a decade of economic stagnation, following rampant real estate and currency speculation.

Software entrepreneurs grew astoundingly rich, however, through the digitally powered Information Revolution, and big-box stores in the malls of America brought consumers cheaper goods based on third-world labor and global transfers of credit. Despite resistance from Great Britain and Denmark, the European Union established a single market currency, the euro. Speeding and enlarging communication, digital cameras outsold film equipment, and cellular phones became common for both the urbane and the poor citizen with sparse landlines. Access to the Internet was, for the first time, seen as essential to basic education. Was all this good news or bad news? Merely managing the onslaught of information was a challenge of the 1990s. Design definitions were varied. Some designers seized on the era's technological innovations; some looked back and extended the effervescent spirit of the 1980s; some sought art-world status for their limited-edition works. Others looked back and sought to dematerialize Modernist forms; still others addressed ecological issues, which globalization was making more urgent. The 1990s recalled the '70s in the plurality of design and art styles, yet among the many differences was the new seriousness accorded design in its many roles.

With particular agility, Frank Gehry exploited current computer technology to generate the sculptural forms of his public buildings and chose high-tech materials to sheathe them. Acclaimed by critics, art tourists, and the public, his Guggenheim Museum in Bilbao, Spain, completed in 1997 (figs. 1–2), gave this gritty industrial city a cluster of canted, curvaceous titanium structures for exhibiting contemporary art. The architecture exploded all Modernist norms and has proved more memorable than any Guggenheim loans exhibited there: it established the new museum—among the largest possible designed objects—as a cultural destination and local economic booster.

Computer-aided design (CAD) was also employed to create designs as different as a wiry architectonic chair and streamlined futuristic seating (pp. 393, 407): it allowed designers to visualize and explore their conceptions quickly and in three dimensions and to calculate the behavior of materials selected for their virtual objects. Compared to the older, many-step methods of handwork and model making, CAD/CAM (computer-aided manufacturing) saved time, money, and many mistakes while liberating formal invention. It let designers alter specifications and tooling easily during manufacture, and it promised to change products to suit changing needs and niche markets.

A tuned-in exhibition of 1995 at The Museum of Modern Art surveyed current explorations of new synthetic materials, new techniques, and new uses of traditional materials, as seen in Karim Rashid's three-tiered laminated-glass coffee table (p. 358), which was prominently displayed. About the contents of *Mutant Materials in Contemporary Design*, exhibition curator Paola Antonelli wrote that "new technologies are being used to customize, extend, and modify the physical properties of materials and invent new ones endowed with the power of change." Rashid's table, for example, could be ordered in one of twenty-seven variants, and synthetic fibers on view could "remember" the shape of the user's body. "Materials are being transformed from adjuncts in passive roles to active interpreters of the goals of engineers and designers."[1] By the late twentieth century, plastics were defined, as Antonelli pointed out, either by composition (polyurethanes and silicones) or by technology (thermoplastics). In their "mature years," plastics were "acquiring flexibility and a quiet beauty."[2]

Plastics continued to be a protean means to realize Postmodern ideas, which were still crowd-pleasing in the 1990s. Polyurethane foam made it relatively easy for Masanori Umeda to fabricate his flowerlike chair, reminiscent of Pop art's gigantic transformations (p. 400). But newer materials also inspired new visions of color and light (translucent polypropylene for containers, p. 361; methacrylate for a fountain, p. 407), and new structures that were lightweight but strong (injection-molded magnesium for a chair, p. 407).

Some signature styles that had captured attention in the 1980s were extended, with Massimo Iosa Ghini and Philippe Starck, for example, demonstrating their continued loyalty to Futurism and Surrealism (pp. 405–06). In 1999 Starck moved from his native France to New York, which he saw as the world center for promoting and selling new design. As for other celebrity designers of the '80s, Ettore Sottsass survived the obituaries written for Memphis, notably when couturier Karl Lagerfeld, a pioneer supporter of the Milanese group, auctioned his collection in 1991.[3] Sottsass, Andrea Branzi, and Alessandro Mendini continued to flaunt their decorative invention (pp. 367–70, 384) and to gather laurels in turn: Sottsass was honored by a retrospective at the Centre Georges Pompidou in Paris in 1994, and Branzi was selected to curate the surveys *Italian Design 1964–1972* and *Italian Design 1973–1990* for the Milan Triennale in 1996 and 1999.

In 1996 planning began for a permanent collection of design to be installed in the Triennale's extensive buildings, and three exhibitions followed on how design should be collected and displayed. The decade saw the establishment of design museums in Toronto and Chicago; and in 1990 the Vitra Design Museum in Germany, designed by Gehry, opened with a display of the furniture company's corporate collection. Vitra began originating and circulating exhibitions of twentieth-century furnishings, as well as hosting summer workshops in France with leading designers.

Design also attracted broader interest from art enthusiasts and the public. Toward the end of the 1990s, furniture trade fairs opened in Cologne and Barcelona on the

1 Frank O. Gehry, Guggenheim Museum, Bilbao, Spain.
2 Computer rendering of Guggenheim Museum, Bilbao, design.

1

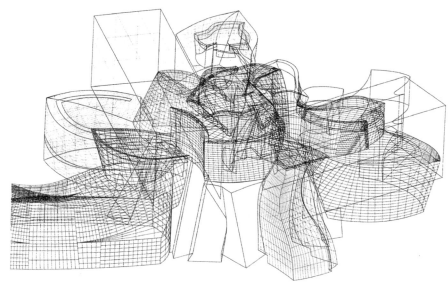

2

3

4

5

model of the Milan Triennale, which had its nineteenth presentation in 1996. In Milan itself, the Salone del Mobile, an annual event since 1961, sparked related displays outside the official area, in showrooms and alternative spaces: among the most creative were those mounted by Design Gallery Milano. Ingo Maurer and Ron Arad presented their work together, both at the Salone and off-site, dramatizing by contrast Maurer's magical lighting and Arad's aggressive furnishings in sheet steel (pp. 394–95, 408–09).

Arad, who had founded his gallery-studio One Off in 1981 in London, emerged by the early '90s as arguably the foremost of the British "metal bashers." In this post-punk generation, including Marc Newson, Tom Dixon, and Nigel Coates (pp. 386, 393), Arad's chairs and lounges were most surprising in their forms, resilience, and unexpected comfort. His choice of tempered steel and his play with its patinas, polishes, and welding associated his work with one-of-a-kind sculpture. Yet his success with plastics for Vitra and the Italian firms Kartell and Alessi in the 1990s underlined the functional ingenuity of his industrial designs. In the new millennium, his and Newson's expressionist metal designs in limited editions would become coveted art objects promoted by contemporary art galleries.

At the opposite pole from these English residents were designers who could be called Neominimalists. Eschewing both cold metal in rough overscale shapes and Postmodernism's cacophonous patterns and colors, they favored transparency, unadorned planar surfaces, delicate pastel hues, and simplified outlines. The aesthetic was visible in new buildings. The Museum of Modern of Art's 1995 exhibition *Light Constructions* took a punning title to describe international contemporary architecture in which structures seem both lightweight and filled with light, reinterpreting early Modernism with the new sensibility of the design world. French architect Jean Nouvel's building for the Fondation Cartier pour l'art contemporain in Paris seemed paradigmatic. Its curtain wall appears as a separate veil in front of the building—not as part of a glass box in Mies van der Rohe's style. The installation there of the exhibition *Issey Miyake: Making Things* in winter 1998–99 was the perfect marriage with Nouvel's architecture (fig. 3). Miyake's fashions, moving up and down on motorized hangers, added animation, color, and daring shapes in a dialogue with Nouvel's minimal interior.

Miyake's commissions for showrooms from his countryman Shiro Kuramata were cited in the previous chapter. The Japanese designer's furniture and interiors of transparent acrylic were physically strong and extraordinarily heavy but hauntingly poetic in their use of found objects and their visual evanescence (p. 360). In a related reductivist vein were designs by Jasper Morrison of England and Maarten Van Severen of Belgium (figs. 4–5, p. 363), whose twenty-year career was devoted to paring forms down to their diagrammatic essences. This and his dedication to geometries gave Van Severen's work a puritanical air, while his unusual proportions and dimensions made experiencing his designs memorable.[4] His aesthetic refinement of design types from the 1930s through mid-century suggests the new life that a different generation was giving the legacy of the Eameses, George Nelson, and others. Jasper Morrison put it flippantly in 1999: "Looking back, there was nothing wrong with modernism, it just needed an oil change."[5]

As scholarly exhibitions of the careers of the Eameses and Mies van der Rohe educated young observers, Herman Miller reissued the furnishings it had licensed from these and other designers in the 1950s. For consumers on more modest budgets, IKEA

3 Jean Nouvel, Fondation Cartier, with Issey Miyake's exhibition *Making Things* on view, October 13, 1998, to February 28, 1999.
4 Jasper Morrison, *Some new items for the house—part I*, DAAD Gallery, Berlin, 1988.
5 Maarten Van Severen, *Blue Bench*, 1/1 installation at Encore Bruxelles, May 1997.

made the utilitarian simplicities of "Scandinavian Modern" available to millions of homes through its international stores and mail-order system. Founded in the 1950s, IKEA was offering over twelve thousand home products by the 1990s, selling low-cost quality furniture and housewares in twenty-six nations.[6] Good Design as defined in the 1950s at last found its intended audience, though one that demanded less refinement and durability than its grandparents had.

An enlarged definition of Good Design had "green design" as a corollary. Governments, designers, and consumers took more seriously their responsibility to conserve resources and nature. Recycling laws were passed in industrialized countries; by the mid-1990s, about 6,600 cities in the United States had such laws, and the federal Environmental Protection Agency claimed that approximately one-fifth of all waste products were recycled. The *Green Newsletter* reported that, by 1994, 10.5 percent of new products claimed a green feature,[7] suggesting that environmentally conscious design added value to products.

Droog Design linked such concerns to idiosyncratic minimalism. Introduced at the 1993 Salone del Mobile in Milan, Droog was a Dutch collaborative of designers with a shared mission of experimentation. Their furnishings, lighting, and housewares struck a chord with serious consumers and proved to be moderately successful commercially. "Droog" means "dry" in Dutch, with connotations the group wanted: "Strong and clear like a good Martini, the desert, or a pointed remark in conversation."[8] The group saw itself as emblematic of the 1990s in refusing to acknowledge the traditional identification of important design with a single style. The company cofounder Renny

6 Shigeru Ban, *Paper Loghouse*, Nagata-Ku, Kobe, Japan, 1995, built for people who lost their homes to the Hanshin earthquake.

Ramakers wrote: "We certainly don't see [our products] as the definitive solution to a problem or the one direction to take but as the door to any number of possibilities."[9] The various idioms of artists such as Sigmar Polke and Martin Kippenberger were analogous.

Recycling is an ongoing theme for some designers in the 1990s (pp. 378, 380) and for Droog, as seen in their chest of drawers, piled and belted together, and hanging lamp of milk bottles (pp. 374–75, 379). For Droog, found objects were not nihilistic, as they had been for Dada or Pop, but moralistic: Droog's products were meant to proclaim "waste not, want not" to a culture of overabundance.

On a small scale, a Droog project at the end of the decade illustrated its designers' social concern. The historic town of Oranienbaum, freed from the Iron Curtain and part of reunified Germany, invited Droog to propose designs made with local materials by local manufacturers, in order to revive its severely depressed economy and renew its cultural identity. Droog's slogan, revising the 1970s motto, was "act locally, think globally." Its many design ideas, appealingly modest and environmentally engaged, included a lollipop of local orange candy on a curved poplar stick with an orange seed, suggesting that the consumer eat the candy and plant the seed. "Restoration, revival and innovation are the three pillars supporting the [Droog] concept," wrote one of the Oranienbaum organizers, "the guiding purpose of which was to give the complex its soul back."[10] His belief, on the eve of a new millennium, was optimistic: that thoughtful design could restore a community's soul.

Responding to more drastic needs, the Japanese minimalist Shigeru Ban sought elemental forms on both social and aesthetic grounds. The architect's *Paper Loghouse* of 1995 (fig. 6) was intended for the victims of the Hanshin earthquake that devastated Kobe, Japan. The requirements were for a cheap building that anyone could assemble and dismantle, one insulated against both summer and winter weather. Ban's achievement was a 172-square-foot unit costing less than $2,000. The cardboard materials were easily disposed of or recycled.[11] Ban, who could design graceful Neomodernist furnishings with cardboard tubing (p. 385), had already created emergency shelters in 1994 to help meet the needs of the more than two million people made homeless by the civil war in Rwanda.

A cardboard shelter for disaster housing, a lollipop of local candy—these functional designs were not the most photogenic or controversial of the 1990s, but they demonstrated the growing awareness in the decade of design's role in problem-solving for all society.

Karim RASHID

(born 1960)

Coffee table
Aura
Designed 1990
Glass, coated steel rods
48.3 x 91.5 x 69.9 cm
Produced by Zeritalia,
Pesaro, Italy
The Montreal Museum of Fine
Arts, D98.179.1a–d, gift of Zeritalia

In the 1990s avant-garde designers such as Rashid used the most recent industrial materials and technology for different purposes from their mid-century counterparts. They sought individual expression to replace universal ideals, and adopted technology as a tool. For *Aura* Rashid explored new laminated glass technologies for its three tiers in three different colors and shapes. Each piece of glass has three layers. "A super high-pressure laminating press fused the three layers into a pertectic state (between a solid and liquid) and metamorphosed the sandwich into a solid sheet, whose edges were polished to hide the film layer." The table could take twenty-seven different configurations as the client assigned navy, peach, and yellow to the oval, hourglass, and rectangular glass pieces, and had them positioned on the top, middle, and bottom levels of the table.[12] Not only could the table assume twenty-seven different looks, but its perceived colors and the tinted shelves it cast could be highly individualized. No Platonic solids here: Rashid made technology serve as many variables and changes in human perception as he could.

Shiro KURAMATA

(1934–1991)

Stool

Acrylic Stool with Feathers
Designed 1990
Acrylic, aluminum, stained alumite
finish, feathers
54 x 30.9 x 40.5 cm
Produced by Ishimaru Co., Ltd.,
Tokyo, Japan
The Montreal Museum of
Fine Arts, D98.145.1

Kuramata has transformed this stocky, angled stool, one of the oldest of seating forms, by using transparent acrylic to dematerialize the design. The feathers, symbolic of lightness and the soul, float suspended. The design is sensuous, reflecting the surrounding light. An aluminum cylinder serves as a minimal backrest and contrasts with the geometric cube with its outwardly canted front. Kuramata had played with romantic symbolism using the same technique in his earlier armchair, *Miss Blanche*, which contained artificial roses embedded in the acrylic. Here, he uses actual soft feathers that appear to fall delicately in the air.

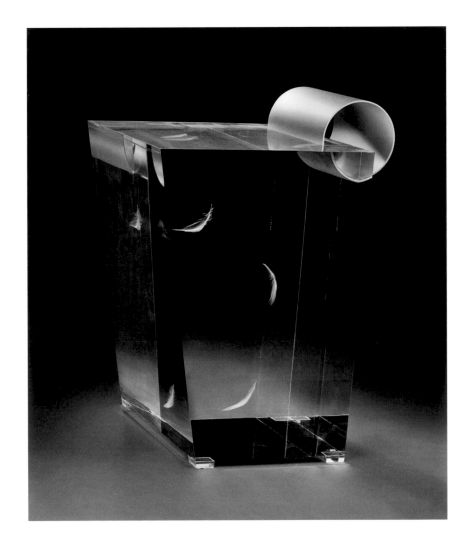

Andrea ANASTASIO

(born 1961)

Chest of drawers
Alba (Dawn)
Designed 1999
Lacquered wood, aluminum
laminate, methacrylate
121 x 126 x 50 cm
Produced for Design Gallery
Milano, Milan, Italy
The Montreal Museum of
Fine Arts, D99.163.1

Although the simplest of rectilinear forms, this chest of drawers is a studied work of art, reminiscent of the Minimalist sculptural boxes of Donald Judd. Yet the chest functions, even as Anastasio transforms the usually bulky form of the traditional type into a light, ethereal design. The support for the drawers is a structure hidden at the rear, allowing them to appear to float, an effect enhanced by the silvery facing in pink-tinted aluminum laminate. The designer plays with what we know—a storage piece requires balancing heavy weights and supports—and what we see—a trio of levitating forms aptly called *Alba,* Italian for "dawn." The nearly square-fronted chest was produced in an edition of twelve commissioned by Design Gallery Milano.

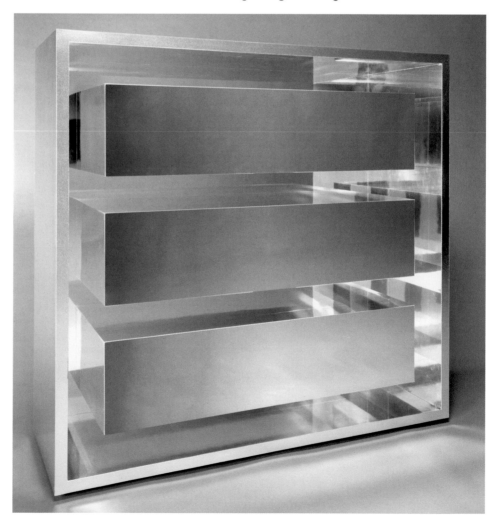

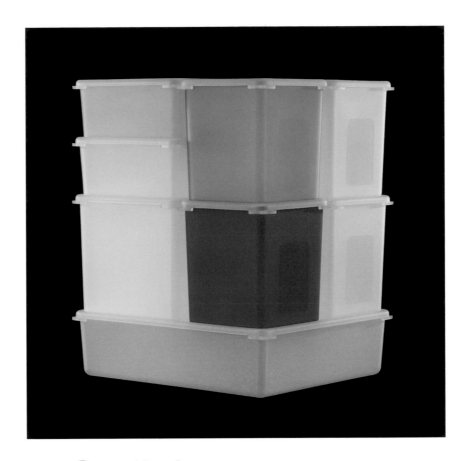

Constantin BOYM
Laurene Leon BOYM

(born 1955) and **(born 1964)**

Food containers
Use It
Designed 1995
Polypropylene
22.8 x 18.9 x 16.2 cm (assembled)
Produced by Authentics,
Holzgerlingen, Germany
The Stewart Program for
Modern Design, 2007.5.1–8

The Authentics company is known for products of translucent polypropylene and designs demonstrating its thinness, fine texture, and luminous color effects. Authentics commissioned the Boyms to conceive "a universal set of plastic containers." Constantin Boym wrote: "The containers had to become dignified enough to escape a cheap connotation of kitchen objects. Our work on the project attempted to simplify and eliminate every unnecessary articulation or detail. . . . In the end, our series of modular toy-like blocks looked almost generic, reminiscent of Wilhelm Wagenfeld's glass cubes or the American refrigerator ware of the 1940s. New was their immaterial lightness and ethereal translucent colors, which the company changed every season."[13] These qualities gave the containers' association with Tupperware a distinctly contemporary inflection.

Gijs BAKKER

(born 1942)

Bracelet
Shot
Designed and executed 1995
Anodized aluminum
8 x 8 cm
The Montreal Museum of Fine
Arts, D98.142.1, gift of Helen Drutt

Trained as a jewelry designer, Bakker created a wide range of industrial products, but jewelry has remained his focus. In 1966, he married Emmy Van Leersum, and they worked in partnership designing jewelry. After her death in 1984, he continued to make jewelry and to explore new concepts. In 1993, he and Renny Ramakers established Droog Design, an industrial design collaborative in which he continued to participate until 2009. Bakker usually works in a series, exploring a particular concept, such as incorporation of photography into his jewelry designs. This bracelet, created using digital technology, is related to his *Holes* project in industrial designs (p. 410) and also seen in the VIP room at the De Flint Amersfoort theater (below). The series of *Shot* jewelry "breaks away from the visually static character of the *Holes* project by adding the dynamism of movement. Imaginary gunshots into a thick disc create holes in the surface and bulges on the edge," hence the name. "Bullets of different caliber result in an oval form reflecting the cross-section of the hand." [14]

BELOW, LEFT Gijs Bakker, VIP room at the De Flint Amersfoort theater, Amsterdam, 1994.

Maarten VAN SEVEREN

(1956–2005)

Stacking chair
No. 3
Designed 1999
Polyurethane foam, aluminum
76.2 x 52.7 x 38.1 cm
Produced by Vitra, Weil am
Rhein, Switzerland
The Stewart Program for
Modern Design, 2008.31

Trained as an architect, Van Severen began designing furniture in 1985. He approached it as an architect, and pursued a minimalist aesthetic, emphasizing line and simplifying form. *No. 3* is related to archetypal modernist designs of the 1930s, such as a simplified steel and rubber chair of 1930 by René Herbst. Unlike visually similar prototypes, however, this austere chair is technically complex. "The secret lies in the unseen steel springs incorporated into the polyurethane, which both strengthen it and maintain its flexibility. It all makes the construction even more unexpected."[15] The unusual technology adds comfort to the chair, his first industrially produced design. It is available in several colors and in a stacking version as well.

Tore SVENSSON

(born 1948)

Two brooches
Designed and executed 1995
140.1: Iron, gold, silver
140.2: Iron, gold
7 x 7 cm (each)
The Montreal Museum of
Fine Arts, D98.140.1–2,
gift of Helen Drutt

After studying art from 1972 to 1974, Svensson learned silversmithing at the Konstindustriskolan HKS in Gothenburg, Sweden. He favors iron for many of his jewelry designs because it is inexpensive and strong, and its surface can be manipulated artistically. In these two brooches, he combined iron with silver and gold to create subtle variations in color and texture. The jewelry is part of a series based on rigidly geometric seven-centimeter squares, reminiscent of the black square paintings by the Russian Suprematist artist Kasimir Malevich.[16] The spare geometric design and its surface treatment also evoke Japanese art.

Antonio Glen Oliver CITTERIO LÖW

(born 1950) and **(born 1959)**

Table

Battista (Baptist)
Designed 1991
Thermoplastic technopolymer,
steel, aluminum, rubber
Extended: 68.5 x 100 x 54.5 cm
Folded: 68.5 x 20.3 x 54.5 cm
Produced by Kartell
S.p.A., Milan, Italy
The Montreal Museum of
Fine Arts, D95.194.1

This design was a collaboration between Citterio and the German designer Glen Oliver Löw, who joined Citterio's Milan studio in 1989. The *Battista* table was also the first collaboration between Citterio and Kartell and required more than a year of research and a year to produce.[17] The ingenious accordion supports for the top allow the piece to be compressed to one-fifth its length and its top folded for storage. The large, custom-made wheels, a Citterio and Löw hallmark, swivel in all directions. Though Citterio wrote that he intended the series of carts to bring back "images that have always belonged to household memories,"[18] *Battista* resembles a hospital gurney in its utilitarian appearance.

ABOVE, LEFT Citterio and Löw, *Gastone* and *Battista* tables, 1991.

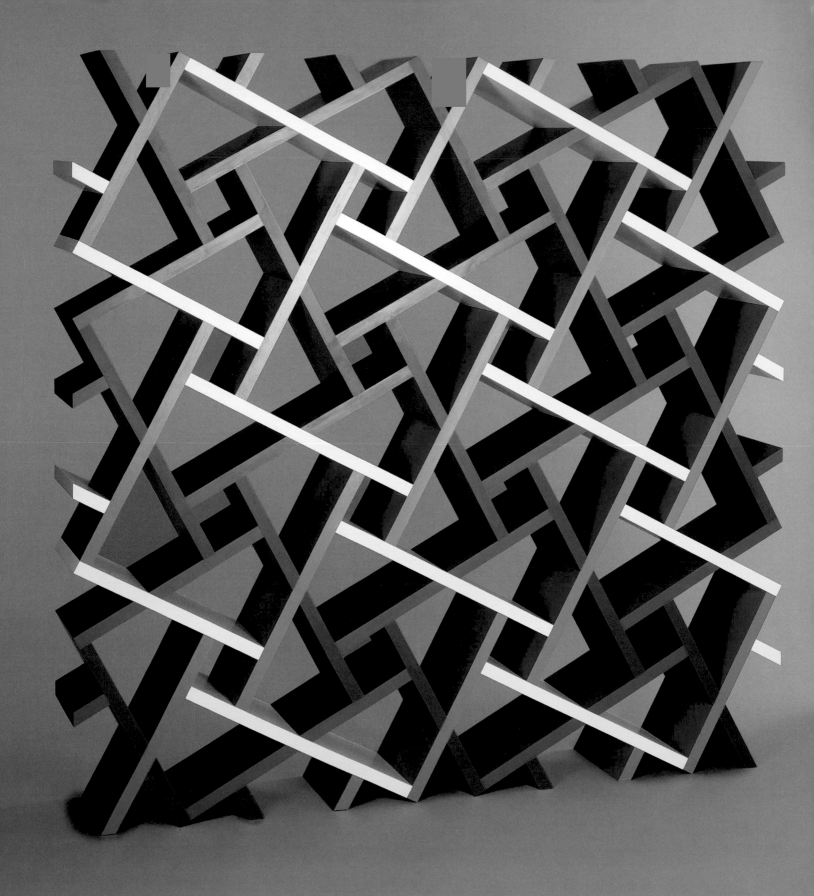

Shigeru UCHIDA

(born 1943)

Shelving
Stormy Weather
Designed 1991
Particle board, Formica
162 x 163 x 25 cm
Produced by Jean-François
Baudouin, Montreal,
Quebec, Canada
The Montreal Museum of Fine
Arts, D99.196.1

Although this shelving unit was designed in 1991, it was not produced until 1999 when the Montreal Museum of Decorative Arts commissioned it.[19] The shelving was inspired by a Mughal-period relief pattern carved on the Agra Fort in Agra, India, which Uchida saw in a book on international design. He was intrigued by the fact that each element was simple and geometric, yet the completed pattern looked complex.[20] The design is composed of stepped identical squares: the first square in the series is higher than the second by a third of its height; the second square is higher than the third by the same distance, and so on. The result is a set of directionals, each a different color, that refuse optical resolutions but create a harmonious whole. The transformation of a decorative motif into a large, hyperkinetically styled furnishing is a legacy of Postmodernism.

Alessandro MENDINI

(born 1931)

Vases
Alchemilla
Designed 1993
Glazed and gilded porcelain
233: 60.5 x 18 x 18 cm
234: 60.5 x 17.5 x 17.5 cm
Produced for Design Gallery
Milano, Milan, Italy
Indianapolis Museum of Art,
2008.233–234,
gift of Dr. Michael Sze to
The Stewart Program for
Modern Design*

From the 1970s on, Mendini celebrated ornament, symbolism, and craftsmanship and rejected the reductive aspects of Modernist design. These vases are part of the *Museum Market* collection he created for Design Gallery Milano. *Alchemilla,* named for a popular garden herb with leaves that radiate in a fan shape, combines Mendini's emphasis on colorful surface decoration with typically unexpected forms. The pleated cone shape appears throughout the collection. The stark contrast between the decorated and undecorated vases calls attention to Mendini's use of ornament, which he derives from various older cultures.[21] The decoration originates in painted African designs.

Alessandro MENDINI

(born 1931)

Chest of drawers
Nigritella Nigra
Designed 1993
Lacquered and stained
mahogany, Abet plastic laminate,
gold leaf, glass mosaic tile
110 x 97 x 50 cm
Produced for Design Gallery
Milano, Milan, Italy
The Montreal Museum of
Fine Arts, D94.318.1,
gift of Caroline Moreau

Named after a European black orchid, this ziggurat-like chest of drawers is exotic in its elaborate decorative scheme. The individual drawers are based on one of the oldest forms in the useful arts: the simple lidded wooden box. Here each box was constructed and decorated separately, then they were assembled and screwed together. A total of twelve chests were made, and the top box of each was decorated with a drawing by Lucio Giudici. The elaborate display of craftsmanship and patterning of this series typifies the luxuriousness of much Postmodern design in Italy. Part of an exhibition called *Museum Market*, commissioned by Design Gallery Milano, the series was, according to Mendini, inspired by a thought that he should simplify his designs, so he began a "classification of the thousands of forms, signs, colors, types, structures, and materials developed by us over the years."[22]

Ann WÅHLSTRÖM

(born 1957)

Vase prototype
Labyrinth
Designed 1992
Glass
40.3 x 21.5 x 21.5 cm
Produced by Kosta Boda,
Kosta, Sweden
The Montreal Museum of Fine
Arts, D93.102.1, gift of the
designer and Kosta Boda

Born in Stockholm, Wåhlström learned the techniques of glassblowing in the glass schools at the Orrefors factory in Sweden, and the Pilchuck Center in Washington State, U.S.A. From 1986 to 2005, she designed glass for Kosta Boda in Sweden, but she has also designed ceramics, metalware, and textiles for other companies. The spiral pattern—more reminiscent of the works of Memphis than of traditional Swedish glass—is sandwiched between layers of glass in this simple vase form. Wåhlström says this "very graphic" pattern is "a symbol I always return to. . . . It starts much smaller and follows the blowing process when air is blown into the glass. I like that it gets a little distorted."[23] *Labyrinth* is the prototype for an edition of twenty-five vases that were made to celebrate the 250th anniversary of the Kosta factory in 1992.

Roseline DELISLE

(1952–2003)

Covered jars

Quadruple 9.95, Triptyque 11.95, Triptyque 12.95
Designed and executed 1995
Partially glazed porcelain
Quadruple 9.95:
56.3 x 12.3 x 12.3 cm
Triptyque 11.95: 27 x 12.3 x 12.3 cm
Triptyque 12.95: 37 x 20.1 x 20.1 cm
The Montreal Museum of
Fine Arts, D95.212.1a–b,
D95.215.1a–c, D95.213.1a–c

Roseline Delisle graduated from the Institute of Fine Arts in Montreal in 1969, and in 1978 left her native Quebec to move to California, where she opened a studio in Santa Monica. She is known for her simple, elegant vessels with unusual proportions, wheel-thrown in sections and joined together. She uses a restricted palette—blues, black, and white—with linear decoration on forms that appear machine-perfect. According to the artist, "My work evolves from the concept of the unity of opposites . . . black and white, strength and fragility, movement and stillness. . . . Still maintaining the minimal qualities but desiring to add color, I experimented with vitreous engobes [liquid clay slips]. Wishing to obtain the same smooth surface, I applied the engobes to the vessel while on the wheel. The stripe pattern was a natural outgrowth of the application process. It seems to capture the spinning quality which refers back to [the vessels'] initial means of conception."[24]

Tejo REMY

(born 1960)

Chest of drawers
You Can't Lay Down Your Memories
Designed 1991
Maple; recycled drawers of wood, plastic, metal, and cardboard; cotton belt
134.5 x 136 x 69 cm
Produced by Droog Design, Amsterdam, The Netherlands
The Montreal Museum of Fine Arts, D99.159.1–41

This chest is a cacophonous display composed of twenty drawers gathered from old and recently made furniture in different sizes and facings, held together by a furniture mover's belt. It is put together and disassembled by the consumer. The total is metaphor for life's transience and the temporary nature of ownership, as well as the contingency of commodities themselves. This Dadaist work, which Remy conceived when he was a graduate student, has become one of the icons of the Dutch collaborative Droog Design, with which he has been associated since its founding in 1993. Remy's choice of discarded, everyday furniture parts and his disdain of costly-looking manufacturing processes reflect Droog's attitude toward the environment and technology. "Partly, this represented a revolt against the dictates of trendy design, but it was also because existing objects add an extra dimension."[25]

Marcel WANDERS

(born 1963)

Chair
Geknoopte stoel (Knotted Chair)
Designed 1995
Carbon and Aramid
fibers, epoxy resin
74.8 x 50.5 x 66 cm
Produced by Cappellini, S.p.A.,
Como, Italy, for Droog Design,
Amsterdam, The Netherlands
The Montreal Museum of
Fine Arts, D99.138.1,
gift of Cappellini, S.p.A.

Wanders made *Geknoopte stoel* by the ancient method of macramé—
knotting string without the use of tools—but he employed a high-tech
string of his own invention composed of carbon and Aramid fibers.
After the string was hand-knotted, the limp chair form was treated
with epoxy, carefully arranged into the desired shape, and then hung
to dry.[26] Lacy and lightweight, the knotted chair, launched in 1996
by Droog, is both rigid and strong. Because the design can be realized
by minimally skilled workers, and production requires no fuels, it has
become emblematic of the 1990s' concern for ecological issues
and inequities for global laborers.

Marcel WANDERS

(born 1963)

Vase

Egg
Porcelain
Designed 1992
14 x 12 x 11 cm
Produced by Rosenthal for Moooi
Studio, Breda, The Netherlands
The Stewart Program for
Modern Design, 2008.9

The egg, considered a perfect form by designers, has inspired modern objects large and small. Most have Platonic aspirations, but not this vase. Wanders is known for his ironic and provocative designs, which blur the distinctions between craft and industry. He created this by stuffing hard-boiled eggs into a latex condom, creating an asymmetrical, tilted, and tumescent vase form, then dipping and firing the piece. This unusual and oddly beautiful vessel was produced in three different sizes.[27] Wanders sought to go beyond the production technology learned from the Bauhaus and "to tell a different story—one that is more interesting, inspiring and valuable, which gives a new meaning and not only matches but expands our view of the world."

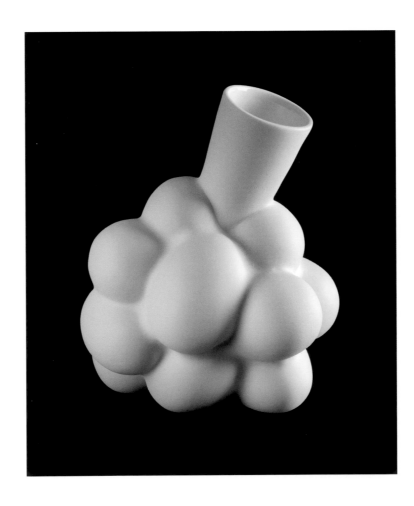

Fernando CAMPANA
Humberto CAMPANA

(born 1961) and **(born 1953)**

Tables
Designed 1995
Plastic, aluminum pizza
pans, aluminum
44.5 x 41 x 41 cm (each)
Produced by Fernando and
Humberto Campana,
São Paulo, Brazil
The Montreal Museum of Fine Arts,
D99.105.1, D99.125.1

Working together as partners since 1989, the Campana brothers have explored the craft traditions of their native Brazil as well as industrial materials. Their furnishings, often made from materials found on the streets of São Paulo, are stylistically eclectic as they focus on concept rather than image. These low tables are created by sandwiching an inflatable plastic form between two recycled pizza pans. Perched on three legs, reminiscent of 1950s Good Design, the drum-like tables are inexpensive to manufacture and easy to deflate and ship. In addition to functioning well, the tables provide humor and unpretentious pleasure.

Tejo REMY

(born 1960)

Hanging lamp
*Melkflessenlamp
(Milk-Bottle Lamp)*
Designed 1991
Recycled glass milk bottles,
stainless steel
28.5 x 36 x 27 cm
Produced by DMD (Development
Manufacturing Distribution,
Rotterdam BV), Voorburg,
The Netherlands
The Montreal Museum of Fine Arts,
D99.124.1, gift of Murray Moss

Remy created this lamp of recycled milk bottles—like the reused drawers in *You Can't Lay Down Your Memories* (pp. 374–75)—as part of his final exam in design at the Utrecht College for the Fine Arts. His goal was to counter the overwhelming abundance of different products in the 1980s and their costly materials by exploring the lyricism and beauty of the simple milk bottle. The container connoted a simpler, older way of life that included home delivery of milk in glass bottles. The straightforwardness of this lamp's assembly is part of its appeal. Four rows of bottles are arranged three deep, as in Dutch milk crates. Remy frosted them to diffuse the light and imitate older bottles. Stainless-steel fittings replace the original caps and hold the sockets and bulbs. *Melkflessenlamp* signaled a new directness in design that would lead to the formation of the Droog collaborative in 1993.

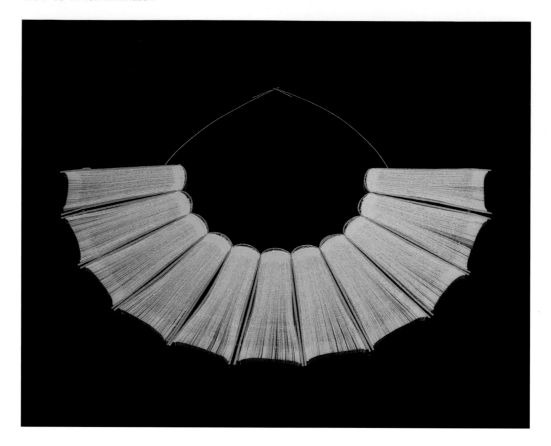

Janna SYVÄNOJA

(born 1960)

Necklace
Books
Designed and executed 1990
Book slices, wire
29.7 x 36.9 x 1 cm
The Montreal Museum of
Fine Arts, D92.155.1

While studying interior design at the University of Industrial Arts in Helsinki from 1982 to 1993, Syvänoja began making and selling jewelry. Her work countered the excessive consumerism of the late 1980s in her use of ephemeral, often recycled materials. For this necklace, she cut, shaped, and sewed together slices of a discarded book, using a fretsaw, drill, and sewing machine, and then strung them onto a steel wire. She wanted, she said, "to continue the life-span of material, to bring forth what had once existed and to demonstrate new connections. My works are prolonged moments."[28] The thin slices of the book are transformed into abstract shapes, and they flare into a kind of collar. "When you open a book and start to interpret it," Syvänoja wrote, "you find an adventure, a trip to jump into. I wanted to open this usual object in an unusual way, as we cut a fruit and find the seeds."[29]

Konstantin GRCIC

(born 1965)

Portable lamp
Mayday
Designed 1998
Polypropylene
53 x 21.5 x 21.5 cm
Produced by Flos, Milan, Italy
The Stewart Program for
Modern Design, 2007.59

Grcic, a graduate of the Royal College of Art in London, set up his own practice in 1991. This straightforward design, intended for multiple uses, was inspired by the emergency worker's portable lamp, transferring the form to domestic use for the mobility of a contemporary lifestyle. "People like it," Grcic explained, "because they can relate to it very directly. They immediately understand how to use it. In the end that's what made it a successful product."[30] The orange handle allows the lamp to be hung or carried easily, and the electrical cord can be cleated around it. *Mayday* is named after the S.O.S. call, which comes from the French *m'aidez* ("help me"), and, Grcic says, it is "handy for all sorts of expected/unexpected situations."[31] Its plastic makes it lightweight. In 2001, *Mayday* won the Compasso d'Oro, the internationally prestigious industrial design award presented annually by the Associazione per il Disegno Industriale.

Frank O. GEHRY

(born 1929)

Armchair prototype
Cross Check
Designed 1990
Maple-faced plywood, metal
94.5 x 88.5 x 65 cm
Produced by Gehry Studio, Los
Angeles, California, for Knoll
International, New York,
New York, U.S.A.
The Montreal Museum of Fine
Arts, D92.115.1, gift of the designer
and The Knoll Group

In a studio/workshop adjacent to his architectural office, Gehry and his colleagues developed a new bentwood furniture line for Knoll over a two-and-a-half year period. Inspired by a simple woven wood basket, Gehry's team produced and tested 120 full-scale prototypes, a group of which were donated to the Montreal Museum of Decorative Arts. As with the other chairs in this line, *Cross Check* is named after a type of foul in ice hockey—Gehry's favorite sport. Gehry said that "all of the bentwood furniture to this point . . . always had a heavy substructure and then . . . an intermediary structure for the seating. The difference in my chairs is that the support structure and the seat are formed of the same lightweight slender wood strips, which serve both functions. The material forms a single and continuous idea. What makes this all work and gives it extraordinary strength is the interwoven, basketlike character of the design."[32]

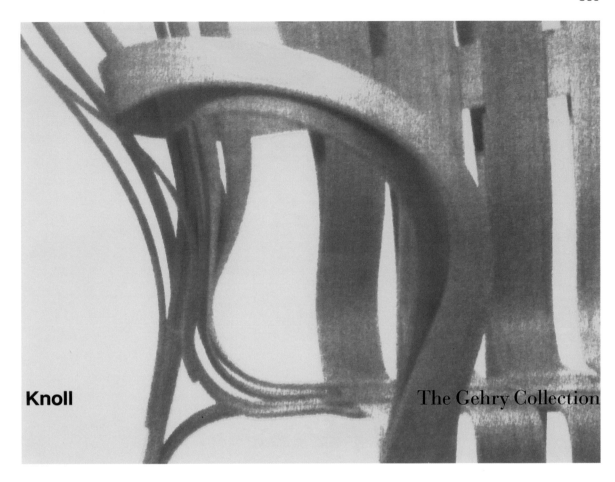

Knoll

The Gehry Collection

Bruce MAU

(born 1959)

Poster
The Gehry Collection
Designed 1991
Printed paper
59.5 x 76 cm
Produced for The Knoll Group,
New York, New York, U.S.A.
The Stewart Program for
Modern Design, 2009.7

Mau studied at the Ontario College of Art and Design in Toronto, but left before graduation to work for design firms, including Pentagram, an acclaimed graphics partnership based in London. In 1985 he established his own firm, which gained international recognition for its innovative research, environmental signage, and exhibition and product design. Frank Gehry found in Mau's graphic designs an experimental spirit sympathetic to his architecture, and in 1991 they collaborated on this poster and the exhibition catalogue, *Frank Gehry: New Bentwood Furniture*.[33] In the spirit of Herbert Matter's posters of the 1950s, this elegant, simple graphic design focuses on a detail of *Cross Check* (opposite), one of the architect's chair designs for Knoll, juxtaposed with the company name. The reverse side presents Gehry's explanation of his interest in designing furniture.

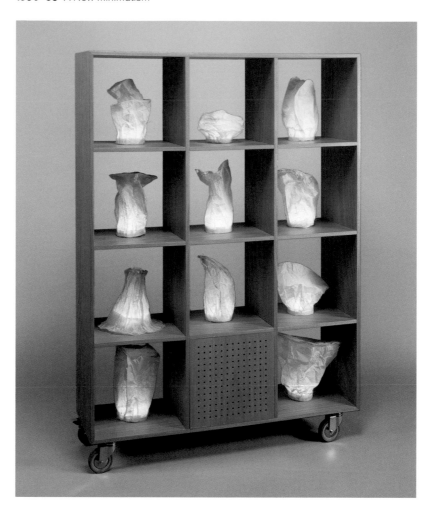

Andrea BRANZI

(born 1938)

Shelf/lighting
Wireless
Designed 1996
Walnut, rice paper,
aluminum, rubber
137.2 x 95.2 x 29.8 cm
Produced for Design Gallery
Milano, Milan, Italy
The Montreal Museum of Fine
Arts, D97.100.1a–m

Branzi's *Wireless* is a combination of shelving, lighting unit, and room divider, yet its appearance is less functional than poetic and sculptural. Eleven open compartments provide settings for freeform lamps, each different and covered with crushed handmade rice paper. The light glows from within these forms without any external wiring: the lamps are powered by rechargeable batteries concealed in the central compartment at the base. Without concern for access to electrical outlets, the unit is mounted on casters so it can be moved easily. *Wireless*, Branzi explained, is an object that corresponds "to a condition of existence in which we all live today: a condition where the 'ties' of the old knowledge systems are breaking, where the 'wires' of the old ideologies have disappeared."[34]

Shigeru BAN

(born 1957)

Bench and folding screen
Carta
Designed 1998
Cardboard tubes, plywood, fabric
Bench: 37 x 185 x 60 cm
Screen: 180 x 247 x 4.5 cm
Produced by Cappellini S.p.A.,
Milan, Italy
The Montreal Museum of
Fine Arts, 2001.44–45,
gift of Cappellini S.p.A.

Ban is known internationally for his innovative architectural work with recycled cardboard tubes, which he used to compose quick, easy-to-assemble housing for disaster victims (see p. 356, fig. 6). He wrote, "Even in disaster areas, as an architect I want to create beautiful buildings. I want to move people and to improve people's lives. If I did not feel this way, it would be impossible to create meaningful architecture and to make a contribution to society at the same time."[35] That inexpensive cardboard could be handsome (as well as ecological) is evident in his *Carta* series of furniture, including this bench and folding screen. The simplifed forms are reminiscent of designs at mid-century: the screen, for example, recalls curvilinear models by both Aalto and the Eameses (pp. 102–03).

Marc NEWSON

(born 1963)

Chair
Wicker Chair
Designed 1990
Wicker, steel
77 x 66 x 88 cm
Produced by Idée Co. Ltd.,
Tokyo, Japan
The Montreal Museum of
Fine Arts, D99.166.1

From 1989 to 1992, Newson lived in Tokyo, working for the design entrepreneur Teruo Kurosaki, president of Idée, the progressive Japanese furniture manufacturer. "Kurosaki sent me off to Bangkok for three months to work on some wicker pieces," Newson recalled. "I thought of this really beautiful shape and went out to the factory in the countryside, full of oxen, to make it. Each one took four hundred man hours of work."[36] When the design was presented, a contemporary critic wrote that Newson mixed the swollen, organic shapes of 1950s industrial styling with his enthusiasm for surfing from his native Australia.[37] Although this chair appears to be made of a single piece of woven wicker, underneath there is a steel frame and at the back a strut for support. This combination of a traditional material and an aerodynamic shape anticipated much contemporary design that was to follow.

Cindy SHERMAN

(born 1954)

Soup tureen and tray

Madame de Pompadour
Designed 1990
Glazed and painted porcelain,
photo-silkscreen transfer
36.8 x 55.9 x 29.9 cm
Produced by the Ancienne
Manufacture Royale de Limoges,
France, for Artes Magnus,
New York, New York, U.S.A.
The Montreal Museum of
Fine Arts, 2009.3.1–3

Since the 1970s, this Postmodern camera artist has dealt with how female identity is constructed in various periods and media, from the contemporary to the historical. In most of her work, Sherman alters her appearance with makeup and costume and then photographs herself acting in a role: here she applied her considerable directorial skills to the decorative arts. In the design of this porcelain tureen, she supplied a photograph of herself, disguised as Madame de Pompadour, the famed mistress of Louis XV, to replace the Pompadour portrait in the original service. At the Limoges factory, the Sherman image was transferred by means of a complex process of photo silkscreens, and an edition of one hundred porcelain tureens was produced as part of a complete service, similar to the original ordered by Madame de Pompadour in 1756 from the Manufacture Royale de Sèvres[38]. The personality of Pompadour may have appealed to Sherman, as both were associated with the arts and cultivated witty role-playing. Here the New Yorker's "patronage" helped the current business of the Ancienne Manufacture Royale, as Pompadour had aided a predecessor.

Gaetano PESCE

(born 1939)

Table lamp
Verbal Abuse
Designed 1993
Polyurethane, lead, graphite
fishing rods, steel
65 x 37 x 63 cm
Produced by Fish Design,
New York, New York, U.S.A.
The Montreal Museum of
Fine Arts, D98.169.1

This lighthearted design looks like a looming, big-footed cartoon figure, and its behavior is humanoid. The table lamp, made in an edition of six, is based on Pesce's technical knowledge of polyurethane, which he developed through experimentation in his studio and in cooperation with industry.[39] Graphite fishing rods are set between steel rods and inserted into a pair of lead "feet"; the body of the figure was created by pouring red resin over the rods, and a horizontal wire, representing the arms, is placed at the level of the sensor light switch. The red body and light-fixture head are bowed by lead weights at the ends of the two chains. Creating functional yet playful objects was not a new idea for Pesce in the 1990s: he had been producing expressive, imaginative interpretations of everyday objects since the '60s, and this lamp, which Pesce says represents a victim of verbal abuse, is no exception.

Joyce SCOTT

(born 1948)

Necklace
Frosted
Designed and executed 1995
Glass beads, plastic beads
34.5 x 28.5 x 4 cm
The Montreal Museum of
Fine Arts, D95.179.1

Scott has worked in jewelry, sculpture, performance, and installation art during her career. Although some of her beaded necklaces are confrontational and political, representing her African-American experience, this example is more subdued, and is described by the artist as "pink dreams, kind of light; frosty daylight, crystal. Lady sleeping but barely awake . . . hazy colors of spring."[40] She began using beads in the mid-1970s after working with Native American and African artists at the Haystack Mountain School of Crafts in Deer Isle, Maine. Her jewelry has no backing for support: she builds fluid figures, as if in bas-relief, by using a traditional Native American peyote stitch to sew thousands of colored beads.[41]

Dale CHIHULY

(born 1941)

Bowls

*Cadmium Yellow Seaform
Set with Red Lip Wraps*
Designed and executed 1990
Glass
43.2 x 61 x 91.5 cm
The Montreal Museum of
Fine Arts, D90.219.1a–j,
gift of Jay Spectre*

In the 1960s Chihuly's glass designs were functional, and in 1968 he made the first of many visits to Venice to work at the Murano glass factories. He soon began to move from functional to sculptural designs in glass (p. 252). In 1980 he initiated the *Seaform* series, in which he imitated the movement of the sea in vividly colored, ruffle-edged bowls. This example is in bright yellow, red, and orange, and the different pieces can be displayed separately or nested. "The piece is always moving while it's in progress, and one has to make decisions very quickly," Chihuly wrote, "I like the work to reflect those quick decisions, the end result being a frozen fluid thought—as direct as drawing. My work . . . relies on spontaneous combinations of fire, molten glass, air, and gravity."[42] By the 1990s, Chihuly had become the most famous glass artist in the world, and his studio a manufactory of environmentally scaled glass sculptures. He recalled learning about the teamwork required for such an enterprise from his experience at Murano.

BELOW Dale Chihuly, *Saffron & Red Tower,* 2000, Rutherford, California.

Jacopo FOGGINI

(born 1966)

Floor lamp
Dancing Sculpture
Designed 1998
Methacrylate, lacquered
wood, iron
178.5 x 64 x 65 cm
Produced by Jacopo Foggini for
Design Gallery Milano,
Milan, Italy
The Montreal Museum of
Fine Arts, D.98.1.34.1

A descendant of a Baroque sculptor at the Medici court, Foggini is a sculptor and designer. His colorful organic light sculptures are made of methacrylate, a plastic material used for road signs and car reflectors. He melts the methacrylate at a high temperature (300°C/572°F) and spins thin filaments, shaping them on a turntable into attenuated organic forms. *Dancing Sculpture* gathers and intensifies ambient light like a highway reflector, emitting light from a bulb within. The lamp rests on a remote-controlled motor that turns it, providing changing views of its wave-like forms. These soft shapes evoke the sea, which the artist loves, especially along the coast of Greece. The lamp is one of an edition of ten commissioned by Design Gallery Milano for its 1998 exhibition at the time of the Milan Furniture Fair.

Tom DIXON

(born 1959)

Chair
Pylon
Designed 1991
Painted steel
126.5 x 57.3 x 55.5 cm
Produced by Cappellini
S.p.A., Como, Italy
The Montreal Museum of
Fine Arts, D99.137.1,
gift of Cappellini S.p.A.

At the beginning of his career in the early 1980s, Dixon was among the London artists known as "metal bashers" who enjoyed the New Brutalist look of metal objects roughly welded together. He moved to more organic forms in metal and rattan (p. 330), and then to this dematerialized design, which represented a dramatic turn in his work. The symmetrical, structural seating "consists of nothing but open wire, zig-zagging skywards in a crazy matrix of welds, until its backrest appears to hover above the sitter like a mantis."[43] Constructed of thin steel rods welded into triangles, the overall structure is reminiscent of the Eiffel Tower. Monumental in conception, the chair is quite small in actuality. Initially made and sold in a limited edition by his own company, Space, the chair was put into production by Cappellini in 1992.

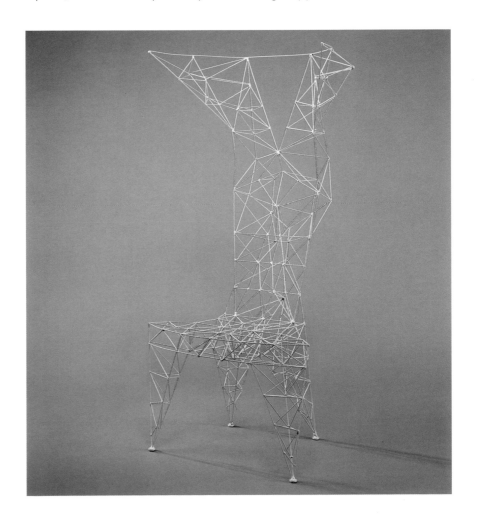

Ron ARAD

(born 1951)

Bookcase
One Way or Another
Designed 1993
Steel
255 x 180 x 30 cm
Produced by One Off Ltd.,
London, England
The Montreal Museum of Fine
Arts, D93.311.1, gift of Mr. and Mrs.
Roger Labbé

With *One Way or Another*, Arad challenged the conventional bookcase form, which is rectilinear and stationary. This work's blackened, tempered steel sheets are among Arad's favorite materials: he explored the strong but very flexible sheets in his challenging work after he began his own company, One Off, in 1981. Considering the resilience of the steel in his predecessor for this bookcase, Arad wrote: "Nothing is fixed solidly, so although it is locked, it still moves and is still allowed to spring. Gravity helps shape it as well; when you remove a book from the library, the whole coil is still breathing for a while."[44] Arad's daughter named this bookcase *One Way or Another* because of its tendency to sway from left to right in response to use.[45]

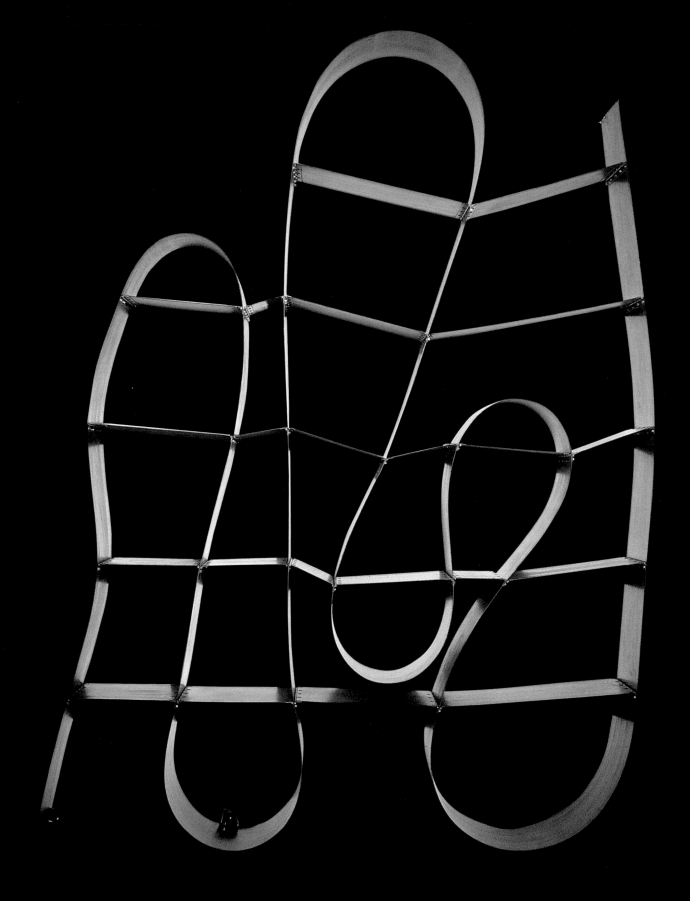

Andrea BRANZI

(born 1938)

Vases
Amnesie (Amnesia) Series
Designed 1991
Aluminum
44.2 x 11.4 x 11.4 cm (largest)
Produced for Design Gallery
Milano, Milan, Italy
The Montreal Museum of
Fine Arts, D93.297.1–5,
gift of Paul Leblanc

These vases were commissioned for Branzi's 1991 exhibition *Amnesie* at Design Gallery Milano in collaboration with architect and designer Monica Moro. Branzi explained that the title of the series means "free break" through "(temporary) memory collapse."[46] Produced on computer-controlled lathes in an edition of fifty, the *Amnesie* series displays the precision of the machine and some of the forms generated by lathe-turning. Exploiting the sheen of aluminum, the vases give an impression of vibrant rotation.[47] The vases can stand alone, or their related forms allow them to be grouped, establishing a linear rhythm. Each vase was named for the number of grooves per vase, preceded by the letter A for *Amnesie*: here are shown, left to right, A 56, A 38, A 28, A 51, and A 46.

Karim RASHID

(born 1960)

Ice bucket
Tor
Designed 1999
Stainless steel
24.5 x 24.6 x 23.7 cm
Produced by Magppie for Karim
Rashid, Inc., New York,
New York, U.S.A.
The Stewart Program for
Modern Design, 2007.68

Rashid has explored slanted forms over a period of years, beginning with his *Leaning Clocks* and serving pieces of 1995 for Nambé.[48] In addition to this ice bucket, his line for Magppie includes a slanted wine cooler, cocktail shaker, and champagne cooler. These departures from the vertical are unexpected and provide whimsical humor for the cocktail hour. The canted cylinder of the bucket melts like ice into a fluid, tapering base, and the rounded top has an amusing droplet-shaped finial. Like all his receptacles, this derives its sensuousness from Rashid's display of unadorned materials and his eye for appealing silhouettes.

Ronan BOUROULLEC

(born 1971)

Vases

Sans Titre (Untitled)
Designed 1997
Plastic polycarbonate
20 x 14 x 14 cm (each)
Produced by Cappellini,
Milan, Italy
The Stewart Program for
Modern Design, 2008.23.1–2

Resembling a spinning-top toy, *Sans Titre* vases can be grouped and interlocked in a linear composition, or used separately. This vase was designed by Ronan Bouroullec two years before he formed a partnership with his brother, Erwan, in 1999. Like their *Cloud* shelving system of 2004, also produced by Cappellini, *Sans Titre* can be assembled by the owner in configurations to suit individual needs. The Bouroullec brothers' work is notable for its experimental nature and striving for perfection. They considered the grouping of these vases as a still life without concern for function. "It's a complex subject to forget about function, to produce an object solely for the eye," the Bouroullecs wrote. "Λ still life . . . is based on formal qualities of proportions and colours . . . it works through more cultural, symbolic references."[49]

Ole JENSEN

(born 1958)

Teapot
Ole
Designed 1993
Glazed porcelain
22.5 x 15 x 19 cm
Produced by Royal Copenhagen,
Copenhagen, Denmark
The Stewart Program for
Modern Design, 2008.5a–b,
gift of Dr. Michael Sze

The Danish designer Ole Jensen graduated from the School of Art in Kolding, Denmark, in 1985 and the Royal Academy of Arts, Copenhagen, in 1989. His playful biomorphic forms such as this teapot reflect a new direction for the manufacturer Royal Copenhagen, a long-established company under royal patronage since 1775 and known primarily for its blue-and-white wares in traditional forms. This engaging, three-legged teapot, which was also produced in a bright yellow, is both organic and streamlined with its forward thrust and continuous curves. Its black wavy lid trails back onto its flared handle, adding a touch of whimsy.

Masanori UMEDA

(born 1941)

Armchair
Getsuen (Moonlit Garden)
Designed 1990
Cotton velvet, polyurethane foam,
Dacron, polyethylene, lacquered
iron, steel
83.2 x 100.4 x 92.1 cm
Produced by Edra S.p.A.,
Pisa, Italy
The Montreal Museum of
Fine Arts, D93.259.1,
gift of Maurice Forget

Umeda conceived this chair in the form of the kikyo, a Chinese bellflower, a favorite of the designer. He was concerned about the harm that industrialization brought to his native Japan, destroying not only nature but also the country's historical heritage. "This sad reality," he wrote, "has made me try to love animals, plants and nature . . . just like the Japanese used to do. That's why my designs are full of [such] motifs."[50] Though fanciful in form, *Getsuen* is supported by an elaborate steel frame, and its fluorescent green rear castor gives it mobility. In 1967, Umeda left Japan to work in Milan for the Castiglioni brothers, and he remained there until 1969. In the 1970s he met Ettore Sottsass, who invited him to participate in the first Memphis exhibition in 1981, for which Umeda created his famous "boxing ring" seating. *Getsuen* continues in this vein of humor and fantasy.

David PALTERER

(born 1949)

Armchairs
Tritrono (Three Thrones)
Designed 1990
Ebonized ash
71.7 x 72.3 x 72 cm; 71.7 x 76 x
73.5 cm; 71.7 x 74.5 x 84.5 cm
Produced for Edizioni Galleria
Colombari, Milan, Italy
The Montreal Museum of
Fine Arts, D91.409.1–3

This tripartite seating design is based on the nineteenth-century tête-à-tête, a type found in Victorian drawing rooms. Palterer updated the design by creating it of three organically sculpted armchairs that can be joined together or used separately. The extensions of the crest rails compose one curvilinear shelf when the chairs are placed back to back and facing outward. Trained as an architect at the University of Florence, the Israeli-born Palterer made these three chairs as part of a limited, handcrafted edition for the Colombari Gallery in Milan, an enterprise specializing in adventurous twentieth-century design.

Danny LANE

(born 1955)

Fountain maquette
Shora'a Ala El-Nil (Sail on the Nile)
Designed and executed 1998
Glass, chromium-plated steel
72 x 74 x 49 cm
The Montreal Museum of
Fine Arts, 2008.397

Born in Urbana, Illinois, Lane moved to London in 1975. In 1981 he opened his own studio in the West End, and soon became one of England's best-known artists in glass. He has created furniture, sculpture, and site-specific pieces in glass—a material he often combines with metal. Characteristic of Lane's work is his use of stacked and fractured glass, recycled broken glass, and twisted or rusted steel. Between 1983 and 1985, Lane exhibited with Tom Dixon at Ron Arad's One Off gallery presenting furniture characterized as "either genuinely found or deliberately reduced to an advanced stage of picturesque decay."[51] This maquette is for a water sculpture that was erected in the center of the foyer of the Conrad Hotel in Cairo, commissioned by Bechtel/Hilton Hotels Corp. The spiraling form is mounted on a fractured glass base.

BELOW The *Shora'a ala El Nil* fountain, in the foyer of the Conrad Hotel in Cairo.

David PALTERER

(born 1949)

Vase
Orsa Minore (Little Dipper)
Designed 1991
Glass
71.7 x 26.4 x 34.3 cm
Executed by Pino Signoretto,
Murano, Italy, for Edizioni Galleria
Colombari, Milan, Italy
The Montreal Museum of
Fine Arts, D91.429.1

For this expressive multilimbed vase, Palterer was inspired, he says, by the Greco-Roman wine vessel, the "classical amphora, again in memory of the very, very archetype of vases."[52] But there is a difference. The amphora is perfectly symmetrical and lacks a base (being placed in racks), while this handblown vase stands on five root-like legs—an excess of support, added for animation rather than necessity. In his ebullient designs for glass, Palterer has a kinship with Bořek Šípek, and in fact the two formed a partnership in 1983 they called Alterego to design and produce works in glass. *Orsa Minore* is part of a limited edition commissioned by Galleria Colombari in Milan.

Philippe STARCK

(born 1949)

Stool

W.W. (Wim Wenders)
Designed 1990
Varnished sandblasted aluminum
97 x 56 x 53 cm
Produced by Vitra GmbH,
Weil am Rhein, Germany
The Montreal Museum of Fine
Arts, D93.204.1, gift of Vitra
International AG

In the late 1970s and '80s Starck became famous for his restaurant designs in Paris and his interiors for chic hotels such as the Royalton in New York. He initially designed this stool for the office of the German film director Wim Wenders, and it has been in production by Vitra since 1992. Starck wrote that "Wim Wenders said to me something like: 'either I sleep or I work standing up, maybe with a kind of stool.'"[53] In response, Starck's sensuous anthropomorphic design was more a metaphor than a functional stool; the three-pronged piece of sandblasted cast aluminum barely allows sitting, but can serve as a form to lean upon. On the straighter leg, the angular spur offers a footrest. Both animal and vegetable in its aura, the slightly menacing design is a hip conversation piece.

Massimo IOSA GHINI

(born 1959)

Sunglasses
Designed 1991
4.6 x 15.5 x 15.3 cm
Plastic
Produced by Silhouette
Modelbrillen, Linz, Austria
The Montreal Museum of Fine
Arts, D94.169.1a,
gift of the designer

"Designer" sunglasses have been fashionable since the 1960s, and flowing shapes, like this single sweep of plastic, are recurrent stylizations. This example is the most aerodynamic in the line, with its extended oval reminiscent of the nose of an airplane. It represents a continuation of Iosa Ghini's obsession with streamlined forms, which he announced in 1982 when he gathered likeminded designers to found the Bolidist group.[54] In addition to these glasses, Iosa Ghini also conceived sculptural displays for the manufacturer's eyewear.

Ross LOVEGROVE

(born 1958)

Armchair
Go Chair
Designed 1999
Magnesium-aluminum alloy,
polycarbonate plastic
77.5 x 58.4 x 68.6 cm
Produced by Bernhardt Design,
Lenoir, North Carolina, U.S.A.
The Stewart Program for
Modern Design, 2004.6,
gift of Bernhardt Design

This streamlined, aerodynamic armchair was the first seating to be mass-produced in injection-molded magnesium, a metal lighter than aluminum yet equally strong. Asked what inspired the *Go Chair*, Lovegrove replied: "Body form, sensuality, anatomical base, high technology: I want to make things which can only exist today. . . . I am an absolute committed futurist. I actually don't live in the time zone I stand in; I don't look back."[55] The *Go Chair* looks to the future with the continuous swoop of its front legs, arms, and crest rail. Styled for the space age, it is nonetheless comfortable for today's user.

Ingo MAURER
Dagmar MOMBACH

(born 1932) and **(born 1958)**

Floor lamp
Babadul from *MaMo Nouchies* series
Designed 1998
Paper, stainless steel, stone, silicone, plastic
133.5 x 14 x 22 cm
Produced by Ingo Maurer, Munich, Germany
Liliane Stewart Collection

This lamp was designed in homage to Isamu Noguchi and inspired by his *Akari* series of paper lamps of the 1950s (see p. 138–39). The ultimate source for both lamps is traditional Japanese paper lanterns, and both provide light as well as sculptural art for a room. The series name *MaMo Nouchies* is a play on the last names of the two designers and Noguchi. The series of thirteen lamps was a collaboration between Maurer and Mombach, who developed the technique for making the minutely pleated, stiffened paper by hand.[56] *Babadul* resembles a cocoon hanging from a tree: its lyrical form is created by the simple folding over of the pleated paper, which is loosely attached to the thin steel rod that supports the light bulbs.

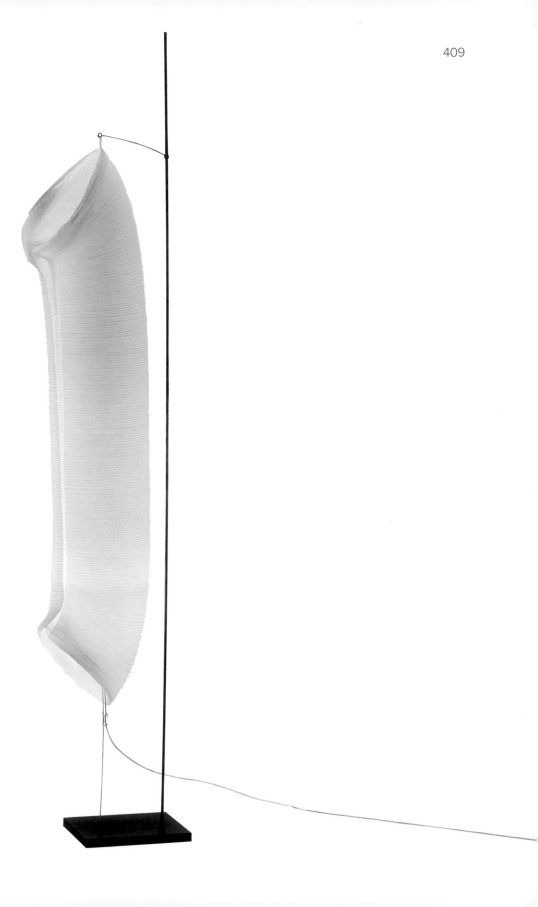

Gijs BAKKER

(born 1942)

Tablecloth
Non Cloth
Designed 1991
Linen
148 x 148 cm
Produced by DMD (Development
Manufacturing Distribution),
Tilburg, the Netherlands
The Stewart Program for
Modern Design, 2009.23

This tablecloth is part of Bakker's *Holes* project, a collection of perforated objects, including a table, chair, candlestick, vase, bracelet, cake cover, and wallpaper. "I discovered that it is not the hole, but what is behind the hole that is important. In this case, instead of hiding your table with your tablecloth, you reveal parts of it."[57] The holes made all Bakker's objects lighter and saved material, yet the objects remained strong enough to fulfill their purpose, the ultimate in minimalism. The designer saw the project as a criticism of the volume of wasted materials in our consumer society. "I have never been interested in handmade things, and I am, in fact, suspicious of their charm. It's the idea that matters."

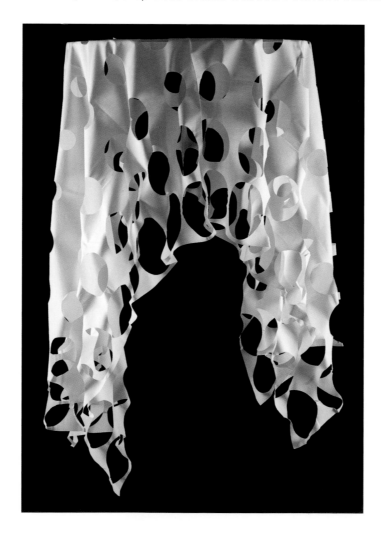

Bořek ŠÍPEK

(born 1949)

Armchair
Steltman
Designed 1994
Plywood, cherry, leather
86 x 61 x 52 cm
Produced by Steltman
Galleries, Amsterdam,
the Netherlands
The Stewart Program for
Modern Design, 2009.16

Šípek received his architectural training at the celebrated Ulm School in Germany and became an international celebrity for his designs in furniture, glass, and metalwork, often reinterpreting historic forms. *Steltman* is a lighthearted fantasy whose amusement derives from the contrast of its two disparate elements: the seat and front legs derived from a traditional chair form, and the extravagant back composed of a single piece of perforated, painted wood serving as back, rear support, and arms. It is surprisingly comfortable: "I wanted my things to be functional," Šípek wrote, "but I didn't want them to be boring."[58] *Steltman* is named after the gallery that represents Šípek's work, and this example is number nine from an edition of fourteen.

2000
2009

The New Millennium:
Celebrity, Technology, Ecology

International celebrations and anxious anticipation about the new millennium notwithstanding, the world slipped relatively quietly into the twenty-first century. Some cities engaged designers to mark the turn into 2000 with public structures, most notably London, which commissioned the Millennium Dome from Richard Rogers Partnership (fig. 1). Equally gargantuan public architecture became global news a year later, when the World Trade Center in New York was destroyed by terrorist attacks. The twin towers, designed by Minoro Yamasaki and completed in 1971, were targeted on September 11, 2001, as an emblem of capitalism and Western power. Their destruction was an unforgettable demonstration of the power of design symbols to arouse primal emotions.

The first decade of the twenty-first century also witnessed what economists have called the worst financial crisis since the Great Depression in the 1930s. Beginning globally in 2008, and continuing through most of 2009, the "Great Recession" could not but affect design at the end of the decade. With unemployment running at 10 percent in the United States and more in other industrialized countries, with less money for general consumers to spend, the demand for new mass-marketed products dropped. But a budget-conscious economy can inspire innovation, as it did during World War II. In January 2009, Paola Antonelli, design curator at The Museum of Modern Art, forecast optimistically: "What designers do really well is work within constraints, work with what they have . . . there will be less design, but much better design."[1]

Public-spirited problem-solving design has gained energy in the new millennium, especially environmentally conscious or "green" design and "universal design"— ergonomically engineered products to meet the needs of handicapped, elderly, and average adults alike. Technological advances in synthetic materials and digitally powered production methods further such responsible design and also continue to inspire new forms at various price points, whether for a broad public or the recession-proof elite. Correspondingly, the star designers and architects of the 1980s and 1990s seem to be flourishing, and "Design Art" has enlarged its cachet in cutting-edge galleries, international art fairs, and the art and lifestyle press. *Celebrity, technology,* and *ecology* are watchwords for design for the first decade of the twenty-first century. *Globalism* characterizes the world of designers, while *emotionalism* radiates from their conceptions as they seek to serve needs beyond the practical.

Design Art has its detractors, as it giddily recalls the economic exuberance of the 1980s, when limited editions or one-offs of furniture and other designs were produced as expensive *objets d'art* for an exclusive market of very rich customers. Such galleries as Néotù in Paris (1984–2001) and Art + Industry (founded 1979) and the Peter Joseph Gallery (1991–97) in New York promoted these precious objects as art, although they were often functional. Design Art re-emerged with the astonishing boom in the contemporary art market in 2000–2007, and auction houses and galleries seized the moment to sell unique and limited-edition furniture. In addition, the rising tide of international art fairs, such as Miami-Basel, has found Design Art a commodity for the growing number of knowledgeable collectors created by new wealth throughout the world. Even priced at six figures, Design Art is more reasonable to purchase than hyped contemporary art, and it requires no grasp of art theory for its appreciation and use.

Not surprisingly, such high-end designs have overshadowed affordable products in the media, which often cover new designs as counterparts to fashion and entertainment. Marc Newson's *Lockheed Lounge* of 1985 (fig. 2), a sculptural beauty of aluminum and fiberglass, sold at Phillips de Pury & Co. in 2009 for $1.6 million, a record for contemporary design. Newson's edition of ten "retro-futurist" lounges was made to order for the super-heated Design Art market; and the Gagosian Gallery, one of that market's highest-flying suppliers, added Newson to its stable of contemporary artists. Designers such as Ron Arad and architects including Zaha Hadid have also collaborated with galleries to create costly objects, affordable by few customers, and they take commissions that allow them to explore novel forms, materials, and processes without concern for public tastes or the limits of function and manufacturing. Such designs can be more experimental, according to their defenders, because the designer is freed from the restrictions of mass production. Design Art objects are too costly to be junked and too few in number to threaten the environment through their manufacture. On the other hand, according to design critics Charlotte and Peter Fiell, their development "is beginning to monopolize the time and attention of some of our most creative designers, the very people we need to develop urgent real-world solutions."[2]

Technology has proven as helpful to responsible design as it has to Design Art. As the twenty-first century began, it was the unusual architect and designer who did not use CAD (computer-aided design) and CAM (computer-aided manufacturing) software in their design of products and their production of drawings, models, and prototypes. Processes such as RP (rapid prototyping), a digital information-printing technology, and 3-D stereo lithography allow them to experiment without the heavy investments in model-making, tooling, and factory-worker training that had previously been required for mass production. Using ISDN (integrated services digital network) files, designers send computer-generated designs directly to RP facilities capable of immediate production. In laser-sintering, as used in the production of Patrick Jouin's chair (p. 420–21), a laser beam is fired into a vat of nylon powder, which heats the nylon and fuses it into a precisely cut solid—all without mold-making. Before, the economy of mass production required simplifying the production process, with consequent simplifications in the materials, molds, and labor used and often in the appearance of the final product. With the new technology, more complex forms can be achieved and at a reasonable price. Technology has enabled the expansion of a protean and ornamental aesthetic.

1 Millennium Dome, London, designed by Richard Rogers Partnership, 1999.
2 Marc Newson, *Lockheed Lounge*, aluminum over fiberglass and metal, 1985, sold at Phillips de Pury & Company, London, April 30, 2009, for a record-breaking £1,105,250.

In some instances of rapid prototyping, the process and results are expressionistic and improvisatory. For example, the team at Front Design, established in 2004 in Sweden, has developed a method of realizing actual forms through free sketches or strokes made in the air with a pen tool (fig. 3). These strokes are recorded with motion-capture video technology and then digitized into a 3-D computer model. The digital files are then sent to a rapid-prototyping facility that uses computer-controlled laser-sintering to print the objects in plastic, creating their *Sketch Furniture*, a clear translation of drawings into objects.[3] At the opposite pole, RP can be used to generate intricate geometric permutations, as in Platform's *Fractal* table, (p. 464–65).

Computers with advanced software are also being used by those willing to call themselves craftspeople, with the result that divisions between crafts and industrial design can no longer be defined by handwork. Designers who once used a jeweler's loupe for close-up work may now "draw" on their PCs and simply zoom in. What distinguishes their work is its self-expression for a limited audience and therefore its aura as art. Like Newson's *Lockheed Lounge*, limited-edition and one-off works by jeweler Eva Eisler and ceramicist Gustavo Perez, for example (pp. 430, 458), deserve the term "Design Art." Symptomatic of design's advancing status is the name change of New York's former American Craft Museum, which since 2002 has called itself the Museum of Arts and Design.

3 Front Design, *Sketch Furniture*, 2005. Process demonstrated by Acron Form Service AB, Sweden.

Meanwhile, "craft" techniques, vernacular materials, and marks of the maker have re-entered experimental design since the 1990s, and they humanize products in a slick-surface world of identical things. The works are unique in Maarten Baas's *Clay Furniture* series (p. 457) because he hand-models lumpy clay over their metal structures. While Fabio Novembre's table is mass-produced, its multiple hanging rope "legs" make it as homely and endearing as an old-fashioned floor mop (p. 455). Countering the "soulless perfection" of the machine-made, Hella Jongerius incorporates errors and signs of process in her manufactures; her handwritten instructions to the printer are included in her final textile (p. 425).

Where computers are used to mass-produce designs, they can introduce irregularities into each one as easily as they insure strict uniformity for all. With some add-on designs, the buyers personalize the product by expanding it and installing it to their liking (pp. 438–39, 452–53). The materials are high-tech, but the metaphor is organic, and the forms are as luxuriant and charming as Victorian cut-paper ornaments. Technology and design invention combine to allow customizing on a scale never seen before. Consumers, designers, and manufacturers interact, and with increasing speed. On Nike's website, for example, the giant shoe manufacturer lets consumers choose from a large range of variables to create what are virtually custom-made shoes.

The consequence of more individualized designs may simply be more design, however, and therefore more use of fossil fuels in conventional production and more hazardous wastes at the end of a product's useful lifetime. Former Vice-President Al Gore's 2006 book and Oscar-winning documentary film *An Inconvenient Truth* was a milestone in establishing international awareness of the causes and consequences of global warming. In growing numbers, thoughtful designers are attempting to appraise how their work, in its cycle from conception through obsolescence, relates to the ongoing assault on the environment—an issue accelerated since the 1970s. Green design has gathered new advocates, as the world's population and consumption have exploded.

New devices, like lighting with energy-efficient LEDs (light-emitting diodes) (pp. 422–23), have become more widely marketed. Public service graphics promote restricted driving and smaller carbon footprints (p. 467). Materials are recycled and incorporated into new designs, sometimes with amusing transformations and social climbing (p. 454). The conceptually rich designs of the Dutch firm Droog in the 1990s have attracted adherents, who value their narratives and occasional use of low-tech manufacturing methods and found objects. Former Droog member Marcel Wanders has become a design superstar, and he argues for designs with longer life spans, including traditional furniture forms, which he is currently exploring. He seeks, he says, "durability in the field of ideas, relationships, objects and so on, not only to create a world that is less wasteful but also to create deeper and more meaningful relationships with our environment."[4] Calling himself a designer of "sensual minimalism," Karim Rashid remarks: "In the controversial arguments about excess, sustainability, and market seduction, I believe that every new object should replace three. *Better products edit the marketplace*."[5]

Maximum usefulness is the keynote of "universal design," with its focus on social inclusion. It aims to create products for everyone, rather than objects specifically for the handicapped or the elderly. Designers and manufacturers of universal design work from the conviction that everyone will eventually benefit from the accommodating features now found in designs for clients with special needs. More focused on comfort than on the beautiful or stylish, universal designs are intended to appeal to everyone.

4 Smart Design: Davin Stowell and Steven Allendorf, Mixing bowls: *Good Grips*, designed 1992, Santoprene, rubber, largest: 15 x 29 x 23 cm, The Stewart Program for Modern Design, 2007.29.
5 Yves Behar with Nicholas Negroponte and MIT Media Lab, *$100 Laptop for Children*, plastic, 2006, The Stewart Program for Modern Design, 2008.6, gift of George R. Kravis, II.
6 Smart Cities Group at MIT Lab, *CityCars*, 2007.

Oxo's *Good Grips* kitchenwares, for instance, were early in embodying the standards of universal design (fig. 4).[6]

A similar conscience about inclusiveness motivates some designers to create for the less privileged. In 2006, Yves Behar designed a reasonably priced laptop for children (fig. 5), in conjunction with Nicholas Negroponte and the MIT Media Lab. Their product was for One Laptop Per Child (OLPC), a non-profit organization devoted to bringing technology and education to millions of children worldwide.

Designs with a conscience may be one benefit of globalization and its handmaidens, international travel and instantaneous Internet communication. Adventurous designers have left their countries—most easily as citizens of the European Union—and migrated to study in design centers such as London and Milan, where the Royal College of Art and the Domus Academy faculties feature celebrities such as Jasper Morrison, Ross Lovegrove, and Alessandro Mendini. A surprising number of designers represented in this chapter are graduates of and/or teachers at the Royal College, which offers graduate degrees in art and design.

Another magnet is the Design Academy Eindhoven in The Netherlands, where Droog member-graduates continue to teach. Major designers on staff, such as Gijs Bakker, attract talented students to the programs, which are strengthened by government funding. The longtime liberalism and multiculturalism of this small nation have combined with the influence of Eindhoven to make The Netherlands a new center for design experiment.

While peripatetic designers respond to widespread conditions around the world, some draw on the design traditions of their birthplaces. In the 1990s the Campana brothers of Brazil introduced a global audience to a funky idiom from Saõ Paulo's streets. In the new decade, Front Design revitalizes Royal Delft porcelain, prized in their native Sweden in the eighteenth century (p. 470–71), and the London-based Satyendra Pakhalé recycles industrial glass in baskets based on the ancient container forms of his native India (pp. 462–63). The stylistically diverse results reward the educated consumer who can recognize allusions to vernacular, aristocratic, and traditional cultures of various nations. Fears that globalization will produce bland, homogenous styles appear overblown.

Indeed, today's buyers are presented with a bewildering multiplicity of products, in various idioms, and they can use them to express a more faceted individuality than ever before. Each of us can choose green features, heeding the warnings of designers and their press about the impact of consumerism on the environment—or not. Nonetheless, the environment may be a common ground for innovative designers, for in the face of growing threats of terrorism, financial meltdowns, and the like, green design may be perceived as the one thing they can control, in an undivided spirit of public service.

The *CityCar* prototype, a project developed at MIT Media Lab with the sponsorship of General Motors, is a small but hopeful example (fig. 6). These toy-like two-passenger electric vehicles can be stacked and recharged next to public transportation, where users can rent them and drop them off like airport luggage carts. *CityCars* thus supplement other means of urban transport and help limit their emissions, while contributing none of their own, and they embody the problem-solving of the most promising current designs.

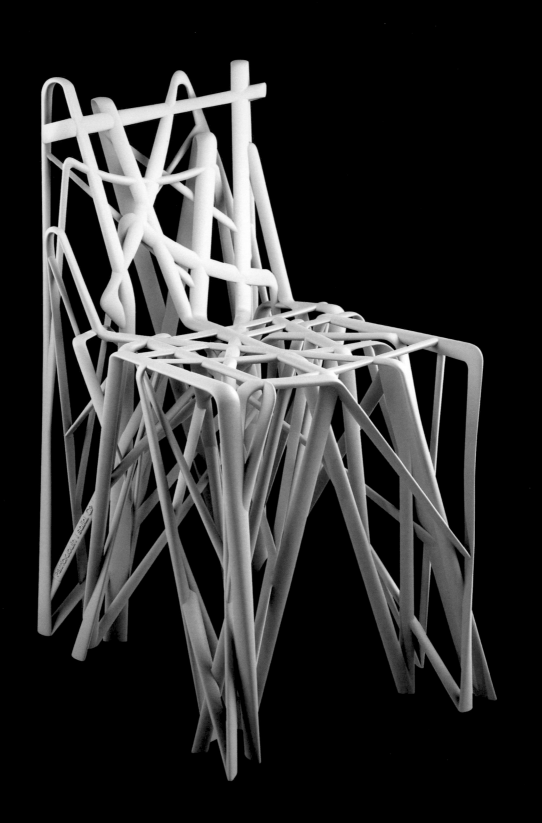

Patrick JOUIN

(born 1967)

Chair
C2, from the Solid Collection
Designed 2004
Epoxy resin
77.5 x 39.5 x 50.8 cm
Produced by Materialise.MGX,
Louvain, Belgium
The Montreal Museum of
Fine Arts, 2008.23

In this revolutionary design/production process, the designer begins with a freehand, three-dimensional sketch that is converted into a digital code and sent to a computer. The computer, in turn, directs a laser to transform the data into a solid object. Like a magic wand, the laser beam makes contact with either liquid resin or, in this case, nylon powder and hardens it instantly, building tiny layers of material like a stalagmite. Free to stretch the imagination, the designer can create forms shaped by electronic information that are otherwise impossible to fabricate. Referring to older treatments of synthetics, Jouin describes this freedom of creation as "emancipation from the limitations of the molds."[7] Using the power of the computer and rapid manufacturing, he achieves a complex design inspired by criss-crossing blades of grass.

Yves BEHAR

(born 1967)

Lamp
Leaf Light
Designed 2005
Aluminum, plastic
51 x 47.5 x 22 cm
Produced by Herman Miller,
Zeeland, Michigan, U.S.A.
The Stewart Program for
Modern Design, 2008.6

In this adjustable lamp, Behar exploits the miniaturization and sharp focus made possible by LEDs (light-emitting diodes). Small but ultra-efficient in lighting specific areas, the LEDs in Behar's grid provide a broad spectrum of light, from a golden glow to pure white, because he has employed ten cool-hued and ten warm-hued bulbs. The leaf-like shaft of twisted metal with a hinged arm is balanced delicately on a circular base and appears to float. Behar wrote about his lamps, "What I pursue is the fusing of storytelling and form where the potential for technology and poetry, commerce and culture, merge with the physical world."[8]

APPLE Design Team

MP3 Player
iPod Shuffle
Designed 2005
Polycarbonate, ABS plastic
8.5 x 2.5 x 0.8 cm
Produced by Apple Computer,
Inc., Cupertino, California, U.S.A.
The Stewart Program for
Modern Design, 2008.18,
gift of Dr. Michael Sze

The *iPod Shuffle* is a digital audio player designed to be easily loaded with a selection of hundreds of songs, which can be played in any order. Instead of storing data on a hard disk, this is the first *iPod* to use "flash" memory. The miniaturization of the memory storage device, developed for computer use, allows for this sleek, ultra-thin design, which is intended to fit comfortably in the user's hand or pocket. The *iPod* typifies Apple's designs since Its epochal entry into digital competition in 1984 with the Macintosh computer: both friendly and futuristic, these seemingly irresistible commodities make communication of all kinds pleasurable.

ABOVE, LEFT A pedestrian passes a wall covered with Apple *iPod* advertisements, July 14, 2005, in San Francisco, California.

Hella JONGERIUS

(born 1963)

Textile
Repeat Dot Print
Designed 2001
Cotton, polyester, rayon
222.3 x 143.5 cm
Produced by Maharam,
New York, New York, U.S.A.
The Stewart Program for
Modern Design, 2008.16,
gift of Maharam

Over two meters long, the huge repeat on this cotton print is unusual, but the print itself isn't. The combination of bands and dots of different sizes may recall "Mid-century Modern" patterns and even archetypal forms—allusions that Jongerius often makes in her designs for textiles, ceramics, and other eco-friendly media. "When I get a commission from Maharam," she says, "I don't rush to my drawing board to design a snazzy new pattern. I pore through the archives, use existing patterns, and add a new concept to them."[9] Whether or not consumers recognize the references, here the cotton can give a custom look to upholstery. Using current technology to individualize design typifies Droog, the Dutch design collaborative, of which she was a member in the 1990s, after studying in Eindhoven from 1988 to 1993. Since 2000, Jongerius has worked independently in Rotterdam.

BELOW, LEFT Maharam's showroom at the NeoCon trade fair in Chicago, June 2002.

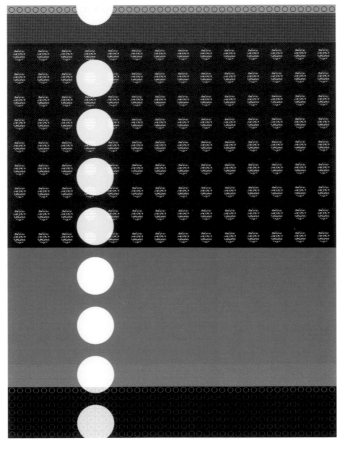

David A. HOLCOMB

(born 1953)

Vegetable steamer

SleekStor VeggiSteam
Designed 2006
Silicone, stainless steel
6.5 x 29 x 21 cm
Produced in China for Chef'n
Corporation, Seattle,
Washington, U.S.A.
The Stewart Program for
Modern Design, 2007.53,
gift of Dr. Michael Sze

Made of heat- and stain-resistant silicone, the three-legged *VeggiSteam* is designed for ease of use and safety in steaming foods. The flexible, two-handled form fits into small or medium-sized pots; it does not damage nonstick coatings, and it withstands heat up to 340°C (650°F). It is available in three colors—cherry red, avocado, and translucent white—and, at a retail price of $10, this steamer is exemplary of low-cost good design. With a wide, shallow shape and handles, it recalls a Greek kylix vase or drinking vessel. Designer David A. Holcomb is the founder and CEO of Chef'n Corporation, a Seattle-based housewares company that has introduced some three hundred innovative tools to the kitchen.[10]

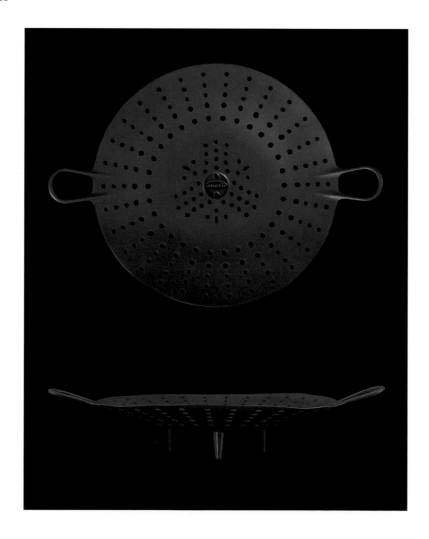

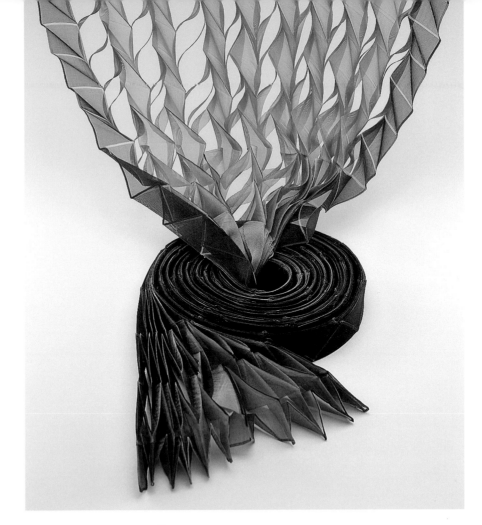

Reiko SUDO

(born 1953)

Textile
Tanabata
Designed 2005
Polyester
452.1 x 129.5 cm
Produced by Nuno
Corporation, Tokyo, Japan
The Stewart Program for
Modern Design, 2008.21

Tanabata is the name of the Japanese star festival, celebrating the moment when, according to folklore, two lovers separated by the Milky Way meet again. Sudo's textile resembles the large hanging decorations of cut paper that the Japanese create for the festival.[11] The Nuno Corporation, of which Sudo is a founder and chief designer, has a patent on the "origami pleating" process used to create the fabric, which can be used artistically for clothing and draperies.[12] According to the designer, "The original idea for this came about quite unremarkably as one of the Nuno staff members sat absent-mindedly folding her lunch receipt into a strikingly 'geodesic' series of accordion ridges. And since we're always thinking, 'what if this were fabric?' we decided to give it a try."[13] A paper pattern is folded to the desired shape; a polyester sheet of the same size is tucked into its folds and heat is applied to create permanent pleats in the polyester. Paper transfer dye is ironed onto the edges of the polyester sheet to shade its existing color.

Mathias BENGTSSON

(born 1971)

Armchair
Slice Vertical
Designed 2001
Corrugated cardboard
83.5 x 95 x 70 cm
Produced by Mathias Bengtsson,
London, England
The Montreal Museum of
Fine Arts, 2003.279

Bengtsson is part of Panic, a group of young Danish furniture designers who gathered in London in 1999, the year he graduated from London's Royal College of Art. His *Slice* series of sculptural furniture combines the latest computerized laser-cutting techniques with handwork, making the most of current technology and craftsmanship.[14] First executed in plywood, then adapted for aluminum, his chairs evolved into this example: 388 sheets of laser-cut corrugated cardboard, each three millimeters thick, are hand-glued together in layers to make an organic form like a giant vertebra. Frank Gehry's cardboard furniture of the 1970s establishes a precedent (p. 251), but the refinement of process and the bony surrealism of form in this chair are individual to Bengtsson.

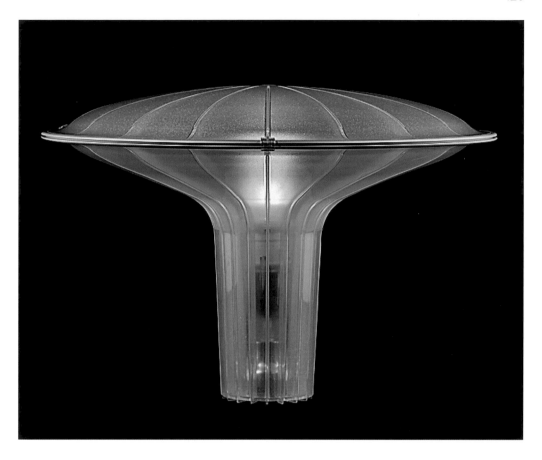

Ross LOVEGROVE

(born 1958)

Table lamp
Agaricon
Designed 2001
Polycarbonate plastic, aluminum
28 x 41 x 41 cm
Produced by Luceplan,
Milan, Italy
The Stewart Program for
Modern Design, 2008.26,
gift of Dr. Michael Sze

Named after a type of mushroom, *Agaricon* is an injection-molded polycarbonate light with a touch-sensitive circuit around its entire circumference. The light source is encased in the wide, flared, translucent shade—which is available in different colors— revealing the interior components. The user can switch the light on or off and control the brightness by touching any point on the circular metal rim. The organic form looks and functions like a device for a séance, but it is also a reflection of Lovegrove's interest in science and technology. He maintains, "There is no simple methodology to achieve the balance of materials, technology and form, only a process of internalization of the object derived from an intuitive sensibility, designing from the inside out and outside in to find a harmony between all things considered."[15]

Eva EISLER

(born 1952)

Bracelet
Möbius
Designed and executed 2005
Stainless steel
6.5 x 10.8 x 10.8 cm
The Stewart Program for
Modern Design, 2006.16

Eisler's jewelry, distinctive for its forceful yet minimal geometric forms, is often compared to architecture or sculpture. She based this series on the mathematical Möbius strip, twisting strips of steel and attaching the ends to produce continuous loops in a shape reminiscent of José de Rivera's *Möbius* sculptures of the 1970s. Her goal was to create an object that is "proportionally, aesthetically and technically perfect. The focus is on the free-flowing line of the strip's surface and its edges."[16] Eisler was trained in Bauhaus principles at the School of Building Technology and Architecture in Prague, and, after first working as an architect, she turned to freelance design, applying her knowledge to jewelry. Living in New York from 1983 on, she taught in the metals department at Parsons from 1987 to 1990. She has extended the Möbius concept to nearly fifty-meter-long sculptures.

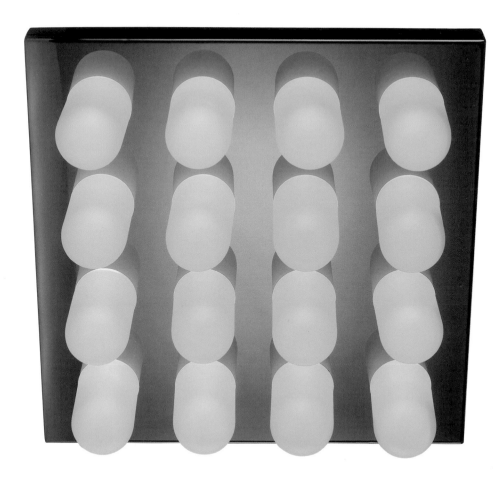

Johanna GRAWUNDER

(born 1961)

Ceiling lamp
LED
Designed 2005–06
Polished stainless steel,
chromium-plated steel,
frosted glass
5.2 x 56.3 x 56.3 cm
Produced for Design Gallery
Milano, Milan, Italy
The Stewart Program for
Modern Design, 2002.10.1

This ceiling fixture, which is from a limited edition of twelve, was part of an exhibition of Grawunder's work held at Design Gallery Milano in April 2002. According to a contemporary article, her designs for the show were "the result of a classic design translated into original and dimensionally impressive pieces. Touching on the artistic in their vibrations of colour, they pay discreet homage to Dan Flavin and are created primarily from the repletion of a single element transformed into a weave—or, to quote Grawunder, into texture."[17] The lamp is reminiscent of the work of Sottsass in the 1980s, with its geometric composition and sixteen chartreuse, capsule-shaped lights contrasting with the reflective steel ground. Grawunder worked at Sottsass Associates in Milan after graduating from California State Polytechnic University in 1984. She became a partner of the firm in 1989, and in 2001 opened her own studios, operating in both Milan and San Francisco.

Garry Knox BENNETT

(born 1934)

Necklace
California Cockdor No. 4
Designed and executed 2001
Copper, brass, sterling silver,
23k-gold plate, silver plate,
blown glass
4 x 18 x 33 cm
The Stewart Program for
Modern Design, L2001.12,
promised gift of Paul D. Leblanc

This necklace is made of three elements: a bottom layer of polished brass cut in joyous, Matisse-like leaves; a commercial metal scouring pad as the middle section; and a third and central section of sterling silver cast from the artist's glans penis. This last element recalls the sexual revolution of the 1970s, when Knox conceived the jewelry, as does his title, which refers to the vernacular for its central form. The second syllable of the title comes from efforts at that time to save the giant California condor, visually represented in the large wings and neck-ruff. The artist completed three necklaces in the series in 1973–74, but left the elements for a fourth unused until Liliane Stewart asked him, in 2001, to make a new work for the collection. He added a droplet of red glass to represent the threat of AIDS and the danger of human extinction.

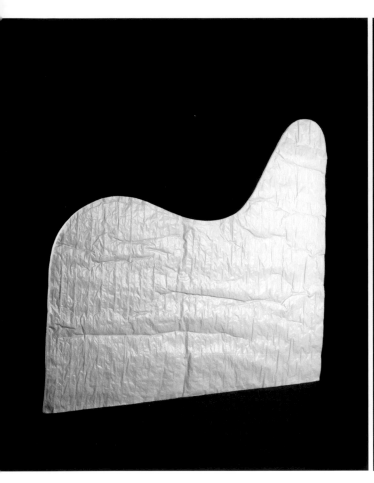

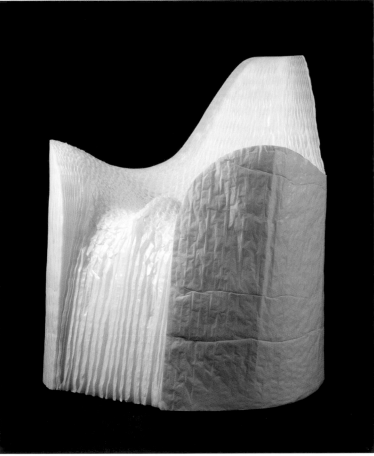

Tokujin YOSHIOKA

(born 1967)

Armchairs
Honey-Pop
Designed 2000
Glassine paper
81.5 x 70.5 x 76 cm (open)
81 x 92 x 1.9 cm (folded)
Produced by Tokujin Yoshioka
Design, Tokyo, Japan
The Montreal Museum of
Fine Arts, 2003.283

The honeycomb structure of this chair is made of 120 sheets of glassine paper piled together and cut so that they open like an accordion, not unlike whimsical paper decorations that unfold to create three-dimensional forms, such as holiday bells. The cells in the outermost layer are compressed when a person sits in the chair, making a permanent impression and creating the seat's final form.[18] Yoshioka's earlier collaborations with couturier Issey Miyake and designer Shiro Kuramata are apparent in the use of surprising, apparently fragile materials, the emphasis on pleating, and the imaginative sense of play. The two examples in the Stewart Collection show the object in flattened and opened form.

Konstantin GRCIC

(born 1965)

Tables
Diana A, E, and *F*
Designed 2002
Painted steel
Diana E (orange): 52.5 x 61 x 39 cm
Diana F (blue): 44 x 65 x 25 cm
Diana A (yellow): 42.5 x 53 x 25 cm
Produced by Classicon,
Munich, Germany
The Stewart Program for
Modern Design, 2008.3.1–3

Grcic's three *Diana* tables are part of a family of brightly colored end tables that can be used singly or together. While they relate in scale and angular composition, each is a variation on the design of bent sheet steel and has a different but equally vivid color; they are almost musical in their relationships and the multiple possibilities of combination. Grcic says the earliest *Diana* designs were complicated, some even with a swivel tabletop mechanism as seen in the orange table here, but "the more I worked on the project the more I understood that even a few simple folds were sufficient to create a beautifully three-dimensional form."[19] Grcic won the Composso d'Oro in 2001.

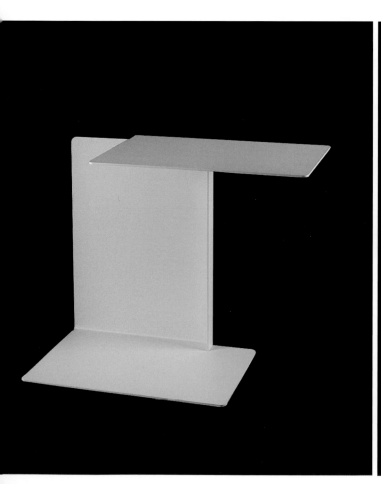

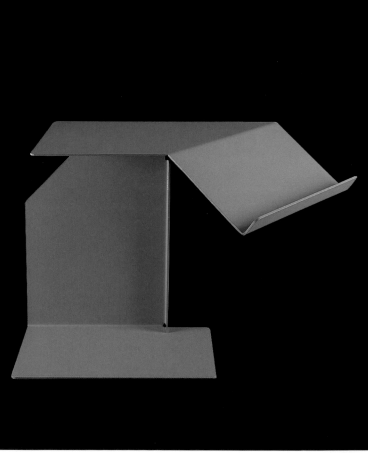

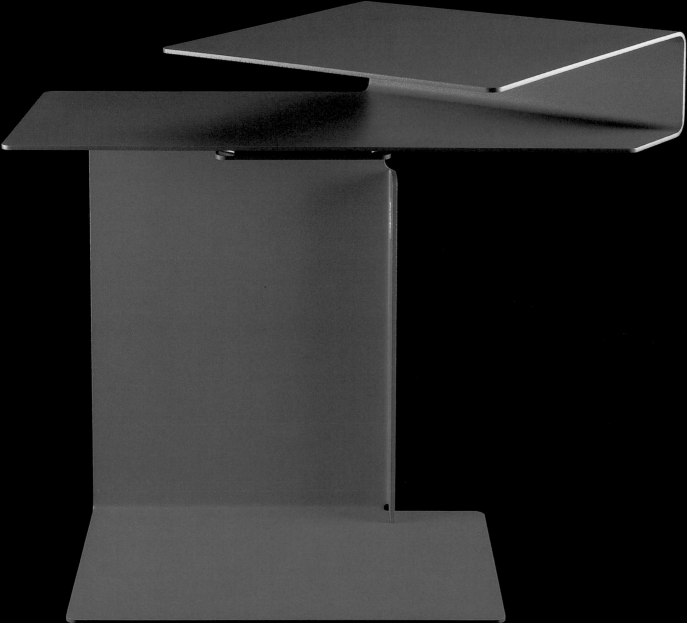

Philippe STARCK

(born 1949)

Armchair
Louis Ghost
Designed 2002
Polycarbonate plastic
94 x 54 x 55 cm
Produced by Kartell,
Noviglio, Italy
Liliane Stewart Collection

Philippe Starck is a self-proclaimed design star, an inventor, and a lifestyle philosopher. Internationally celebrated since the 1980s for his chic hotel and restaurant interiors, he is equally known for a large body of furniture and product designs, especially in plastic for Kartell. Despite its seeming fragility, the *Louis Ghost* chair is comfortable, lightweight, and durable. Like many of his works, it was inspired by an older design—a Louis XVI-style chair. Starck preserves the silhouette of the late-eighteenth-century design, but he transforms the chair through the use of a new material and a modern production method: polycarbonate injected into a single mold. The chair is available in a variety of pale tints and some opaque colors; this colorless transparent model recalls the acrylic furniture widely popular in the 1960s.

Jean NOUVEL

(born 1945)

Flatware place setting
Designed 2004
Stainless steel
Knife: 22.5 x 1.8 cm
Produced by Georg Jensen,
Copenhagen, Denmark
The Stewart Program for
Modern Design, 2008.22.1–5

One of the world's most famous contemporary architects, Nouvel won the distinguished Pritzker Prize for his buildings in 2008. The jury praised his "persistence, imagination, exuberance, and, above all, an insatiable urge for creative experimentation."[20] Nouvel's flatware is distinguished by its simplicity and striking silhouettes of slightly futuristic, clean, sharp, and graceful lines. The pointed spoons are unusual and dramatic, as is the knife, shaped in a single, elegant swoop. The set looks back to the design of another architect: Arne Jacobsen's *AJ* flatware of 1957. Nouvel created this pattern in celebration of the one-hundredth anniversary of the Georg Jensen silver firm. It is a reminder that minimalism is a recurring modern taste, and that Jensen has commissioned progressive designs in silver since 1904.

Tord BOONTJE

(born 1968)

Hanging lamp
Garland Light
Designed 2002
Brass
25.4 x 25.4 cm, variable
Produced by Artecnica, Los
Angeles, California, U.S.A.
The Stewart Program for
Modern Design, 2008.19,
gift of Dr. Michael Sze

This romantic lamp is created from a continuous strip of leaves and flowers cut out of Tyvek, the insulating material, or, as in this example, paper-thin sheets of brass, wrapped around and clipped to the base of a light bulb. Boontje began with a paper model that he draped around his young daughter's bedroom light. Seeing that it was lovely but flammable, he had a factory make twelve in nonconductive material. "I had no idea it would be successful," he wrote about its commercial production.[21] Habitat, the home-furnishings chain, began selling *Garland Light* in 2002, and since 2004 Artecnica in Los Angeles has produced and marketed it in large numbers. It is a beautiful and poetic work of art.

ABOVE Boontje, *Garland Light,* sheet of garland as shipped.

Monika MULDER

(born 1972)

Watering cans
Vållö, PS Collection
Designed 2002
Polypropylene
32.9 x 34.5 x 12.6 cm (each)
Produced by IKEA,
Almhult, Sweden
The Montreal Museum of
Fine Arts, 2007.31.1–6

This is based on the traditional form of a watering can, but what an exotic flower! Made in a single mold with injected polypropylene, this watering can has a continuous curvilinear silhouette in which the upward sweep of the spout, open so that the flow of water is visible, contrasts with the downward movement of the arc-shaped handle. The playful design is practical, too: the can's high sides deter spillage. Available in six colors, stackable, and modestly priced, the vessel recalls another Scandinavian crowd-pleaser in plastic: Vernon Panton's S-shaped stacking chairs of 1960—67 (p. 196). Mulder's cans also look alluring on store shelves, a benefit to IKEA, the global home-furnishings chain. Mulder has been a member of IKEA's in-house design team since 1998, joining the firm only a year after graduating from the Design Academy Eindhoven in The Netherlands.

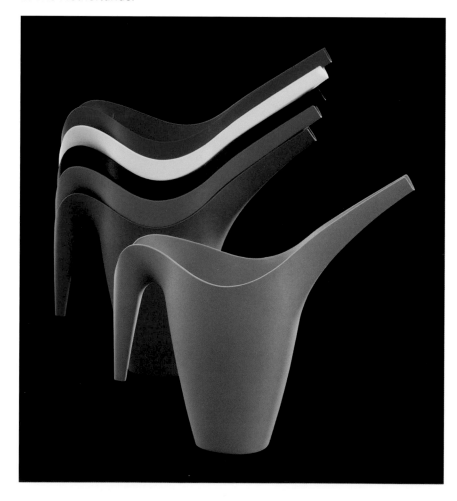

Ross LOVEGROVE

(born 1958)

Chairs

Supernatural
Designed 2005
Polyamide plastic
81.5 x 47.5 x 47 cm
Produced by Moroso, Milan, Italy
The Stewart Program for
Modern Design, 2008.4.1–2

One of Britain's best-known designers today, Welsh-born Lovegrove received a master's degree in design from the Royal College of Art in London in 1983. He experiments at the intersections of design, architecture, science, and technology and describes this chair as representing "a new vision of form, generated by digital data, resulting in a chair to be used every day, slender, lively and healthy. The liquid, organic nature of its form combines the beauty of the human anatomy with the most advanced process of industrialization of twenty-first-century polymers."[22] He notes that the perforations, which allow a handhold, add an additional sensory effect, as light passing through them creates shadows and an unexpected beauty.

Zaha HADID

(born 1950)

Vases
Crevasse
Designed 2005
Stainless steel
42 x 8 x 6 cm each
Produced by Alessi, Milan, Italy
The Stewart Program for
Modern Design, 2008.28,
gift of Dr. Michael Sze

After earning a degree in architecture, Hadid worked with her former teacher, Rem Koolhaas, at his Office for Metropolitan Architecture and became a partner in 1977. She established her own practice in London in 1980. Although her designs were innovative, incorporating multiple perspective points and fragmented geometry, she initially went unrecognized, but with computer technology she has completed many successful commissions around the world, most notably the MAXXI (Museum of Art for the XXI Century) in Rome. The *Crevasse* vases reflect her architecture, which creates dynamic spaces, through their interrelations of forms. Here the title signals the importance of the space between the turned but slightly different twisted columns. The dialogue of shapes and void, pleasingly complicated by stainless steel's reflections, can be varied, of course, by juxtaposing the vases differently.

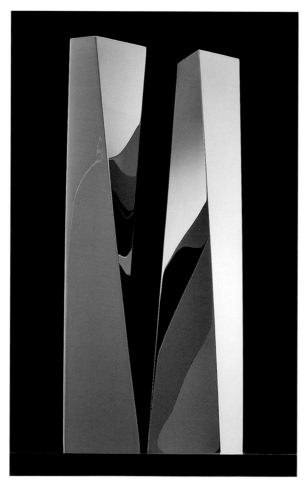

Massimiliano FUKSAS
Doriana MANDRELLI

(born 1944) and **(born 1957)**

Vase
E-Li-Li
Designed 2005
Stainless steel
30 x 24.5 x 9 cm
Produced by Alessi, Milan, Italy
The Stewart Program for
Modern Design, 2008.15

This vase, produced in stainless steel and black ceramic versions, is an object of the most reductive and elegant simplicity, a persistent characteristic of modern design. The folding of a rhombus-shaped piece of paper is the basis for the design, which is joined at the sides and given a bottom to form a container. In its gleaming planar surfaces and sharp silhouette, the vase looks back to Müller-Munk's *Normandie* pitcher (p. 58), which was formed using a similar technique. The monumentality of the vase may reflect the more than twenty-year partnership of this couple as architects. At the Fuksas architectural firm, Mandrelli is in charge of the design section.

Nathalie JEAN

(born 1963)

Screen
Ajikata
Designed 2002
Macassar ebony veneer
199 x 245 x 80 cm
Produced for Design Gallery
Milano, Milan, Italy
The Montreal Museum of
Fine Arts, 2005.18.

Jean was one of the leading contemporary architects chosen for the annual Design Gallery Milano exhibition in 2002. She had moved to Milan fifteen years earlier, and worked for Sottsass Associates and with the architect Aldo Cibic before opening her own studio in 1993. A native of Montreal, where she earned a degree in architecture, she continues to create interior and exhibition designs. Her cubistic constructions are strongly sculptural. With its veneered surface, a screen like this evokes deluxe decorative designs of the Art Deco period because of the angular forms and the exotic material, an African wood especially favored by the French *ébénistes* of the 1920s and '30s. Nonetheless, the imposing scale and flat planes of *Ajikata,* named after a village in Japan, identify it with late twentieth-century sculpture.

Ted MUEHLING

(born 1953)

Bowl
Moon Snail White
Designed 2000
Partially glazed porcelain
13 x 36.5 x 19 cm
Produced by Porzellan-
Manufaktur Nymphenburg,
Munich, Germany
Indianapolis Museum of Art,
2008.336

This bowl is part of a line of fine porcelain modeled after sea snails and shells, designed for one of Germany's famous porcelain manufacturers. Its quiet tranquility makes it, like much of Muehling's work, an object that is also a contemplative work of art. Known for his natural organic forms in ceramics, jewelry, and glass, Muehling says, "Rocks, shells, eggs, and insects all inspire me and humble me as a designer." As he explains, "I try to keep shapes restrained, abstracting forms in nature, transforming them through the imperative to make objects that look beautiful." Muehling was trained as an industrial designer and has been working in many media since 1976. He opened his first shop in New York in 1990.[23]

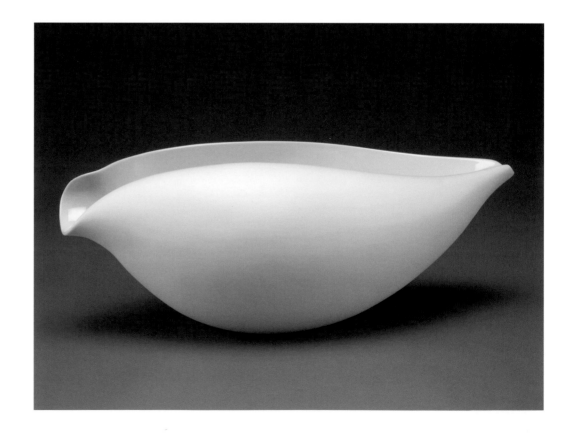

David WATKINS

(born 1940)

Bracelet
In the Gardens of Arqua Petrarca 2
Designed and executed 2003
Stainless steel
14.5 x 14.5 cm
The Stewart Program for
Modern Design, 2003.15

Watkins was head of the department of goldsmithing at the Royal College of Art, London, from 1984 to 2006, and is known for his lectures on contemporary jewelry. In his own oeuvre he incorporates innovative structures and materials and creates geometric compositions that emphasize both complexity and simplicity.[24] This bracelet illuminates his aesthetic, which takes line as a decorative and constructive element, and links two concentric circles by a leafy form, like a delicate drawing. In the mid-1960s, he started his own jewelry business, producing painted and silkscreened jewelry in acrylic and paper. The interest of many modern jewelry designers in non-precious materials is a Bauhaus legacy strengthened by the 1960s counterculture.

Oki SATO

(born 1977)

Chair
Cabbage Chair
Designed 2007
Paper, resin
71 x 74 x 67 cm
Produced by Nendo,
Tokyo, Japan
The Stewart Program for
Modern Design, 2010.2.1

The Canadian-born designer Oki Sato founded the architecture and design firm Nendo in 2002. Known for fresh, lighthearted, minimal designs, the company created this chair for the 2008 Tokyo exhibition *XXI*[st] *Century Man*, organized by Issey Miyake.[25] The exhibition explored how things would be made in the future and included a broad range of objects and media, many addressing environmental concerns. Miyake invited Nendo to create furniture from the leftover paper backing he used to manufacture his fabric, *Pleats Please*. "Our solution to his challenge," wrote Oki Sato, "transformed a roll of pleated paper into a small chair that appears naturally as you peel away its outside layers, one layer at a time."[26] Shipped as a roll for the buyer to "peel" or as an already formed chair, this design requires neither internal structural for support nor any hardware for assembly. Available in several colors, the chair is comfortable, as the pleats give it a springy resilience.

BELOW *Cabbage Chair* on display in the exhibition *XXIst Century Man* at 21_21 Design Sight, Tokyo, Japan, 2008.

Liv BLÅVARP

(born 1956)

Necklace
Memory of Where
We Used to Swim
Designed and executed 2000
Tarata, birch, nylon cord
3 x 28.5 x 26 cm
The Montreal Museum of
Fine Arts, 2004.147

Blåvarp first studied metalsmithing in Oslo and then, in 1983 and '84, jewelry-making at the Royal College of Art, London. Her necklaces in various woods reflect the longstanding craft traditions of her native Norway. In this spiraling design, which clasps between the two fish, she combines Norwegian birch with more exotic tarata, from a New Zealand tree, and dyed elements to create rhythmic movement and warm color harmony. According to Jorgen Schou-Christensen, "Using wood as a material for jewelry naturally leads to volume, plasticity, and also to mobility and body friendliness. Wood as a material also provides art jewelry with the possibility for rich and varied surface treatment, inlaying, colouring, and painting. It is Liv Blåvarp who has managed to tackle these aspects with the greatest variation and refinement."[27]

Stefan LINDFORS

(born 1962)

Armchair
MX200
Designed 2000
Steel, plastic resin
94.5 x 87 x 82 cm
The Montreal Museum of
Fine Arts, 2002.9

This construction of welded steel rods may recall the 1950s experiments of Harry Bertoia and the Eameses, but Lindfors prefers an irregular handcrafted look to their sleek industrial aesthetic for furnishings. For this insectile armchair, he merges the role of sculptor and industrial designer, using the industrial material plastic resin in a painterly manner for its translucency and sheen. This chair resembles a butterfly, but it is less fanciful than the work of many contemporary designers, such as Umeda's *Moonlit Garden* chair in the form of a flower (p. 400).

Ronan BOUROULLEC
Erwan BOUROULLEC

(born 1971) and **(born 1976)**

Modular clipping system
Algue (Algae)
Designed 2004
Polypropylene
Variable dimensions
Produced by Vitra, Weil
am Rhein, Germany
The Stewart Program for
Modern Design, 2008.17,
gift of Dr. Michael Sze

Like much of the Bouroullec brothers' work, this screen is whimsical, inventive, and accessible. It is made of plastic elements in the form of algae that can be snapped together at nineteen eyelet perforations to create a screen or room divider in endless combinations of branching structures. The ingenious design is made to sell at low cost, in packs of various quantities, and it is easily assembled and disassembled. While practical, the screen is also mysterious and evocative, recalling the physical experience of a gentle sea. Though they are referring to their modular shelving system, *Clouds*, of 2002, the brothers could easily have been discussing *Algue* when they wrote, "they are the proliferation of a shared abstract form, like a growing plant, stubbornly repeating its structure of nodes."[28]

BELOW *Algue* assembled into a screen.

Matali CRASSET

(born 1965)

Waste paper basket
Artican
Designed 2000
Polymethacrylate, aluminum,
polypropylene
61 x 41.9 x 41.9 cm
Produced by Matali Crasset
Productions, Paris, France
The Stewart Program for
Modern Design, 2009.13

In her designs, Crasset seeks a dialogue between the artificial and natural, as seen in *Artican*. "Continuing my work in recycling," she wrote, "I have designed a waste paper basket made out of the plastic bristles from brooms used by the street sweepers of the City of Paris."[29] This mundane ingredient becomes part of an unexpected fantasy. Though this basket form is derived from earlier open-grid wire examples, it is more obviously a little forest that reclaims paper, made from trees, for what one hopes is new life. Crasset graduated from the École Nationale Supérieure de Création Industriale in Paris, and worked for Philippe Starck before establishing her own company in 1998.

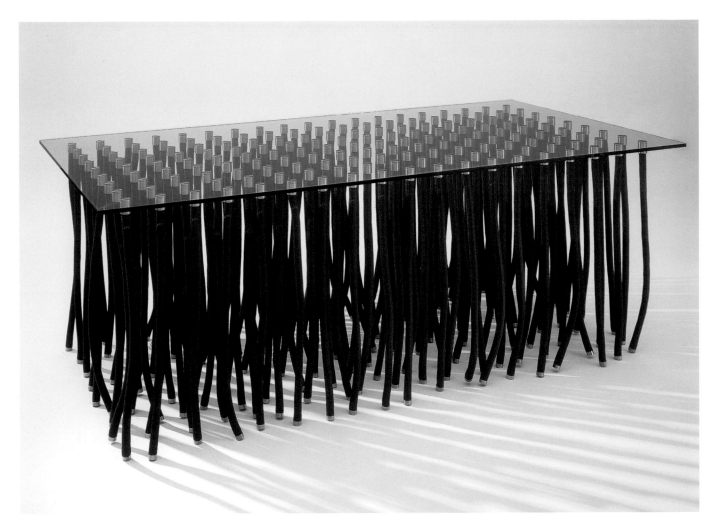

Fabio NOVEMBRE

(born 1966)

Table
Org
Designed 2001
Glass, polypropylene, steel, cord,
brushed stainless steel
73.2 x 200 x 100 cm
Produced by Cappellini,
Milan, Italy
The Montreal Museum of
Fine Arts, 2002.57.1

Novembre is one of several emerging Italian designers whose work is known through Cappellini's manufacture. Trained as an architect, he is recognized for his imaginative contract designs for bars, shops, and restaurants. *Org* is part of a series of tables he designed for Cappellini with similar structures supporting glass tops. Bristling with legs like a centipede, this has a total of four structural supports with internal metal rods, while the rest are suspended pieces of rope, creating an amusing, colorful design that teases about our wish to have normal furniture legs provide strong support. The name *Org* derives from the fact that the table is "like a living organism."[30]

Zak KYES

(born 1983)

Poster
The Fall/02.12.05
Designed 2005
Lithograph
83.5 x 58 cm
The Stewart Program for
Modern Design, 2009.15

Swiss-American, Zak Kyes received a BFA in Graphic Design from California Institute of the Arts in 2005, the same year he started his own studio, moved to London, and designed this poster for the December 2 concert of the rock group The Fall. Kyes writes: "Shortly after moving to London I saw my first concert by The Fall. This poster appeared in the exhibition *All That Is Solid Melts into Air* (solo show at Kemistry Gallery, 2006) using lyrics from the track 'Youwanner'—a track in which I particularly like the line 'There's always work in progress/You're always a work in progress.'"[31] The extension of some letters into black verticals, made easy by software, and the jump of words from one line to another in a phrase produces the graphic equivalent of conversations half-heard on the street. The total underlines what graphic artists have exploited since the 1980s: the computer-aided ability to invent fonts and make them expressive as forms as well as letters—here in a kind of "concrete poetry."

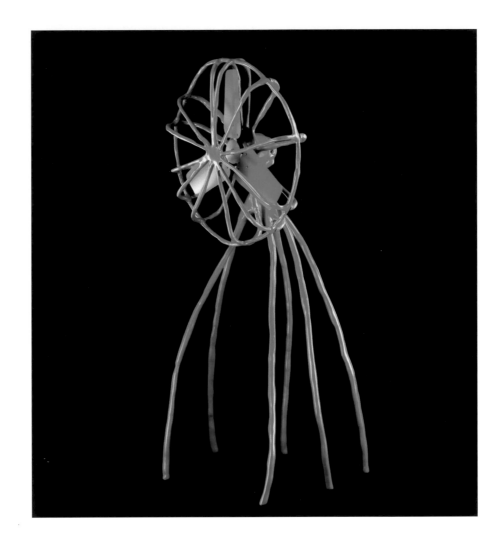

Maarten BAAS

(born 1978)

Floor fan
Clay Furniture Series
Designed 2006
Lacquered industrial clay
152.4 x 48.3 x 48.3 cm
Produced by Baas & den Herder,
Eindhoven, The Netherlands
The Montreal Museum of
Fine Arts, 2007.601

To graduate from the Design Academy in Eindhoven in 2002, Baas created the *Smoke* furniture collection, for which he set fire to old chairs and tables before coating them in an epoxy resin to preserve the charred remains. Stripping away ornament, diminishing "design" as precious, he carries the idea of imperfection further in the *Clay* series. The structure of this furniture is a metal skeleton on which Baas models clay composite. Each example is unique, thanks to Baas's modeling by hand, and the series is available in eight standard colors. They function effectively, like conventional fans, but in their cartoonish designs and irregular surfaces, they question the necessity of a Machine Age look for machines.[32]

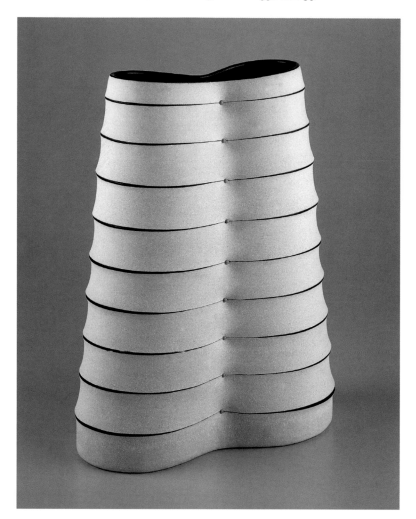

Gustavo PEREZ

(born 1950)

Vase
Designed and executed 2000
Partially glazed stoneware
43.2 x 31.5 x 14.5 cm
The Montreal Museum of
Fine Arts, 2002.81

Illusion is the key element in Perez's vases, as well as the tension between interior and exterior surfaces. In this tall vessel, the matte sandy-colored surface contrasts with a glossy, black-glazed interior, and a vertical row of what resemble upholstery buttons pinch the form as if it were a stack of thick fabric bands. With immense care the edges of these "bands" are glazed in black, and the "buttons" are highlighted and shadowed with subtle changes in the exterior slip glaze. This combination of bold conception and nuanced execution typifies Perez's work, which has won international recognition, particularly in The Netherlands and the United States. He is Mexican by birth and works in his native country.

Maria Grazia ROSIN

(born 1958)

Two bottles
Detergens WC and
Detergens Spray
Designed 2000
Glass, plastic
WC: 30.5 x 12.1 x 6.4 cm
Spray: 31.8 x 10.1 x 6.4 cm
Executed by Vittorio Ferro,
Murano, Italy
The Stewart Program for
Modern Design, 2009.12.1–2

With a Pop sensibility, Rosin here transforms common household plastic spray containers into brilliant colored glass by Vittorio Ferro.[33] The leaping of boundaries between "low" and "high" art began with Warhol's Brillo boxes and Campbell's soup cans in the 1960s, and was expanded by Italian Postmodern designs in particular in the '80s, when Rosin was studying at the Academy of Fine Arts in Venice. After graduating in 1983, she initially worked in graphic design and advertising. In 1992 she participated in the *Progetto Vetro* (Glass Project), in which eight artists from the Veneto region of Italy who were new to glass worked with its master glass blowers on the island. That was her first collaboration with Vittorio Ferro, with whom she later worked on the *Detergens*. Though centuries old, the Vittorio Ferro glassworks has reached out to progressive designers and artists since the 1940s, when it first presented glass in the quirky shapes and vivid hues to which Rosin's *Detergens* series alludes.

Sophie COOK

(born 1974)

Bottles
Pod and Teardrop
Designed 2003, executed 2008
Glazed porcelain
1: 54 x 8.5 x 8.5 cm
2: 42 x 9 x 9 cm
3: 26 x 14 x 14 cm
The Stewart Program for
Modern Design, 2008.10.1–3

Cook's delicate porcelain bottles are handcrafted in series and come in a variety of colors. She takes pleasure in the ways that "differing light can subtly change their appearance and sometimes create luminosity around their silhouette, emphasizing the light translucency of the porcelain."[34] Cook is one of several contemporary artists who look back to mid-century Murano glass. Although her pod and teardrop forms are similar, her color palette is different in its pastel nuances, and the attenuated necks of these bottles are thinner and more elongated. She says, "Porcelain is such a fluid medium on the wheel. I can throw up to six pieces a day but rarely, if ever, do all six survive the making and firing processes." Function (and economy) are far less important than artistic form to her. Ideally, one acquires several bottles "to be seen as a three-dimensional still life that, when viewed from different angles, creates new relationships between the pieces."[35]

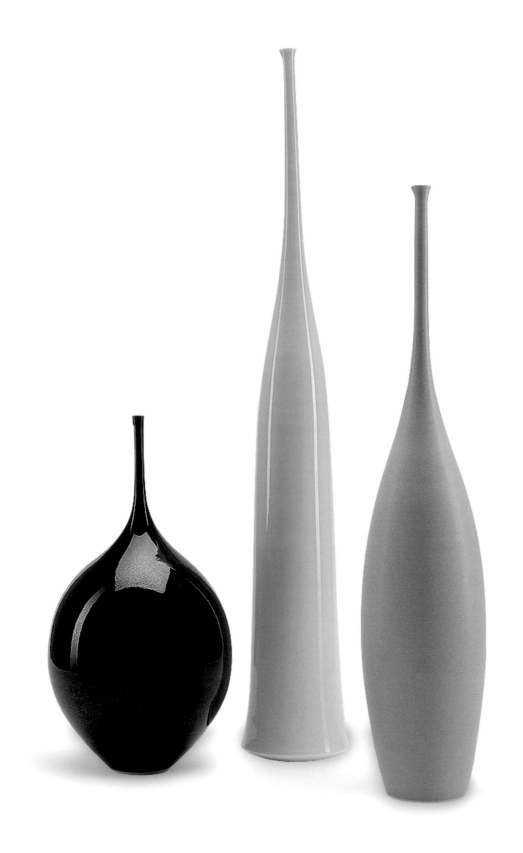

Satyendra PAKHALÉ

(born 1967)

Baskets
Akasma
Designed 2002
Glass
15 x 53 x 50 cm
Produced by RSVP-Curvet,
Ambienti, Italy
The Stewart Program for
Modern Design, 2009.6.1–3

Pakhalé coined the name *Akasma* for these vessels, which, as he wrote for the retail product literature, "means as if something happened suddenly . . . the objects look as if they were just born with ease and almost by chance." However, producing the pieces was challenging, as the glass had to be cut to the profile he desired, then heated and bent to the form sought and finally glued together. This line of baskets is based on ancient containers that he discovered in his native India, and he transposed the forms into contemporary designs by industrial processes, produced by the auto glassmaker RSVP. He thus called attention to both craft traditions and modern industry, whose supposed opposition he tries to heal.

Satyendra PAKHALÉ

(born 1967)

Vase
B.M. (Bel Metal)
Designed 2001
Bel metal
27.2 x 16.7 x 15 cm
Produced by Atelier Satyendra
Pakhalé, Amsterdam,
The Netherlands
The Stewart Program for
Modern Design, 2009.2.2

Fruit Basket
B.M. (Bel Metal)
Designed 2001
Bel metal
12.5 x 29.2 x 29.2
Produced by Atelier Satyendra
Pakhalé, Amsterdam,
The Netherlands
The Stewart Program for
Modern Design, 2009.2.1

Trained as a mechanical engineer and industrial designer in his native India, Pakhalé initially worked as an industrial designer in Puna, India, before moving to Europe in 1992. He was employed at Frog Design and Philips Design before setting up his own practice in Amsterdam in 1998. At the Design Academy Eindhoven, he is head of the Masters program in humanitarian design. On visits to India, he explored craft traditions in metalwork, wood, marble, and ceramics. These two containers reflect his interest in the forms and materials of objects of the past, in this case traditional Indian woven baskets, which he transposes into long-lasting bel metal, a mixture of copper and tin similar to bronze, using contemporary manufacturing technology, thus updating the aesthetic in a more durable material.[36]

PLATFORM with Matthias Bär

(founded 2007)

Table

Fractal
Designed 2007
Epoxy resin
42.5 x 99.5 x 59 cm
Produced by Materialise MGX,
Louvain, Belgium
The Stewart Program for
Modern Design, 2009.25

Like the Jouin side chair, the *Fractal* table is created through rapid-prototyping stereo lithography. The inspiration for this table came from growth patterns seen in nature, specifically the branches of trees.[37] Several modules are joined together, each consisting of four epoxy resin arms emerging from a square base that splits into four more arms, which split again and again, becoming thinner and thinner, as they rise to form a fine, lacy surface resembling the stylized top of a tree. This design, by far the most ambitious attempted using rapid prototyping, was created by the London-based studio Platform, headed by Gernot Oberfell and Jan Wertel, in cooperation with Matthias Bär, and was first presented at the 2008 Milan Furniture Fair.

Rafael ESQUER

(born 1966)

Poster
Vote
Designed 2004
Lithograph
104 x 68.3 cm
The Stewart Program for
Modern Design, 2008.27.1,
gift of the designer

During the 2004 American presidential election, the AIGA (American Institute of Graphic Arts) asked designers from across the country to create posters as part of the "Get Out the Vote 2004" campaign. "There is no single message, although the intent is a call to action, motivating people to register and to turn out to vote. The visuals and the text of the message must be nonpartisan—AIGA is supporting the basic democratic premise of citizen participation." Esquer conveys his message clearly and simply: bold red lettering contrasts with the corpse-like bound figure, illustrating the consequence of failing to vote. A single strong image with a single line of text is a combination reminiscent of mid-century poster designs. "Good Design makes choices clear" refers to the Florida ballots of the 2000 election in which poor design confused some voters and their votes were disqualified, arguably leading to Al Gore's defeat. Born in Mexico, Esquer moved to Los Angeles and graduated from the Art Center College of Design in 1996. In New York, he established Alfalfa Studio in 2004.[38]

M-A-D

(founded 1989)

Exhibition poster
Fuelicide
Designed 2003
Archival digital print
111.8 x 83.5 cm
The Stewart Program for
Modern Design, 2008.20.1,
gift of the designers

Both designers, Erik Adigard and Patricia McShane, graduated from the California College of Arts and Crafts, Oakland, in 1987 with degrees in graphic design. In 1989, they founded M-A-D, an interdisciplinary firm for the design of print and interactive media. M-A-D has produced award-winning graphics and illustrations, most notably the well-known editorial design and logo for *Wired* magazine, as well as websites for *WiredDigital*.[39] This poster, which was created for AIGA's annual competition, cleverly adapts the stylized, international symbols for a man and a fuel pump, implying that every person pumping gas for a car is in effect committing suicide. The collaged photograph shows a distressed child trying to stop this suicide for the sake of the next generation and our planet.

EL ULTIMO GRITO

(founded 1997)

Stool
Mico (Monkey)
Designed 2006
Polyurethane
39.5 x 67 x 67 cm
Produced by Magis, Milan, Italy
The Stewart Program for
Modern Design, 2008.24

With its comic, humanoid form, this stool was designed for use by children, but it also delights adults. It invites inventive positions and ideas, and takes on new forms depending on how the child places it and where its multiple points come to rest. *Mico* is durable, fine for outdoor use, welcoming imaginative interpretations. A child might ride, kick, throw, or mimic it, only a few among the many responses it encourages. The designers, Roberto Feo and Rosario Hurtado, from Madrid, established El Ultimo Grito, Spanish for "the last shout," in 1997 in London, where Feo teaches at the Royal College of Art. The firm name signals their desire to give their products names that convey the objects' essences and witty charm.

Maria BERNTSEN

(born 1961)

Insulated jug
Quack
Designed 2002
Plastic, aluminum, zinc
16 x 22 x 14.5 cm
Produced for Georg Jensen,
Copenhagen, Denmark
The Stewart Program for
Modern Design, 2008.12

For this insulated jug, Berntsen began with the idea of a compact object that would rest solidly on a table.[40] The design is her take on 1930s streamlining, with its dramatic forward thrust suggesting a speeding vehicle or a bird in flight, and a lifted handle like a tail flying in the wind. Yet the jug's contemporary origins are visible in its muted, earthy colors— beige (seen here), green, and chocolate brown—and its squat ovoid form, which softens the streamlined effect and humorously evokes the duckling of its name, *Quack*.

FRONT DESIGN

(founded 2004)

Vase
Blow Away
Designed 2008
Porcelain
30.5 x 32 x 26 cm
Produced for Moooi, Breda,
the Netherlands
The Stewart Program for
Modern Design, 2009.22

From an eighteenth-century Royal Delft vase, Front Design created a digital replica using CAD (computer-aided design) software and then subjected it to a virtual wind force. Then the designers paused the animation and had technicians use the still frame to model a new form and develop a physical mold of it to allow production. The vase in its new porcelain form is a cartoon come to life, startling in its defiance of material properties.[41] The Stockholm-based Front Design group—Sofia Lagerkvist, Charlotte von der Lancken, Anna Lindgren, and Katja Sävström—is known for its innovative computer design methods, including a technique by which freehand strokes in the air are recorded to create their *Sketch Furniture* line.[42] The vase refers both to its old Delft prototype and to new technology, in which the effects of invisible phenomena (like wind) can be made material and can be used to generate mass-produced objects.

Notes

The Liliane and
David M. Stewart Collection
Inspired Enterprise

1. Art Association of Montreal, *Reports for 1916 being the fifty-fifth report*, 1917, 5–6, quoted in Georges-Hébert Germain, *A City's Museum: A History of the Montreal Museum of Fine Arts* (Montreal: The Montreal Museum of Fine Arts, 2007), 66.
2. Liliane M. Stewart in *All for Art! In Conversation with Collectors*, exh. cat. (Montreal: The Montreal Museum of Fine Arts, 2007), 236.

The Creation of a Collection

1. Mr. Stewart's interest in history had already led him in 1955 to create a museum celebrating the discovery of the New World—now known as the Stewart Museum—on St. Helen's Island in the city's old fort. The decorative arts museum reflected Mrs. Stewart's particular interest.
2. The collection had been assembled in the early 1980s by Mark Isaacson, Mark McDonald, and Ralph Cutler, who were partners in New York's Fifty/50 Gallery, the premier showcase in North America for mid-century design at that time.
3. Martin Eidelberg, ed., *Design 1935–1965: What Modern Was,* exh. cat. (New York: Harry N. Abrams, with the Montreal Museum of Decorative Arts, 1991; repr. 2001).
4. Georges-Hébert Germain, *A City's Museum: A History of the Montreal Museum of Fine Arts* (Montreal: Montreal Museum of Fine Arts, 2007), 227.

1900–1929
An Introduction to Modernism

1. Edgar Kaufmann, Jr., *What is Modern Design?* (New York: Museum of Modern Art, 1950), 7.
2. Christopher Wilk, *Marcel Breuer: Furniture and Interiors* (New York: Museum of Modern Art, 1981), 79.
3. Sybil Gordon Kantor, *Alfred H. Barr, Jr. and the Intellectual Origins of the Museum of Modern Art* (Cambridge, Mass.: MIT Press, 2002), 262. Barr first visited the Bauhaus in 1927; Johnson in 1929.

4. Russell Lynes, *Good Old Modern: An Intimate Portrait of the Museum of Modern Art* (New York: Atheneum, 1973), 28.

1930–1939
Modes of Modernism

1. Paul Johnson, *Modern Times: The World from the Twenties to the Eighties* (New York: Harper & Row, 1983), 246–47.
2. Philip Johnson, "Machine Art," *Bulletin of The Museum of Modern Art* 3 (November 1933): 2.
3. Philip Johnson, *Machine Art*, exh. cat. (New York: Museum of Modern Art, 1934), n.p.
4. On streamlining, see Jeffrey L. Miekle, *Twentieth Century Limited: Industrial Design in America, 1925–1939* (Philadelphia: Temple University Press, 1979, repr. 2001), and the most recent survey of the form, David A. Hanks and Anne Hoy, *American Streamlined Design: The World of Tomorrow* (Montreal: Flammarion for the Stewart Program for Modern Design, 2005).
5. Kathryn B. Hiesinger and Stanley H. Marcus, *Landmarks of Twentieth-Century Design: An Illustrated Handbook* (New York: Abbeville, 1993), 116, 130.
6. Arthur Loomis Harmon, quoted in R. Craig Miller, *Modern Design in the Metropolitan Museum of Art, 1890-1990* (New York: Metropolitan Museum of Art, 1990), 26–27.
7. Anon., "Contrast in Design," *Creative Design in Home Furnishings* 3 (September 1938): 31.
8. Hiesinger and Marcus, *Landmarks of Twentieth-Century Design*, 135, 141.
9. For more on the differences, see David A. Hanks and Anne Hoy, "Streamlining and Art Deco in American Industrial Design," *The Magazine Antiques* (October 2004): 114–23.
10. Lewis Mumford, *Technics and Civilization* (London: Routledge, 1934), 356.
11. William S. Lieberman, "Modern French Tapestries," *The Metropolitan Museum of Art Bulletin* (January 1948): 112.
12. Alice Zrebiec, in *What Modern Was*, 231.

13. Leonard Griffin and Louis K. and Susan Pear Meisel, *Clarice Cliff: The Bizarre Affair* (New York: Harry N. Abrams, 1988), 52.
14. Letter from Anne Gross, Christofle, Paris, to Lenore Newman, David A. Hanks & Associates, April 21, 1995. Archives, The Montreal Museum of Fine Arts.
15. Joan Kahr, "Gilbert Poillerat: A Half-Century of Ironwork Design," *Metalsmith* 12 (Summer 1992): 33.
16. Letter from Yvonne Bruhammer, former director of Musée des arts décoratifs, Paris, to Luc d'Iberville Moreau, director, Musée des arts décoratifs, Montreal, July 25, 1994.
17. Walter Dorwin Teague, "Industrial Art and Its Future," *Art and Industry* 22, no. 131 (May 1937): 194.
18. Jean Puiforcat, quoted in *Design 1900–1940*, ed. Kathryn B. Hiesinger and George H. Marcus (Philadelphia: Philadelphia Museum of Art, 1987), 40.
19. *Deutsche Warenkunde* (Berlin: Kunst-Dienst, c. 1935), 430, provided in June 1984 by Dr. Christian Wolsdorff of the Bauhaus-Archiv, Berlin, Germany.
20. Letter to Caroline Stern of David A. Hanks & Associates from Dr. Christian Wolsdorff, June 13, 1984. Archives, The Montreal Museum of Fine Arts.
21. Magdalena Droste, *Bauhaus 1919–1933* (Berlin: Bauhaus Archiv, 1990), 178.
22. "The Wilbour Library, Brooklyn Museum, Brooklyn, New York," *American Architect*, December 1935.
23. Donald Albrecht, Robert Shonfeld, and Lindsay Stamm Shapiro, *Russel Wright: Creating American Lifestyle*, exh. cat. (New York: Harry N. Abrams and Cooper-Hewitt, National Design Museum, Smithsonian Institution, 2001), 26.
24. Mary Schoeser, *Marianne Straub*, exh. cat. (London: The Design Council, 1984), 48–49.
25. *Design Paper*, no. 9 (no date), n.p.
26. Anna Venini Diaz de Santillana, *Venini: Catalogue Raisonné 1921–1986* (Milan: Skira, 2000), 25.
27. Arlette Barré-Despond, *Dictionnaire International des arts appliqués et du design* (Paris: Editions du Regard, 1996), 253.
28. Catalogue, Montreal Museum of Decorative Arts, Archives, Montreal Museum of Fine Arts.

29. Nathan George Horwitt, "Reasoned Design," *Creative Art* 8, no. 5 (May 1931): 377.
30. Christopher Wilk, in *What Modern Was*, 81.
31. Judith Nasby, *Rolph Scarlett: Painter, Designer, Jeweller* (Montreal: McGill-Queens University Press, 2004), 49.
32. Christopher Wilk, *Marcel Breuer Furniture and Interiors* (New York: Museum of Modern Art, 1981), 150-151.
33. *Modern Plastics* 15, no. 10 (June 1938): 24.
34. *What Modern Was*, 36.

1940–1949
Creativity in the War Years

1. Edgar Kaufmann, Jr., *Prize Designs for Modern Furniture* (New York: Museum of Modern Art, 1950), 8.
2. Walter R. Hagedohm, "New Developments," *Arts & Architecture* (June 1944): 31.
3. Quoted in *Les Années UAM, 1929–1959*, exh. cat. (Paris: Musée des Arts Décoratifs, 1989), 100.
4. For a survey of biomorphism within modern design, see Eidelberg, *What Modern Was*, 88–93.
5. "Registering a New Trend," *Everyday Art Quarterly* (Fall 1946): 6–7.
6. Wilk, in *What Modern Was*, 54.
7. "New Furniture," *Arts & Architecture*, 65, no. 7 (July 1948).
8. Christa C. Mayer Thurman, in *What Modern Was*, 61.
9. See Christa C. Mayer Thurman, "Textiles," in *Design in America: The Cranbrook Vision 1925–1950* (New York: Harry N. Abrams, for the Detroit Institute of Art and The Metropolitan Museum of Art, 1983), 201–205.
10. Knoll Associates, Inc., sales catalogue designed by Herbert Matter (New York: Knoll Associates, and H. G. Knoll International, 1950), 20.
11. *House Beautiful*, October 1947.
12. Ruth Adler Schnee, letter to Montreal Museum of Decorative Arts, September 17, 1984. Archives, The Montreal Museum of Fine Arts.
13. David A. Hanks, *Innovative Furniture in America* (New York: Horizon Press, 1981), 104.
14. Exhibition brochure, "Angelo Testa," The George Walter Vincent Smith Art Museum, March 2–20, 1949. Correspondence from Ryan Paveza,

The Art Institute of Chicago, to David Hanks, July 31, 2009, regarding research by Christa Thurman, Stewart Program Archives.
15. Letter from Angelo Testa to David A. Hanks, September 19, 1983. Archives, The Montreal Museum of Fine Arts.
16. David Bourdon, *Calder/Mobilist/ Ringmaster/Innovator* (New York: Macmillan, 1980), 49–51.
17. Sam Kramer, "Creating Spontaneous Jewelry," *Design* 53 (May 1951): 181.
18. Janet Fiske Mitarachi, "Kåge's Fractured Forms," *Interiors* 112 (June 1953): 81.
19. Marielle Ernould-Gandouet, "Galeries: Paris: Fulvio Bianconi," *L'Oeil* 371 (June 1986): 85.
20. Salvador Dalí, quoted in Lida Livingston, ed., *Dalí: A Study of His Art-in-Jewels—The Collection of the Owen Cheatham Foundation* (Greenwich, Conn.: Graphic Society, 1959), 12.
21. Diaz de Santillana, *Venini: Catalogue Raisonné*, 217.
22. Dan Klein, *Glass: A Contemporary Art* (New York: Rizzoli, 1989), 87–88.
23. Axel Salto, *Forces of Nature: Axel Salto*, exh. cat. (New York: Antik Gallery, 1999), 5.
24. Eidelberg, in *What Modern Was*, 70.

1950–1959
"Good Design"
1. Edgar Kaufmann, Jr., *What is Modern Design?*, 9.
2. "Useful Gifts 1950," *Everyday Art Quarterly* 17 (Winter 1950–51): 1.
3. The Eameses' fiberglass LAR (Low ARm) Chair sold for $38 in 1957; their rosewood-veneered, leather-upholstered Lounge Chair and Ottoman then cost a hefty $634. See David A. Hanks and Anne Hoy, *Design for Living: Furniture and Lighting 1950–2000*, and ed. Martin Eidelberg (Paris: Flammarion for the Montreal Museum of Decorative Art, 2000), 57.
4. Philip B. Meggs and Alston W. Purvis, *Meggs' History of Graphic Design* (Hoboken, N.J.: John Wiley & Sons, 2006) devotes chapter 18 to the style.
5. Quoted in "Design and Theory: Two Points of View," *Design since 1945*, ed. Kathryn B. Hiesinger and George H. Marcus (New York: Rizzoli and the

Philadelphia Museum of Art, 1983), 3.
6. Reyner Banham, "A Throw-Away Esthetic," *Industrial Design* (March 1960): 62–63.
7. László Moholy-Nagy, *Vision in Motion* (New York: Paul Theobald, 1947, repr. 1969), 91.
8. Dorothy Liebes, "Designing Textiles for Industry," *Craft Horizons*, 12, no. 3 (May–June 1952): 20.
9. Isamu Noguchi, "Akari—Isamu Noguchi," *Arts and Architecture* 72 (May 1955): 14.
10. Grey Art Gallery, New York, *The Geometry of Hope: Latin American Abstract Art from the Patricia Phelps de Cisneros Collection,* exhibition, 2008.
11. Jack Lenor Larsen, letter to David A. Hanks, April 2009. Archives, The Stewart Program for Modern Design.
12. Olga Gueft, "The Exhilarated World of Eszter Haraszty," *Interiors* 115, no. 11 (June 1956): 94.
13. Charlotte and Peter Fiell, eds., *1000 Lights: 1879 to 1959* (Cologne: Taschen, 2005), 401.
14. Hiesinger and Marcus, *Landmarks of Twentieth-Century Design*, 170.
15. Rosa Barovier Mentasti, *Anzolo Fuga: Murano Glass Artist: Designs for A.V.E.M., 1955–1968* (New York: Acanthus Press with Lobel Modern, 2005), n.p.
16. Meyric R. Rogers, *Italy at Work: Her Renaissance in Design Today* (Rome: Comagnia Nazionale Artigiana, 1950), 30.
17. Peter Todd Mitchell, "Textile Design as a Career," 1946, typewritten manuscript, from Priscilla Cunningham, who also provided information about this drawing. Archives, The Montreal Museum of Fine Arts.
18. Meggs and Purvis, *Meggs' History of Graphic Design*, 364.
19. Vivianna Torun Bülow-Hübe, letter to Toni Lesser Wolf, September 16, 1989. Archives, The Montreal Museum of Fine Arts.
20. Kathryn B. Hiesinger and Felice Fischer, *Japanese Design: A Survey Since 1950* (Philadelphia: Philadelphia Museum of Art in association with Harry N. Abrams, New York, 1994), 227.

1960–1969
Contradictory Visions
1. Quoted in Christopher Mead, ed., *The Architecture of Robert Venturi*

(Albuquerque: University of New Mexico Press, 1989), 4–5.
2. C. Ray Smith, *Supermannerism: New Attitudes in Post-Modern Architecture* (New York: E. P. Dutton, 1977), 270.
3. See J. R. G., "Fourteen Is an Awkward Age," *Industrial Design* 15 (October 1968): 51–53.
4. Arata Isozaki, as quoted in Andrea Branzi, *The Hot House: Italian New Wave Design* (Cambridge, Mass.: MIT Press, 1984), 4–5.
5. Emilio Ambasz, ed., *Italy: The New Domestic Landscape: Achievements and Problems of Italian Design* (New York: Museum of Modern Art, 1972), 19.
6. *Ibid.*, 21.
7. Quoted in Rachel Gotlieb and Nina Munk, *The Art of Clairtone: The Making of a Design Icon 1958–1971* (Toronto: McClelland & Stewart/Design Exchange, 2008), 17.
8. Gloria A. Collinson, 1964 press release "Project G—Fact Sheet," printed in Munk and Gotlieb, *The Art of Clairtone*, 76.
9. *Phaidon Design Classics: 333 of 999 Objects, Volume II* (London: Phaidon, 2006), n.p., object no. 574.
10. Marianne Aav, ed., *Marimekko: Fabrics Fashion Architecture* (New Haven: Yale University Press, 2003), 159.
11. Ambasz, *Italy: The New Domestic Landscape*, 95–97.
12. Gaetano Pesce, as quoted in Alexander von Vegesack, Peter Dunas, and Mathias Schwartz-Clauss, *100 Masterpieces from the Collection of the Vitra Design Museum* (Weil am Rhein: Vitra Design Museum, 1995), 50.
13. Wilk, in *What Modern Was*, 314.
14. François Burkhardt with Juli Capella and Francesca Pichhi, *Why Write a Book on Enzo Mari* (Milan: Federico Motta, 1997), 121–22.
15. Virgilio Vercelloni, *The Adventure of Design: Gavina* (New York: Rizzoli, 1987), 16.
16. Gianfranco Frattini, letter to the Montreal Museum of Decorative Arts, January 25, 1995. Archives, The Montreal Museum of Fine Arts.
17. Hiesinger and Marcus, *Landmarks of Twentieth-Century Design*, 246.
18. See Branzi, *The Hot House*, 67.

19. Elisabeth Vedrenne and Anne-Marie Fevre, *Pierre Paulin* (Paris: Dis Voir, 2001), 61.
20. Giampiero Bosoni, ed., *Contemporary Domestic Landscapes: 1945–2000* (Milan: Skira, 2001), 227.
21. Eric Larrabee and Massimo Vignelli, *Knoll Design* (New York: Harry N. Abrams, 1981), 117.
22. Eidelberg, in *What Modern Was*, 339.
23. Kaj Kalin, et al., *Kaj Franck: Designer* (Helsinki: Werner Söderström Osakeyhtiö, 1992).
24. Letter from Gaetano Pesce to David A. Hanks, Stewart Program for Modern Design, March 3, 2009.
25. Acquisition research report, February 23, 2001, Montreal Museum of Fine Arts Archives.
26. Bruno Martinazzi, "Autobiography of Bruno Martinazzi, Goldsmith and Sculptor, Professor at the Accademia di Belle Arti de Torino," *Goldsmiths' Journal* 4 (August 1978): 37.
27. Cindi Strauss, *Ornament as Art: Avant-garde Jewelry from the Helen Williams Drutt Collection* (Stuttgart, Germany: Arnoldsche Art Publishers in association with The Museum of Fine Arts, Houston, 2007), 208.
28. Robert Ebendorf, letter to jewelry scholar Toni Greenbaum, June 5, 1994, Montreal Museum of Fine Arts Archives.
29. Ambasz, *Italy: The New Domestic Landscape*, 94.
30. Paola Antonelli, *Objects of Design from The Museum of Modern Art* (New York: Museum of Modern Art, 2003), 258.
31. Piero Gilardi, as quoted in Elisa V. Massai, "Youth Power," *Home Furnishings Daily*, May 17, 1968.
32. Enrico De Munari, letter to the Montreal Museum of Decorative Arts, January 19, 1995. Archives, The Montreal Museum of Fine Arts.
33. Marvin Lipofsky, quoted in Suzanne Baizerman, ed., *Marvin Lipofsky: A Glass Odyssey* (Oakland, Calif.: Oakland Museum of California, 2003), 119.
34. Magdalena Abakanowicz, quoted in Jasia Reichardt, *Magdalena Abakanowicz* (Chicago: Museum of Contemporary Art, 1982), 48.
35. Meggs and Purvis, *Meggs' History of Graphic Design*, 429.

474

36. Beth Levine, interview with Montreal Museum of Decorative Arts, October 14, 1993. Archives, The Montreal Museum of Fine Arts.
37. Paco Rabanne, *Trajectoire: d'une vie à l'autre* (Paris: Édition n° 1/Michel Lafon, 1991), 137–38.
38. Quoted in Shirley Kennedy, *Pucci: A Renaissance in Fashion* (New York: Abbeville, 1991), 95.
39. Ibid., 103.
40. Meggs and Purvis, *Meggs' History of Graphic Design*, 439.
41. Ray Grover and Lee Grover, *Contemporary Art Glass* (New York: Crown, 1945), 73.
42. "Millinery Mobiles Are Displayed in Art Gallery in New York," *Toledo Blade*, February 8, 1959.
43. Utility patent 3,317,722 for an "Electroluminescent Lamp," application filed April 26, 1965, and granted May 2, 1967.
44. Quoted in Terence Conran, *Printed Textile Design* (New York: Studio Publications, 1957), 40.
45. Eddie Squires, letter to the Montreal Museum of Decorative Arts, June 27, 1994. Archives, The Montreal Museum of Fine Arts.
46. Bevis Hillier, *The World of Art Deco* (New York: E. P. Dutton, 1971), 19.
47. Benjamin Loyauté, *Pierre Cardin Evolution* (Paris: Flammarion, 2006), 7.
48. Andrea Branzi, *The Hot House Italian New Wave Design* (Cambridge, Mass.: MIT Press, 1984), 59.

1970–1979
Pluralism and Responsibility

1. Penny Sparke, ed., *The Plastics Age: From Modernity to Post-modernity* (London: Victoria and Albert Museum, 1990), 151.
2. Joe Colombo in Ambasz, *Italy: The New Domestic Landscape*, 172.
3. Branzi, *The Hot House*, 69.
4. Hiesinger and Marcus, *Landmarks of Twentieth-century Design*, 250.
5. Charles Jencks, *Architecture Today* (New York: Harry N. Abrams, 1982), 247.
6. Kyo Toyoguchi, "Design Organizations," in Heisinger and Fischer, *Japanese Design*, 25.
7. Barbara Bloemink, *Design ≠ Art: Functional Objects from Donald Judd to Rachel Whiteread,* exh. cat. (London: Merrell, with Cooper-Hewitt, National

Design Museum, New York, 2004), 37.
8. Ibid., 39.
9. Joan Kron and Suzanne Slesin, *High Tech: The Industrial Style and Source Book for the Home* (New York: Clarkson N. Potter, 1978).
10. Carrie Rickey, "Art of Whole Cloth," *Art in America* 67 (November 1979): 79.
11. Frank Gehry, interview with David A. Hanks, May 24, 1991, quoted in *Frank Gehry: New Bentwood Furniture,* exh. cat. (Montreal: Montreal Museum of Decorative Arts, 1992), 42.
12. Francesco Dal Co and Kurt W. Forster, *Frank O. Gehry: The Complete Works* (New York: Monacelli, 1998), 210.
13. Dan Klein, *Artists in Glass: Late Twentieth Century Masters in Glass* (London: Mitchell Beazley, Octopus Publishing Group, 2001), 38.
14. Flavio Barbini, interview with Montreal Museum of Decorative Arts, December 14, 1994. Archives, The Montreal Museum of Fine Arts.
15. Jack Lenor Larsen, letter to the Montreal Museum of Decorative Arts, June 2, 1995. Archives, The Montreal Museum of Fine Arts.
16. William C. Seitz, *The Responsive Eye* (New York: Museum of Modern Art, 1965), 26.
17. Meggs and Purvis, *Meggs' History of Graphic Design*, 405.
18. Paul Rand, "The Rebus," *Design Quarterly* 123 (1984): 24.
19. France Vanlaethem, *Gaetano Pesce: Architecture, Design, Art* (New York: Rizzoli, 1989), 66.
20. Andrea Branzi, letter to the Montreal Museum of Decorative Art, July 22, 1993. Archives, The Montreal Museum of Fine Arts.
21. Sergio Asti, letter to the Montreal Museum of Decorative Arts, October 20, 1994. Archives, The Montreal Museum of Fine Arts.
22. Vanni Pasca, *Vico Magistretti: Elegance and Innovation in Postwar Italian Design* (London: Thames and Hudson, 1991), 69.
23. For illustrations of other pieces in the *Birillo* series, including a small table, armchair, and ottoman, see Ignazia Favata, *Joe Colombo and the Italian Design of the Sixties* (Cambridge, Mass.: MIT Press, 1988), 77.

24. See Lella and Massimo Vignelli, *Design: Vignelli* (New York: Rizzoli, 1981), 82.
25. Jewel Stern, *Modernism in American Silver: 20th-Century Design* (Dallas: Dallas Museum of Art, and New Haven: Yale University Press, 2005), 298–301.
26. Giotto Stoppino, quoted in Daniele Baroni, *Giotto Stoppino: dall'architettura al design* (Milan: Electa Editrice, 1983), 39.
27. Tom Patti, quoted in Dan Klein, *Glass: A Contemporary Art* (New York: Rizzoli, 1989), 65.
28. Quoted in *Currents 24: Tom Patti,* exhibition brochure, St. Louis Art Museum, 1984.
29. Strauss, *Ornament as Art*, 478.
30. Quoted in George H. Marcus, *Masters of Modern Design: A Critical Assessment* (New York: Monacelli, 2005), 152.
31. Helmut Ricke and Eva Schmitt, *Italian Glass 1930–1970* (Munich: Prestel, 1997), 246–47.
32. David Revere McFadden, ed., *Scandinavian Modern Design 1880-1980* (New York: Harry N. Abrams, 1982), 178–79.
33. Paola Antonelli, *Objects of Desire from the Museum of Modern Art* (New York: Museum of Modern Art, 2003), 228.
34. Neal Benezra, *Robert Arneson: A Retrospective* (Des Moines, Iowa: Des Moines Art Center, 1985), 56.
35. Ibid., 67.
36. Helen Drutt, interview by David A. Hanks, July 7, 2009. Archives, The Stewart Program for Modern Design.
37. Gijs Bakker, letter to David A. Hanks, February 28, 2009. Archives, The Stewart Program for Modern Design.
38. Strauss, *Ornament as Art*, 508.
39. Ambasz, *Italy: The New Domestic Landscape*, 20.
40. Cesare Birignani, ed., *Marzio Cecchi: Fancy Designs 1969–1979* (Florence: Studio Most, 1995), n.p.
41. Donato D'Urbino, letter to Montreal Museum of Decorative Arts, November 3, 1995. Archives, The Montreal Museum of Fine Arts.
42. Helena Hernmarck, letter to David A. Hanks, Stewart Program for Modern Design, March 3, 2009.

43. John R. Berry, *Herman Miller: The Purpose of Design*, 139.
44. Meggs and Purvis, *Meggs' History of Graphic Design*, 425.
45. Guido Drocco, letter to the Montreal Museum of Decorative Arts, June 3, 1995. Archives, The Montreal Museum of Fine Arts.
46. U.S. Patent 4,328,991 filed March 26, 1980.
47. Giampiero Bosoni, ed., *Il Modo Italiano: Italian Design and Avant-garde in the 20th Century,* exh. cat. (Milan: Skira in association with The Montreal Museum of Fine Arts, 2006), 277.

1980–1989
Postmodernism and Other Currents

1. Robert Venturi, quoted in David B. Brownlee, David G. De Long, and Kathryn B. Hiesinger, *Out of the Ordinary: Robert Venturi, Denise Scott Brown and Associates* (Philadelphia: Philadelphia Museum of Art in association with Yale University Press, 2001), 201.
2. Andrea Branzi, quoted in Richard Horn, *Memphis: Objects, Furniture, Patterns* (Philadelphia: Running Press, 1985), 17.
3. Ettore Sottsass, quoted in Joe Dolce, "Profiles: Four Designers," *I.D.: The International Design Magazine* 36 (January/February 1989): 56.
4. Barbara Radice, *Memphis: Research, Experiences, Results, Failures and Successes of New Design* (Milan and New York: Gruppo Editoriale Electa and Rizzoli, 1984), 26.
5. See Dorothy Mackenzie, *Green Design: Design for the Environment* (London: Lawrence King, 1991), passim.
6. Alessandro Mendini, letter to the Montreal Museum of Decorative Arts, November 30, 1995. Archives, The Montreal Museum of Fine Arts.
7. Gaetano Pesce, interview with Montreal Museum of Decorative Arts, March 11, 1993.
8. Ramón Puig Cuyás, letter to Toni Greenbaum, June 5, 1994.
9. Cerchio is a town in Italy with Roman origins; it included a small group of houses constructed around a theater (*circo*), a plan perhaps suggestive of the pattern of this textile.
10. Radice, *Memphis*, 88.

11. Ralph Bacerra, letter to Michael McTwigan, ceramic historian, March 2, 1994. Archives, The Montreal Museum of Fine Arts.

12. Dorothy Hafner, interview with the Montreal Museum of Decorative Arts, December 15, 1994. Archives, The Montreal Museum of Fine Arts.

13. Suzanne Slesin, "Sottsass' Oversize Collection: Is It Furniture or Art?" *The New York Times*, October 29, 1987. Archives, The Montreal Museum of Fine Arts.

14. Niki de Saint-Phalle, letter to the Montreal Museum of Decorative Arts, April 28, 1996. Archives, The Montreal Museum of Fine Arts.

15. The Museum of Contemporary Art, Los Angeles, letter to the Montreal Museum of Decorative Arts, March 26, 1996. Archives, The Montreal Museum of Fine Arts.

16. Blake Gopnik, "Leopold Foulem's Conceptual Pottery," *American Ceramics* 12, no. 2 (1996): 26.

17. Radice, *Memphis*, 141.

18. Dan Friedman, *Dan Friedman: Radical Modernism* (New Haven and London: Yale University Press, 1994), 11.

19. Alberto Alessi, ed., *Alessi: The Design Factory* (Chichester, England: Academy Editions, John Wiley & Sons, 2nd ed., 1998), 95.

20. Kathryn B. Hiesinger in *Out of the Ordinary*, 201–11.

21. Robert Venturi and Denise Scott Brown, as quoted in *Knoll Venturi Collection* (New York: Knoll International, c. 1984), n.p.

22. Hiesinger in *Out of the Ordinary*, 223–24.

23. Cleto Munari, memorandum to R. Craig Miller, Denver Art Museum, July 6, 2001, Denver Art Museum Archives.

24. See Françoise de Bonneville, *Jean Puiforcat* (Paris: Éditions du Regard, 1986), 123.

25. Michael Graves, quoted in Annette Tapert, *Swid Powell: Objects by Architects* (New York: Rizzoli, 1990), 40.

26. Hugh Cumming in *The Post-Modern Object, An Art & Design Profile*, Andreas C. Papadakis, ed. (London: Academy Group, 1987), 24.

27. Alessi, *The Design Factory*, 39.

28. See Radice, *Memphis*, 63.

29. Philippe Louguet and Dagmar Sedlicka, *Bořek Šípek* (Paris: Dis Voir, 1998), 67.

30. Julia Manheim, letter to David A. Hanks, April 21, 2009. Archives, The Montreal Museum of Fine Arts.

31. Issey Miyake, as quoted in Peter Popham, "The Emperor's Clothes," *Blueprint*, no. 15 (March 1986): 16.

32. Strauss, *Ornament as Art*, 268.

33. Gerd Rothman, letter to Toni Greenbaum, December 30, 1993. Archives, The Montreal Museum of Fine Arts.

34. *Lella and Massimo Vignelli: Design is One* (Mulgrave, Victoria, Australia: Images House, 2004), 99.

35. Tom Dixon, letter to the Montreal Museum of Decorative Arts, October 18, 1993. Archives, The Montreal Museum of Fine Arts.

36. Peter Cook and George Rand, *Morphosis: Buildings and Projects* (New York: Rizzoli, 1989), 155.

37. Philip B. Meggs in *US Design: 1975–2000*, ed. R. Craig Miller (Munich: Prestel, 2001), 203.

38. Robert Bell in David Revere McFadden, et al., *Elegant Fantasy: The Jewelry of Arline Fisch* (Stuttgart: Arnoldsche, 1999), 23.

39. Paola Antonelli, *Mutant Materials in Contemporary Design* (New York: Museum of Modern Art, 1995), 82.

40. Gaetano Pesce, interview with the Montreal Museum of Decorative Arts, March 11, 1994. Archives, The Montreal Museum of Fine Arts.

41. Deyan Sudjic, *Ron Arad* (London: Laurence King, 1999), 56.

42. Adelle Lutz, letter to the Montreal Museum of Decorative Arts, October 5, 1995. Archives, The Montreal Museum of Fine Arts.

43. Massimo Iosa Ghini, interview with the Montreal Museum of Decorative Arts, April 14, 1994. Archives, The Montreal Museum of Fine Arts.

44. Matteo Thun, letter to the Montreal Museum of Decorative Arts, December 22, 1994. Archives, The Montreal Museum of Fine Arts

45. Philippe Starck, letter to the Montreal Museum of Decorative Arts, November 7, 1995. Archives, The Montreal Museum of Fine Arts.

46. Alessi, *The Design Factory*, 101.

47. Association Française d'Action Artistique, *Sylvain Dubuisson*, exh. cat. (Paris: AFAA, 1992), 66.

48. Carlo Forcolini, quoted in Nally Belati, *New Italian Design* (New York: Rizzoli, 1990), 68.

49. Shigeru Uchida, quoted in Hiesinger and Fischer, *Japanese Design*, 162.

1990–1999
A New Minimalism

1. Antonelli, *Mutant Materials in Contemporary Design*, 9.

2. Ibid., 11.

3. Sotheby's, Monaco, October 13, 1991.

4. Geert Bekaert, *Maarten Van Severen* (Ghent, Belgium: Ludion, 2000), 67.

5. Jasper Morrison, ed., *International Design Yearbook 1999* (New York: Abbeville, 1999), 5.

6. Francesca Picchi, "Projects: IKEA: Ingvar Kamprad," *Domus* 775 (October 1995): 70.

7. Tedi Bish and Suzette Sherman, "Design to Save the World: A Practical Guide to Green Design," *I.D.: The International Design Magazine* 37 (November/December 1990). 48.

8. Paola Antonelli, "Nothing Cooler than Dry," in Renny Ramakers and Gijs Bakker, eds., *Droog Design: Spirit of the Nineties* (Rotterdam: 010 Publishers, 1998), 12.

9. Renny Ramakers, Foreword, *Droog Design*, 9.

10. Thomas Weiss et al., *Couleur Locale: Droog Design for Oranienbaum* (Rotterdam: 010 Publishers, 1999), 13.

11. Emilio Ambasz and Shigeru Ban, *Shigeru Ban* (Princeton: Princeton Architectural Press, 2001), 107.

12. Antonelli, *Mutant Materials in Contemporary Design*, 88.

13. Constantin Boym, Peter Hall, and Steven Skov Holt, *Curious Boym* (New York: Princeton Architectural Press, 2002), 138.

14. Ida van Zijl, *Gijs Bakker and Jewelry* (Stuttgart: Arnoldsche, 2005), 43.

15. Bekaert, *Maarten Van Severen*, 90.

16. Strauss, *Ornament as Art*, 505.

17. Alberto Bassi, *Industrial Designer Antonio Citterio* (Milan: Electa, 2004), 108.

18. Andrée Putman, ed., *The International Design Yearbook* 7 (London: Abbeville, 1992), 42.

19. The design for the shelving unit was illustrated in *The International Design Yearbook* for 1993, but the Japanese manufacturer Chairs had not put it into production. Uchida sent design drawings to the Montreal Museum of Decorative Arts so that *Stormy Weather* could be produced for the Stewart Collection.

20. Minako Morita, Assistant to Shigeru Uchida, Studio 80, letters to the Montreal Museum of Decorative Arts, September 3 and 28, 1999. Archives, The Montreal Museum of Fine Arts.

21. Alessandro Mendini, *Museum Market*, exh. cat. (Milan: Design Gallery Milano, 1993), n.p.

22. Ibid.

23. Ann Wåhlström, letter to David A. Hanks, April 17, 2009. Archives, The Montreal Museum of Fine Arts.

24. Roseline Delisle, letters to the Montreal Museum of Decorative Arts, June 26 and 27, 1995. Archives, The Montreal Museum of Fine Arts.

25. Quoted in Ida va Zijl, *Droog Design 1991–1996* (Utrecht, The Netherlands: Centraal Museum, 1997), 197.

26. Het Kruithuis, *Wanders Wonders: Design for a New Age* (Rotterdam: Museum of Contemporary Art, 1999), 45.

27. Quoted in Shonquis Moreno, *Marcel Wanders: Behind the Ceiling* (Berlin: Die Gestalten Verlag, 2009), 66.

28. Quoted in Strauss, *Ornament as Art*, 506.

29. Janna Syvänoja, letter to the Montreal Museum of Decorative Arts, January 27, 1995. Archives, The Montreal Museum of Fine Arts.

30. Florian Böhm, ed., *KGID: Konstantin Grcic Industrial Design* (London: Phaidon, 2005), 23.

31. Konstantin Grcic, www.konstantin-grcic.com.

32. Quoted in Martin Filler, intro., *Frank Gehry: New Bentwood Furniture Designs*, exh. cat. (Montreal: Montreal Museum of Decorative Arts, 1992), 43.

33. See Filler, intro., *Frank Gehry*.

34. Andrea Branzi, quoted in François Burkhardt and Cristina Morozi, *Andrea Branzi* (Paris: Dis Voir, 1996), 77.

35. Shigeru Ban, intro., in Ambasz and Ban, *Shigeru Ban*, xi.

36. Alice Rawshorn, intro., *Marc Newson* (London: Booth-Clibborn Editions, 1999), 60.

37. Putman, *The International Design Yearbook* 7, 67.

38. Diane Charbonneau, "Ceramic Art: Upheaval in the Centre of the Table," *M: The Magazine of the Montreal Museum of Fine Arts* (January–April 2009), 25.

39. Joyce Scott, interview with the Montreal Museum of Decorative Arts, October 31, 1995. Archives, The Montreal Museum of Fine Arts.

40. Strauss, *Ornament as Art*, 284.

41. *Gaetano Pesce: The Presence of Objects*, exh. brochure (Montreal: The Montreal Museum of Decorative Arts, 1998), n.p.

42. Dale Chihuly, as quoted in Barbaralee Diamonstein-Spielvogel, "From a Seattle Boathouse Dale Chihuly Floats Ideas in Glass," *House and Garden* 165 (July 1993): 32.

43. Rick Poynor, ed., *The International Design Yearbook* 8 (New York: Abbeville, 1993), 68.

44. Ron Arad, interview with the Montreal Museum of Decorative Arts, April 15, 1994. Archives, The Montreal Museum of Fine Arts.

45. Sudjic, *Ron Arad*, 105.

46. Andrea Branzi, letter to the Montreal Museum of Decorative Arts, July 22, 1993. Archives, The Montreal Museum of Fine Arts.

47. Andrea Branzi, *Amnesie (e altri luoghi)*, exh. cat. (Milan: Design Gallery Milano, 1991), n.p.

48. Karim Rashid, ed., *Karim Rashid: I Want to Change the World* (New York: Universe, 2001), 24–25.

49. Erwan Bouroullec, Ronan Bouroullec, Rolf Fehlbaum, and Giulio Cappellini, *Ronan and Erwan Bouroullec* (London: Phaidon, 2003), 98.

50. Masanori Umeda, letter to the Montreal Museum of Decorative Arts, June 15, 1994. Archives, The Montreal Museum of Fine Arts.

51. Danny Lane, quoted in Jennifer H. Opie, *Danny Lane: Breaking Tradition,* exh. cat. (London: Mallett, 1999), 16.

52. David Palterer, interview with the Montreal Museum of Decorative Arts, April 15, 1994. Archives, The Montreal Museum of Fine Arts.

53. Philippe Starck, letter to the Montreal Museum of Decorative Arts, November 7, 1995. Archives, The Montreal Museum of Fine Arts.

54. Maurizio Corrado, *Massimo Iosa Ghini: 15 Years of Projects* (Milan: Electa, 2001), 13.

55. Ross Lovegrove, interview, July 2001, on www.design-engine.com.

56. Thomas Happel, Ingo Maurer GmbH, Munich, letter to David Hanks, April 7, 2009. Stewart Program Archives.

57. Gijs Bakker, letter to David A. Hanks, June 8, 2009. Stewart Program Archives.

58. Philippe Louguet and Dagmar Sedlicka, *Bořek Šípek* (Paris: Éditions Dis Voir, 1998), 74.

2000–2009
Celebrity, Technology, Ecology

1. Quoted in Michael Cannell, "Design Loves a Depression," *New York Times,* January 3, 2009.

2. Charlotte and Peter Fiell, *Design Now!* (Cologne: Taschen, 2007), 9.

3. Paola Antonelli et al., *Design and the Elastic Mind* (New York: Museum of Modern Art, 2008), 67.

4. Marcel Wanders, Foreword in Marcus Fairs, *21st Century Design: New Design Icons from Mass Market to Avant-Garde* (London: Carlton Books, 2006), xx.

5. Quoted in Marcus Fairs, *21st Century Design: New Design Icons from Mass Market to Avant-Garde* (London: Carlton Books, 2009), 407.

6. George H. Marcus, *What is Design Today?* (New York: Harry N. Abrams, 2002), 93.

7. Cara McCarty, *Currents 101: Patrick Jouin,* exh. brochure (St. Louis: St. Louis Art Museum, 2007), n.p.

8. Designboom.com, interview, June 20, 2005.

9. Louise Schouwenberg, *Hella Jongerius* (London: Phaidon, 2003), n.p.

10. Jessica Ahlering, Chef'n Corporation, Seattle, letter to David A. Hanks, The Stewart Program for Modern Design, October 3, 2008. Archives, The Stewart Program for Modern Design.

11. Chad Patton, Nuno Corporation, letter to David A. Hanks, October 4, 2008. Archives, The Stewart Program for Modern Design.

12. Leslie Millar, ed., *2121: The Textile Vision of Reiko Sudo and Nuno* (Epsom, Surrey, England: University College for the Creative Arts, 2005), 8.

13. Reiko Sudo, quoted in Chad Patton, Nuno Corporation, letter to David A. Hanks, October 4, 2008. Archives, The Stewart Program for Modern Design.

14. R. Craig Miller, Penny Sparke, and Catherine McDermott, *European Design Since 1985: Shaping the New Century* (London: Merrell, 2009), 103.

15. Ross Lovegrove, *Supernatural: The Work of Ross Lovegrove* (New York: Phaidon, 2004), 151.

16. Quoted in Andrea Dinoto, "Eva Eisler," *American Craft* 64, no. 5 (October/November 2004): 72.

17. "Tessiture di luce," *Domus* (May 2003): 859.

18. Ryo Niimi, *Tokujin Yoshioka Design* (London: Phaidon, 2006), 130.

19. Florian Böhm, ed., *KGID: Konstantin Grcic Industrial Design* (London: Phaidon, 2005), 100.

20. www.pritzkerprize.com/laureates/

21. Martina Margetts, *Tord Boontje* (New York: Rizzoli, 2006), 126.

22. Ross Lovegrove, quoted on www.bonluxat.com.

23. Susan Yelavich, *Ted Muehling: A Portrait by Don Freeman* (New York: Rizzoli, 2008), n.p.

24. Strauss, *Ornament as Art*, 509.

25. Miyake, Issey, et al., *XXIst Century Man* (Tokyo: Kyuryudo Art-Publishing, 2008), 1983.

26. www.nendo.jp

27. Jorgen Schou-Christensen, quoted in Strauss, *Ornament as Art*, 90.

28. Ronan and Erwan Bouroullec, *Ronan and Erwan Bouroullec* (London: Phaidon, 2003), 86.

29. Matali Crasset, letter to Angéline Dazé, The Stewart Program for Modern Design, Montreal, April 16, 2009.

30. Beppe Finessi, *Novembre* (Milan: Skira, 2008), 181.

31. Zak Kyes, letter to David A. Hanks, Stewart Program for Modern Design, July 13, 2009.

32. Diane Charbonneau, "Maarten Baas: From Fire to Earth," *M: The Magazine of the Montreal Museum of Fine Arts* (September–December 2008): 22.

33. Maria Grazia Rosin, *Gelatine Lux* (Padua, Italy: Il Poligrafo, 2007), 86.

34. www.sophiecook.co.uk

35. Ibid.

36. Simona Giacomelli, Atelier Satyendra Pakhalé, letters to David A. Hanks, December 2008. Archives, The Stewart Program for Modern Design.

37. Fairs, *21st Century Design*, 141.

38. Rafael Esquer, letters to David A. Hanks, September 2008. Archives, The Stewart Program for Modern Design.

39. Patricia McShane, M-A-D, letter to David A. Hanks, October 30, 2008. Archives, The Stewart Program for Modern Design.

40. Georg Jensen, "*Quack* Serving Jug" product information sheet. Archives, The Stewart Program for Modern Design.

41. Moooi publicity materials, 2009. Archives, The Stewart Program for Modern Design, Montreal.

42. Antonelli et al., *Design and the Elastic Mind*, 67.

Index

Acknowledgements

The Stewart Collection was created by many talented individuals, including those who worked at the Montreal Museum of Decorative Arts from its inauguration in 1979 until its merger with the Montreal Museum of Fine Arts in 2000, as well as staff at both the Montreal Museum of Fine Arts and the Stewart Program for Modern Design who continue to strengthen the collection.

Over the last thirty years, the collection has benefited from the advice of several dedicated individuals with curatorial expertise in twentieth-century design. Of the people responsible for the initial development of the collection, special recognition should be given to Luc d'Iberville-Moreau, Director of the Montreal Museum of Decorative Arts from 1980 to 2000, who played an active role in collecting examples of both mid-twentieth-century design and contemporary works. Trained in the history of art at the Institute of Fine Arts in New York and the Courtauld Institute in London, d'Iberville-Moreau brought to the Stewart Collection an exceptional eye for aesthetic quality in design and an inquiring mind in search of new and creative talents in today's design.

Curators Martin Eidelberg and David A. Hanks in New York have been loyal advisors to for the collection since its inception, and Mrs. Stewart has also relied on an advisory committee of experts—George Beylerian, Helen Drutt English, Jack Lenor Larsen, and Toshiko Mori—as well as professionals in specialized fields of design, such as Yvonne Brunhammer and Toni Greenbaum. All of these curatorial voices established the critical dialogue that helped to form the collection.

Since 2000, Rosalind Pepall, Senior Curator of Decorative Arts at the Montreal Museum of Fine Arts, and her colleague Diane Charbonneau, Curator of Contemporary Decorative Arts, have continued to shape the collection at the museum, through astute acquisitions and presentations of selections from the collection in changing installations in the Stewart Pavilion.

In addition to those who are responsible for creating the Stewart Collection, we would like to acknowledge the individuals responsible for the production of this book. It is a pleasure to thank the staff of the Montreal Museum of Fine Arts. The museum's two directors, Nathalie Bondil and Paul Lavallée, have been enthusiastic supporters of the project from the beginning. We are very grateful to Diane Charbonneau, who was in charge of coordinating the selections from the museum for this publication, for her advice on many of the objects she oversees. Special thanks also go to Rosalind Pepall; Danièle Archambault, Registrar and Head of Archives; Danielle Blanchette, Documentation Technician; Anne-Marie Chevrier, Loans and Acquisitions Technician; Sandra Gagné, Head of Exhibitions; Marcel Marcotte, Exhibition Technician; and Charles Blouin, Exhibition Inventory Clerk; Natalie Vanier, Cataloguer; Marie-Claude Saia, Technician, Photographic Services and Copyright; and Jeanne Frégault, Photographic Services Clerk. Linda-Anne d'Anjou, Technician, Photographic Services and Copyright, worked meticulously and indefatigably to obtain rights and permissions for images used in this publication, and in so doing also secured new information about our designs and designers; for this we owe her our gratitude

The complex task of producing a publication in French and English editions has been ably carried out by the staff at Flammarion, longtime publishing partners for books on the Stewart Collection. The French translation was done by Jacques Bosser. The handsome design was created by Bernard Lagacé, Paris, with whom it has always been a pleasure and a privilege to work. Nathalie Chapuis at Éditions Flammarion coordinated the production of this book, and her time, care, and generosity have been most appreciated. Suzanne Tise-Isoré, Editorial Director of the Styles and Design Collection at Flammarion, provided the initial concept for this project as well as considerable expertise in facilitating the production of this book.

Denis Farley of Montreal carried out special photography for this publication, bringing great sensitivity to the interpretation of the objects, with guidance from Bernard Lagacé. At the Montreal Museum of Fine Arts, Christine Guest and Jean-François Brière also provided new photography of selected objects. Many of the existing photographs used in this book were produced by Giles Rivest of Montreal.

The responsibility of creating a publication with such a tight deadline has not fallen to any one person. The selection of the objects was carried out by David Hanks and Martin Eidelberg in collaboration with Diane Charbonneau. The writing and editing of this publication were carried out by a team of skilled individuals. David Hanks created the initial manuscript, writing new text and adapting existing text from past publications of the Stewart Collection: *Design 1935–65: What Modern Was; Messengers of Modernism: American Studio Jewelry 1940–1960; Designed for Delight: Alternative Aspects of Twentieth-Century Decorative Arts; and Designed for Living: Furniture and Lighting 1950–2000.* The specific contribution of the scholars responsible for the research and text of those publications is acknowledged in the Source Credits. Adele Silver was responsible for editing and shaping the initial essays. Martin Eidelberg lent his exceptional skill and experience in developing the conceptual framework of the book. Anne Hoy made extensive authorial contributions to the chapter introductions and was responsible for the expression of the book as a whole, as well as copyediting and proofreading. Her skillful rewriting of the object descriptions has made them more accessible to the general public. Final copyediting and proofreading were carried out by Kate Clark.

The staff of the Macdonald-Stewart Foundation offered great assistance and encouragement: Bruce Bolton, Executive Director; Lucille Riley, Administrative Assistant; Guy Ducharme, Director of Public Affairs; Dora Santschi, Controller; Françoise Lambert, Accounting Clerk.

This project would not have moved forward without Angéline Dazé, Registrar of the Stewart Program for Modern Design, whose tireless were as exceptional as her grace and good nature. Among many tasks, she coordinated the new photography, assembled existing photography, verified registrarial data, and facilitated the new acquisitions made for this publication. Also vital to the creation of this book was the extensive work of Kate Clark of David A. Hanks & Associates, New York, on many aspects of the project, including research, editing, photographic permissions, and assembling the manuscript and images.

Members of the design community, as well as designers whose work is represented here, were generous in providing information. We thank, in particular, Gijs Bakker, Rafael Esquer, Gianfranco Fini, Helena Hernmarck, Jack Lenor Larsen, Ruth Adler Schnee, and Judy Skoogfors.

Staff members of several institutions and private individuals have contributed their knowledge and assistance for this project: Jennifer Belt, Art Resource; Yasmée Faucher and Josée Noël of Cartgo Museological Services; Stephen Harrison, Cleveland Museum of Art; Laura Bennison at the Denver Art Museum; Jennifer Olshin, Friedman Benda Gallery; Mandy Williams, The Geffrye Museum; Linda Baron and Mike Stuk, Herman Miller Archives; Claudia Johnson, R. Craig Miller, and Ruth V. Roberts, Indianapolis Museum of Art; Nathalie Roy and Paul Chénier, Library of the Canadian Centre for Architecture, Montreal; Annette Schaich, Maharam; Andres Lepik, Museum of Modern Art; Christopher Wilk, Victoria and Albert Museum; Lisa Li, The Wolfsonian—Florida International University; Marino Barovier; Priscilla Cunningham; Helen Drutt; Judith Nasby; Bernard Paré; Ryan Paveza; Daniele Renosto; Jan Spak; and Jewel Stern.

We are indebted to the Council for Canadian American Relations (formerly the American Friends of Canada) and wish to acknowledge their generosity over the past thirty years; many of their donations are illustrated in this book (indicated with an asterisk).

Finally, we thank Mrs. Stewart most gratefully for her vision, her generosity, and her faith in this project. Her support for this, as for past projects, has been indispensable.

Photographic credits and copyright information